Volume 1: Concepts

TUTORIAL: **Object-Oriented Computing**

Gerald E. Peterson

COMPUTER SOCIETY ORDER NUMBER 821
LIBRARY OF CONGRESS NUMBER 87-80433
IEEE CATALOG NUMBER EH0257-6
ISBN 0-8186-0821-8
SAN 264-620X

THE COMPUTER SOCIETY OF THE IEEE

THE INSTITUTE OF ELECTRICAL AND ELECTRONICS ENGINEERS, INC.

COMPUTER SOCIETY PRESS

Published by Computer Society Press of the IEEE
1730 Massachusetts Avenue, N.W.
Washington, D.C. 20036-1903

Cover designed by Jack I. Ballestero

Computer Society of the IEEE Order Number 821
Library of Congress Number 87-80433
IEEE Catalog Number EH0257-6
ISBN 0-8186-0821-8 (Paper)
ISBN 0-8186-4821-X (Microfiche)
SAN 264-620X

Order from: Computer Society of the IEEE   IEEE Service Center   Computer Society of the IEEE
    Terminal Annex   445 Hoes Lane   13, Avenue de l'Aquilon
    Post Office Box 4699   P.O. Box 1331   B-1200 Brussels
    Los Angeles, CA 90080   Piscataway, NJ 08855-1331   BELGIUM

 THE INSTITUTE OF ELECTRICAL AND ELECTRONICS ENGINEERS, INC.

IEEE

Preface

Object-oriented computing is a style of computing in which data and associated procedures are encapsulated to form an *object*. An object is a useful computing entity existing at a higher level than procedures or data structures.

Object-oriented computing has gained considerable interest in the last few years. This interest is being fanned by the U. S. Department of Defense's push of Ada, a common (partially) object-oriented language.

This tutorial should be of interest to that group of computer professionals who have heard the term "object-oriented," know it is important, and want to obtain a more substantial understanding of the concept. This group includes:

- software engineers,
- AI professionals,
- professors and students of programming language and computer architecture courses,
- those who are building or proposing new computer languages or architectures.

Most of the papers are at the level of the practicing computer engineer. Some papers, especially those in Chapters I and II of Volume 1, are accessible to the computer-knowledgeable layman.

All aspects of object-oriented computing are considered, including object-oriented languages, object-oriented design and development, examples of object-oriented programming, object-oriented databases, and object-oriented computer architectures.

Volume 1 presents the basic concepts of object-oriented programming and describes several object-oriented languages.

An overview of the fundamental ideas of object-oriented programming is given in Chapter 1.

Smalltalk is a language based entirely on the use of objects. Everything in the language, including integers, is an object. A great deal of knowledge about object-oriented computing can be obtained by studying Smalltalk. Chapter 2 is devoted exclusively to this language.

Other languages are supportive of the object philosophy. These languages include Ada, in which objects can be created as packages; Modula-2, in which objects are created as modules; and some dialects of Lisp. The manner in which the object-oriented philosophy can be incorporated in these languages is considered in Chapters 3 and 4.

Volume 2 is devoted to the manner in which programs are implemented using object-oriented methods, and the manner in which object-oriented languages are themselves implemented.

It has been found that many problems decompose naturally into objects and messages that pass between them. Object-oriented development is the process of decomposing a problem into objects and messages and maintaining these structures in the implementation. Object-oriented development techniques and examples of their use are presented in Chapter 1.

Much insight into the nature of object-oriented programming can be obtained by studying examples where it was successfully put to use. Several examples of object-oriented programming are considered in Chapter 2.

The biggest problem with languages that fully support the object-oriented philosophy is efficient implementation. On a dedicated processor costing in the neighborhood of $100K, Smalltalk runs satisfactorily. On less expensive machines, however, Smalltalk implementations have been too slow to be practical for large programs. Chapter 3 contains many ideas about how to overcome this problem.

Several important concepts and issues that did not fit in other chapters are considered in Chapter 4.

Object-oriented computer architectures have also been studied and implemented in recent years. Chapter 5 describes principles, such as capability-based addressing, which have guided these implementations. Several examples of object-based architectures are described in Chapter 6. These include the Intel iAPX 432 and the IBM System/38.

Gerald E. Peterson

Acknowledgments

The author wishes to thank the McDonnell Douglas Astronautics and Aerospace Information Services Companies for providing a pleasant climate in which this work could be undertaken. This tutorial resulted from studies which were undertaken in order to improve the manner in which software is developed at McDonnell Douglas Corporation.

Table of Contents

Chapter 1: Introduction to Object-Oriented Computing

An *object* is a computer structure similar to a procedure or a data structure. In fact, objects normally contain both data and related procedures. Therefore, objects provide a coarser level of granularity for program decomposition than is available by using data or procedures.

Using objects for decomposition is usually more natural than using data or function. The idea of using objects has come from many years of experience in attempting to find a natural high-level structuring device. The key concept is that a collection of data and the operations that are normally performed on that data are very closely related and should be treated as a single entity rather than as separate things.

For example, stacks, queues, file interfaces, sensor interfaces, numbers, character strings, robot interfaces, compilers, and operating systems are naturally occurring programming structures that can be considered to be objects.

Objects are often referred to as computer abstractions. To understand the nature of an object better, it is helpful to consider first the nature of an abstraction. To do so, consider the purposes of some real world structures such as houses, automobiles, or chests of drawers:

- Some are structured so that the commonly used things (like water faucets) will be conveniently available, but those not frequently needed (like plumbing pipes) are hidden.
- They protect so that the rain and wind and other people will not harm the things enclosed.

Computer structures are built for the same reasons.

Examples of computer structures that have these purposes are variables, data structures, and procedures. These kinds of structures are called abstractions. This means that the structuring is done so that the most useful features are abstracted (made conveniently available) while the features that are not ofter needed or are conceptually unnecessary are deliberately hidden.

The idea of abstraction is an extremely important one not only in computer science but in all of life. Progress is made by concentrating on the important and ignoring the rest.

Objects are natural abstractions that may exist at a higher level than procedures or data. Most objects contain data and procedures that are naturally associated together. However, objects that consist of data alone or procedures alone are also possible.

There are simple and complex objects. There are also hierarchies of objects.

A tree together with the operations of adding an element, deleting an element, locating an element, and outputting the elements in preorder would constitute one example of an object. This example would normally be abbreviated and referred to simply as a tree.

An object simpler than a tree is a single integer together with the operations of addition, subtraction, multiplication, and division.

A more complex object is a dictionary organized as a binary tree. The dictionary operations could be *create, look-up, add*, and *delete*.

There could be many trees in a single program, each with the same capabilities. A description of the capabilities of an object is called an object *type* or *class*. Each tree object is an *instance* of the tree class.

There can be literally hundreds of objects in large programs. For example, in a program that controls a missile, some naturally occurring objects are the sensor interfaces, the files and their interfaces, the interface to the data bus, the direction cosine matrix and associated operations, and the collection of standardized earth data.

The papers in this chapter were chosen to help the reader obtain a basic understanding of object-oriented computing.

"Object-Oriented Software Systems," by David Robson is an excellent introduction to the subject. It is somewhat specific to the Smalltalk system in its definitions, but the major ideas of object-oriented computing are carefully and clearly presented. This article should be accessible to anyone who has picked up this tutorial, even for browsing.

The key ideas are as follows:

Traditional software development takes the point of view that there are procedures and there are data structures, and these are treated as independent entities. An object-oriented system has a single type of entity, the object, that represents both.

Unlike data, an object can act. It can determine what to do when a message is received. The same message when received by different objects can cause completely different actions.

Many different objects are nearly identical in their capabilities. These objects can be collectively defined by defining a class (i.e. a description of similar objects.)

In Smalltalk, even a class is an object. When a class receives the message "new," a new object with the capabilities described in the class is created.

Classes are organized into a tree structure, with the parent of each class called its *superclass*. When an instance of a class is created with the "new" method, the object created inherits from the superclass (and all ancestors of the superclass) each of its methods unless there is a method of the same name in the class.

The paper by B. J. MacLennan, "Values and Objects in Programming Languages," presents a philosophical discussion pertaining to the difference between value and object. Values are timeless abstractions: They do not exist in time and therefore can be neither created nor destroyed. An example is the number 2. It always exists. Objects, on the other hand, exist in time and can be created and destroyed. An example is the representation of the number 2 in the storage of a computer. Mathematics deals with values; computer science with objects. This may be a fundamental distinction between the two disciplines. This paper presents an extremely interesting and very valuable point of view that helps to position object-oriented computing in its proper relation with other scientific disciplines.

Geoffrey A. Pascoe, in "Elements of Object-Oriented Programming," describes the distinguishing features of languages that fully support the object-oriented philosophy. These features are *information hiding*, *data abstraction*, *dynamic binding*, and *inheritance*. Ada and Modula-2 possess the first two of these features but lack the other two. Smalltalk incorporates all four. Pascoe also discusses the advantages and disadvantages of using an object-oriented language. The primary advantage is that the inheritance mechanism of object-oriented languages allow code to be reused in a convenient manner, and this can improve programmer productivity. The primary disadvantage is the run-time cost of using object-oriented languages. However, it is argued that this run-time increase in cost is not very significant, and there may even be a decrease in cost for large applications.

Pascoe's paper leads to the question of whether or not one should use the term *object-oriented* when considering languages such as Ada and Modula-2 that do not fully support the object-oriented philosophy. In this tutorial, Ada and Modula-2 are considered to be object-oriented mainly because there are structures in these languages (packages in Ada, modules in Modula-2) that can be thought of as objects, even though they do not possess all the properties of objects in Smalltalk. These structures do allow some of the object-oriented technology to be incorporated in Ada or Modula-2 programs.

Tim Rentsch's paper, "Object Oriented Programming," contains the following remarkable forward-looking quotation: "Object-oriented programming will be in the 1980's what structured programming was in the 1970's. Everyone will be in favor of it. Every manufacturer will promote his products as supporting it. Every manager will pay lip service to it. Every programmer will practice it (differently). And no one will know just what it is."

This prediction is being fulfilled, except that we can and should know what object-oriented programming is.

Rentsch presents a characterization of object-oriented systems similar to the other papers presented in this chapter, and then he compares various object-oriented systems (Smalltalk, Sketchpad, Simula, Lisp frames, Alphard, Ada, and CLU) that were available in 1982. The language CLU comes out as the most object-oriented next to Smalltalk.

In "Software-ICs," by Lamar Ledbetter and Brad Cox, object-oriented programming is compared to the building of hardware by using integrated circuits (ICs). Objects in software correspond to ICs in hardware. These software ICs are the key to creating truly reusable software. To achieve the goal of reusability, languages must support the concept of inheritance, and standards for software ICs must be developed. A market for software ICs that can be "plugged" into existing software systems to provide added functionality is beginning to emerge. Actual customer experience with Objective-C have resulted in code bulk reductions of between 2.5-1 and 5-1. The coming widespread use of software ICs should improve software productivity much as the use of hardware ICs did in the hardware world.

Additional References

These are primarily books and collections that pertain to object-oriented programming in general.

B.J. Cox, *Object-Oriented Programming: An Evolutionary Approach*, Addison-Wesley, Reading, Massachusetts, 1986.

Cox carefully explains the reasons for object-oriented programming. The basic concepts are explained along with comparisons of various languages that support objects. Common classes such as Collection and Array are described. A substantial example is presented in the latter part of the book. Probably the best single reference for object-oriented computing.

Byte, Volume 11, Number 8, August 1986.

Special issue on object-oriented programming.

Object-Oriented Programming Workshop, June 9-13, 1986, *SIGPLAN Notices*, ACM, Inc., New York, New York, Volume 21, Number 10, October 1986.

Nineteen papers about object-oriented computing.

OOPSLA '86: Conference on Object-Oriented Programming Systems, Languages and Applications, SIGPLAN Notices, ACM, Inc., New York, New York, Volume 21, Number 11, November 1986.

Fifty technical papers on topics related to object-oriented computing.

B.J. MacLennan, "Abstraction in the Intel iAPX-432 Prototype Systems Implementation Language," *SIGPLAN Notices*, ACM, Inc., New York, New York, Volume 18, Number 12, December 1983, pages 86-95.

Describes a language that embodies some of MacLennan's ideas from his paper included here.

D.T. Ross, "Toward Foundations for the Understanding of Type," *SIGPLAN Notices*, ACM, Inc., New York, New York, Volume 11, 1976 Special Issue, pages 63-65.

An early reference to the compound word *object-oriented*, perhaps the earliest. The term *object* was used much earlier. Paper presented at the *Conference on Data: Abstraction, Definition and Structure*, Salt Lake City, Utah, March 22-24, 1976.

K.J. Schmucker, *Object-Oriented Programming for the Macintosh*, Hayden, Hasbrouck Heights, New Jersey, 1987.

Reprinted with permission from *BYTE*, Volume 6, Number 8, August 1981, pages 74–86. Copyright © 1981 by David Robson.

Object-Oriented Software Systems

David Robson
Learning Research Group
Xerox Palo Alto Research Center
3333 Coyote Hill Rd
Palo Alto CA 94304

This article describes a general class of tools for manipulating information called object-oriented software systems. It defines a series of terms, including software system and object-oriented. The description is greatly influenced by a series of object-oriented programming environments developed in the last ten years by the Learning Research Group of Xerox's Palo Alto Research Center, the latest being the Smalltalk-80 system. The article describes object-oriented software systems in general, instead of the Smalltalk-80 system in particular, in order to focus attention on the fundamental property that sets the Smalltalk-80 system apart from most other programming environments. The words "object-oriented" mean different things to different people. Although the definition given in this article may exclude systems that should rightfully be called object-oriented, it is a useful abstraction of the idea behind many software systems.

Many people who have no idea how a computer works find the idea of object-oriented systems quite natural. In contrast, many people who have experience with computers initially think there is something strange about object-oriented systems. (I don't mean to imply that computer-naive users can create complex systems in an object-oriented environment more easily than experienced programmers can. Creating complex systems involves many techniques more familiar to the programmer than the novice, regardless of whether or not an object-oriented environment is used. But the basic idea about how to create a software system in an object-oriented fashion comes more naturally to those without a preconception about the nature of software systems.) I had had some programming experience when I first encountered an object-oriented system and the idea certainly seemed strange to me. I am assuming that most of you also have some experience with software systems and their creation. So instead of introducing the object-oriented point of view as if it were completely natural, I'll try to explain what makes it seem strange compared to the point of view found in other programming systems.

Software Systems

A software system is a tool for manipulating informa-tion. For the purposes of this article, I'm using a very broad definition of information.

Information: *A representation or description of something.*

There are many types of information that describe different things in different ways. One of the great insights in computer science was the fact that information can (among other things) describe the manipulation of information. This type of information is called *software*.

Software: *Information describing the manipulation of information.*

Software has the interesting recursive property of describing how to manipulate things like itself. Software is used to describe a particular type of information-manipulation tool called a *software system*.

Software system: *An information-manipulation tool in which the manipulation is described by software.*

A distinction is made in information-manipulation tools between *hardware* systems and *software* systems. A hardware system is a physical device like a typewriter, pen, copier, or television set. The type of manipulation performed by a hardware system is built in and can only be changed by physical modification. The type of manipulation performed by a software system is not built in—it is determined by information, which can be manipulated.

The virtue of software systems is that the mechanism developed for manipulating information can be used to manipulate the mechanism itself. Software systems that actually manipulate other software systems are called *programming environments*.

Programming environment: *A software system that manipulates software systems. An environment for the design, production, and use of software systems.*

Thus, a programming environment is also recursive: it *is* what it manipulates. The fact that software systems can be manipulated is both good news and bad news. Since a text editor is a software system, it is not "cast in concrete" and you can change it to conform to your style of interacting with text more closely than it does now (using a programming environment). However, you also may reduce it to the proverbial "pile of bits" (not a text editor at all).

Data/Procedure-Oriented Software

The traditional view of software systems is that they are composed of a collection of *data* that represents some information and a set of *procedures* that manipulates the data.

> **Data:** *The information manipulated by software.*
>
> **Procedure:** *A unit of software.*

Things happen in the system by invoking a procedure and giving it some data to manipulate.

As an example of a software system, consider a system for managing windows that occupy rectangular areas on a display screen. The windows contain text and have titles. They can be moved around the screen, sometimes overlapping each other. (The details of this system are not important. Its main purpose is to point out the differences between the structure of a data/procedure system and an object-oriented system.)

A window-management system implemented as a data/procedure system would include data representing the location, size, text contents, and title of each window on the screen. It would also include procedures that move a window, create a window, tell whether a window overlaps another window, replace the text or title of a window, and perform other manipulations of windows on a display. To move a window, a programmer would call the procedure that moves windows and pass to it the data representing the window and its new location.

A problem with the data/procedure point of view is that data and procedures are treated as if they were independent when, in fact, they are not. All procedures make assumptions about the form of the data they manipulate. The procedure to move a window should be presented with data representing a window to be moved and its new location. If the procedure were presented with data representing the text contents of a window, the system would behave strangely.

In a properly functioning system, the appropriate choice of procedure and data is always made. However, in an improperly functioning system (eg: one in the process of being developed or encountering an untested situation), the data being manipulated by a procedure may be of an entirely different form from that expected. Even in a properly functioning system, the choice of the appropriate procedure and data must always be made by the programmer.

These two problems have been addressed in the context of the data/procedure point of view by adding several features to programming systems. Data typing has been added to languages to let the programmer know that the appropriate choice of data has been made for a particular procedure. In a typed system, the programmer is notified when a procedure call is written using the wrong type of data. Variant records allow the system to choose the appropriate procedure and data in some situations.

Object-Oriented Software

Instead of two types of entity that represent information and its manipulation independently, an object-oriented system has a single type of entity, the *object*, that represents both. Like pieces of data, objects can be manipulated. However, like procedures, objects describe manipulation as well. Information is manipulated by sending a *message* to the object representing the information.

> **Object:** *A package of information and descriptions of its manipulation.*
>
> **Message:** *A specification of one of an object's manipulations.*

When an object receives a message, it determines how to manipulate itself. The object to be manipulated is called the *receiver* of the message. A message includes a symbolic name that describes the type of manipulation desired. This name is called the message *selector*. The crucial feature of messages is that the selector is only a *name* for the desired manipulation; it describes *what* the programmer wants to happen, not *how* it should happen. The message receiver contains the description of how the actual manipulation should be performed. The programmer of an object-oriented system sends a message to invoke a manipulation, instead of calling a procedure. A message names the manipulation; a procedure describes the details of the manipulation.

Of course, procedures have names as well, and their names are used in procedure calls. However, there is only one procedure for a name, so a procedure name specifies the exact procedure to be called and exactly what should happen. A message, however, may be interpreted in different ways by different receivers. So, a message does not determine exactly what will happen; the receiver of the message does.

If the earlier example of the window-management system were implemented as an object-oriented system, it would contain a set of objects representing windows. Each object would describe a window on the screen. Each object would also describe the manipulations of the window it represents—for example, how to move it, how to determine whether it overlaps another window, or how to display it. Each of these manipulations would correspond to a selector of a message. The selectors could include move, overlap, display, delete, width, or height. (In this article, an alternate typeface is used for words that refer to specific elements in example systems.)

In addition to a selector, a message may contain other objects that take part in the manipulation. These are called the message *arguments*. For example, to move a window, the programmer might send the object representing the window a message with the selector move. The message would also contain an argument representing the new location. Since this is an object-oriented system, the selector and argument are objects: the selector representing a symbolic name and the argument representing a location or point.

The description of a single type of manipulation of an object's information (the response to a single type of message) is a procedure-like entity called a *method*. A method, like a procedure, is the description of a sequence of actions to be performed by a processor. However, unlike a procedure, a method cannot directly call another method. Instead, it must send a message. *The important thing is that methods cannot be separated from objects.* When a message is sent, the receiver determines the method to execute on the basis of the message selector. A different kind of window could be added to the system with a different representation and different methods to respond to the messages move, overlap, display, delete, width, and height. Places where messages are sent to windows do not have to be changed in order to refer to the new kind of window; whichever window receives the message will use the method appropriate to its representation.

Objects look different from the outside than they do from the inside. By the outside of an object, I mean what it looks like to other objects with which it interacts (eg: what rectangles look like to other rectangles or to windows). From the outside, you can only ask an object to do something (send it a message). By the inside of an object, I mean what it looks like to the programmer implementing its behavior. From the inside, you can tell an object how to do something (in a method). For example, a window can respond to messages having the selectors move, overlap, display, delete, width, or height. However, nothing is known outside the window about how it responds to these messages. (It is known that a window will move when asked to, but it is not known how it accomplishes the move.)

The set of messages an object can respond to is called its *protocol*. The external view of an object is nothing more than its protocol; the internal view of an object is something like a data/procedure system. An object has a set of variables that refers to other objects. These are called its *private variables*. It also has a set of methods that describes what to do when a message is received. The values of the private variables play the role of data and the methods play the role of procedures. This distinction between data and procedures is strictly localized to the inside of the object.

Methods, like other procedures, must know about the form of the data they directly manipulate. Part of the data a method can manipulate are the values of its object's private variables. For example, we might imagine three ways that a window represents its location and size (internally). The private variables might contain:

- four numbers representing the x and y location of the center, the width, and the height
- two points representing opposite corners of the window
- a single rectangle whose location and size are the same as the window's

The method that moves a window (the response to messages with the selector move) assumes that a particular representation is used. If the representation were changed, the method would also have to be changed. Only the methods in the object whose representation changed need be changed. All other methods must manipulate the window by sending it messages.

A message must be sent to an object to find out anything about it (ie: our concept of manipulation includes inquiring about information, as well as changing information). This is needed because we don't want the form of an object's inside known outside of it. The response to a message may return a value. For example, a window's response to the message width returns an object that represents its width on the display (a number). The method for determining what to return depends on the form of the window's private variables. If they are represented as the first alternative listed above (four numbers), the response would simply return the value of the appropriate private variable. If the second alternative is used (two points), the method would have to determine the width from the x coordinates of the two corners. If the third alternative is used (one rectangle), the width message would simply be passed on to the rectangle and the rectangle's response would become the window's response.

Classes and Instances

Most object-oriented systems make a distinction between the description of an object and the object itself.

Many similar objects can be described by the same general description. The description of an object is called a *class* since the class can describe a whole set of related objects. Each object described by a class is called an *instance* of that class.

> **Class:** *A description of one or more similar objects.*

> **Instance:** *An object described by a particular class.*

Every object is an instance of a class. The class describes all the similarities of its instances. Each instance contains the information that distinguishes it from the other instances. This information is a subset of its private variables called *instance variables*. All instances of a class have the same *number* of instance variables. The *values* of the instance variables are different from instance to instance. An object's software (ie: the methods that describe its response to messages) is found in its class. All instances of a class use the same method to respond to a particular type of message (ie: a message with a particular selector). The difference in response by two different instances is a result of their different instance variables. The methods in a class use a set of names to refer to the set of instance variables. When a message is sent, those names in the invoked method refer to the instance variables of the message receiver. Some of an object's private variables are shared by all other instances of its class. These variables are called *class variables* and are part of the class.

The programmer developing a new system creates the classes that describe the objects that make up the system. The programmer of the window-management system would create a class that contained methods corresponding to the message selectors move, display, delete, width, and height. This class would also include the names of the instance variables referred to in those methods. These names might be frame, text, and title, where:

> frame is a rectangle defining the area on the screen,
> text is the string of characters displayed in the window, and
> title is the string of characters representing the window's name

The classes representing rectangles and strings of characters are included in most systems, so they don't need to be defined.

In a system that is uniformly object-oriented, a class is an object itself. A class serves several purposes. In a running system, it provides the description of how objects behave in response to messages. The processor running an object-oriented system looks at the receiver's class when a message is sent to determine the appropriate method to execute. For this use of classes, it is not necessary that they be represented as objects since the processor does not interact with them through messages (preventing a nasty recursion). In a system under development, a class provides an interface for the programmer to interact with the definition of objects. For this use of classes, it is extremely useful for them to be objects, so they can be manipulated in the same way as all other descriptions. Classes also are the source of new objects in a running system. Here again, it is useful for the class to be an object, so object creation can be accomplished with a simple message. For example, the message new might be sent to a class to create a new instance.

Inheritance

Another mechanism used for implicit sharing in object-oriented systems is called *inheritance*. One object inherits the attributes of another object, changing any attributes that distinguish the two. Some object-oriented systems provide for inheritance between all objects, but most provide it only between classes. A class may be modified to create another class. In such a relationship, the first class is called the *superclass* and the second is called the *subclass*. A subclass inherits everything about its superclass. The following modifications can be made to a subclass:

- adding instance variables
- providing new methods for some of the messages understood by the superclass
- providing methods for new messages (messages not understood by the superclass)
- adding class variables

As an example, the window-management system might contain windows that have a minimum size. These would be instances of a subclass of the ordinary class of windows that added an instance variable to represent the minimum size and provided a new method for the message that changes a window's size.

Conclusion

The realization that information can describe the manipulation of information is largely responsible for the great utility of computers today. However, that discovery is also partially responsible for the failure of computers to reach the utility of some predictions made in earlier times. On the one hand, it can be seen as a unification between the manipulator and the manipulated. However, in practice, it has been seen as a distinction between software and the information it manipulates. For small systems, this distinction is harmless. But for large systems, the distinction becomes a major source of complexity. The object-oriented point of view is a way to reduce the complexity of large systems without placing additional overhead on the construction of small systems. ■

VALUES AND OBJECTS IN PROGRAMMING LANGUAGES*

B. J. MacLennan
Computer Science Department
Naval Postgraduate School
Monterey, CA 93943

1. INTRODUCTION

The terms *value-oriented* and *object-oriented* are used to describe both programming languages and programming styles. This paper attempts to elucidate the differences between values and objects and argues that their proper discrimination can be a valuable aid to conquering program complexity. The first section shows that *values* amount to timeless abstractions for which the concepts of updating, sharing and instantiation have no meaning. The second section shows that *objects* exist in time and, hence, can be created, destroyed, copied, shared and updated. The third section argues that proper discrimination of these concepts in programming languages will clarify problems such as the role of state in functional programming. The paper concludes by discussing the use of the value/object distinction as a tool for program organization.

2. VALUES

Values are applicative. The term *value-oriented* is most often used in conjunction with *applicative* programming. That is, with programming with pure expressions and without the use of assignment or other *imperative* facilities. Another way to put this is that value-oriented programming is programming in the absence of side-effects. This style of programming is important because it has many of the advantages of simple algebraic expressions. *viz.* that an expression can be understood by understanding its constituents, that the meaning of the subexpressions is independent of their context, and that there are simple interfaces between the parts of the expression that are obvious from the syntax of the expression. That is, each part of an expression involving values is independent of all the others. One reason for this is that values are *read-only*. i.e., it is not possible to update their components. Since they are unchangeable, it is always safe to share values for efficiency. That is, they exhibit *referential transparency*: there is never any danger of one expression altering something which is used by another expression. Any sharing that takes place is hidden from the programmer and is done by the system for more efficient storage utilization. Avoiding updating eliminates dangling reference problems and simplifies deallocation [3].

What are values? We have discussed a number of properties of values. What exactly are they? The best examples of values are mathematical entities, such as integer, real and complex numbers, hence we can understand values better by understanding these better.

One characteristic of mathematical entities is that they are *atemporal,* in the literal sense of being timeless. To put it another way. the concept of time or duration does not apply to mathematical entities any more than the concept color applies to them; they are neither created nor destroyed. When we write 2+3 there is no implication that 5 has just come into existence and that 2 and 3 have been consumed. What is it about numbers that give them this property?

Values are abstractions. The fundamental fact that gives mathematical entities and other values their properties is that they are *abstractions.* (universals or concepts). Although a full explication of mathematical entities is beyond the scope of this paper it should be fairly clear that the number 2 is an abstraction that subsumes all particular pairs. This universal nature of abstractions makes them atemporal, or timeless. The number 2 can neither be created nor destroyed because its existence is not tied to the creation or destruction of particular pairs. Indeed, the concept of existence, in its usual sense, is not applicable to the number 2. It is the same with all values, because all values correspond to abstractions: they can neither be created nor destroyed.

The work reported herein was supported by the Foundation Research Program of the Naval Postgraduate School with funds provided by the Chief of Naval Research. This paper is a condensation and revision of [6], to which the reader is referred for further information.

It is also the case that abstractions, and hence values, are immutable. Although values can be operated on, in the sense of relating values to other values, they cannot be altered. That is, $2+1 = 3$ states a relation among values; it does not alter them. When in a programming language we assign x the value 2, $x := 2$, and later add one to x, $x := x+1$, haven't we changed a number, which is a value? No, we haven't; the number 2 has remained the same. What we have changed is the number that the name 'x' denotes. We can give names to values and we can change the names that we give to values, but this doesn't change the values. The naming of values and the changing of names is discussed in a later section.

Values cannot be counted. A corollary of the above is that there is not such a thing as "copies" of a value. This should be clear from mathematics: it is not meaningful to speak of this 2 or that 2; there is just 2. That is, the number 2 is uniquely determined by its value. This is because an abstraction is uniquely determined by the things which it subsumes, hence, anything which subsumes all possible pairs is the abstraction 2. Therefore, the concept 'number' is not even applicable to abstractions; it makes no sense to ask how many 2's there are. In a programming language, it is pointless to make another copy of a value; there is no such thing. There is also no reason to make such a copy since values are immutable. (It is, of course, possible to make copies of a representation of a value; this is discussed later.)

It is also meaningless to talk about the sharing of values. Since values are immutable, cannot be counted, and cannot be copied, it is irrelevant whether different program segments share the same value or different "copies" of the value. Of course, there might be implementation differences. If a long string value is assigned to a variable it will make a big difference whether a fresh copy must be made or whether a pointer to the original copy can be stored. While this is an important implementation concern, it is irrelevant to the semantics of values.

Values are used to model abstractions. We have discussed a number of the characteristics of values but have not discussed whether values should be included in programming languages, or, if they are, what they should be used for. The answer to this question lies in the relation we have shown between values and abstractions: values are the programming language equivalent of abstractions. Thus, values will be most effective when they are used to model abstractions in the problem to be solved. This is in fact their usual use, since **integer** and **real** data values are used to model quantities represented by integer and real numbers. Similarly, the abstraction 'color' might be modeled by values of a Pascal or Ada enumeration type, (RED, BLUE, GREEN). On the other hand, it is not common to treat compound data values, such as complex numbers or sequences, as values. If done, this would eliminate one source of errors, namely, updating a data structure that is unknowingly shared [3]. Value-oriented languages, such as the languages for data-flow machines and functional programming, have only values. Is there any need for objects at all? This is answered in the following sections.

3. OBJECTS

Computing can be viewed as simulation. It has been said that computing can be viewed as simulation [4]. This is certainly obvious in the case of programs that explicitly simulate or model some physical situation. The metaphor can be extended to many other situations. Consider an employee data base: each record in the data base corresponds to an employee. The data base can be said to be a simulation, or model, of some aspects of the corporation. Similarly, the data structures in an operating system often reflect the status of some objects in the real world. For instance, they might reflect the fact that a tape drive is rewinding or in a parity-error status. The data structures can also reflect logical situations, such as the fact that a tape drive is assigned to a particular job in the system.

A data structure is needed for each entity. Simulation is simplified if there is a data structure corresponding to each entity to be simulated, since this factors and encapsulates related information. This is exactly the approach that has been taken in object-oriented programming languages, such as Smalltalk [4,7]. The usual way to structure a program in such a language is to create an object for each entity in the system being modeled. These entities might be real-world objects or objects that are only real to the application, such as figures on a display screen. The messages these objects respond to are just the relevant manipulations that can be performed on the corresponding real entities. Given this relationship between programming language objects and real world objects, we will try to clarify the notion of an object.

What is an object? In our programming environment we have objects and in the real world we have objects. Just what is an object? When we attempt to answer this question we immediately find ourselves immersed in age-old philosophical problems. In particular, what makes one object different from another? One philosophical answer to this question is to say that while the two objects have the same *form,* they have different *substance.* To put this is more concrete terms, we could say that the two objects are alike in every way except that they occupy different regions of space.

We find exactly the same situation arising in programming languages. We might have two **array** variables that contain exactly the same values, yet they are two different variables. What makes them different? They occupy different locations. So by analogy, the form of the array variable is the order and value of its elements while its substance is the region of memory it occupies.

Objects can be instantiated. There is also a less philosophical way in which we distinguish real world objects: we give them proper names. We find an exactly analogous situation in programming languages. Programming objects, such as the array variables already mentioned, generally have a unique name: the reference to the object. This is generally closely related to the region of storage the object occupies. This is not necessary, however, as we can see by considering a file system. It is easy to see that files are objects; it is quite normal to have two different files with the same contents. Of course, if the files are to be distinguished, then they must have distinct names. For our purposes, we will not be too concerned about what *individuating* element is used to distinguish objects; whether it is some form of unique identification (such as a capability), or whether it is implicit in the region of storage occupied; we will assume that each object is different from every other object even if they contain the same data values. In general, we can say that the uniqueness of an object is determined by its *external* relations and is independent of its *internal* relations and properties. This is opposed to a value, which is completely determined by its internal relations and properties (e.g., a set is completely determined by its elements). Thus there might be any number of *instances* of otherwise identical objects. This leads to a number of further consequences.

Objects can be changed. We have said that the identity of an object is independent of any of its internal properties or attributes. For instance, even if all of the elements of an array variable are changed, it is still the same variable (because it occupies the same region of storage). This is of course like real world objects, for they too can change and retain their identity. Values, on the other hand can never change. For instance, if we add 5 to $1+2i$, we don't change $1+2i$, we compute a different value, $6+2i$. This changeability, this fact that an object might have one set of properties at one time and a different set at another time, is a distinctive feature of objects (and of programs).

Objects have state. This changeability of objects leads to the idea of the *state* of an object: the sum total of the internal properties and attributes of an object at a given point in time. Thus, we can say that the state of an object can be changed in time. State is of course a central idea in computer science, so it is not surprising to find that objects are at the heart of computer science. Since the state of an object can change in time, it is certainly the case that objects exist "in time," i.e., they are not atemporal like values.

Objects can be created and destroyed. The fact that objects are not atemporal leads to the conclusion that they can be both created and destroyed. This is familiar in programming languages where, for instance, a variable might be created every time a certain block is entered and destroyed every time it is exited. Many languages also provide explicit means for creating and destroying objects (e.g., Pascal's 'new' and 'dispose'). Since values are atemporal, it is meaningless to speak of their being either created or destroyed.

Objects can be shared. Since there can be any number of instances of otherwise identical objects and since objects can change their properties in time, it is a crucial question whether an object is shared or not. This is because a change made to the object by one sharer will be visible to the other sharer. Such side-effects are common in programming and are often used by programmers as a way of communicating. People also frequently use shared objects as means of communication. For instance, two persons might communicate by altering the state of a blackboard.

Recall that in our discussion of values we found that the issue of sharing didn't apply. Whether a particular implementation chooses to share copies of values or not is irrelevant to the semantics of the program; it is strictly an issue of efficiency. Sharing is a crucial issue where objects are concerned.

Computer science as objectified mathematics. We can see now an important difference between the domain of mathematics and the domain of computer science. Mathematics deals with things such as numbers, functions, vectors, groups, etc. These are all abstractions, i.e., values. It has been said that the theorems of mathematics are timeless, and this is literally true. Since mathematics deals with the relations among values and since values are atemporal, the resulting relations (which are themselves abstractions and values) are atemporal. Conversely, much of computer science deals with objects and with the way they change in time. State is a central idea. It might not be unreasonable to call computer science objectified mathematics, or object-oriented mathematics.

It has frequently been observed that the advantage of applicative programming is that it is more mathematical and eliminates the idea of state from programming. We can see that this means that applicative programming deals only with values (indeed, several languages for applicative programming are called "value-oriented" languages). Really, applicative programming is just mathematics.

These ideas can be summarized in two observations:

- Programming is object-oriented mathematics.
- Mathematics is value-oriented programming.

These two principles show the unity between the two fields and isolate their differences.

4. VALUES AND OBJECTS IN PROGRAMMING LANGUAGES

Most languages confuse them. Both values and objects are accommodated in most programming languages, although usually in a very asymmetric and *ad hoc* way. For example, a language such as FORTRAN supports values of several types, including integers, reals, complex numbers and logical values. These are all treated as mathematical values; for example, it is not possible to "update" the real part of a complex number separately from the imaginary part. Of course, it is possible to store all of these values in variables, but that is a different issue, as we will see later. On the other hand, FORTRAN provides objects in the form of updatable, sharable arrays. This pattern has been followed with few variations in most other languages. All of these languages unnecessarily tie the value or object nature of a thing to its type, usually by treating the atomic data types as values and the compound data types as objects. We will argue below, that this confusion complicates programming.

Programming languages are most often deficient in their treatment of compound values; in particular, they rarely provide recursive data types as Hoare described them [3]. They tend to confuse the logical issue of whether a thing should be an object (i.e., it is shared, updatable, destroyable, etc.) with the implementation issue of whether it should be shared for efficiency. We will see how this can be solved later.

Mathematics deals poorly with objects. We have said that mathematics is value-oriented; that is, it deals with timeless relations and operations on abstractions. Concepts that are central to objects (and computer science), such as state, updating and sharing, are alien to mathematics. This is not to say that it is impossible to deal with objects in mathematics; it is done every day, only indirectly. For instance, it is common to deal in physics with systems that change in time; they are represented mathematically by functions of an independent variable representing time. The relationships between objects can be represented as differential equations (or difference equations if state changes are quantized). Similarly, mathematics can distinguish instances of an object by attaching a unique name (generally a natural number) to each instance of a value. These techniques work but are awkward. A more fully developed attempt to apply the concepts of mathematics to the description of objects can be seen in denotational semantics. Here the state is explicitly passed from function to function to represent its alteration in time.

Fen theory deals poorly with values. In our *fen* theory [5] we attempted to deal with objects more directly by developing an axiomatic theory of objects. This was done in two ways: (1) we discarded the axiom of set theory that forces two sets with the same values to be identical. This permitted multiple instances of the same set. (2) An axiom was inserted that required there to be at least a countable infinity of instances of each set. The result was an object-oriented theory of sets and relations. This worked well for describing many of the properties of objects and for defining the semantics of those programming language constructs that are object-oriented. Unfortunately, it suffered from the dual problem of mathematics: it was awkward to deal with values. What is 2? Is it the name of some distinguished object that we have chosen to represent 2 or does it denote any object with a certain structure? There are related problems with operations on values. For instance, which 5 does 2+3 return? These are all problems of attempting to deal with values in an object-oriented system. Values are inherently *extensional* while fen theory is inherently *intensional* (see [2], p. 109). The solution adopted in fen theory was to treat values as equivalence classes of objects in the supporting logic. This was possible because that logic was extensional (i.e., value-oriented).

Computers use objects to represent values. These are exactly the issues that must be faced in dealing with values on a computer. Abstractions are not physical objects (except so far as they exist in our brains), so to deal with them they must be represented or encoded into objects. We do this when we represent the number 2 by the numeral '2' or the word 'two' on a piece of paper. Once a value has been represented as an object it acquires some of the attributes of objects. Clearly, whenever a value is to be manipulated in a computer it must be represented as the state of some physical object. Typically, there will be many such representing objects in a computer at a time. For instance, 2 can be represented by a bit pattern in a register and in several memory locations. Therefore, everything "in" a computer is an object; there are no values in computers. This does not imply, however, that values should be discarded from programming languages.

Programmers need values. Most conventional languages have both values and objects, although a purely object-oriented programming language could be designed. This could be done by storing everything in memory and then only dealing with the addresses of these things. It would be like having a pointer to every object. It would then be necessary for the programmer to keep track of the different instances of what were intuitively the same value so that he wouldn't accidently update a shared value or miss considering as equal two instances of the same value. Some languages actually come close to this, such as Smalltalk. Unless such a language were carefully designed, it would be almost impossible to deal with values such as numbers in the usual way.

Programmers need objects. Conversely, programmers need objects in their programming languages. There have, for sure, been completely value-oriented programming languages. These include the FP and FFP systems of Backus [1]. It is interesting to note, however, that Backus went on to define the AST system, which includes the notion of state (and implicitly, of objects). Applicative languages were originally developed in reaction to what was surely an overuse of objects and imperative features in programming. Yet, it seems clear that we cannot eliminate them from programming without detrimental effect. For example, it is not uncommon to see applicative programs pass large data structures, which represent the state of the computation, from one function to the next. The result in such a case is not greater clarity, but less. We should not be surprised to have to deal with objects in programming; as we argued before, this is a natural outgrowth of the fact that we are frequently modeling real world objects. A better solution than banning objects is to determine their proper application and discipline their use.

We should use appropriate modeling tools. This suggests that programmers should be clear about what they are trying to model and then use the appropriate constructs. If they are modeling an abstraction, such as a number, then they should use values; if they are modeling an entity or thing that exists in time, then they should use an object. This implies that languages should support both values and objects and the means to use them in these ways. To put it another way, we must develop an appropriate discipline for using values and objects and linguistic means for supporting that discipline.

Names should be fixed. How can we arrive at such a discipline? How can we tame the state? One of the motivations for value-oriented programming is the incredible complexity that can result from a state composed of hundreds or thousands of individual variables, all capable of being changed (the Von Neumann bottleneck). We can see a possible solution to this problem by looking at natural languages. Generally, a word has a fixed meaning within a given context. This holds whether the word is a common noun or a proper name. We do not use a word to refer to one abstraction one moment and another the next, or to refer to one object one moment and another the next. Yet this is exactly what we do with variables in programming languages. To the extent that we need temporary identifiers, natural languages provide pronouns. These are automatically bound and have a very limited scope (generally a sentence or two).

Can these ideas be applied to programming languages? It would seem so; let's consider the consequences. Suppose that names in programming languages were always bound to a fixed value or object within a context; effectively all names would be constants. Similarly, whenever an object was created it could be given a name that would refer to that object until it was destroyed. There would be no "variables" that can be rebound from moment to moment by an assignment statement. Variables in the usual sense would only be allowed as components of the state of an object and the only allowable assignments would be to these components.

Would it be possible to program in such a language, or would it be too inconvenient? Without actually designing it is difficult to tell. We can only point to the fact that a considerable amount of good mathematics has been done without the aid of variables, not to mention a considerable amount dealing with real world objects. Such a language could provide, as does mathematics, mechanisms for declaring constants of very local scope. Some languages do provide these mechanisms already (e.g., 'let $t = (a+b)/2$ in ...', or '$\sin(t)+\cos(t)$ where $t = ...$'). As suggested by natural languages, it might be possible to provide some sort of pronoun facility. Hence, what we are describing is a programming language that is variable-free, but does not do away with objects, values, or names.

5. CONCLUSIONS

In this paper we have distinguished the two concepts 'value' and 'object'. We have shown that values are abstractions, and hence atemporal, unchangeable and non-instantiated. We have shown that objects correspond to real world entities, and hence exist in time, are changeable, have state, are instantiated, and can be created, destroyed, and shared. These concepts are implicit in most programming languages, but are not well delimited.

We claim that programs can be made more manageable by recognizing explicitly the value/object distinction. This can be done by incorporating facilities for handling values and objects in programming languages.

REFERENCES

[1] Backus, J., Can programming be liberated from the Von Neumann style? A functional style and its algebra of programs, *CACM 21*, 8, August 1978, pp. 613-641.

[2] Flew, A., *A Dictionary of Philosophy*, St. Martin's Press, New York, 1979.

[3] Hoare, C.A.R., *Recursive Data Structures*, Stanford University Computer Science Department Technical Report STAN-CS-73-400 and Stanford University A.I. Lab. MEMO AIM-223, October 1973.

[4] Kay, Alan C., Microelectronics and the personal computer, *Scientific American 237*, 3, September 1977, pp. 230-244.

[5] MacLennan, B. J., Fen - an axiomatic basis for program semantics, *CACM 16*, 8, August 1973, pp. 468-471.

[6] MacLennan, B. J., *Values and Objects in Programming Languages*, Naval Postgraduate School Computer Science Department Technical Report NPS52-81-006, April 1981.

[7] Schoch, J., An overview of the language Smalltalk-72, *Sigplan Notices 14*, 9, September 1979, pp. 64-73.

ELEMENTS OF OBJECT-ORIENTED PROGRAMMING

BY GEOFFREY A. PASCOE

What features must a language have to be considered an object-oriented language?

THERE ARE AS many different views of what object-oriented programming is as there are computer scientists and programmers. Because the term was first used to describe the Smalltalk programming environment developed at Xerox PARC (see references 1–5), this article will present object-oriented programming concepts, terminology, and characteristics from that perspective. I will stress the differences between an object-oriented programming style and the more conventional procedure-oriented style. I hope to show that a language must have four elements to support object-oriented programming: information hiding, data abstraction, dynamic binding, and inheritance. (Some languages that have one or two of these elements have been improperly called object-oriented.) I will follow this with a discussion of the advantages and disadvantages of object-oriented programming languages.

DATA PROCEDURES VS. OBJECT MESSAGES

Most programming languages support the "data-procedure" paradigm.

Active procedures act on the passive data that is passed to them. A typical example might be a square root function, sqrt(x), that takes a number and returns its square root.

In a strongly typed language such as Pascal, it would be typical to have a different version of sqrt(x) for each data type of x, usually returning a floating-point result. A late-binding language such as LISP detects x's data type at run time and performs the appropriate operations for that data type. Such generic operations are generally primitives restricted to a small class of data types such as numbers, or they are functions defined in terms of such primitives.

Object-oriented languages employ a data or object-centered approach to programming. Instead of passing data to procedures, you ask objects (data) to perform operations on themselves. To emphasize this difference I will use an object-oriented expression syntax of my own invention. The object name is followed by :operation, followed by any further arguments, and terminated by a period (in some ways the syntax is similar to that of Small-

talk-80, though simpler). For example, an expression to take the square root of x will look like this:

x :sqrt.

The implication is that x is asked to perform the :sqrt operation on itself. You say that x is the *receiver* of the *message* :sqrt.

A more complicated example would be the dot-product operation. The dot-product of two one-dimensional vectors, x and y, is computed, producing a scalar result:

x :dot y.

Here, x is told to perform a dot-product operation with itself and the argument y. You could take the square root of the dot product of x and y and assign the result to the variable z in the following manner

z ← (x :dot y) :sqrt.

Geoffrey A. Pascoe (1027 Scituate Harbor, Pasadena, MD 21122) is a researcher in the Department of Defense's Computing Systems Research Division and comoderator of the Smalltalk conference on BIX.

using parentheses to indicate the order of evaluation, although the parentheses are really not needed here, assuming left-to-right evaluation.

Some Terminology

The basic terminology of object-oriented programming is illustrated in the text box "Data Structures" on page 142. The object that I have been referring to (i.e., x, in the sqrt example) is an *instance* of a *class*. The class provides all the information necessary to construct and use objects of a particular kind, its instances. (For this reason, a class is sometimes called a *factory*.) Each instance has one class; a class may have multiple instances.

The class also provides storage for *methods*. Methods are simply procedures that are invoked by sending *selectors* to a class's instances (also called sending messages). The methods reside in the class to save storage, since all instances of a class have an identical set of methods. Methods may allocate temporary variables for use during the execution of the method. These temporary variables are much like local variables in Pascal procedures in that their value is lost when you leave the method.

Each instance has storage allocated for maintaining its individual state. The state is referenced by *instance variables*. Instance variables may be primitive data types such as integers, other objects, or both, depending on the language. Each object has its own set of instance variables. Both temporary and instance variables may be freely referenced within the scope of an object's method, but unlike temporary variables the value of instance variables is not lost when you leave the object's method.

Computation is performed by sending messages to objects, which invokes a method in the object's class. Typically, a method sends messages to other objects, which invokes other methods, etc., until you reach the point where a *primitive method* is invoked. Here ends the chain of message-sends. Each message-send eventually returns a result to the sender (e.g., x :sqrt returning the square root of x). The end result of all these message-sends is usually the changing of the state of one or more objects. Sometimes, however, a message is sent simply to invoke some primitive having a side effect external to the world of objects, for example, accessing an external file system or controlling hardware.

To fully support object-oriented programming a language must exhibit four characteristics: information hiding, data abstraction, dynamic binding, and inheritance. I will examine two languages, Ada and Modula-2, that have been mistakenly called object-oriented in order to illustrate why all four characteristics are necessary and why conventional procedure-oriented languages cannot adequately support object-oriented programming.

Information Hiding

Information hiding is important for ensuring reliability and modifiability of software systems by reducing interdependencies between software components. The state of a software module is contained in private variables, visible only from within the scope of the module. Only a localized set of procedures directly manipulates the data. In addition, since the internal state variables of a module are not directly accessed from without, a carefully designed module interface may permit the internal data structures and procedures to be changed without affecting the implementation of other software modules.

Most modern languages, even FORTRAN, to some degree, support information hiding. ISO (standard) Pascal is one notable exception, since it provides no way to declare static variables within the scope of a procedure.

Data Abstraction

Data abstraction could be considered a way of using information hiding. A programmer defines an abstract data type consisting of an internal representation plus a set of procedures used to access and manipulate the data. Modula-2 provides excellent data abstraction mechanisms. Listing 1 is a fragment of Modula-2 module that implements a stack as an abstract data type (called an *opaque type* in Modula-2 terminology. See reference 6). Variables of type Stack may be declared and manipulated in other program units.

Modula-2's data abstraction mechanism provides a certain degree of protection since no direct access to the internal state of a stack is provided. The stack is manipulated through the module's processing and query procedures. But there are a couple of problems with the Modula-2 solution. One is that the procedures used by a module must have either unique or qualified names. For example, if a module uses (imports) two different abstract data types, Stack and Queue, and variables of these types must be initialized, then the initialization procedures defined for these types must have different names, such as InitializeStack and InitializeQueue, or their usage must be qualified, as in Stack.Initialize and Queue.Initialize. This makes the resulting program less versatile. But more important than the need for unique identifiers is the drawback that Modula-2 abstract data types can operate on only one type of data. Stack, therefore, can store only integers.

Ada partially solves both these problems through two language features: operator overloading and generic program units (see reference 7). Operator overloading permits a program to use multiple operators with the same name. The distinction between operators can be determined at compile time by examining the types and number of parameters, just as + can be used to add either integer or real numbers in most modern languages. Generic program units permit the definition of a module to be used with different data types. The generic program unit is a procedural template that can be parameterized with actual types during compilation of programs using its capabilities.

A problem still exists if you wish to use the stack to store heterogeneous elements. Neither compile-time solution, operator overloading or generic program units, is sufficient. The solution is dynamic binding.

Dynamic Binding

Dynamic binding is needed to make full use of this code for stacking other types of data. Consider the addition of a procedure, Print, to the Stack-Handler module that prints the contents of a stack. If you use the stack for storing integers, floating-point numbers, character strings, etc., a traditional procedure-oriented approach dictates that you include a case statement to check at run time that the correct printing procedure for an element's type is used. Trying to print an integer with a procedure designed to print character strings is potentially disastrous. The resulting problem is that every time you add a new type of data to the software sys-

---

Listing 1: *Definition and implementation modules for the abstract data type* Stack.

```
DEFINITION MODULE StackHandler;

TYPE
  Stack; (* Opaque type *)

  StackType = INTEGER;

PROCEDURE Initialize(VAR s: Stack): BOOLEAN;

PROCEDURE Push(s: Stack;
              value: StackType): BOOLEAN;

PROCEDURE Pop(s: Stack;
             VAR value: StackType): BOOLEAN;

PROCEDURE IsEmpty(s: Stack): BOOLEAN;

PROCEDURE IsEmpty(s: Stack): BOOLEAN;

PROCEDURE IsFull(s: Stack):BOOLEAN;

END StackHandler.
-------------------------------------
IMPLEMENTATION MODULE StackHandler;

  FROM SYSTEM IMPORT TSIZE;

  FROM storage IMPORT Allocate, Available;

  CONST

    BufferSize = 1000;

TYPE

  IndexRange = [0..BufferSize];

  StackRecord =
    RECORD
      index: IndexRange;
      buffer: ARRAY [1..BufferSize] of StackType
    END;

  Stack = POINTER TO StackRecord;

(* code for implementation part of Initialize,
Push, Pop, IsEmpty, and IsFull goes here *)
        .
        .
        .

BEGIN (* StackHandler *)             .
  (* No Initialization Required *)
END StackHandler.
```

tem, you must modify all such case statements and recompile—a time-consuming and error-prone procedure. Ideally, additions should require only additions, not modifications.

The object-oriented approach pushes the responsibility for printing elements onto the objects themselves. Each object is sent the exact same message selector, Print, so that it will print itself in the proper way. This is known as *polymorphism*, since the same message can elicit a different response depending on the receiver. Operator overloading in Ada does not exhibit this form of dynamic polymorphism since the address of the procedure invoked is fixed at compile time.

This model of object-oriented programming can be improved. As presented thus far, the addition of a new type of object requires writing entirely new procedures for common operations such as Print. What's worse is that there will be a great deal of similarity between different Print methods, requiring continual rewrites of methods that differ slightly or not at all. This burden is likely to be so great that programmers would avoid the creation of new object types, significantly reducing the practical usefulness of object-oriented programming systems. Inheritance is a mechanism that largely relieves programmers of this burden.

INHERITANCE
Inheritance enables programmers to create classes and, therefore, objects that are specializations of other objects. For example, you might create an object, Trumpet, that is a specialization of a BrassInstrument, which is a specialization of a WindInstrument, which is a specialization of MusicalInstrument, etc. A Trumpet inherits behavior that is appropriate for BrassInstruments, WindInstruments, and MusicalInstruments.

Creating a specialization of an existing class is called *subclassing*. The new class is a *subclass* of the existing class, and the existing class is the *superclass* of the new class. The subclass inherits instance variables, class variables, and

methods from its superclass. The subclass may add instance variables, class variables, and methods that are appropriate to more specialized objects. In addition, a subclass may override or provide additional behavior to methods of a superclass. Methods are overridden when you provide a new method for an old method's selector.

The mechanism to add new behavior to an existing method tends to be language-dependent. In those languages most closely modeled after Smalltalk, this is accomplished by embedding a message-send to the *pseudovariable* super in the new definition of a method (see the text box "Pseudovariables" on page 144). For example, suppose you have an initialization method, initialize, defined in a superclass. If a subclass adds some instance variables, x and y, that must also be initialized to zero, then both initialization behaviors will be exhibited by the following method:

initialize
  super initialize.
  $x \leftarrow y \leftarrow 0$.

The initialization in the superclass is performed, followed by the added initialization behavior. Depending on the placement of the message-send to super, the new behavior may precede, follow, or surround the existing behavior.

Inheritance enables programmers to create new classes of objects by specifying the differences between a new class and an existing class instead of starting from scratch each time. A large amount of code can be reused this way.

ADVANTAGES
Object-oriented languages have many advantages over more traditional procedure-oriented languages. Information hiding and data abstraction increase reliability and help decouple procedural and representational specification from implementation. Dynamic binding increases flexibility by permitting the addition of new classes of objects (data types) without having to modify existing code. Inheritance coupled with dynamic binding permits code to be reused. This

DATA STRUCTURES

The class data structure in figure A contains information needed to construct and use object instances. The first and second fields indicate the number of instance variables and their names, respectively. The names are needed so that when methods are compiled, the instance variable names can be identified as referring to instance variables.

The third field of the class data structure is a flag that indicates whether an instance contains a variable number of indexable instance variables. Arrays are examples of objects that may have a variable number of instance variables. The instance variables of an array are accessed by indexing instead of by names. Since arrays of different sizes will respond to the same protocol (the set of messages to which an object responds), it does not make sense to have different classes for each array size.

The class variable field contains storage for variables shared by all instances. Class variable names are also stored here. Class variables can be convenient for storing information that should be common to all instances of the class. Not only does this save storage, but it greatly simplifies changing shared information. Otherwise, all instances of a class would have to be located to change an instance variable.

The method dictionary contains pairs of selectors and methods. When a message is sent to an object, the class's method dictionary is searched for a method to execute.

The superclass field points to the superclass of this class. The superclass is another class data structure that has all the same fields as this class. Other instance variables, class variables, and methods may be defined in the superclass.

If during a message-send a method is not found in the instance's immediate class, the superclass method dictionary is searched. If it is not found there, the superclass's superclass method dictionary is searched, and so on, until the class at the root of the hierarchy (most often called Object) is searched and found not to have a matching selector. In this case an error is returned.

Note that each instance contains a

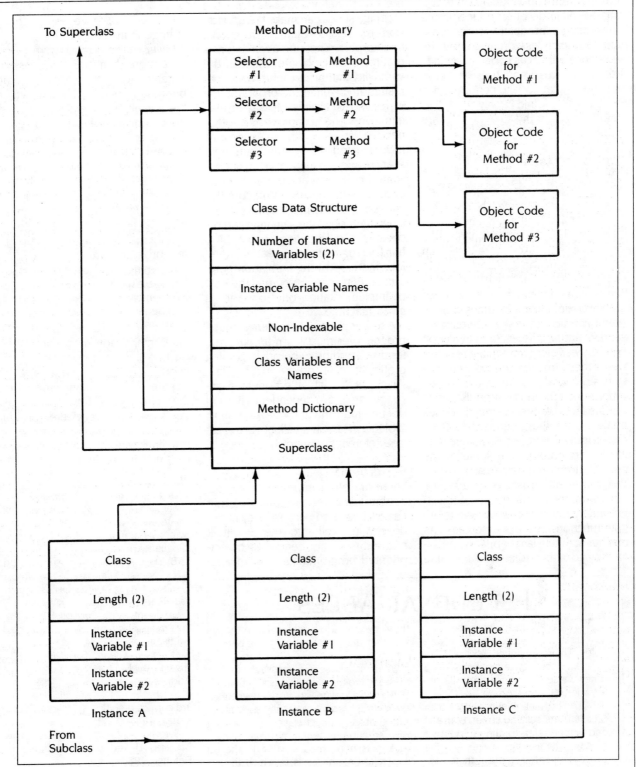

Figure A: *Data structures illustrating concepts related to object-oriented programming. Arrows indicate pointers.*

pointer to its class and a field indicating the length of the instance. The pointer to the class is needed so that the class, and therefore an object's methods, may be easily located when the instance is sent a message. Storing length information in the instance aids the storage manager and is useful when dealing with indexable instances.

has the attendant advantage of reducing overall code bulk and increasing programmer productivity, since you have to write less original code. Inheritance enhances code "factoring" (see references 1 and 2). Code factoring means that code to perform a particular task is found in only one place, and this eases the task of software maintenance.

DISADVANTAGES

Object-oriented languages have a few characteristics that are considered disadvantages by some. The one most often debated is the run-time cost of the dynamic binding mechanism. A message-send takes more time than a straight function call. Some studies have shown that with a well-implemented messager this overhead is approximately 1.75 times a standard function call (see references 8 and 9). Actual differences in execution speed between traditional languages and their object-oriented counterparts, however, do not prove to be very significant. This is most likely due to the fact that the overhead applies only to message-sends and that message-sends accomplish more than a function call. Often, some of the work done automatically by a message-send must be done by the programmer anyway using code surrounding function calls or even multiple function calls. In fact, a case can be made that in large applications the ability to standardize and fine-tune

the functionality supplied with the message-sends can make the application run faster than a traditional counterpart. The primary reason is that messaging obviates much of the variability in function setup code that results from different programming styles and skill levels. Messaging also eliminates the complex code often needed when traditional programs have to simulate dynamic binding.

Another disadvantage often cited is that implementation of object-oriented languages is more complex than comparable procedure-oriented languages, since the semantic gap between these languages and typical hardware machines is greater. Therefore more software simulation is required. Fortunately, you pay the cost of implementation only once for a given machine.

Another potential problem is that a programmer must learn an often extensive class library before becoming proficient in an object-oriented language. As a result, object-oriented languages are more dependent on good documentation and development tools such as Smalltalk-80 browsers (see references 2 and 4).

CONCLUSION

There are other important concepts in object-oriented programming that I haven't covered because they either do not fit well into the Smalltalk model or are not central to object-oriented programming. Two that re-

quire at least abbreviated mention are multiple inheritance and automatic storage management.

Multiple inheritance allows a class to have more than one superclass. The potential for code sharing is greater, but the possibility of conflicts between multiple superclasses increases the complexity of such systems. Certain flavors of LISP get a great deal of power by using multiple inheritance.

Automatic storage management, though not necessary, is so useful that it almost qualifies as a fifth major element. Automatic storage management techniques such as reference counting and garbage collection permit programmers to ignore details concerning the release of an object's storage. Application code becomes cleaner, and the overall system becomes more reliable.

Object-oriented programming provides major advantages in the production and maintenance of software: shorter development times, a high degree of code sharing (good factoring), and malleability. These advantages make object-oriented programming an important technology for building complex software systems now and in the future. ∎

REFERENCES
1. Ingalls, Daniel H. *The Smalltalk-76 Programming System Design and Implementation*. Conference Record of the Fifth Annual Symposium on Principles of Programming Languages.
2. BYTE, Smalltalk Issue, August 1981.
3. Goldberg, Adele, and Dave Robson. *Smalltalk-80: The Language and Its Impementation*. Reading, MA: Addison-Wesley, 1983.
4. Goldberg, Adele. *Smalltalk-80: The Interactive Programming Environment*. Reading, MA: Addison-Wesley, 1984.
5. Krasner, Glenn. *Smalltalk-80: Bits of History, Words of Advice*. Reading, MA: Addison-Wesley, 1983.
6. Wirth, Niklaus. *Programming in Modula-2*, 3rd corrected edition. New York: Springer-Verlag, 1985.
7. *Reference Manual for the Ada Programming Language*. United States Department of Defense, 1980.
8. Cox, Brad J. "Object-oriented Programming in C." *Unix Review*, October/November, 1983.
9. Cox, Brad J. "Message/Object Programming: An Evolutionary Change in Programming Technology." IEEE *Software*, vol. 1, no. 1, January 1984.

PSEUDOVARIABLES

Syntactically, pseudovariables are treated the same as normal variables. Their semantics, however, are different since they cannot be assigned a new value during any particular invocation of a method.

Two important pseudovariables in Smalltalk are self and super. Both self and super refer to the object that received the message currently being processed. For example, if there happen to be 22 different rectangle objects currently existing and one of them is sent the center message, then the system will set both the pseudovariables self and super to refer to that rectangle. The difference between

these two pseudovariables lies in the way that the message lookup is performed.

When self is sent a message, the message lookup algorithm is identical to the way a lookup is performed when the message is sent externally, starting in the object's direct class.

When super is sent a message, the lookup is performed starting in the superclass of the class in which the method that is currently executing is found. Note that this is not necessarily the superclass of the object's class. This pseudovariable mechanism gives objects a controlled way of accessing superclass methods.

Object Oriented Programming

Tim Rentsch
Computer Science Department
University of Southern California
Los Angeles, California 90089-0782

Recently I had the opportunity to read the Intel manual introducing the iAPX 432 architecture. The manual is an amalgam of an informal overview of the hardware, a quick tutorial review of computer architectures in general, an introduction to the advanced concepts of the 432 in particular, and marketing hype proclaiming the advantages of the 432 over its competition. The 432's architecture has many interesting, unusual characteristics, and Intel is wise to introduce them in a form which is quickly assimilable. What most caught my interest is the claim that the 432 supports the "object oriented design methodology."

What is object oriented programming? My guess is that object oriented programming will be in the 1980's what structured programming was in the 1970's. Everyone will be in favor of it. Every manufacturer will promote his products as supporting it. Every manager will pay lip service to it. Every programmer will practice it (differently). And no one will know just what it is.

Surely there's a better way. I hope this paper will clarify object oriented programming by characterizing its more important aspects. These characterizations, while not a definition *per se*, should at least provide a better understanding, and ideally a commonly held one. Thus I hope we can avoid the deplorable and confusing situation just described.

History

The immediate ancestor of object oriented programming is the programming language Simula. The Smalltalk programming system carried the object oriented paradigm to a smoother model. Although other systems have definitely shown some object oriented tendencies, the explicit awareness of the idea – including the term "object oriented" – came from the Smalltalk effort. Furthermore, Smalltalk is still the strongest representative of object oriented programming in the sense of being the most unified under a single (object oriented) paradigm. Comments on some related efforts will be given in a later section. For now it is enough to note that object oriented programming arose when Smalltalk was developed and therefore the history of Smalltalk serves as the history of object oriented programming.

Smalltalk is the software half of an ambitious project known as the Dynabook. The Dynabook is a sort of computer holy grail, with the goal of being a truly personal computer. The Dynabook ultimately is expected to handle with equal facility any and all kinds of information management, and to be all (computer type) things to all people. Accordingly Smalltalk has to carry quite a burden of expressiveness and convenience.

Alan Kay is the man chiefly responsible for the vision of the Dynabook. In the late 1960's he did work on a preliminary version, known in that incarnation as the Flex machine. Then in the early 1970's he went to the Xerox Palo Alto Research Center and there formed the Learning Research Group. Alan's goal was still a truly useful personal computer, with the Xerox Alto being the interim hardware for the Dynabook, and with LRG doing Smalltalk as the software.

Smalltalk drew heavily from Flex, which in turn was an "Eulerized" version of Simula. While a LISP influence is clearly evidenced in the deeper structure of Smalltalk, the *class* notion from Simula dominated the design. The language became completely based on the notion of a class as the sole structural unit, with instances of classes, or *objects*, being the concrete units which inhabit the world of the Smalltalk system. Smalltalk did not completely give up its LISP heritage; rather that heritage is felt more as a flavor of the system than as specific ideas of the programming language.

Relationship of Smalltalk to Object Oriented Programming

More than a programming language, Smalltalk is a complete programming environment, all of which reflects the object oriented philosophy. Object oriented programming is so much a part of Smalltalk that it is difficult to tell where one leaves off and the other begins. While the entire Smalltalk system is worthy of investigation in its own right, we are now concerned only with object oriented *programming*, which is just a part of the Smalltalk system. A brief discussion will make clear the distinction and remove confusion about which term means what.

> Note: this paper is not a tutorial on the Smalltalk language. I will discuss the internals and specifics of Smalltalk only insofar as they relate to the topic at hand. Readers unfamiliar with Smalltalk may wish to read the references first, although I have tried to make this unnecessary. I suggest to the confused reader that he finish reading this paper, then consult the references to clear up any confusion, then (optionally) read this paper again.

Smalltalk may be thought of as comprised of four pieces, *viz.*, a programming language kernel, a programming paradigm, a programming system, and a user interface model. These pieces are fuzzily defined and not explicit within the actual Smalltalk system. They are basically hierarchical, though there is overlap and some convolution. Thus the user interface is built on the programming system, which is built following the programming paradigm and using the programming language kernel.

The *programming language kernel* is the syntax and semantics as determined by the Smalltalk compiler. The *programming paradigm* is the style of use of the kernel, a sort of world view or "meaning" attached to the entities in the kernel. The *programming system* is the set of system objects and classes that provides the framework for exercising the programming paradigm and language kernel, the things necessary to make programming possible and convenient. The *user interface model* is the use and usage of the systems building materials in order to present the system to the user – in other words, the given user interface plus the user interface "flavor." The combination of these four pieces is the Smalltalk system.

> Although I have represented the pieces as separate and independent, they are not, really. In fact they are inseparable and very interdependent. Not only could each piece itself not exist in a vacuum, the design for each piece influenced the design for all the other pieces, i.e., each design could not exist in a vacuum. A more faithful representation would be as interrelated aspects of the Smalltalk system. Following the note, however, I shall continue to consider them as "pieces" rather than "aspects."

Using this view of the Smalltalk world, imagine a line drawn within the programming system piece such that the objects and classes relating to the user interface model are on one side and the objects and classes relating to the programming paradigm and language kernel are on the other. We now find Smalltalk divided naturally into two parts: a user interface part, and another part. This other part is the object oriented programming aspect of Smalltalk. With the understanding that by "Smalltalk" I mean only as much of Smalltalk as is below the line of the user interface part, I shall henceforth use the terms "Smalltalk" and "object oriented programming" interchangeably.

Characterizing Object Oriented Systems

Object oriented programming is *not* programming using a Simula-like class concept, just as structured programming is not GOTO-less programming. Most of the definitions of structured programming fail to impart any real understanding of the term. We can do better by *characterizing* object oriented programming rather than giving a formal definition.

No explanation of object oriented programming could get off the ground without a discussion of objects. In characterizing such systems we are interested not in what an object is but in how an object appears. In what follows an object is always viewed from outside (the characterization of objects), not from inside (what objects "are").

It is no accident that in explaining object oriented programming objects are viewed from outside. The shift of viewpoint from inside to outside is itself an essential part of object oriented programming. In my experience this shift occurs as a quantum leap, the "aha!" that accompanies a flash of insight. In spite of this, I am convinced that the view from outside is the natural one – only my years of training and experience as a programmer conditioned me to "normally" view objects from inside. Probably due to the influence of formal mathematics, programmatic behavior was originally thought of as extrinsic. For understanding complex systems, however, intrinsic behavior provides a better metaphor, because people think that way (for example, children learn Smalltalk very quickly.) As Dijkstra cautions, we must be careful not to think something is convenient just because it is conventional. The first principle of object oriented programming might be called *intelligence encapsulation*: view objects from outside to provide a natural metaphor of intrinsic behavior.

Objects

The Smalltalk world is populated by items seen uniformly to be "objects." These "objects" are the sole inhabitants of an otherwise empty universe. This is not just a trick of nomenclature; the items are uniform in a number of ways, that uniformity producing the items' "objectivity." In what ways are objects uniform?

Objects are uniform in that all items are objects. An item found floating in the void of Smalltalk's universe is certain to be an amorphous blob. The blob has the properties of *objectness*: inherent processing ability, message communication, and uniformity of appearance, status, and reference. The item being amorphous means that no other properties are evident. The object may possess properties outside objectness, but these are made available by the whim of the object – any such properties are not visible to an outside observer.

Objects are uniform in that all objects are equally objectlike. What this means is that all objects communicate using the same metaphor, namely message passing. Objects send messages to communicate with objects. (Message sending is discussed later in the paper.)

Objects are uniform in that no object is given any particular status. Thus, "primitive" objects, such as integers, are objects just like any other. Also, "system" objects, such as class *Class*, are objects just like any other. Finally, user defined objects are objects just like any other. There are no "second class citizens."

Not only are objects themselves uniform, the means of referring to objects is uniform. An object is always dealt with as a whole, by using its (system internal) name; a given name may name any object, since all objects have the same kind of names. It follows that there is no way of opening up an object and looking at its insides, or updating ("smashing") its state. What is more important is that the concept of opening up an object does not exist in the language. (This is like trying to imagine that something is true that can't be thought of in the first place.)

Of course it is possible for the object itself to act as if it could be opened up. With suitable methods an object can choose to provide behavior that duplicates, say, a Pascal record. Pascal records can certainly have their insides looked at, or their state updated (or smashed). The distinction is that the object itself has chosen to provide this behavior – it is not part of the language. Furthermore, most objects do not normally provide such behavior. In a true object oriented system, this is as true of the system philosophy as of the actual mechanisms.

Processing, Communication, and Message Sending

For a processing system to be a useful one, processing activity must take place. In Smalltalk, the processing activity takes place inside objects. An object, far from being inert matter, is an active, alive, intelligent entity, and is responsible for providing its own computational behavior. Thus processing capability is not only inside the object, it is everpresent within and inseparable from the object.

The other property essential to a programming system is communication. An object in process may at times be entirely self sufficient, but when it is not it must have some way of interacting with objects outside of itself. Also, the user wants processing done to bring about his wishes. Both of these are needs of communication, and both are served by the mechanism of message passing.

Objects process and send messages to effect the user's desires as well as their own. A user asks an object to carry out some processing activity by sending to the object a message. The object may in turn ask other objects for information, or for some computational work to be done, by sending them messages, and so on.

Message sending serves as the uniform metaphor for communication in the same way that objects serve as the uniform metaphor for processing capability and synthesis. This uniformity is an important part of Smalltalk. In what ways is message sending uniform?

Message sending is uniform in that all processing is accomplished by message sending. The same mechanism serves to do addition, compute arctanh, request the most complicated file service operation, or provide whatever behavior is available from a user defined object. No other mechanism – such as "operating on data" – is available.

Message sending is uniform in that one message is just like another. By this I do not mean that all messages are identical, or that all messages have the same format, but that messages are sent the same way irrespective of the recipient. An example should clarify this: the message " + " to an integer, denoting addition, is sent the same way as the message " + " to a dictionary, (possibly) denoting adding an entry.

The distinction between communicating and accomplishing processing is a fine one in Smalltalk. Objects react to messages sent to accomplish processing by sending messages to accomplish processing. The buck has to stop somewhere (and indeed it does), but it seems as if it could be passed on indefinitely. A corollary of messages all being sent the same way is that each object potentially can respond to any message by sending other messages in turn. The principle as it applies to object oriented programming is: any object can accomplish processing requested by any message by directing message flow to other objects.

Messages

As the sending of a message is the only way of communicating, the message itself must be the information to be communicated. Conceptually a message is the text of the message-request. Additionally a message may be parameterized by sending along with the text one or more object names. The object name parameters are part of the language of discourse and are different from the text in that the text is constant whereas the parameters may vary. An object responds to a message with a *reply*, which is an object name.

A message serves to initiate processing and request information. The text of the message informs the object what is requested. The parameters supply any additional necessary information or computational ability. The reply confirms activity completed and returns the information requested.

There is a subtle but important distinction between a conventional procedure call, which denotes an action, and sending a message, which makes a request. In a typical procedural programming language it is hard to give up the notion that the caller of a procedure is somehow "in control." The caller and callee share a language, a set of procedural interfaces, by which the caller directs the callee to perform actions. In Smalltalk, on the other hand, a message is a request of what the sender wants with no hint or concern as to what the receiver should do to accomodate the sender's wishes. The sender, presuming all objects to be quite intelligent, trusts the receiver to do "the right thing" without worrying about exactly what the right thing is. Thus assured, the sender relinquishes control philosophically as well as actually, so that the interpretation of the message is left entirely up to its recipient. This notion, a sort of *call by desire*, is central to the object oriented philosophy.

Sharing

In order to meet the goals of the Dynabook project, Smalltalk must do more than provide computational activity *in situ*. A successful personal computer system will be understandable, usable, modifiable, and adaptable. All of these requirements can be met by a facility for *sharing*.

Sharing allows understanding because it is a good match to the way people think. For example, the earth and a basketball are different, yet each has the property *round*. There isn't one "round" that belongs to the earth and another that belongs to the basketball; the common attribute round is shared. People model the universe by collecting together archetypal attributes and allowing them to be shared by the things to which they are common.

Sharing makes for a usable system by facilitating *factoring*, the property of one thing being in only one place. Successful factoring produces brevity, clarity, modularity, concinnity, and synchronicity, which in turn provide manageability in complex systems. In a project as ambitious as the Dynabook, manageability is essential to usability.

Sharing increases the ease of making modifications. This may sound paradoxical, since changing shared parts increases the chance of producing unforeseen consequences. The paradox disappears on realizing that sharing is not a binary decision but a spectrum from totally shared to totally individual. One can choose an appropriate place for a modification by moving around in the sharing spectrum, whereupon consequently the level of detail is neither too great nor too trivial. To put this another way, you can concentrate on what must be changed, not what must be left alone. This is made possible by an explicit framework providing a spectrum of sharing.

Sharing provides for adaptation by being variable along another dimension, the dimension of individuality. What this means is that attributes can be shared by a group while allowing for individuals within the group to reinterpret some "shared" behavior *as it applies to the individuals themselves*. The previous sharing spectrum varies as to which objects share which collections of attributes; the dimension of individuality determines to what extent individuals within a given collection actually share the "common" attributes. The result of allowing individual variability is that, given something close to what you want, it is easy to produce exactly what you want by overriding shared behavior with individual behavior – to *adapt*. This situation of "I want something just like that, except ..." invariably arises in real use. Adaptation is supported by sharing in this form and is referred to as *differential programming*.

Smalltalk meets the goals of sharing by providing a framework of classing, subclassing, and superclassing, collectively referred to as *inheritance*. In relation to object oriented programming what is important is not the mechanism of classing and sub-superclassing but the provision for the merits of sharing. Inheritance is also an excellent paradigm – probably any particular framework would be – for *elucidation*, providing as it does a sort of road map for the system universe. The conclusion: object oriented systems provide an explicit framework for sharing so as to accrue the attendant advantages.

Notes on Related Systems

Smalltalk remains the model object oriented system. But no programming language is an island, and a mention of other systems is clearly called for. Following is a capsule summary of relevant systems. The point here is to view the work as it relates to object oriented programming, not to appraise the merits of the various systems.

A group of installations with Burroughs B220's used a clever scheme to insure portability of files from one installation to another, in order to get around the difficulty of not having operating systems. A file was arranged as a transfer vector with relative pointers, followed by actual B220 code, followed by data. Although the code and representation of data varied from installation to installation, the desired effect could be obtained by reading the file into a standard memory location and branching indirectly through the appropriate location in the transfer vector. This idea was later carried over into the operating system of the B5000. Indeed, the entire architectural concept of the B5000 pointed in this direction, offering the first hardware implementation of what are now known as capabilities. Unfortunately, the B5000 is almost legendary for being ahead of its time, unappreciated, and misunderstood, and so the impact of the earliest object oriented ideas was hardly felt.

The Sketchpad system of the early 1960's is an object oriented system that apparently was programmed using an object oriented style. But Sketchpad is a graphical interaction system, not a programming system. While Sketchpad was one of the earliest object oriented systems, its application to programming systems was not widely appreciated, perhaps because the object oriented philosophy was not explicit enough.

The programming language Simula is an ALGOL based simulation language which first introduced the class concept. Simula certainly can be used with a style which is highly object oriented. But old ideas die hard, and Simula's extensions over ALGOL were used in support of simulation features with traditional ALGOL style programming taking up the slack. In practice, Simula falls short of realizing object oriented programming for several reasons. One, primitive data types, system data types, and user data types do not all have equal status. Two, the extensions to ALGOL, while including the class concept, also included many "features" such as INSPECT and IN, which are contrary to the object oriented philosophy. Three, the object oriented metaphor has not really caught on in the Simula community, due to the roots of the language in ALGOL. Four, the typing mechanism in Simula often makes it difficult to realize the free-spiritedness of object oriented programming. If Sketchpad is an object oriented system without the language, Simula is an object oriented language which is rarely used in an object oriented fashion.

The LISP-AI notion of frames captures well the idea that behavior rides along with the thing whose behavior is being described. Also, the resemblance of the common/default mechanism of frames to the inheritance mechanism of Smalltalk is striking. I think of frames as an object oriented extension to LISP. Similar to Simula, however, the problem with frames is that the LISP notion very strongly remains, so that the inclination towards the object oriented philosophy is not nearly so strong, nor as clearly defined, as in a completely object oriented system.

The programming language Alphard is related but still in a rather uncertain state. After more use the character of Alphard will be clearer, but generally speaking Alphard centers on abstraction, which is roughly evenly divided between data encapsulation and abstract data types. If anything Alphard leans to the abstract data types side, though not so far as, for example, algebraic axiomatic specification. One clear oversight is that Alphard does not use inheritance in any strong fashion.

The programming language ADA, though still in the implementation stages, is clearly centered and focused on data encapsulation. The sense of operating on data is very strong in ADA, from syntax to operator overloading to separation of types from modules. Generic procedures capture some, but not nearly all, of the polymorphism inherent in object oriented programming, and ADA's facility for inheritance is weak at best. ADA has followed traditional (i.e., ALGOL style) language design principles so that the issues of implementation and usage would be clear at the outset. ADA is one of the few languages that was designed with extensive, specific requirements definitely given *a priori*; none of these requirements mentions object oriented programming.

The programming language CLU makes a serious effort in the object oriented direction. The sense of unification of reference mode is very strong in CLU, narrowing the distinction between different object categories. CLU falls a little short on the syntax side, which is still a conventional functional (i.e., data oriented) format. Also, the typing mechanism of CLU doesn't give a sense of freedom to the "receiver" of a message, since the particular response mechanism is specified by the type, which is known and explicit in the source at the call site. This restriction shifts the sense of control from the receiver (object oriented) to the sender (data oriented). Furthermore, CLU resembles Alphard and ADA in lacking a good inheritance mechanism. As with Alphard, CLU tries to balance abstract data types with data encapsulation by centering on abstraction, but CLU leans to the data encapsulation side more than Alphard does. Even so, CLU remains as the strongest "traditional" contender for supporting object oriented programming.

Conclusions

It is usual to understand new ideas in terms of familiar ones. Object oriented programming might be (and probably already has been) likened to abstract data types, data encapsulation, information hiding, and modularization. This may be more palatable to some audiences, but it ducks the issue. These comparisons neither do justice to, nor capture the essence of, the object oriented methodology. To quote Alan Kay:

> "Though Smalltalk's structure allows the techniques now known as data abstraction to be easily (and more generally) employed, the entire thrust of its design has been to supercede the concept of data and procedures entirely; to replace these with the more generally useful notions of activity, communication, and inheritance."

Object oriented programming holds great promise, but is not yet widely understood. In spite of object oriented programming just now becoming popular, the term of its use is already in danger of being overworked and misunderstood. My goal has been to argue for an understanding of object oriented programming, not just a dogmatic definition. Let us hope that we have learned our lesson from structured programming and find out what the term means *before* we start using it.

Acknowledgements

My thanks to all the people who have cheerfully let me express their ideas as though they were my own.

References

Dynabook and Related

Kay, A., "The Reactive Engine," Ph.D. Thesis, University of Utah, September, 1969

Kay, A., "A Personal Computer for Children of All Ages," ACM Nat'l Conf., Boston, Aug., 1972

Kay, A., and A. Goldberg, "Personal Dynamic Media," Computer, March, 1977

Kay, A., "Microelectronics and the Personal Computer," Scientific American, September, 1977

Other systems mentioned

Birtwhistle, *et al.*, *Simula Begin*, Petrocelli/Charter, 1975

Ichbiah, J.D., *et al.*, "Preliminary ADA Reference Manual," ACM SIGPLAN Notices 14, 6A, June, 1979

Intel Corporation, *Introduction to the iAPX 432 Architecture*, Manual Number 171821-001

Intel Corporation, *iAPX 432 Architecture Reference Manual*, Manual Number 171860-001

Liskov, B., *et al.*, *CLU Reference Manual*, MIT-TR 225, October, 1979

McKeag, R.M., "Burroughs B5500 Master Control Program," Queens University of Belfast, Northern Ireland, 1971

Roberts, B., and I. Goldstein, "The FRL Manual," MIT-TR 409, September, 1979

Sutherland, I., "Sketchpad," Ph.D. Thesis, MIT, 1963

Wulf, London, and Shaw, "An Introduction to the Construction and Verification of ALPHARD Programs," IEEE Transactions on Software Engineering SE-2, 4, 1976

Smalltalk

Byte special issue on Smalltalk, BYTE, August 1981 (primarily the following articles)

    Xerox Learning Research Group, "The Smalltalk-80 System"

    Robson, D., "Object-Oriented Software Systems"

    Tesler, L., "The Smalltalk Environment"

    Ingalls, D., "Design Principles Behind Smalltalk"

    Goldberg, A., and J. Ross, "Is the Smalltalk-80 System for Children?"

Ingalls, D., "The Smalltalk-76 Programming System: Design and Implementation," 5th Annual ACM Symposium on Principles of Programming Languages, January, 1978

P·R·O·G·R·A·M·M·I·N·G T·E·C·H·N·I·Q·U·E·S

SOFTWARE-ICs

BY LAMAR LEDBETTER AND BRAD COX

A *plan for building reusable software components*

THE SOFTWARE WORLD has run headlong into the Software Crisis—ambitious software projects are hard to manage, too expensive, of mediocre quality, and hard to schedule reliably. Moreover, all too often, software delivers a solution that doesn't meet the customers' needs. After delivery, if not before, changing requirements mean that systems must be modified.

We must build systems in a radically different way if we are going to satisfy tomorrow's quantity and quality demands. We must learn to build systems that can withstand change.

Some system developers are already building software much faster and of better quality than last year. Not only that, the systems are much more tolerant of change than ever before, as a result of an old technology called message/object programming. This technology, made commercially viable because of the cost/performance trends in hardware, holds the key to a long-awaited dream—software reusability. A new industry is developing to support the design, development, distribution, and support of reusable Software-ICs (integrated circuits). A forthcoming

series in *UNIX/World* will address message/object programming.

MESSAGE/OBJECT PROGRAMMING AND SOFTWARE-ICS

In this article we'll look at the concepts of message/object programming and how they support the building of "Software-ICs," as we call them, by satisfying the requirements for reusability.

A Software-IC is a reusable software component. It is a software packaging concept that combines aspects of subroutine libraries and UNIX filter programs. A Software-IC is a standard binary file produced by compiling a C program generated by Objective-C.

The notion of *objects* that communicate by *messages* is the foundation of message/object programming and fundamental to Software-ICs. An object includes data, a collection of procedures (*methods*) that can access that data directly, and a selection mechanism whereby a message is translated into a call to one of these procedures. You can request objects to do things by sending them a message.

Sending a message to an object is exactly like calling a function to operate on a data structure, with one

crucial difference: Function calls specify not *what* should be accomplished but *how*. The function name identifies specific code to be executed. Messages, by contrast, specify what you want an object to do and leave it up to the object to decide how.

REQUIREMENTS FOR REUSABILITY

Only a few years ago, hardware designers built hardware much as we build software today. They assembled custom circuits from individual electrical components (transistors, resistors, capacitors, and so on), just as we build functions out of low-level components of programming languages (assignment statements, conditional statements, function calls, and so on). Massive reusability of hardware designs wasn't possible until a packaging technology evolved that could make the hardware environment of a chip (the circuit board and adjoining electrical components) rela-

Lamar Ledbetter is director of special projects and Brad Cox is vice president of Productivity Products International (27 Glen Rd., Sandy Hook, CT 06482), which produces Objective-C.

tively independent of the detailed workings of that chip. The IC quickly developed to the point that multiple chip vendors now vie to sell their hardware design effort in a market for reusable hardware designs.

One concept that stands out in hardware systems is that many of the components perform unique services. Services are provided upon request, and the requester need not be concerned with the internal methods or data used, only the result. The equivalent software concept, *encapsulation*, is fundamental to success in software reusability. Encapsulation defines a data structure and a group of procedures for accessing it. Users access the data structure only through a set of carefully documented, controlled, and standardized interfaces.

The concept of *messaging* is also prevalent in the hardware world. It is through messaging that the loose coupling of components is achieved and the division of responsibility between the user and the supplier is defined and enforced.

The hardware industry has also achieved a high degree of reusability through the development of standards. There are standards for interconnection, power, and processing, for example. In contrast, in the software world standards for the syntax and semantics of only a few languages have been defined and adhered to across a range of hardware. There have also been many unsuccessful attempts to define standards for the implementation of software algorithms and applications (such as GOTO-less programming, no global data, loose coupling, tight binding, and data hiding, among others). Stressing strict static "type checking" as a standard helps solve the problems of integration and debugging but does not change the basic operator/operand concept embodied in most languages; it only moves it to a higher level of abstraction. To reuse modules developed using the operator/operand concept, you have to hope that the output of one module is compatible with the "type" of the input of the receiver, redefine the type of the operands in either the receiver or sender, or transform the operands. Because of the complexity, there has been little progress in the definition of standards for reusability in the operator/operand model. In contrast, useful standards for reusability are in use or being developed in organizations that have embraced the message/object paradigm.

In the hardware world, the functions of standard components are well defined and identifiable. Given a knowledge of the functions available and a high level of standardization, hardware designers routinely integrate reusable hardware components into new systems. Standard functions are easy to identify because they map into the real-world model of hardware systems. In the software world, the definition of standard, identifiable functions is still a dream, even with our "standard" utility libraries. If software reusability is to become a reality, languages must support a more direct mapping from the model of the real-world functions to the implementation.

Hardware components are delivered in an unmodifiable form. That means that standard functions are protected. If Software-ICs are to become a reality, the languages and standards must support the delivery of components that operate as advertised and are immune to modification

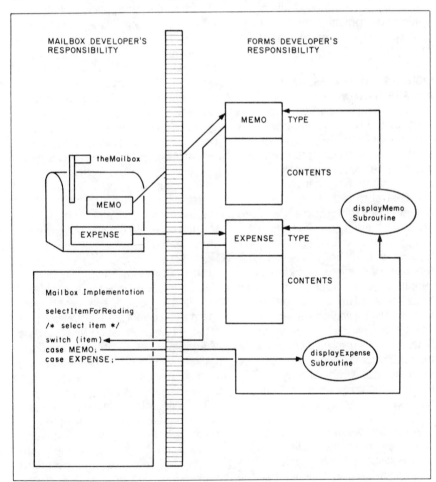

Figure 1: *Mailbox using the operator/operand model. The Mailbox developer must specify how to display the form by checking the form type and calling the correct subroutine. As a result, every form type must be enumerated and the implementation changed as form types are added or deleted.*

by the system builder. If the system builder wants different functions, he must go back to a Software-IC "foundry" for a new component.

Reusability can have several meanings in both the hardware and software worlds. A hardware designer would never think (as we do in software) of starting the design of a modification with a blank piece of paper or by looking at the design of all of the connecting components. A designer also doesn't worry about needing to modify the interfaces or components not affected by the change. Modified components "inherit" most of the previous implementation and contain only the changes necessary to provide the required new behavior. The inheritance of already-working methods by a new Software-IC has tremendous productivity implications.

WHY DIDN'T SOFTWARE-ICs EXIST BEFORE?

One of the main reasons Software-ICs didn't exist before is that the cost performance of hardware did not support the requirement that computer cycles must be used ("wasted") to enhance software reusability. The cycles were too expensive, and performance optimization was necessarily a primary goal. Strict implementations such as Smalltalk-80 consume orders of magnitude in performance. Less revolutionary implementations of the message/object paradigm, such as Objective-C, while paying some performance price, are viable for commercial systems and are in use today in companies building major software systems.

Most of us have been taught to think within the conceptual framework of operators and operands. That framework has led many to conclude that the complexity involved in reusing a software component far exceeds the possible benefits.

In order for Software-ICs to work, the manner in which systems evolve has to be fundamentally different. The concept of *inheritance*, discussed in detail later, is that fundamental difference. The concept of Software-ICs

Encapsulation is fundamental to success in software reusability.

also demands a level of standardization in system implementation that has not been feasible until recently. Finally, the market for Software-ICs is a recent reality created by the recognition that what I call the Software Crisis can be solved only by fundamental changes in the way we build systems. It is no longer competitively viable to ignore the products of previous development efforts if there is any way to reuse or reapply those products.

OBJECTS, MESSAGES, AND ENCAPSULATION

The distinction between specifying what should be done as opposed to how it should be done is subtle and often misunderstood. It is, however, a crucial one because, as has been demonstrated in the hardware world, it is central to reusability.

By way of example, imagine a programmer building an electronic mailbox in an electronic office system, and focus on the mailbox developer's role as a user of services provided by his supplier, the developer of the forms being mailed. The mailbox developer must provide a way to implement the intention to display the selected item. If he does this using the conventional operator/operand model and specifying how, not what, as depicted in figure 1, the code given in listing 1a results.

Notice the separation of responsibilities. Because the mailbox developer is responsible for deciding how to implement the function that is called selectItemForReading, the code must enumerate every data type the forms developers might provide. This results in code that is inherently nonreusable; the case labels explicitly

state that this mailbox is useless except for memo and expense contents.

Now notice what happens in the rewritten code (listing 1b) using messages and objects as depicted in figure 2. The message expression, item display, commands the object, item, to display itself, thus specifying only what the object is to do. How the object is to do it is decided by the forms developers so the mailbox code becomes independent of its contents.

The technical term for this is *dynamic binding*. Dynamic binding and encapsulation are at the root of the reusability provided by this variety of message/object programming.

Some modern programming languages (Ada, Modula-2, and CLU, for example) provide a different form of encapsulation by binding statically at compile time. While this certainly is an improvement over traditional languages like C and Pascal, it provides no new help in solving the reusability problem. The mailbox example coded in any of these languages would still need the switch statement.

The notion of a Software-IC, in which reusable code is built and tested by a supplier and then delivered to consumers in binary form, is not possible without dynamic binding.

USING SOFTWARE-ICs

We will demonstrate the use of Software-ICs by building a simple program that counts the unique words in a file. For the sake of comparison, we will discuss two different solutions based on reuse of existing software and then turn our attention to the Software-IC solution.

The subroutine-library solution would reuse library functions for managing files, printing results, and comparing strings. Custom software would be required for the word parser, hash function, hash table/collision handling, counting words in the hash table, and printing the formatted results. Much of the significant new development and debugging effort concerns algorithms that have been

Listing 1: *Operator/operand versus message/object implementations. Listings 1a and 1b are, respectively, examples of portions of code that create an electronic Mailbox using conventional (operator/operand) and message/object models. Comparing the two illustrates the difference between the Mailbox developer specifying "how" versus "what."*

(1a)

```
selectItemForReading(theMailbox) {
    .
    .
    .
    /* Select an item in theMailbox and . . . */
  /* check the item type flag */
    switch(item->type)
  /* Now call the appropriate display subroutine */
  {
    case MEMO:      displayMemo(item); break;
    case EXPENSE:  displayExpense(item); break;
    .
    .
    .
    default: error("unknown contents"); break;
  }
    .
    .
    .
}
```

(1b)

```
selectItemForReading(theMailbox) {
    . . .
    /* Select an item in theMailbox and . . . */
    [item display];    /* Send item a message to display itself */
    .
    .
}
```

Listing 2: *Using Software-ICs. This message/object program counts the unique words in a file using preexisting Software-ICs from the Objective-C library:* Set *and* String.

```
// Reads words from stdin and counts unique ones main( ) {
    extern id String, Set;      // Specify object (instance) factory ids
    id uniqueWords, currentWord;      // Local object (instance) ids
    char buf[MAXBUF];          // Word buffer

    uniqueWords = [Set new];      // Create a new empty set instance
    while (nextWord(buf) != EOF) {      // forEachWord . . .
      currentWord = [String str:buf];  // Create a string instance for each word
      [uniqueWords filter:currentWord];// Store unique ones in set
    }
    printf("The number of unique words is %d \ n", [uniqueWords size]);
}
```

implemented in many previous applications. Once working, however, the implementation should be fairly efficient.

A UNIX-style solution would consist of small "tools" connected by pipes. The off-the-shelf utilities that could be reused include tr (translate characters), sort (sorting utility), and wc (word-count utility). The programmer would have to custom-build a script for assembling the utilities. This particular problem requires a good working knowledge of applicable UNIX utilities but no custom software. The implementation would be noticeably slower than both the subroutine library and Software-IC solutions.

The Software-IC solution involves assembling two prefabricated Software-ICs from a library of components. A String is used to hold words, and a Set can be used to hold the unique words. Both are standard components in the library released with Objective-C. The performance of the Software-IC solution would not be as good as the first solution, but it would certainly be acceptable and could be optimized by tuning. The full text for this solution, except for the small function nextWord( ), which parses words from the input stream, is presented in listing 2.

The two external symbols Set and String identify a pair of *factory objects* whose function is to produce instances of their *classes* (Software-ICs). Each class defines behaviors and declares data for (a) its factory object and (b) its instances. The two local symbols uniqueWords and current-Word identify instances, which will be manufactured by Set and String at run time.

The notion of a Software-IC is not possible without dynamic binding.

In this example, String responds to a str: message by allocating enough space to hold the characters in the message argument buf. The next statement commands the set unique-Words to perform the filter: function on currentWord.

How are reusable sets possible, since they must work properly with many different kinds of contents? For example, the same Set code may need to compare strings, points, symbols, and so on, often within the same application. The answer is that dynamic binding allows the Set to legitimately consider equality testing, for example, none of its business. Instead, it pushes that decision back onto its contents. When it needs to test the equality of two items, it mere-ly commands one of them to report whether it isEqual: to the other.

CLASSES, METHODS, AND INHERITANCE

So far we have focused primarily on encapsulation. This technology should be thought of as an aid to using the services in a system. It also provides some advantages for the suppliers (builders) of message/object systems as well. Consider the job facing the builders of three familiar components of an office-automation system: Mailbox, Envelope, and File-Folder.

At one level a Mailbox is very different from a FileFolder, but they are similar in that they are kinds of containers. Each will have some amount of code involved in managing collections of other objects.

Inheritance allows containment code to be built, stockpiled, and thereafter reused as often as needed. This is done by building a class named Container, whose methods support the operations we expect of containers: adding elements, removing them, expanding and shrinking their internal capacity as needed. Thereafter, specialized container classes like Mailbox, Envelope, and FileFolder are built by describing only how each subclass differs. They may differ by having additional private data fields or by having additional (or modified) behaviors. Figure 3 depicts a typical inheritance hierarchy.

To design a new capability, the pro-

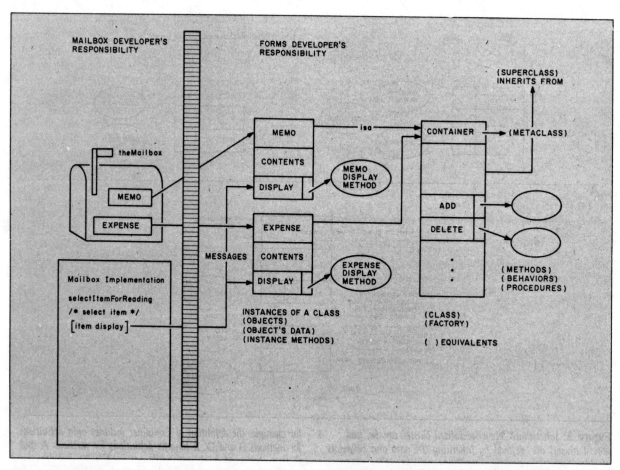

Figure 2: *Mailbox using the message/object model. The Mailbox developer specifies what the form should do by sending it a message to display itself. As a result, form types can be added or deleted without changing the Mailbox implementation.*

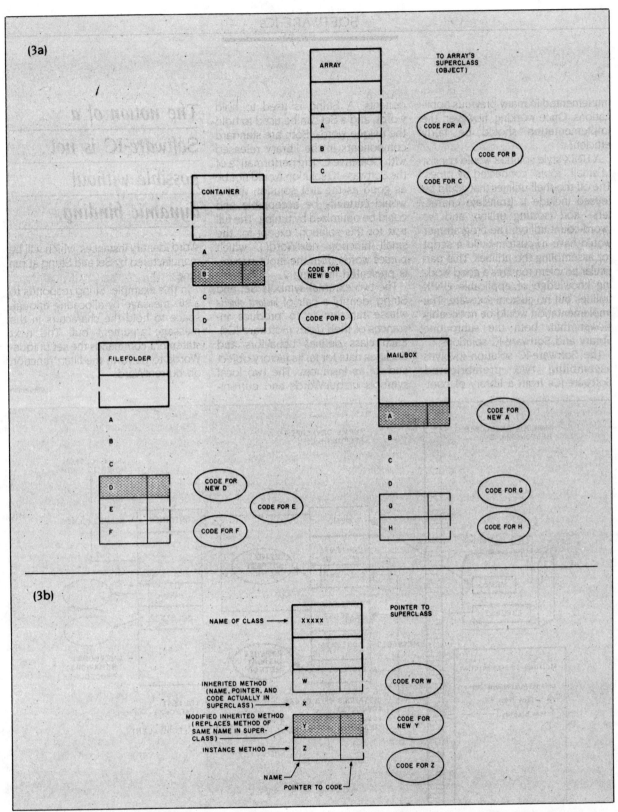

Figure 3: *Inheritance. New specialized classes can be, and almost always are, defined by inheriting the data and behaviors of older generic classes, then specifying only how the new ones differ. Figure 3a shows how the classes Container, FileFolder, and Mailbox are created; 3b explains the notation used. Note that, for example, the definition of Container includes only definitions for methods B and D. It inherits definitions for methods A and C from Array; these definitions do not need to be explicitly specified by the programmer, nor do they take any room in the definition of Container.*

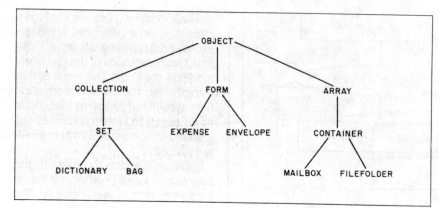

Figure 4: *Opportunities to reuse work emerge. As the design proceeds, similarities to previously developed Software-ICs become apparent, and a large degree of reuse results.*

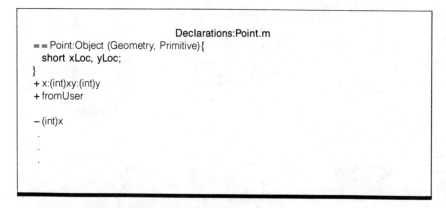

```
                        Declarations:Point.m
== Point:Object (Geometry, Primitive){
    short xLoc, yLoc;
}
+ x:(int)xy:(int)y
+ fromUser

- (int)x
.
.
.
```

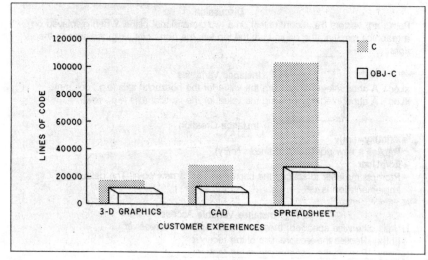

Figure 5: *Productivity experiences. Actual decreases in lines of code experienced by PPI customers using Objective-C in three different application areas.*

The manner in which systems evolve has to be fundamentally different.

grammer's thoughts turn immediately to "What do I already have that is most like the thing I need?" (see figure 4). For example, to develop an Envelope the programmer focuses on describing how Envelopes should differ from Containers. Envelopes differ from Containers by, for example, having additional data variables such as returnAddress, targetAddress, and stamp. Envelopes also differ by exhibiting additional behaviors (or methods), for example, mailTo:, open, and discard. Note that no methods need be defined for adding and removing contents from envelopes because they, and the data variables that support them, are acquired automatically, or *inherited*, from Container.

FileFolders and Mailboxes will have their own distinctive implementations. However, only their differences from a Container need to be designed, coded, tested, documented, delivered, and maintained. Their containment abilities were developed once and thereafter reused. Containment is defined consistently, systemwide. You add a letter to a Mailbox in precisely the same manner as you add a letter to a FileFolder.

SYSTEM BUILDING WITH SOFTWARE-ICs

System requirements normally model data, data flow, and actions on data. In traditional system building, the system requirements must then be mapped into the operator/operand model in order to optimize the implementation on a computer. Message/object programming allows a more direct representation of the real-world

OBJECTIVE-C

Objective-C, a PPI product (Productivity Products International Inc., 27 Glen Rd., Sandy Hook, CT 06482), is a hybrid language that combines the reusability, modeling power, and complexity-reducing attributes of Smalltalk-80 with the portability, efficiency, compatibility, and access to machine details of the C language. As shown in figure A, the Objective-C compiler transforms the Objective-C language into standard C statements. The message/object code examples use the Objective-C syntax.

While Smalltalk-80 attempts to revolutionize programming, Objective-C seeks to change it through evolution. Objective-C provides a thin layer of new structure over its C substrate by adding classes, objects, messages, encapsulation, and inheritance. No C-language capabilities are eliminated,

and none are changed. The programmer can choose conventional C-language tools when efficiency and portability are paramount and message/object power tools when encapsulation, inheritance, and dynamic binding are needed to enhance reusability and reduce code bulk and complexity.

The hybrid approach of Objective-C does breach the purity of the message/object paradigm. This means that the design and implementation rules are not as clearly defined but must evolve through experience. The hybrid approach will also require more management diligence if the amount of reusable code is to be optimized. The criteria for choosing messages/objects or writing functions in C should be clearly defined and enforced. This will require standards and control.

> *Message/object programming allows a more direct representation of the real-world model in the code.*

model in the code. The result is that the normal radical transformation from system requirements (defined in users' terms) to system specifications (defined in computer terms) is greatly reduced.

Software-ICs directly support the concept of rapid prototyping (or, in hardware terms, *breadboarding*). The ability to demonstrate a subset of a system's final functionality (particularly the human interface) in a rapid prototype helps ensure that the system built is the system needed.

No matter how well the delivered system satisfies the requirements, people usually have an immediate desire to change/evolve the system. Fortunately, as we have seen, it is possible to build changeable systems.

System builders using Objective-C employ a combination of aids to enhance the reusability of their Software-ICs. The standard libraries, for example, are documented using a catalog composed of Software-IC specification sheets. Table 1 summarizes the specification sheet for a Software-IC called Point.

CONCLUSIONS

The tools exist today in the software world to build Software-ICs. They are in use in a number of major companies and have demonstrated (see figure 5) code bulk reductions of between 2.5-1 and 5-1.

As the use of Software-ICs spreads, productivity in the software world should improve much as hardware ICs improved productivity in the hardware world. The use of Software-ICs

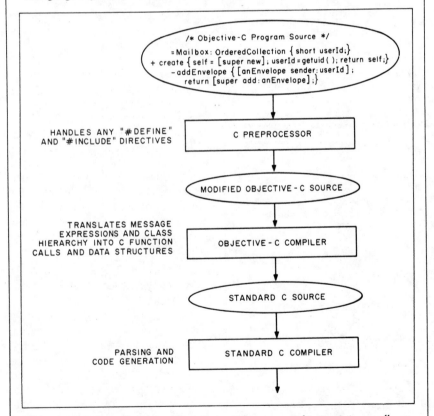

```
/* Objective-C Program Source */

= Mailbox: OrderedCollection { short userId;}
+ create { self = [super new]; userId = getuid ( ); return self;}
- addEnvelope { [anEnvelope sender: userId] ;
    return [super add: anEnvelope] ;}
```

HANDLES ANY "#DEFINE" AND "#INCLUDE" DIRECTIVES → C PREPROCESSOR

→ MODIFIED OBJECTIVE-C SOURCE

TRANSLATES MESSAGE EXPRESSIONS AND CLASS HIERARCHY INTO C FUNCTION CALLS AND DATA STRUCTURES → OBJECTIVE-C COMPILER

→ STANDARD C SOURCE

PARSING AND CODE GENERATION → STANDARD C COMPILER

Figure A: *Objective-C—a superset of the C language. Objective-C is actually a hybrid language whose message/object syntax is changed to standard C syntax by the Objective-C compiler.*

Table 1: *Software-IC specification sheets. This is a condensed version of the specification sheet for the* Point *Software-IC. The complete version contains 21 methods (versus the 9 shown).*

Point

Instance variables: { short xLoc, yLoc; }

Inherits: Object
Inherited by:
Referenced by: Point Rectangle
Refers to: Geometry Point Primitive __Object__Object__csav msg fprintf lmul sqrt

---

Discussion
Points are vectors (i.e., coordinates) on a two-dimensional plane. When displayed on a graphics terminal, the origin is at the top left; the horizontal axis increases to the right . . .

Instance Variables
xLoc   A short integer specifying the value for the horizontal axis (e.g., column).
xLoc   A short integer specifying the value for the vertical axis (e.g., row).

Instance Creation
+x:(int)xy=(int)y
    Replies a new point at coordinates (x@y).
+fromUser
    Prompts the user to specify the coordinates for a new point. The default implementation is . . .

Instance Variable Access
Unless otherwise specified, these methods reply to the receiver.
−(int)x   Replies the x-coordinate of the receiver.
−(int)y   Replies the y-coordinate of the receiver.
−X:(int)xy:(int)y
    Sets the coordinates of the receiver to (x@y).

Conditionals
In the following, words like "isAbove" or "isLeft" are with respect to a screen-oriented point of reference, not the numerical magnitudes of the coordinates. For example, the point (0, 0) is above and to the left of all other positive coordinates.
−(BOOL)isBelow:aPoint
    Replies YES of receiver is below aPoint.

Equality Testing
−(int)hash
    Replies xLoc ^ yLoc.
−(BOOL)isEqual:aPoint
    The receiver and someObject are equal if and only if they are both points and have equal coordinates.

Printing
−printOn:(IOD)anIOD
    Prints the receiver as: fprintf(anIOD,'')%d@%d)'', xLoc, yLoc);

(continued)

---

also will promote the evolution of optimized system-building methodologies and tools. Just as semiconductor foundries produce both standard and custom ICs, Software-IC foundries will do exactly the same in the software industry. ∎

REFERENCES
1. Love, T. "Application Development in Smalltalk-80." Arlington, VA: *Proceedings of Softfair-83*.
2. *Objective-C Reference Manual*, Version 3.0, Sandy Hook, CT: Productivity Products International, December 1984.

Chapter 2: Smalltalk: An Object-Based Language

Object-oriented programming is partly a point of view. It is possible to some extent in any language. Some languages assist the user in maintaining the object-oriented point of view, and others do not. In this sense, object-oriented programming is similar to structured programming. It is a way of organizing programming tasks and can be accomplished in any language, but it is greatly facilitated by a supportive language.

Smalltalk is the most object-supportive language and is, in fact, totally grounded in the object philosophy.

Objects in an object-based language are like paragraphs in prose or theorems in mathematics: they are the basic higher-level structuring device from which the whole is constructed.

The first paper, "Microelectronics and the Personal Computer," by Alan C. Kay, pertains to the origins of Smalltalk. In fact, Smalltalk grew out of Kay's vision of the dynabook: a graphically-oriented, notebook-size computer for personal use. Kay describes the origins and goals of the Smalltalk language as it relates to the dynabook.

This paper was written about 10 years ago. In the first line it prophesies that "in about a decade many people will possess a notebook-size computer with the capacity of a large computer today." If Kay would have used the word "desktop" rather than "notebook-size," he would have been right on the mark. As you read the paper, you might ask yourself if your personal computer achieves for you the vision Kay had when he wrote the article and, if not, would Smalltalk help?

Kay views the computer as a device that can simulate any process. To get the most from the machine, users will have to do some programming to truly get the machine to respond to their needs. (Kay may have missed the mark here. The versatility of canned programs such as Lotus 123 was not foreseen.) Even children should be able to use the machine effectively. Kay sees the computer as made up of many "activities," that is, entities that exhibit certain behavior when sent a particular message. "The host computer is in effect divided into thousands of computers, each with the capabilities of the whole." This is the vision that led to the object-oriented approach of Smalltalk.

Kay describes three levels of computer languages. The first is that of dealing with procedures and data. The second is Smalltalk, dealing with objects, messages, and families of objects. Interestingly, Kay sees a language level that is higher

than any object-based language, that of the observer language. What constitutes an observer language is, however, only very briefly described.

Kay describes how children relate to computers. He is particularly keen on getting the computer to respond in helpful ways for them. He describes very broadly the features of Smalltalk, including its inherent parallelism. Smalltalk is made up of objects and families of objects. Each object in a family responds to the same messages. Kay's view is much higher than that of Smalltalk alone, but the paper is very worthwhile reading and describes one view of how object-based computing fits in with progress in computing. Smalltalk grew out of the work of an idealistic visionary, Alan Kay.

The paper, "Experience with Smalltalk-80 for Application Development," by Tom Love, is an enthusiastic endorsement for the Smalltalk-80 language and programming environment. Love describes his experience in using Smalltalk to develop an application involving a graphic interface to a wide variety of data. This application required 205 statements in Smalltalk, wheras the same application would require thousands of statements in conventional languages.

Love describes both the strengths and weaknesses of Smalltalk. The strengths include the increase in productivity possible with the language, the excellent user interface, the totally integrated environment, the capability for graphics programming, and the possibility for reusing existing code. The weaknesses include the lack of capabilities for communication (mail), no integrated set of utilities for file management, computation speed too slow, small user population, and only one programming language available within the Smalltalk environment.

Love's conclusion is that Smalltalk-80 "is a solid programming environment that can be used as a base for significant applications."

The August 1981 issue of *Byte* magazine was devoted to Smalltalk. Several articles from that issue were particularly pertinent to object-oriented programming and are reproduced here.

The first of these, "The Smalltalk-80 System," by the Xerox Learning Research Group, is an overview of the language, emphasizing objects, messages, and classes. These fundamental building blocks of the language were borrowed from the first object-oriented language, SIMULA. A set of syntax diagrams for Smalltalk is included. Classes are described by using a template that includes the class name, methods (procedures) available for processing objects of that class, and its superclass. One interesting feature of Smalltalk is that every class inherits methods from its superclass. Metaclasses are described. These are classes from which other classes can be obtained.

Smalltalk includes many built-in classes. These include the class Collection, which has as subclasses, Bag, Set, Ordered-Collection, LinkedList, and IndexedCollection. Indexed-Collection has String and Array as subclasses. Also, there is the class Stream with its subclasses, ReadStream, Write-Stream, and ReadAndWriteStream. These and many other classes were implemented by using the Smalltalk system itself and are available to the programmer to use and modify.

"Design Principles Behind Smalltalk," by Daniel H.H. Ingalls, presents some principles that were observed as the Smalltalk system was being developed. These principles, while clearly related to Smalltalk, may be valuable guides to future work on programming languages. To give the flavor of the paper, two of his principles are repeated here.

Uniform Metaphor: A language should be designed around a powerful metaphor that can be uniformly applied in all areas. Examples of languages that followed this are LISP, which is built around linked lists, and Smalltalk, which is built around the concept of communicating objects.

Operating System: An operating system is a collection of things that do not fit into a language. There should not be one. Smalltalk has no operating system as such. The resources normally supplied by an operating system are made available within the language.

Trygve M.H. Reenskaug, in "User-Oriented Descriptions of Smalltalk Systems," describes the Smalltalk system from a user's point of view. It contains an example showing how real-world objects are mapped into Smalltalk objects and gives a fairly good idea of what it is like to actually program in Smalltalk.

Jim Diederich and Jack Milton, in "Experimental Prototyping in Smalltalk," describe several features of Smalltalk that contributed to its successful use in a prototyping application. They found that the Smalltalk environment greatly enhanced the modifiability of a database system. Significant modifications could be made to the system with relatively little code modification. Their conclusion is that the Smalltalk system promotes "fearless" programming by being:
- *Referenceless*: the system manages pointers to structures;
- *Clutterless*: low-level detail is managed by the system;
- *Typeless*: types are not declared for any language construct;
- *Paperless*: after an acquaintence period, programmers are comfortable relying only on the screen images for examining their work.

These authors present another enthusiastic endorsement for object-oriented programming in Smalltalk.

Smalltalk is a language and user environment that is gaining momentum and has advantages that may help to improve software productivity, usability, understandability, etc. It is the embodiment of the object point of view, taking it to its ultimate (for now, at least) realization. For someone to truly understand the object-oriented point of view, the study of Smalltalk is a must.

Additional References

Books:

A. Goldberg and D. Robson, *Smalltalk-80: The Language and its Implementation*, Addison-Wesley, Reading, Massachusetts, 1983.

This is the definitive guide to the Smalltalk language. Part 1 provides an overview of the Smalltalk-80 programming language. Part 2 provides the bulk of the book and describes eight significant categories of classes in Smalltalk. These categories include linear measures, numbers, collections, streams, and graphics. Part 3 is an example of modeling discrete, event-driven simulations in the Smalltalk system. This modeling includes the problem of coordinating and synchronizing the activities of independent processes. The Smalltalk classes Process, Semaphore, and SharedQueue provide synchronization facilities for such processes. Part 4 describes Smalltalk from the implementer's point of view. This book is the best source of information about what can be accomplished by using Smalltalk for object-oriented programming.

A. Goldberg, *Smalltalk-80: The Interactive Programming Environment*, Addison-Wesley, Reading, Massachusetts, 1984.

A companion volume to Goldberg and Robson's *Smalltalk: The Language and its Implementation*.

G. Krasner, editor, *Smalltalk-80: Bits of History, Words of Advice*, Addison-Wesley, Reading, Massachusetts, 1984.

T. Kaehler and D. Patterson, *A Taste of Smalltalk*, W.W. Norton, New York, New York, 1986.

Excellent introduction to programming in Smalltalk. Guides the reader through several versions of the Tower of Hanoi puzzle. Includes a description of the Smalltalk user interface.

Articles:

A. Bernat, "Review of Smalltalk/V," *AI Expert*, Volume 1, Number 11, November 1986, pages 77-81.

Smalltalk/V's strengths and weaknesses are explored in this review. The author's conclusion: It is an excellent system for learning the basics of object-oriented programming but not the system on which to implement a large package for end-user delivery.

A. Borning and D. Ingalls, "Multiple Inheritance in Smalltalk-80,"*Proceedings of the National Conference on Artificial Intelligence*, The American Association for Artificial Intelligence, 1982, 234-237.

In the standard Smalltalk language, a class may inherit from only one other class, its superclass. In this paper a modification to Smalltalk is described that allows for multiple inheritance.

T. Kaehler and D. Patterson, "A Small Taste of Smalltalk," August 1986, pages 145-159.

This paper is a short tutorial about how to program in Smalltalk. The Smalltalk environment is described in the context of two example programs. The first is the well-known Tower of Hanoi puzzle. Programs are given in Pascal and Smalltalk in order that comparisons can be made. The second is an Animal Game that illustrates the use of trees in Smalltalk.

Y. Yokote and M. Tokoro, "The Design and Implementation of ConcurrentSmalltalk," *OOPSLA '86, SIGPLAN Notices*, ACM Inc., New York, New York, Volume 21, Number 11, November 1986, pages 331-340.

G.A. Pascoe, "Encapsulators: A New Software Paradigm in Smalltalk-80," *OOPSLA '86, SIGPLAN Notices*, ACM Inc., New York, New York, Volume 21, Number 11, November 1986, pages 341-346.

This paper describes *encapsulated* objects. When a message is sent to such an object, a pre-action is performed before the object's method is executed and a post-action is performed before a result is returned. Such objects are useful in many situations.

S.R. Vegdahl, "Moving Structures between Smalltalk Images," *OOPSLA '86, SIGPLAN Notices*, ACM Inc., New York, New York, Volume 21, Number 11, November 1986, pages 466-471.

Implementations:

Smalltalk/V, Digitalk, Inc., 5200 West Century Boulevard, Los Angeles, CA 90045.

Smalltalk/V is a version of Smalltalk for PCs; costs $99. It is a substantial subset of Smalltalk-80 with some of the original Smalltalk-80 classes renamed. The documentation that comes with the package is an excellent introduction to Smalltalk. This package is well worth the money if you want to learn Smalltalk, but it is not a version in which to create substantial applications.

Smalltalk AT, Softsmarts, Inc., 4 Skyline Road, Woodside, CA 94062, smallskip.

This is a full Xerox Smalltalk-80 version 2 implementation for ATs; costs $995.

Xerox markets Smalltalk for its 1100, 1108X, and 1132 workstations.

Tektronics markets Smalltalk for its 4404, 4405, and 4406 workstations.

The University of California, Berkeley, distributes an interpreter written in C that runs on the SUN2 workstation under UNIX.

Apple markets a version of Smalltalk for Macintosh computers.

Microelectronics and the Personal Computer

Rates of progress in microelectronics suggest that in about a decade many people will possess a notebook-size computer with the capacity of a large computer of today. What might such a system do for them?

by Alan C. Kay

The future increase in capacity and decrease in cost of microelectronic devices will not only give rise to compact and powerful hardware but also bring qualitative changes in the way human beings and computers interact. In the 1980's both adults and children will be able to have as a personal possession a computer about the size of a large notebook with the power to handle virtually all their information-related needs. Computing and storage capacity will be many times that of current microcomputers: tens of millions of basic operations per second will manipulate the equivalent of several thousand printed pages of information.

The personal computer can be regarded as the newest example of human mediums of communication. Various means of storing, retrieving and manipulating information have been in existence since human beings began to talk. External mediums serve to capture internal thoughts for communication and, through feedback processes, to form the paths that thinking follows. Although digital computers were originally designed to do arithmetic operations, their ability to simulate the details of any descriptive model means that the computer, viewed as a medium, can simulate any other medium if the methods of simulation are sufficiently well described. Moreover, unlike conventional mediums, which are passive in the sense that marks on paper, paint on canvas and television images do not change in

response to the viewer's wishes, the computer medium is active: it can respond to queries and experiments and can even engage the user in a two-way conversation.

The evolution of the personal computer has followed a path similar to that of the printed book, but in 40 years rather than 600. Like the handmade books of the Middle Ages, the massive computers built in the two decades before 1960 were scarce, expensive and available to only a few. Just as the invention of printing led to the community use of books chained in a library, the introduction of computer time-sharing in the 1960's partitioned the capacity of expensive computers in order to lower their access cost and allow community use. And just as the Industrial Revolution made possible the personal book by providing inexpensive paper and mechanized printing and binding, the microelectronic revolution of the 1970's will bring about the personal computer of the 1980's, with sufficient storage and speed to support high-level computer languages and interactive graphic displays.

Ideally the personal computer will be designed in such a way that people of all ages and walks of life can mold and channel its power to their own needs. Architects should be able to simulate three-dimensional space in order to reflect on and modify their current designs. Physicians should be able to store

and organize a large quantity of information about their patients, enabling them to perceive significant relations that would otherwise be imperceptible. Composers should be able to hear a composition as they are composing it, notably if it is too complex for them to play. Businessmen should have an active briefcase that contains a working simulation of their company. Educators should be able to implement their own version of a Socratic dialogue with dynamic simulation and graphic animation. Homemakers should be able to store and manipulate records, accounts, budgets, recipes and reminders. Children should have an active learning tool that gives them ready access to large stores of knowledge in ways that are not possible with mediums such as books.

How can communication with computers be enriched to meet the diverse needs of individuals? If the computer is to be truly "personal," adult and child users must be able to get it to perform useful activities without resorting to the services of an expert. Simple tasks must be simple, and complex ones must be possible. Although a personal computer will be supplied with already created simulations, such as a general text editor, the wide range of backgrounds and ages of its potential users will make any direct anticipation of their needs very difficult. Thus the central problem of personal computing is that nonexperts will almost certainly have to do some programming if their personal computer is to be of more than transitory help.

To gain some understanding of the problems and potential benefits of personal computing my colleagues and I at the Xerox Palo Alto Research Center have designed an experimental personal computing system. We have had a number of these systems built and have studied how both adults and children make use of them. The hardware is faithful in capacity to the envisioned notebook-

COMPUTER SIMULATIONS generated on a high-resolution television display at the Evans & Sutherland Computer Corporation show the quality of the images it should eventually be possible to present on a compact personal computer. The pictures are frames from two dynamic-simulation programs that revise an image 30 times per second to represent the continuous motion of objects in projected three-dimensional space. The sequence at the top, made for the National Aeronautics and Space Administration, shows a space laboratory being lifted out of the interior of the space shuttle. The sequence at the bottom, made for the U.S. Maritime Administration, shows the movement of tankers in New York harbor. Ability of the personal computer to simulate real or imagined phenomena will make it a new medium of communication.

41

size computer of the 1980's, although it is necessarily larger. The software is a new interactive computer-language system called SMALLTALK.

In the design of our personal computing system we were influenced by research done in the late 1960's. At that time Edward Cheadle and I, working at the University of Utah, designed FLEX, the first personal computer to directly support a graphics- and simulation-oriented language. Although the FLEX design was encouraging, it was not comprehensive enough to be useful to a wide variety of nonexpert users. We then became interested in the efforts of Seymour A. Papert, Wallace Feurzeig and others working at the Massachusetts Institute of Technology and at Bolt, Beranek and Newman, Inc., to develop a computer-based learning environment in which children would find learning both fun and rewarding. Working with a large time-shared computer, Papert and Feurzeig devised a simple but powerful computer language called LOGO. With this language children (ranging in age from eight to 12) could write programs to control a simple music generator, a robot turtle that could crawl around the floor and draw lines, and a television image of the turtle that could do the same things.

After observing this project we came to realize that many of the problems involved in the design of the personal computer, particularly those having to do with expressive communication, were brought strongly into focus when children down to the age of six were seriously considered as users. We also realized that children require more computer power than an adult is willing to settle for in a time-sharing system. The best outputs that time-sharing can provide are crude green-tinted line drawings and square-wave musical tones. Children, however, are used to finger paints, color television and stereophonic records, and they usually find the things that can be accomplished with a low-capacity time-sharing system insufficiently stimulating to maintain their interest.

Since LOGO was not designed with all the people and uses we had in mind, we decided not to copy it but to devise a new kind of programming system that would attempt to combine simplicity and ease of access with a qualitative improvement in expert-level adult programming. In this effort we were guided, as we had been with the FLEX system, by the central ideas of the programming language SIMULA, which was developed in the mid-1960's by Ole-Johan Dahl and Kristen Nygaard at the Norwegian Computing Center in Oslo.

Our experimental personal computer

EXPERIMENTAL PERSONAL COMPUTER was built at the Xerox Palo Alto Research Center in part to develop a high-level programming language that would enable nonexperts to write sophisticated programs. The author and his colleagues were also interested in using the experimental computer to study the effects of personal computing on learning. The machine is completely self-contained, consisting of a keyboard, a pointing device, a high-resolution picture display and a sound system, all connected to a small processing unit and a removable disk-file memory. Display can present thousands of characters approaching the quality of those in printed material.

is self-contained and fits comfortably into a desk. Long-term storage is provided by removable disk memories that can hold the equivalent of 1,500 printed pages of information (about three million characters). Although image displays in the 1980's will probably be flat-screened mosaics that reflect light as liquid-crystal watch displays do, visual output is best supplied today by a high-resolution black-and-white or color television picture tube. High-fidelity sound output is produced by a built-in conversion from discrete digital signals to continuous waveforms, which are then sent to a conventional audio amplifier and speakers. The user makes his primary input through a typewriterlike keyboard and a pointing device called a mouse, which controls the position of an arrow on the screen as it is pushed about on the table beside the display. Other input systems include an organlike keyboard for playing music, a pencillike pointer, a joystick, a microphone and a television camera.

The commonest activity on our personal computer is the manipulation of simulations already supplied by the SMALLTALK system or created by the user. The dynamic state of a simulation is shown on the display, and its general course is modified as the user changes the displayed images by typing commands on the keyboard or pointing with the mouse. For example, formatted textual documents with multiple typefaces are simulated so that an image of the finished document is shown on the screen. The document is edited by pointing at characters and paragraphs with the mouse and then deleting, adding and restructuring the document's parts. Each change is instantly reflected in the document's image.

In many instances the display screen is too small to hold all the information a user may wish to consult at one time, and so we have developed "windows," or simulated display frames within the larger physical display. Windows organize simulations for editing and display, allowing a document composed of text, pictures, musical notation, dynamic animations and so on to be created and viewed at several levels of refinement. Once the windows have been created they overlap on the screen like sheets of paper; when the mouse is pointed at a partially covered window, the window is redisplayed to overlap the other windows. Those windows containing useful but not immediately needed information are collapsed to small rectangles that are labeled with a name showing what information they contain. A "touch" of the mouse causes them to instantly open up and display their contents.

In the present state of the art software development is much more difficult and time-consuming than hardware development. The personal computer will eventually be put together from more or less standard microelectronic components, but the software that will give life to the user's ideas must go through a long and arduous process of refinement if it is to aid and not hinder the goals of a personal dynamic medium.

For this reason we have over the past four years invited some 250 children (aged six to 15) and 50 adults to try versions of SMALLTALK and to suggest ways of improving it. Their creations, as imaginative and diverse as they themselves, include programs for home accounts, information storage and retrieval, teaching, drawing, painting, music synthesis, writing and games. Subsequent designs of SMALLTALK have been greatly influenced and improved by our visitors' projects.

When children or adults first encounter a personal computer, most of them are already involved in pursuits of their own choosing. Their initial impulse is to exploit the system to do things they are already doing: a home or office manager will automate paperwork and accounts, a teacher will portray dynamic and pictorial aspects of a curriculum, a child will work on ways to create pictures and games. The fact is that people naturally start to conceive and build personal tools. Although man has been characterized as the toolmaking species, toolmaking itself has historically been the

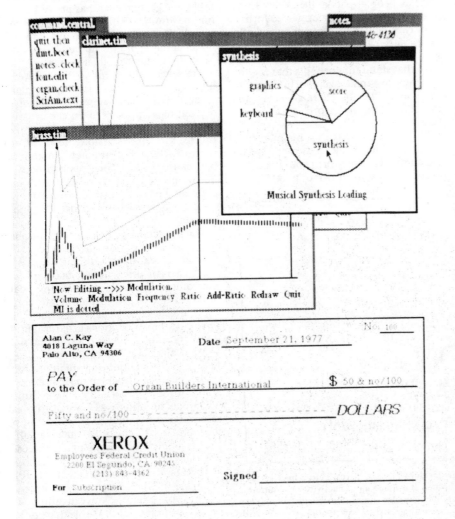

"WINDOWS," display frames within the larger display screen, enable the user to organize and edit information at several levels of refinement. Once the windows are created they overlap on the screen like sheets of paper. When a partially covered window is selected with the pointing device, the window is redisplayed to overlap the other windows. Images with various degrees of symbolic content can be displayed simultaneously. Such images include detailed halftone drawings, analogical images such as graphs and symbolic images such as numbers or words.

One reason is that technologies frequently require special techniques, materials, tools and physical conditions. An important property of computers, however, is that very general tools for using them can be built by anyone. These tools are made from the same materials and with the same effort as more specific creations.

Initially the children interact with our computer by "painting" pictures and drawing straight lines on the display screen with the pencillike pointer. The children then discover that programs can create structures more complex than any they can create by hand. They learn that a picture has several representations, of which only the most obvious—the image—appears on the screen. The most important representation is the editable symbolic model of the picture stored in the memory of the computer. For example, in the computer an image of a truck can be built up from models of wheels, a cab and a bed, each a different color. As the parts of the symbolic model are edited its image on the screen will change accordingly.

Adults also learn to exploit the properties of the computer medium. A professional artist who visited us spent several months building various tools that resembled those he had worked with to create images on paper. Eventually he discovered that the mosaic screen—the indehole out instantly erasable storage of the medium—and his new ability to program could be combined to create rich textures of a kind that could not be created with ink or paint. From the use of the computer for the impoverished simulation of an already existing medium he had progressed to the discovery of the computer's unique properties for human expression.

One of the best ways to teach nonexperts to communicate with computers is to have them explore the levels of abstraction at which images can be manipulated. The manipulation of images follows the general stages of intellectual growth. For a young child an image is something to make: a free mixture of forms and colors unconnected with the real world. Older children create images that directly represent concepts such as people, pets and houses. Later analogical images appear whose form is closely related to their meaning and purpose, such as geometric figures and graphs. In the end symbolic images are used that stand for concepts that are too abstract to analogize, such as numbers, algebraic and logical terms and the characters and words that constitute language.

The types of image in this hierarchy are increasingly difficult to represent on the computer. Free-form and literal images can be easily drawn or painted with lines and halftones in the dot matrix of the display screen with the aid of the mouse or in conjunction with programs that draw curves, fill in areas with tone or show perspectives of three-dimensional models. Analogical images can also be generated, such as a model of a simulated musical intrument: a time-sequenced graph representing the dynamic evolution of amplitude, pitch variation and tonal range.

Symbolic representations are particularly useful because they provide a means of handling concepts that are difficult to portray directly, such as generalizations and abstract relations. Moreover, as an image gets increasingly complex its most important property, the property of making local relations instantly clear, becomes less useful. Communication with computers based on symbols as they routinely occur in natural language, however, has proved to be far more difficult than many had supposed. The reason lies in our lack of understanding of how human beings exploit the context of their experience to make sense of the ambiguities of common discourse. Since it is not yet understood how human beings do what they do, getting computers to engage in similar activities is still many years in the future. It is quite possible, however, to invent artificial computer languages that can represent concepts and activities we do understand and that are simple enough in basic structure for them to be easily learned and utilized by nonexperts.

The particular structure of a symbolic language is important because it provides a context in which some concepts are easier to think about and express than others. For example, mathematical notation first arose to abbreviate concepts that could be expressed only as ungainly circumlocutions in natural language. Gradually it was realized that the form of an expression could be of great help in the conception and manipulation of the meaning for which the expression stood. A more important advance came when new notation was created to represent concepts that did not fit into the culture's linguistic heritage at all, such as functional mappings, continuous rates and limits.

The computer created new needs for language by inverting the traditional process of scientific investigation. It made new universes available that could be shaped by theories to produce simulated phenomena. Accordingly symbolic structures were needed to communicate concepts such as imperative descriptions and control structures.

Most of the programming languages in service today were developed as symbolic ways to deal with the hardware-level concepts of the 1950's. This approach led to two kinds of passive building blocks: data structures, or inert con-

trait name	description
name	box: picture activity
location	□
angle	□
size	□
new	location ← center. angle ← 0. size ← 100.
show	⊘ paint black shape
erase	⊘ paint background. shape
shape	⊘ me goto location: turn angle: down. 1 to 4 do ⊘ go size: turn 90.
grow □	erase. size ← size + □. show

SMALLTALK is a new programming language developed at the Xerox Palo Alto Research Center for use on the experimental personal computer. It is made up of "activities," computer-like entities that can perform a specific set of tasks and can also communicate with other activities in the system. New activities are created by enriching existing families of activities with additional "traits," or abilities, which are defined in terms of a method to be carried out. The description of the family "box" shown here is a dictionary of its traits. To create a new member of the family box, a message is sent to the trait "new" stating the characteristics of the new box in terms of specific values for the general traits "location," "angle" and "size." In this example "new" has been filled in to specify a box located in the center of the screen with an angle of zero degrees and a side 100 screen dots long. To "show" the new box, a member of the curve-drawing family "brush" is given directions by the open trait "shape." First the brush travels to the specified location, turns in the proper direction and appears on the screen. Then it draws a square by traveling the distance given by "size," turning 90 degrees and repeating these actions three more times. The last trait on the list is open, indicating that a numerical value is to be supplied by the user when the trait is invoked by a message. A box is "grown" by first erasing it, increasing (or decreasing) its size by the value supplied in the message and redisplaying it.

⌨ box new named "joe"❗
    box:joe

An offspring of the family "box" is created and is named "joe."

⌨ joe turn 30❗
    ok

The box joe receives the message and turns 30 degrees.

⌨ joe grow –15❗
    ok

Joe becomes smaller by 15 units.

⌨ joe erase❗
    ok

Joe disappears from the screen.

⌨ joe show❗
    ok

Joe reappears.

⌨ box new named "jill"❗
    box:jill

A new box appears.

⌨ jill turn –10❗
    ok

Only jill turns. Joe and jill are independent activities.

⌨ 1 to 10❗
    interval:1 2 3 4 5 6 7 8 9 10

An interval stands for a sequence of numbers.

⌨ forever❗
    interval:1 2 3 4 5 6 7 8 9 10 11...

Forever is the infinite interval. It must be terminated by hitting an escape key.

⌨ 1 to 10 do (joe turn 20)❗
    ok

Joe spins.

⌨ forever do (joe turn 11. jill turn –13)❗
    ok

A simple parallel movie of joe and jill spinning in opposite directions is created by combining forever with a turn request to both joe and jill.

SMALLTALK LEARNING SEQUENCE teaches students the basic concepts of the language by having them interact with an already defined family of activities. First, offspring of the family box are created, named and manipulated, and a second family of activities called "interval" is introduced. Offspring of the interval and box families are then combined to generate an animation of two spinning boxes.

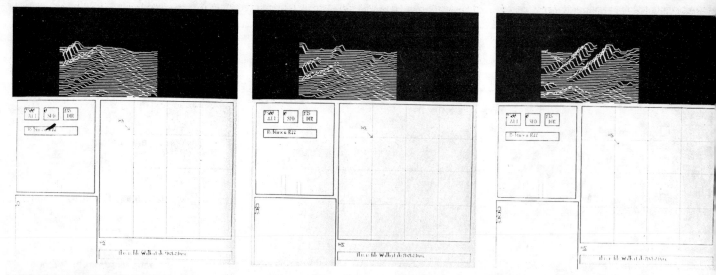

HELICOPTER SIMULATION was developed by a 15-year-old student. The user directs the helicopter where to go with the pointing device, which controls the position of the black arrow on the screen. The window at the top shows the changing topography of the terrain

struction materials, and procedures, or step-by-step recipes for manipulating data. The languages based on these concepts (such as BASIC, FORTRAN, ALGOL and APL) follow their descriptions in a strictly sequential manner. Because a piece of data may be changed by any procedure that can find it the programmer must be very careful to choose only those procedures that are appropriate. As ever more complex systems are attempted, requiring elaborate combinations of procedures, the difficulty of getting the entire system to work increases geometrically. Although most programmers are still taught data-procedure languages, there is now a widespread recognition of their inadequacy.

A more promising approach is to devise building blocks of greater generality. Both data and procedures can be replaced by the single idea of "activities," computerlike entities that exhibit behavior when they are sent an appropriate message. There are no nouns and verbs in such a language, only dynamically communicating activities. Every transaction, description and control process is thought of as sending messages to and receiving messages from activities in the system. Moreover, each activity belongs to a family of similar activities, all of which have the ability to recognize and reply to messages directed to them and to perform specific acts such as drawing pictures, making sounds or adding numbers. New families are created by combining and enriching "traits," or properties inherited from existing families.

A message-activity system is inherently parallel: every activity is constantly ready to send and receive messages, so that the host computer is in effect divided into thousands of computers, each with the capabilities of the whole. The message-activity approach therefore enables one to dynamically represent a system at many levels of organization from the atomic to the macroscopic, but with a "skin" of protection at each qualitative level of detail through which negotiative messages must be sent and checked. This level of complexity can be safely handled because the language severely limits the kinds of interactions between activities, allowing only those that are appropriate, much as a hormone is allowed to interact with only a few specifically responsive target cells. SMALLTALK, the programming system of our personal computer, was the first computer language to be based entirely on the structural concepts of messages and activities.

The third and newest framework for high-level communication is the observer language. Although message-activity languages are an advance over the data-procedure framework, the relations among the various activities are somewhat independent and analytic. Many

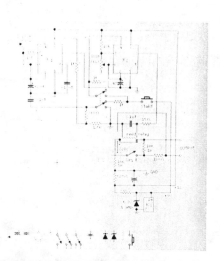
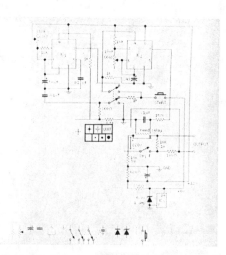
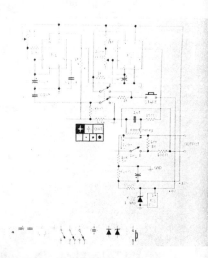

CIRCUIT-DRAWING PROGRAM that was developed by a 15-year-old boy enables a user to construct a complex circuit diagram by selecting components from a "menu" displayed at the bottom of the screen. The components are then positioned and connected with the

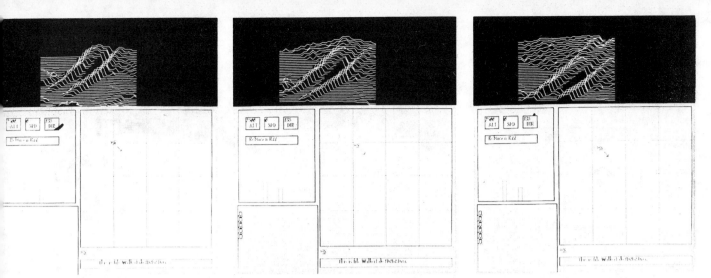

below as the helicopter flies over it. (Actual terrains were obtained from *Landsat* maps.) A third window keeps track of the helicopter's altitude, direction and speed. The variety of events that can be simulated at the same time demonstrates the power of parallel processing.

concepts, however, are so richly interwoven that analysis causes them virtually to disappear. For example, 20th-century physics assigns equal importance to a phenomenon and its context, since observers with different vantage points perceive the world differently. In an observer language, activities are replaced by "viewpoints" that become attached to one another to form correspondences between concepts. For example, a dog can be viewed abstractly (as an animal), analytically (as being composed of organs, cells and molecules), pragmatically (as a vehicle by a child), allegorically (as a human being in a fairy tale) and contextually (as a bone's way to fertilize a lawn). Observer languages are just now being formulated. They and their successors will be the communication vehicles of the 1980's.

Our experience, and that of others who teach programming, is that a first computer language's particular style

and its main concepts not only have a strong influence on what a new programmer can accomplish but also leave an impression about programming and computers that can last for years. The process of learning to program a computer can impose such a particular point of view that alternative ways of perceiving and solving problems can become extremely frustrating for new programmers to learn.

At the beginning of our study we first timidly considered simulating features of data-procedure languages that children had been able to learn, such as BASIC and LOGO. Then, worried that the imprinting process would prevent stronger ideas from being absorbed, we decided to find a way to present the message-activity ideas of SMALLTALK in concrete terms without dilution. We did so by starting with simple situations that embodied a concept and then gradually increasing the complexity of the examples

to flesh out the concept to its full generality. Although the communicationlike model of SMALLTALK is a rather abstract way to represent descriptions, to our surprise the first group and succeeding groups of children who tried it appeared to find the ideas as easy to learn as those of more concrete languages.

For example, most programming languages can deal with only one thing at a time, so that it is difficult to represent with them even such simple situations as children in a school, spacecraft in the sky or bouncing balls in free space. In SMALLTALK parallel models are dealt with from the start, and the children seem to have little difficulty in handling them. Actually parallel processing is remarkably similar to the way people think. When you are walking along a street, one part of your brain may be thinking about the route you are taking, another part may be thinking about the dinner you are going to eat, a third

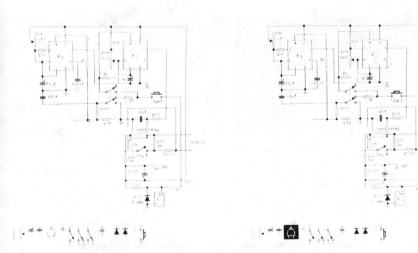

pointing device. An additional menu can be generated on the screen by pushing a button on the pointing device; this menu supplies solid and open dots and lines of various widths. In the sequence shown here two components are selected and added to a circuit diagram.

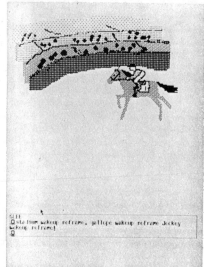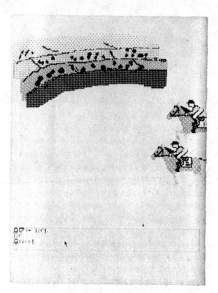
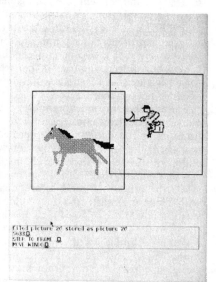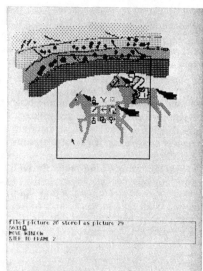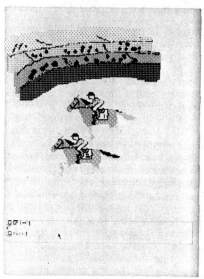
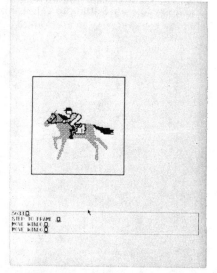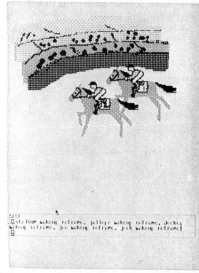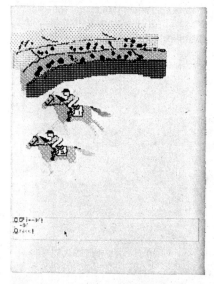

HORSE-RACE ANIMATION shows the capabilities of the experimental personal computer for creating dynamic halftone images. The possible range of such simulations is limited only by the versatility of the programming language and the imagination of the child or adult user. In this sequence, images of horses, riders and background are called up independently from the storage files and arranged for the racing simulation with the pointing device. A single typed command then causes the two horses and riders to race each other across screen.

part may be admiring the sunset, and so forth.

Another important characteristic of SMALLTALK is the classification of objects into families that are generalizations of their properties. Children readily see themselves as members of the family "kids," since they have common traits such as language, interests and physical appearance. Each individual is both a member of the family kids and has his or her own meaning for the shared traits. For example, all kids have the trait eye color, but Sam's eyes are blue and Bertha's are brown. SMALLTALK is built out of such families. Number symbols, such as 2 or 17, are instances of the family "number." The members of this family differ only in their numerical value (which is their sole property) and share a common definition of the different messages they can receive and send. The symbol of a "brush" in SMALLTALK is also a family. All the brush symbols have the ability to draw lines, but each symbol has its own knowledge of its orientation and where it is located in the drawing area.

The description of a programming language is generally given in terms of its grammar: the meaning each grammatical construction is supposed to convey and the method used to obtain the meaning. For example, various programming languages employ grammatical constructions such as (PLUS 3 4) or 3 ENTER 4 + to specify the intent to add the number 3 to the number 4. The meaning of these phrases is the same. In the computer each should give rise to the number 7, although the actual methods followed in obtaining the answer can differ considerably from one type of computer to the next.

The grammar of SMALLTALK is simple and fixed. Each phrase is a message to an activity. A description of the desired activity is followed by a message that selects a trait of the activity to be performed. The designated activity will decide whether it wants to accept the message (it usually does) and at some later time will act on the message. There may be many concurrent messages pending for an activity, even for the same trait. The sender of the message may decide to wait for a reply or not to wait. Usually it waits, but it may decide to go about other business if the message has invoked a method that requires considerable computation.

The integration of programming-language concepts with concepts of editing, graphics and information retrieval makes available a wide range of useful activities that the user can invoke with little or no knowledge of programming. Learners are introduced to SMALLTALK by getting them to send messages to already existing families of activities, such

MUSIC CAN BE REPRESENTED on the personal computer in the form of analogical images. Notes played on the keyboard are "captured" as a time-sequenced score on the display.

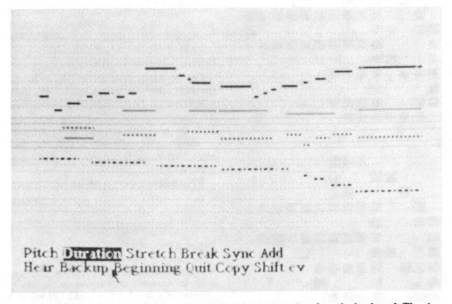

MUSICAL SCORE shown here was generated as music was played on the keyboard. The simplified notation represents pitch by vertical placement and duration by horizontal length. Notes can be shortened, lengthened or changed and the modified piece then played back as music.

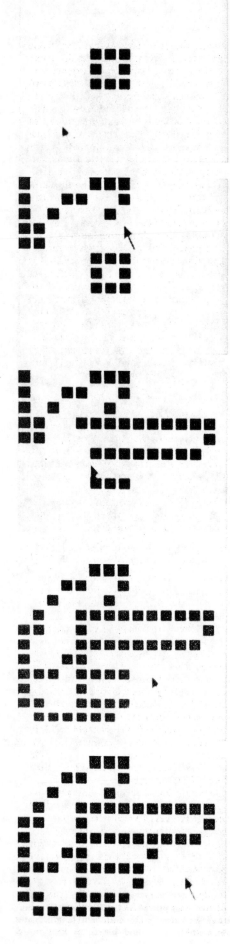

as the family "box," whose members show themselves on the screen as squares. A box can individually change its size, location, rotation and shape. After some experience with sending messages to cause effects on the display screen the learner may take a look at the definition of the box family. Each family in SMALLTALK is described with a dictionary of traits, which are defined in terms of a method to be carried out. For example, the message phrase "joe grow 50" says: Find the activity named "joe," find its general trait called "grow ___" and fill in its open part with the specific value 50. A new trait analogous to those already present in the family definition (such as "grow" or "turn") can easily be added by the learner. The next phase of learning involves elaboration of this basic theme by creating games such as space war and tools for drawing and painting.

There are two basic approaches to personal computing. The first one, which is analogous to musical improvisation, is exploratory: effects are caused in order to see what they are like and errors are tracked down, understood and fixed. The second, which resembles musical composition, calls for a great deal more planning, generality and structure. The same language is used for both methods but the framework is quite different.

From our study we have learned the importance of a balance between free exploration and a developed curriculum. The personal computing experience is similar to the introduction of a piano into a third-grade classroom. The children will make noise and even music by experimentation, but eventually they will need help in dealing with the instrument in nonobvious ways. We have also found that for children the various levels of abstraction supplied by SMALLTALK are not equally accessible. The central idea of symbolization is to give a simple name to a complex collection of ideas, and then later to be able to invoke the ideas through the name. We have observed a number of children between the ages of six and seven who have been able to take this step in their computer programs, but their ability to look ahead, to visualize the consequences of actions they might take, is limited.

Children aged eight to 10 have a grad-

DISPLAY FONTS can be designed on personal computer by constructing them from a matrix of black-and-white squares. When the fonts are reduced, they approach the quality of those in printed material. The image of a pointing hand shown here is a symbol in SMALLTALK representing the concept of a literal word, such as the name associated with an activity.

ually developing ability to visualize and plan and are able to use the concept of families and a subtler form of naming: the use of traits such as size, which can stand for different numerical values at different times. For most children, however, the real implications of further symbolic generality are not at all obvious. By age 11 or 12 we see a considerable improvement in a child's ability to plan general structures and to devise comprehensive computer tools. Adults advance through the stages more quickly than children, and usually they create tools after a few weeks of practice. It is not known whether the stages of intellectual development observed in children are absolutely or only relatively correlated with age, but it is possible that exposure to a realm in which symbolic creation is rewarded by wonderful effects could shorten the time required for children to mature from one stage to the next.

The most important limitation on personal computing for nonexperts appears when they conceive of a project that, although it is easy to do in the language, calls for design concepts they have not yet absorbed. For example, it is easy to build a span with bricks if one knows the concept of the arch, but otherwise it is difficult or impossible. Clearly as complexity increases "architecture" dominates "material." The need for ways to characterize and communicate architectural concepts in developing programs has been a long-standing problem in the design of computing systems. A programming language provides a context for developing strategies, and it must supply both the ability to make tools and a style suggesting useful approaches that will bring concepts to life.

We are sure from our experience that personal computers will become an integral part of peoples' lives in the 1980's. The editing, saving and sifting of all manner of information will be of value to virtually everyone. More sophisticated forms of computing may be like music in that most people will come to know of them and enjoy them but only a few will actually become directly involved.

How will personal computers affect society? The interaction of society and a new medium of communication and self-expression can be disturbing even when most of the society's members learn to use the medium routinely. The social and personal effects of the new medium are subtle and not easy for the society and the individual to perceive. To use writing as a metaphor, there are three reactions to the introduction of a new medium: illiteracy, literacy and artistic creation. After reading material became available the illiterate were those who were left behind by the new medium. It was inevitable that a few creative individuals would use the written word to express inner thoughts and ideas. The most profound changes were brought about in the literate. They did not necessarily become better people or better members of society, but they came to view the world in a way quite different from the way they had viewed it before, with consequences that were difficult to predict or control.

We may expect that the changes resulting from computer literacy will be as far-reaching as those that came from literacy in reading and writing, but for most people the changes will be subtle and not necessarily in the direction of their idealized expectations. For example, we should not predict or expect that the personal computer will foster a new revolution in education just because it could. Every new communication medium of this century—the telephone, the motion picture, radio and television—has elicited similar predictions that did not come to pass. Millions of uneducated people in the world have ready access to the accumulated culture of the centuries in public libraries, but they do not avail themselves of it. Once an individual or a society decides that education is essential, however, the book, and now the personal computer, can be among the society's main vehicles for the transmission of knowledge.

The social impact of simulation—the central property of computing—must also be considered. First, as with language, the computer user has a strong motivation to emphasize the similarity between simulation and experience and to ignore the great distances that symbols interpose between models and the real world. Feelings of power and a narcissistic fascination with the image of oneself reflected back from the machine are common. Additional tendencies are to employ the computer trivially (simulating what paper, paints and file cabinets can do), as a crutch (using the computer to remember things that we can perfectly well remember ourselves) or as an excuse (blaming the computer for human failings). More serious is the human propensity to place faith in and assign higher powers to an agency that is not completely understood. The fact that many organizations actually base their decisions on—worse, take their decisions from—computer models is profoundly disturbing given the current state of the computer art. Similar feelings about the written word persist to this day: if something is "in black and white," it must somehow be true.

Children who have not yet lost much of their sense of wonder and fun have helped us to find an ethic about computing: Do not automate the work you are engaged in, only the materials. If you like to draw, do not automate drawing; rather, program your personal computer to give you a new set of paints. If you like to play music, do not build a "player piano"; instead program yourself a new kind of instrument.

A popular misconception about computers is that they are logical. Forthright is a better term. Since computers can contain arbitrary descriptions, any conceivable collection of rules, consistent or not, can be carried out. Moreover, computers' use of symbols, like the use of symbols in language and mathematics, is sufficiently disconnected from the real world to enable them to create splendid nonsense. Although the hardware of the computer is subject to natural laws (electrons can move through the circuits only in certain physically defined ways), the range of simulations the computer can perform is bounded only by the limits of human imagination. In a computer, spacecraft can be made to travel faster than the speed of light, time to travel in reverse.

It may seem almost sinful to discuss the simulation of nonsense, but only if we want to believe that what we know is correct and complete. History has not been kind to those who subscribe to this view. It is just this realm of apparent nonsense that must be kept open for the developing minds of the future. Although the personal computer can be guided in any direction we choose, the real sin would be to make it act like a machine!

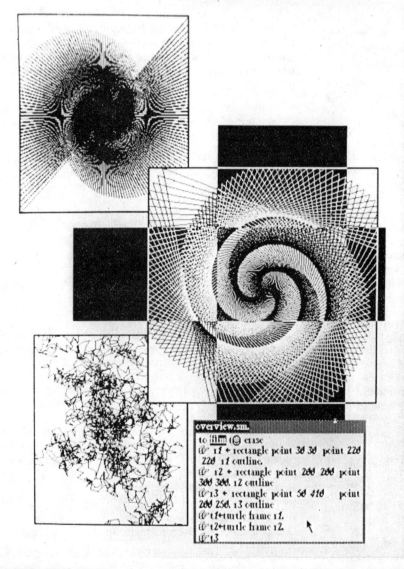

INTRICATE PATTERNS can be generated on the personal computer with very compact descriptions in SMALLTALK. They are made by repeating, rotating, scaling, superposing and combining drawings of simple geometric shapes. Students who are learning to program first create interesting free-form or literal images by drawing them directly in the dot matrix of the display screen. Eventually they learn to employ the symbolic images in the programming language to direct the computer to generate more complex imagery than they could easily create by hand.

Reprinted from *Proceedings of Softfair: A Conference on Software Development Tools, Techniques, and Alternatives*, 1983, pages 61–65. Copyright © 1983 by The Institute of Electrical and Electronics Engineers, Inc.

Experiences with Smalltalk-80™ [1] for Application Development

Tom Love

Schlumberger-Doll Research

This report describes initial experiences using a programming environment and language called Smalltalk-80 to develop an application using a highly graphic interface to a variety of diverse data. The particular data involved included electrical logs, core photographs, stratigraphic sketches, scanning electron micrographs, text reports, and scatter plots.

Smalltalk-80 has surpassed our initial expectations. Order of magnitude reductions in the bulk of code required for certain applications are achievable. Learning the language and user interface is quite easy, but the library of available methods is large (about 4 thousand methods) and often difficult to understand. The computational inefficiencies of the current implementation were not as severe a limitation as originally anticipated.

1. Why Smalltalk?

Smalltalk-80 (ST-80) is an integrated, solitary programming environment conceived and constructed at the Xerox Palo Alto Research Center over the past 12 years. It is integrated in that ST-80 programming is done in a single language and in a single environment which is dealt with consistently by the user. It is solitary in that no support is provided to assist a group of programmers cooperating on a common task.

ST-80 is a state of the art programming environment. It is one of a very small set of environment projects which had the unusual luxury of being able to start from scratch and to continue intact until commercial introduction of the product. The original vision was to build a supportive computer based work environment which pushed the limits of hardware and software technology. From the very beginning the researchers were not substantially constrained by current day costs of hardware or software. Rather the view was to select a base which would be cost effective in 5 to 10 years.

ST-80 became available to commercial customers for the first time in November 1982. Schlumberger had a small headstart in that we were among three clients who

served as a beta test site for ST-80 on the Xerox 1100 (dolphin) workstation. This is the first paper to describe the use of ST-80 as a base for commercial applications.

The Schlumberger-Doll Research Center is responsible for identifying and evaluating promising new hardware and software technologies for possible application within the company. ST-80 was considered a promising new technology due to:

— its sophisticated human engineering of the user interface (offers the promise of being powerful, productive, and reasonable to learn)

— the extensibility of the system (ability to customize the entire system for a particular application)

— the fact that it is the most complete system currently available based upon the concept of objects (objects are a structuring concept for system building and can be thought of as a combination of procedures and data)

— the transportability of the software to other hardware environments without jeopardizing investment in current software (ST-80 has been ported to a VAX at Berkeley under the UNIX operating system and to a Motorola 68000 based Sun workstation)

— it takes a creative and powerful approach to graphics programming

2. Background of the application

A principal business of Schlumberger is to collect, analyze, and interpret measurements from electronics packages lowered into wells. A plot of the response of a particular electronics package within a well is referred to as a log. The electronics package itself is known as a tool. The tools can measure resistivity and density but customers need to locate a zone containing hydrocarbons and to determine the permeability of the zone.

A set of very sophisticated software systems has been developed to analyze a set of tool responses and answer customer problems. Even so it is necessary for a log interpreter to carefully scrutinize every step of this

---

1. A registered trademark of Xerox Corporation.

process and to cope with any additional information available, such as actual rock samples from the well or historical information concerning a particular formation.

The purpose of the application described was to provide a mechanism for accessing and comparing this diverse information electronically.

3. A description of the application

An application has been built with the following capabilities:

1. From a stratigraphic image drawn by a geologist, duplicate the course of a well

   — the image could either be drawn using ST-80 or digitized from a line drawing [2]

2. select a zone within the well and find out what information is available for that zone

   — a zone is selected by moving the mouse to the desired location on the stratigraphic image

   — as the mouse is moved it continuously displays the scaled coordinates of the subsurface environment being depicted in the image

   — the top and bottom of the zone of interest are selected with a button press of the mouse

3. allow the user to select from a menu the desired data and allow the user to move it where he or she wants it on the screen; the variety of data includes:

   — log plots

   — scatter plots

   — simulated digitized photographic images

   — simulated images from instruments such as scanning electron microscopes

   — text reports

   — special programs which can be run if the user chooses; these programs allow the user to integrate data from log plots, images, and text to describe the results on analyses

   — dynamic memos -- memos which include text, graphics, images, simple animation, and programs which may be controlled and manipulated by the user

For example there are methods to plot tool responses for a selected zone. The actual tool response data for a single well has been embedded within a well object. A method of the well class acquires data for a particular

tool within the specified depth interval. The data are then displayed in a user defined window on a labeled grid. Another log can be added to that view or displayed within another view at the same or a different depth interval.

The programmer for this application had never programmed in ST-80 or any object oriented programming language before. The resulting simple application required on!y 205 ST-80 statements and less than 2 months of effort, including training.[3]

To develop the equivalent functionality using only a language such as Fortran or Pascal would probably require 10,000 - 20,000 statements. However, this is not actually a fair comparison because with ST-80 one acquires a rather large library of useful methods and classes; whereas, in more traditional languages one begins with only very primitive operations and data structures.

The distinct tendency of people working in traditional environments is to begin from scratch without building on one of the many existing libraries of useful functions or procedures. It is simply inconceivable that one would choose to do that in ST-80.

4. An Example of ST-80 Code

A simple ST-80 program or method will be presented to demonstrate both the power and the simplicity of the language. This method is simply an example and not actually a part of the application described above.

As shown in Figures 1 - 5, the following method is an interactive program which does a simple plot of data obtained from a log object.

```
1   techRept                                          [Figure 1]
    "This method plots a tool response vertically based upon
     data obtained from the log object."
2   | log penComdr penPlot newLog|

3   penPlot ← Plotter new.
4   penComdr ← Commander new: 11.
5   userRect ← Rectangle fromUser.                    [Figure 2]
6   penComdr north; turn: 180;
        lineUpFrom: userRect origin to: userRect topRight;
        down; go: (userRect height); up; turn: -90;
        lineUpFrom: userRect origin to: userRect bottomLeft;
        down; go: (userRect width); up.               [Figure 3]
7   penPlot north; defaultNib: 3; frame: userRect; up.
8   log ← Logs fromWell: 'OCSG' date: 'dec1982'.
9   newLog ← log getLog: 'sp' minDepth: 1000 maxDepth: 1100.
10  scaledArray ← log scale: newLog to: userRect.
11  scaledArray do:
        [:each | penPlot goto: (userRect origin + each);
        down ].                                        [Figure 4]
```

---

2. This ST-80 application program assumes that files exist containing bit map images for display purposes. In all cases these images are simulated at this time by drawing them with the ST-80 FormEditor. A very modest amount of additional software is required to translate a digitized image to the required form to be used by ST-80.

---

3. A statement was defined to be any single messages or set of messages on a single physical line, any cascaded message (count semicolons), or any block structure. Block structures can of course contain very many statements but all block structures were considered to have at least one statement.

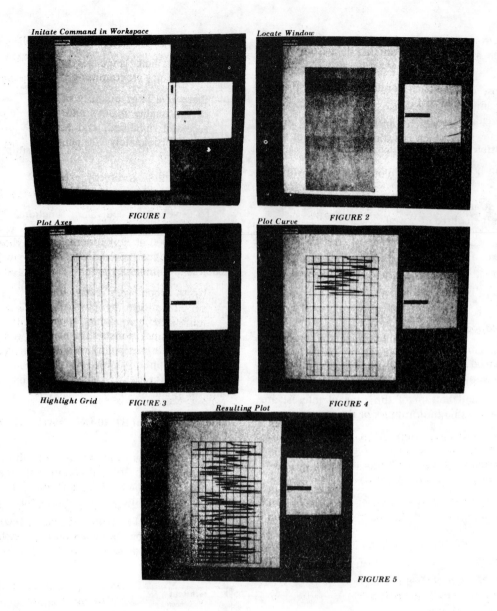

Initate Command in Workspace

FIGURE 1

Locate Window

FIGURE 2

Plot Axes

FIGURE 3

Plot Curve

FIGURE 4

Highlight Grid

Resulting Plot

FIGURE 5

These 24 ST-80 statements will be described to provide the user with a view of the style and form of the language. The program described is intended only as a tutorial example. For a more complete description of ST-80, the reader should see either the August 1981 issue of Byte Magazine or the Addison-Wesley book, **SmalkTalk 80: The Language and Its Implementation** by Adele Goldberg and David Robson of Xerox.

1. *techRept* is the name of the method to be executed.

2. Four names of temporary variables are listed. These variables are local to this method.

3. Create a new object of the class Plotter, named *penPlot*, which responds to all of the methods of Plotter. This is termed creating a new instance of a class.

4. Create a new instance of the class Commander with 11 pens, named *penComdr*. Commander is a class of objects which controls pens, in the sense of pens on a flat bed plotter. penComdr controls 11 pens.

5. Request the user to specify the origin and size of a rectangle on the display. The points which specify this rectangle are stored in the local variable *userRect*.

6. A series of commands are sent to the *penComdr* which has the effect of drawing linear graph paper within the *userRect*. For example, the 11 pens are commanded to line up between the origin and the top right corner of the *userRect;* to lower onto the paper (down); and move a distance equal to the height of the *userRect*.

7. Initialize the direction, pen size, plotting area on

the screen (frame) and position of the plotter.

8. Create a new object which contains data from Well: 'OCSG' on date: 'dec1982'.

9. Create a new object which contains only the sp log within the zone 1000 to 1100.

10. Create a new object which contains the *sp* log data selected above and which is scaled to the size of the *userRect*.

11. Loop through the data and plot each point with a connected line. That is, for each element of the *scaledArray*, plot a line from the previous point to a new point which is the current element of the *scaledArray* plus the origin of the *userRect*.

I hope that this simple 11 instruction example has given the reader a feel for the language and demonstrated the power of ST-80.

5. The ST-80 User Interface

ST-80 was explicitly designed to optimize the productivity of the individual programmer. In my opinion, it is the best solitary environment available within the industry today.

Some of the advantages of the interface include:

— ST-80 a mode-less environment unless one falls out into the ALTO operating system level which happened regularly in the first few weeks of using the system, but which happens about once a month now

— the structure of the interface and the mouse result in fantastically little use of the keyboard; it is not uncommon to realize that you have been working on the system for 30 minutes without have entered a single keystroke

— reasonable first generation tools exist to help the user understand what is actually going on within the system at any given time

— dealing with images is easy and productive under ST-80 unlike any other substantial system I know of

6. Strengths of ST-80

The major strengths of ST-80 are related to the integration of program development tools with graphics. Such integration has begun to appear in other environments such as Interlisp and Lisa.

The following strengths of ST-80 have been observed:

— productivity is substantially enhanced by access to large library of reusable classes and methods and by inheritance (10's of lines of code rather than 1000's)

— the user interface within Smalltalk, while not perfect, is very, very good

— the totally integrated environment allows the sys-

tem to be more accessible to the user and can be mastered by an individual over time

— the Smalltalk language is remarkably productive for graphics programming

— there is a large quantity of existing code which is of reasonable quality and which can be directly accessed, modified, and reused (cost to generate was approximately 100 person years of effort over 12 years)

— Smalltalk-80 is directly extensible so that powerful new application systems can be built in the language of the user

— the base is very good for construction of the remainder of components required for the electronic office (applications, text/graphics, programming, communications)

— based upon very early impressions ST-80 well suited for use by physical scientists and others interested in modeling applications as long as the performance constraints mentioned elsewhere do not result in crippling response time

7. Weakness of ST-80

Obvious weaknesses which have been discovered include:

— lack of any capabilities in the commercial release for multiperson communication or coordination (mail, configuration control, etc.)

— there is no ST-80 file system or integrated set of utilities for file management, file transfer, and manipulation; instead the rather primitive ALTO file system is used outside of ST-80 (a different mode!)

— computation speed is currently a problem for the Xerox 1100 implementation of ST-80 since the computational primitives are not all written in microcode

— available training materials are sparse and inadequate given the radically new environment represented by ST-80

— the user population is extraordinarily small at this time (10's of people)

— hardware to run ST-80 is currently very expensive ($45,000) compared to that found in the typical corporate programmer's office (a $1500 VT-100); Apple's Lisa machine runs ST-80 on a much smaller display screen, but costs only $10,000 for the hardware; (these prices seem to change daily!)

— only one programming language is currently available within the environment; this obviates the possibility of utilizing any previously written software on the workstation itself; network connections to such software are possible

These weaknesses are simply a reflection of the maturity of the product and do not represent fundamental limitations which cannot be overcome.

8. Workstation costs versus software productivity

Workstations to run ST-80 are currently more expensive than we are accustomed to spending on programmer workstations. Any detailed analysis that I can imagine will convincingly demonstrate that for anything resembling the productivity gains which seem possible under ST-80, we could be spending dramatically more for workstations while improving the corporate profitability. The real gains for ST-80 may not just be development productivity but also maintenance productivity. By being succint and readable, we should assume that maintenance costs will be exceptionally low and maintenance turnaround very short.

Every indication is that cost per current day workstation will decrease steadily during the next decade. Personally, though I expect the capabilities of these devices to expand rather than stay constant, so the absolute value may not decrease nearly so rapidly.

9. Summary

ST-80 is a highly productive programming environment and approach to programming. It is non-traditional and represents a discontinuous break from the past. ST-80 combines an integrated programming environment with the object oriented approach to software development. It will fundamentally change the way we think about software environments, the way we develop software, and the amount of money we spend to capitalize programmers.

ST-80 can not longer be considered an interesting toy developed and used within research laboratories. It is a solid programming environment and can be used as a base for significant applications. These applications can be developed, modified, and maintained with dramatically less effort than in any other programming language, programming environment, or operating system. Radical improvements in productivity can now be purchased off the shelf and their seemingly high initial price tags may prove to be very modest indeed.

In conclusion, ST-80 is out of the Xerox research laboratory. It is a reasonably complete first release of a very ambitious software product which is of very high quality. **It has been well worth the rather long wait!**

The Smalltalk-80 System

The Xerox Learning Research Group
Xerox Palo Alto Research Center
3333 Coyote Hill Rd
Palo Alto CA 94304

The Smalltalk-80 system represents the current state of the object-oriented point of view as it has been reduced to practice by the Xerox Learning Research Group. The Smalltalk-80 system is composed of objects that interact only by sending and receiving messages. The programmer implements a system by describing messages to be sent and describing what happens when messages are received.

> *The Smalltalk-80 system is the latest in a series of programming environments that have applied the object-oriented point of view more and more uniformly to the design and production of software systems. The fundamental ideas of objects, messages, and classes came from SIMULA. (See reference 1.) SIMULA allows users to create object-oriented systems, but uses the standard data/procedure-oriented ALGOL language to provide numbers, booleans, basic data structures, and control structures. The Flex system, the Smalltalk-72, Smalltalk-74, and Smalltalk-76 (see references 5, 2, and 4, respectively) systems extended the object-oriented point of view to an increasing number of the elements of a programming environment. For example, in Smalltalk-72, arithmetic, list structures, and control structures were represented as objects and messages, but classes were not. In Smalltalk-74, class descriptions as objects were introduced. The Smalltalk-76 system added the capability to express relationships between classes, and extended the object-oriented point of view to the programmer's interface.*
>
> *This article presents the central semantic features and most of the syntactic features of the Smalltalk-80 system. It was prepared by Dave Robson and Adele Goldberg as scribes for the group effort of designing and implementing the system. Two forthcoming books (see reference 3) provide the full specification of the Smalltalk-80 system; in particular, the books describe the implementation of the interpreter and storage manager, and the graphical user interface.*

Sending Messages—Expressions

Messages are described by *expressions*, which are sequences of characters that conform to the syntax of the Smalltalk-80 programming language. A message-sending expression describes the *receiver, selector,* and *arguments* of the message. When an expression is *evaluated,* the message it describes is transmitted to its receiver. Here are several examples of expressions describing a message to an object. (Note: color has been added to help identify the receivers, selectors, and arguments in the following examples.)

1. `frame` `center`   Key: ☐ Receiver

2. `origin` `+` `offset`   ☐ Selector

3. `frame` `moveTo:` `newLocation`   ▨ Argument

4. `list` `at:` `index` `put:` `element`

Each expression begins with a description of the receiver of the message. The receivers in these examples are described by *variable names:* frame, origin, frame, and list, respectively. Generally, at least one space must separate the parts of an expression.

Messages without arguments are called *unary messages.* A unary message consists of a single identifier called a unary selector. The first example is a unary message whose selector is center.

A *binary message* has a single argument and a selector that is one of a set of special single or double characters called *binary selectors.* For example, the common arithmetic symbols (+ , − , *, and /) are binary selectors; some comparison operations are represented as double characters (eg: = = for equivalence, ~ = for not equal). The second example is a binary message whose argument is offset.

A *keyword message* has one or more arguments and a selector that is made up of a series of *keywords,* one preceding each argument. A keyword is an identifier with

August 1981 © BYTE Publications Inc

a trailing colon. The third example is a single-argument keyword message whose selector is moveTo: and whose argument is newLocation. The fourth example is a two-argument keyword message whose selector is made up of the keywords at: and put: and whose arguments are index and element. To talk about the selector of a multiple-argument keyword message, the keywords are concatenated. So, the selector of the fourth example is at:put:.

The message receivers and arguments in the examples are described by variable names. In addition, they can also be described with *literals*. The two most common kinds of literals are integers and strings. An *integer literal* is a sequence of digits that may be preceded by a minus sign (eg: 0, 1, 156, −3, or 13772). A *string literal* is a sequence of characters between single quotes (eg: 'hi', 'John', or 'the Smalltalk-80 system'). A binary message with an integer literal as its receiver is

45 + count

A keyword message with a string literal as its argument is

printer display: 'Monthly Payroll'

When a message is sent, it invokes a method determined by the class of the receiver. The invoked method will always return a result (an object). The result of a message can be used as a receiver or argument for another message. An example of a unary message describing the receiver of another unary message is

window frame center

Unary messages are parsed left to right. The first message in this example is the unary selector frame sent to the object named window. The unary message center is then sent to the result of the expression window frame (ie: the object returned from window's response to frame).

Binary messages are also parsed left to right. An example of a binary message describing the receiver of another binary message is

index + offset * 2

The result of sending the binary message + offset to the object named index is the receiver for the binary message *2. All binary selectors have the same precedence; only the order in which they are written matters. Parentheses can be used to change the order of evaluation. A message within parentheses is sent before any messages outside the parentheses. If the previous example were written

index + (offset * 2)

the result of the binary message * 2 to offset would be

used as the argument of a binary message with receiver index and selector + .

Unary messages take precedence over binary messages. If unary messages and binary messages appear together, the unary messages will be sent first. In the example

frame center + window offset − index

the result of the unary message center to frame is the receiver of the binary message whose selector is + and whose argument is the result of the unary message offset to window. The result of the + message is, in turn, the receiver of the binary message − index. Parentheses can be used to explicitly show the order of evaluation, eg: ((frame center) + (window offset)) − index. Parentheses can also be used to alter the order of evaluation. In the example

(center + offset) x

the binary message + offset would be sent before the unary message x.

Whenever keywords appear in an unparenthesized message, they compose a single selector. The example

window showText: 'Title' inFont: helvetica
    indented: 15

is a single message whose selector is showText:inFont:indented:. Because of this concatenation, there is no left-to-right parsing rule for keyword messages. If a keyword message is to be used as a receiver or argument of another keyword message, it must be parenthesized. The expression

frame scale: (factor max: 5)

describes two keyword messages. The result of the expression factor max: 5 is the argument for the scale: message to frame.

Binary messages take precedence over keyword messages. When unary, binary, and keyword messages appear in the same expression without parentheses, the unary messages are sent first, the binary messages next, and the keyword messages last. The example

bigFrame height: smallFrame height * 2

is evaluated as if it were parenthesized as follows:

bigFrame height: ((smallFrame height) * 2)

A *cascaded message expression* describes a sequence of messages to be sent to the same object. A simple message expression is a description of the receiver (ie: a variable name, literal, or expression) followed by a message (ie: a unary selector, a binary selector and argument, or a set of keywords and arguments). A cascaded message expres-

August 1981 © BYTE Publications Inc

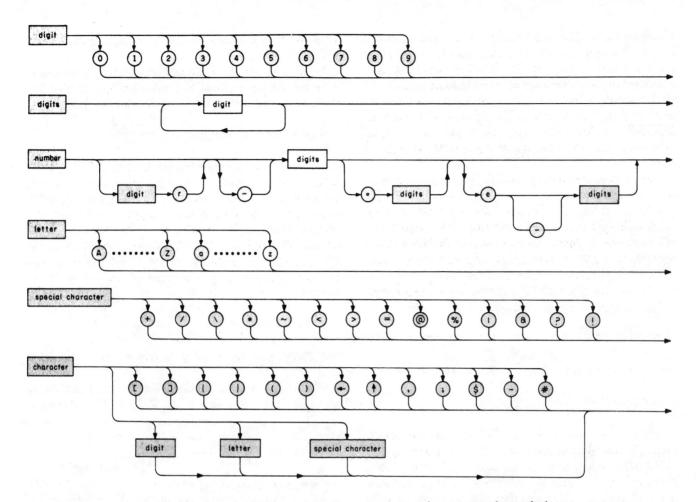

Figure 1: *Syntax diagrams for the Smalltalk-80 language.*

sion is a single description of a receiver followed by several messages separated by semicolons. For example, in the expression

    printer newLine; print: reportTitle; space;
        print: Date today.

four messages are sent to the object named printer. The selectors of the four messages are newLine, print:, space, and print:. In the expression

    window frame center: pointer location;
        width: border + contents; clear

three messages are sent to the object returned from the frame message to window. The selectors of the three messages are center:, width:, and clear. Without cascading, this would have been three expressions

    window frame center: pointer location.
    window frame width: border + contents.
    window frame clear

Assigning Variables

The value of a variable can be used as the receiver or argument of a message by including its name in an expression. The value of a variable can be changed with an *assignment expression*. An assignment expression consists of a variable name followed by a left arrow (←) followed by the description of an object. When an assignment expression is evaluated, the variable named to the left of the arrow assumes the value of the object described to the right of the arrow. The new value can be described by a variable name, a literal, or a message-sending expression. Examples of assignments are

    center ← origin
    index ← 0
    index ← index + 1
    index ← index + 1 max: limit

In the last example, the message + 1 is sent to the value of the variable index, the message max: limit is sent to the result of the + 1 message, and the result of the max: limit message becomes the new value of the variable index.

A number of variables can be assigned in the same expression by including several variable names with left arrows. The expression

    start ← index ← 0

makes the value of both start and index be 0.

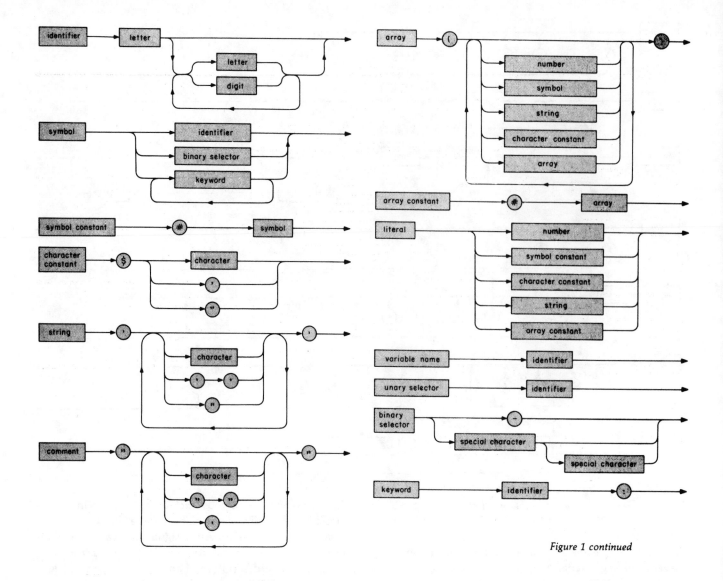

Figure 1 continued

The syntax table in figure 1 is a diagram for parsing well-formed Smalltalk-80 expressions. This table does not specify how *spaces* are treated. Spaces must not appear between digits and characters that make up a single token, nor within the specification of a number. Spaces must appear

- between a sequence of identifiers used as variables or unary selectors
- between the elements of an array in an array constant
- on either side of a keyword in a keyword expression

Spaces may optionally be included between any other elements in an expression. A carriage return or tab has the same syntactic function as a space.

Receiving Messages—Classes

A *class* describes a set of objects called its *instances*. Each instance has a set of *instance variables*. The class provides a set of names that are used to refer to these variables. A class also provides a set of *methods* that describe what happens when its instances receive mes-

sages. A method describes a sequence of actions to be taken when a message with a particular selector is received by an instance of a particular class. These actions consist of sending other messages, assigning variables, and returning a value to the original message.

To create a new application, modify an existing application, or to modify the Smalltalk-80 system itself, a programmer creates and modifies classes that describe objects. The most profitable way to manipulate a class is with an interactive system. Much of the development of the Smalltalk-80 system has been the creation of appropriate software-development tools. (See Larry Tesler's article "The Smalltalk Environment," on page 90.) Unfortunately, to describe a system on paper, a noninteractive linear mode of presentation is needed. To this end, a *basic class template* is provided as a simple textual representation of a class. The basic class template in table 1 shows the name of the class, the names of the instance variables, and the set of methods used for responding to messages.

In table 1, the italicized elements will be replaced by the specific identifiers or methods appropriate to the

August 1981 © BYTE Publications Inc

Figure 1 continued:

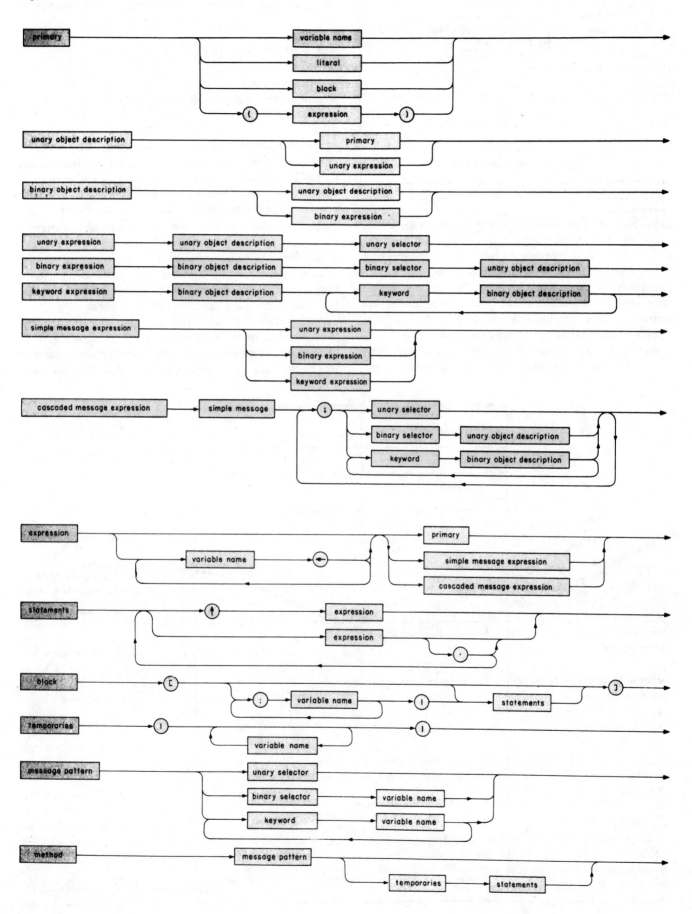

class name	*identifier*		
instance variable names	*identifier*	*identifier*	*identifier*
methods			
method			
method			
method			

Table 1: *The basic class template.*

arithmetic. The details of methods (in particular, the use of '|', '.' and '↑') are the subject of our next discussion.

Methods

A method has three parts:

- a *message pattern*
- some *temporary variable names*
- some expressions

The three parts of a method are separated by vertical bars (|). The message pattern consists of a selector and names for the arguments. The expressions are separated by periods (.) and the last one may be preceded by an up arrow (↑). In the method for selector + in figure 2, the message pattern is + *aPoint*, the temporary variable names are sumX and sumY, and there are three expressions, the last one preceded by an ↑.

Line breaks have no significance in methods; formatting is used only for purposes of aesthetics. The vertical bars and periods are delimiters of significance.

As stated earlier, each message pattern contains a selector. When a message is received by an instance, the method whose message pattern contains the same selector will be executed. For example, suppose that offset were an

class. Names of classes begin with an uppercase letter, and names of variables begin with a lowercase letter. As an example, figure 2 shows the basic template form of a class named Point whose instances represent points in a two-dimensional coordinate system. Each instance has an instance variable named x that represents its horizontal coordinate and an instance variable named y that represents its vertical coordinate. Each instance can respond to messages that initialize its two instance variables, request the value of either variable, and perform simple

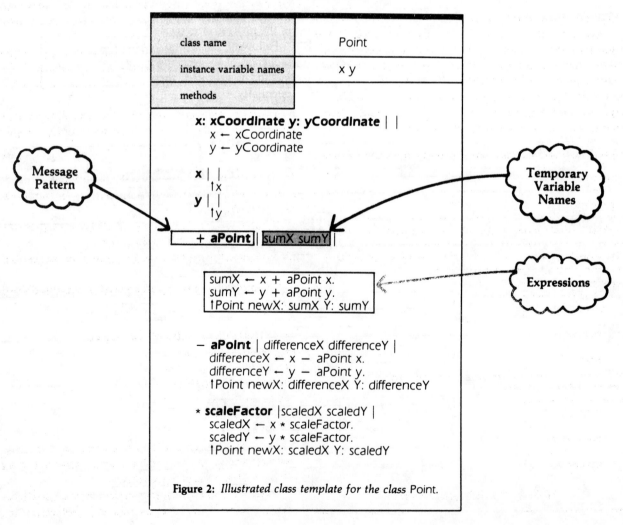

Figure 2: *Illustrated class template for the class* Point.

August 1981 © BYTE Publications Inc

class name	DepositRecord
superclass	Object
instance variable names	date amount
methods	

```
    of: depositAmount on: depositDate | |

        date ← depositDate.
        amount ← depositAmount

    amount | |
        ↑ amount

    balanceChange | |
        ↑ amount
```

Table 2: *Class template for class DepositRecord.*

class name	CheckRecord
superclass	DepositRecord
instance variable names	number
methods	

```
    number: checkNumber for: checkAmount on:
        checkDate | |
        number ← checkNumber.
        date ← checkDate.
        amount ← checkAmount

    of: anAmount on: aDate | .|
        self error:
        'Check records are initialized with
        number:for:on:'

    balanceChange | | ↑ 0 − amount
```

Table 3: *Class template for class CheckRecord.*

instance of Point in the expression

offset + frame center

The method whose message pattern is + aPoint would be executed in response. For selectors that take arguments, the message pattern also contains *argument names* wherever arguments would appear in a message. When a method is invoked by a message, the argument names in the method are used to refer to the actual arguments of that message. In the above example, aPoint would refer to the result of frame center.

class name	identifier		
superclass	identifier		
instance variable names	identifier	identifier	identifier
class variable names	identifier	identifier	identifier
class messages and methods			
method			
method			
method			
instance messages and methods			
method			
method			
method			

Table 4: *The full class template.*

Following the message pattern, a method can contain some *temporary variable names* between vertical bars. When a method is executed, a set of variables is created that can be accessed by the temporary variable names. These temporary variables exist only while the method is in the process of execution.

Following the second vertical bar, a method contains a sequence of expressions separated by periods. When a method is executed, these expressions are evaluated sequentially.

So, there are three steps in receiving a message, corresponding to the three parts of the method. Smalltalk will

1. *Find* the method whose message pattern has the same selector as the message and *create* a set of variables for the argument values.
2. *Create* a set of temporary variables corresponding to the names between the vertical bars.
3. *Evaluate* the expressions in the method sequentially.

Six kinds of variables can be used in a method's expressions:

- the instance variables of the receiver
- the pseudo-variable self
- the message arguments
- temporary variables
- class variables
- global variables

The instance variables are named in the message receiver's class. In the example, x and y refer to the values of the instance variables of offset.

There is an important *pseudo-variable* available in every method, which is named self. self refers to the receiver of the message that invoked the method. It is called a pseudo-variable because its value can be accessed like a variable, but its value cannot be changed using an assignment expression. In the example, self refers to the same object as offset during the execution of the method associated with +.

Arguments and temporary variables are similar, in that the names for both are declared in the method itself and they both exist only during the method's execution. However, unlike arguments, temporary variables are not automatically initialized. The values of temporary variables can be changed with an assignment expression.

Class variables are shared by all instances and the class itself. Names for the class variables are shown in the full class template in an entry called "class variable names" (see table 4). Although they are variables and their values can be changed, they are typically treated as constants, initialized when the class is created, and then simply used by the instances. For example, if the class of floating-point numbers wanted to provide trigonometric functions, it might want to define a variable called pi to be used in any of its methods.

Global variables are shared by all objects. A global dictionary, called Smalltalk, holds the names and values of these variables. The classes in the system, for example, are the values of global variables whose names are the class names. With the exception of variables used to reference system resources, few global variables exist in the Smalltalk-80 system. Programming style that depends on user-defined globals is generally discouraged.

If the last expression in a method is preceded by an ↑, the message that invoked the method takes on the value of this expression. If an ↑ does not precede the last expression, the value of the message is simply the receiver of the message. For example, the x:y: message to a Point (see figure 2) behaves as if it had been written

x: xCoordinate y: yCoordinate | |
    x ← xCoordinate.
    y ← yCoordinate.
    ↑ self

Methods can contain comments anywhere. A *comment* is a sequence of characters delimited by double quotes. Two consecutive double quotes are used to embed a double quote within a comment. The methods in class Point were purposely written in a verbose style to provide examples. The messages for + could have been written

  + aPoint | |
    ↑ Point newX: x + aPoint x Y: y + aPoint y

The basic class template presents only the most important attributes of a class. The complete description of a class is provided by the *full class template*, described in the next section.

Inheritance

The basic template allows a class to be described in-

dependently of other classes. It ignores inheritance among classes. The full class template, however, takes inheritance into account. (See table 4.) With it, a class can be described as a modification of another class called its *superclass*. All classes that modify a particular class are called its *subclasses*. A subclass inherits the instance variable names and methods of its superclass. A subclass can also add instance variable names and methods to those it inherits. The instance variable names added by the subclass must differ from the instance variable names of the superclass. The subclass can *override* a method in the superclass by adding a message with the same selector. Instances of the subclass will execute the method found in the subclass rather than the method inherited from the superclass.

To assemble the complete description of a class, it is necessary to look at its superclass, its superclass's superclass, and so on, until a class with no superclass is encountered. There is only one such class in the system (ie: without a superclass), and its class name is Object. All classes ultimately inherit methods from Object. Object has no instance variables. The set of classes linked through the superclass relation is called a *superclass chain*. The full class template has an entry called "superclass" that specifies the initial link on the class's superclass chain.

As an example, we might describe a class, DepositRecord, whose instances are records of bank account deposits. Each instance has two instance variables representing the date and amount of the deposit. The class template is shown in table 2.

class name	CheckRecord
superclass	DepositRecord
instance variable names	number
class messages and methods	

number: checkNumber for: checkAmount on: checkDate | |
    ↑ self new number: checkNumber
             for: checkAmount
             on: checkDate

instance messages and methods

number: checkNumber for: checkAmount on: checkDate | |
    super of: checkAmount on: checkDate.
    number ← checkNumber

of: anAmount on: aDate | |

    self error: 'Check records are initialized with
        number:for:on:'

balanceChange | | ↑ 0 − amount

Table 5: *Full class template for class CheckRecord.*

August 1981 © BYTE Publications Inc

A class, CheckRecord, whose instances are records of checks written on an account is a subclass of DepositRecord; this new class adds an instance variable that represents the check number. The class template is shown in table 3.

An instance of CheckRecord has three instance variables. It inherits the amount message, adds the number:for:on: message, and overrides the balanceChange and of:on: messages. The of:on: method contains a single expression in which the message error: 'Check records are initialized with number:for:on:' is sent to the pseudo-variable self. The method for error: is found in the superclass of DepositRecord, which is the class Object; the response is to stop execution and to display the string literal argument to the user.

An additional pseudo-variable available in a method's

expressions is super. It allows a subclass to access the methods in its superclass that have been overridden in the subclass description. The use of super as the receiver of a message has the same effect as the use of self, except that the search for the appropriate message starts in the superclass, not the class, of the receiver.

For example, the method associated with number:for:on in CheckRecord might have been defined as

number: checkNumber for: checkAmount on: checkDate | |
    super of: checkAmount on: checkDate.
    number ← checkNumber

Metaclasses

Since a class is an object, there is a different class that describes it. A class that describes a class is called a *metaclass*. Thus, a class has its own instance variables that represent the description of its instances; it responds to messages that provide for the initialization and modification of this description. In particular, a class responds to a message that creates a new instance. The unary message new creates a new instance whose instance variables are uninitialized. The object nil indicates an uninitialized value.

The classes in the system might all be instances of the same class. However, each class typically uses a slightly different message protocol to create initialized instances. For example, the last expression in the method associated with + in class Point (see figure 2) was

    Point newX: sumX Y: sumY

newX:Y: is a message to Point, asking it to create a new instance with sumX and sumY as the values of the new instance's instance variables. The newX:Y: message would not mean anything to another class, such as DepositRecord or CheckRecord. So, these three classes can't be instances of the same class. All classes have a lot in common, so their classes are all subclasses of the same class. This class is named Class. The subclasses of Class are called *metaclasses*.

The newX:Y: message in Point's metaclass might be implemented as

newX: xValue Y: yValue | |
    ↑ self new x: xValue y: yValue

The new message was inherited by Point's metaclass from Class. One reason for having metaclasses is to have a special set of methods for each class, primarily messages for initializing class variables and new instances. These methods are displayed in the full class-template form shown in table 4; they are distinguished from the methods for messages to the instances of the class. The two categories are "class messages and methods" and "instance messages and methods," respectively. Methods in

class name	Point
superclass	Object
instance variable names	x y
class variable names	pi
class messages and methods	

instance creation
newX: xValue Y: yValue | |
    ↑ self new x: xValue
             y: yValue
newRadius: radius Angle: angle | |
    ↑ self new x: radius * angle sin
             y: radius * angle cos

class initialization
setPI | | pi ← 3.14159

instance messages and methods

accessing
x: xCoordinate y: yCoordinate | |
    x ← xCoordinate.
    y ← yCoordinate
x | | ↑x
y | | ↑y
radius | | ↑((x * x) + (y * y)) squareRoot
angle | | ↑(x/y) arctan

arithmetic
+ aPoint | | ↑Point newX: x + aPoint x
                 Y: y + aPoint y
− aPoint | | ↑Point newX: x − aPoint x
                 Y: y − aPoint y
* scaleFactor | | ↑Point newX: x * scaleFactor
                 Y: y * scaleFactor
circleArea | r |
    r ← self radius.
    ↑ pi * r * r

Table 6: *Full class template for class* Point.

the category "class messages and methods" are associated with the metaclass; those in "instance messages and methods" are associated with the class.

If there are no class variables for the class, the "class variable name" entry is omitted. So, CheckRecord might be described as shown in table 5.

It is often desirable to create subcategories within the categories "class messages and methods" and "instance messages and methods." Moreover, the order in which the categories or subcategories are listed is of no significance. (The notion of categories is simply a pretty printing" technique; it has no semantic significance.)

Returning to the example of class Point, if the instance methods of class Point include subcategories *accessing* and *arithmetic*, the template for Point might appear as shown in table 6.

When the class Point is defined, the expression

Point setPi

should be evaluated in order to set the value of the single class variable.

A Point might be created and given a name by evaluating the expression

testPoint ← Point newX: 420 Y: 26

The new Point, testPoint, can then be sent the message circleArea:

testPoint circleArea

or used in a more complex expression:

(testPoint * 2) circleArea

Primitive Routines

The response to some messages in the system may be performed by a *primitive routine* (written in the implementation language of the machine) rather than by evaluating the expressions in a method. The methods for these messages indicate the presence of such a primitive routine by including <primitive> before the first expression in the method. A major use of primitive methods is to interact with the machine's input/output devices.

An example of a primitive method is the new message to classes, which returns a new instance of the receiver.

new | | <primitive>

This particular primitive routine always produces a result. If there are situations in which a primitive routine cannot produce a result, the method will also contain some expressions. If the primitive routine is successful in responding to the message, it will return a value and the expressions in the method will not be evaluated. If the primitive routine encounters difficulty, the expressions will be evaluated as though the primitive routine had not been specified.

Another example of a message with a primitive response is a message with the selector + sent to a SmallInteger

+ **aNumber** | | <primitive>
   self error: 'SmallInteger addition has failed'

One reason this primitive might fail to produce a result is that the argument is not a SmallInteger. In the example, this would produce an error report. In the actual Smalltalk-80 system, an attempt is made to check and see if the argument were another kind of number for which a result could be produced.

Indexed Instance Variables

An object's instance variables are usually given names by its class. The names are used in methods of the class to refer to the values of the instance variables. Some objects also have a set of instance variables that have no names and can only be accessed by messages. The instance variables are referred to by an integral *index*. Indexable objects are used to implement the classes in the system that represent collections of other objects, such as arrays and strings.

The messages to access indexed instance variables have

class name	Array
superclass	IndexedCollection
indexable instance variables	
class messages and methods	

instance creation
with: anElement | |
  ↑(self new: 1) at: 1 put: anElement
with: firstElement with: secondElement
  | anArray |
  anArray ← self new: 2.
  anArray at: 1 put: firstElement.
  anArray at: 2 put: secondElement.
  ↑anArray

instance messages and methods

accessing
at: anInteger | |
  <primitive>
  self error: 'index out of range'

at: anInteger put: anElement | |
  <primitive>
  self error: 'index out of range'

funny stuff
embed | |
  ↑Array with: self

Table 7: *Full class template for class* Array.

August 1981 © BYTE Publications Inc

selectors at: and at:put:. For example

list at: 1

returns the first indexed instance variable of list. The example

list at: 4 put: element

stores element as the value of the fourth indexed instance variable of list. The at: and at:put: messages invoke primitive routines to load or store the value of the indicated variable. The legal indices run from one to the number of indexable variables in the instance. The at: and at:put: messages are defined in class Object and, therefore, can be understood by all objects; however, only certain classes will create instances with indexable instance variables. These classes will have an additional line in the class template indicating that the instances contain *indexable instance variables*. As an example, we show a part of the template for class Array in table 7.

Each instance of a class that allows indexable instance variables may have a different number of them; such instances are created using the new: message to a class, whose argument tells the number of indexable variables. The number of indexable instance variables an instance has can be found by sending it the message size. A class whose instances have indexable instance variables can also have named instance variables. All instances of any class will have the same number of named instance variables.

Control Structures and Blocks

The two control structures in the Smalltalk-80 system described so far are

● the sequential execution of expressions in a method
● the sending of messages that invoke other methods that eventually return values

All other control structures are based on objects called *blocks*. Like a method, a block is a sequence of expressions, the last of which can be preceded by an up arrow (↑). The expressions are delimited by periods; they may be preceded by one or more identifiers with leading colons. These identifiers are the *block arguments*. Block arguments are separated from expressions by a vertical bar.

Whenever square brackets are encountered in a method, a block is created. Evaluation of the expressions inside the square brackets is deferred until the block is sent the message value or a message whose selector is a concatenation of one or more occurrences of the keyword value:. Control structures are implemented as messages with receivers or arguments that are blocks. The methods for carrying out these control-structure messages involve sending the blocks patterns of value messages.

In the Smalltalk-80 system, there are two types of primitive control messages: conditional selection of blocks, ifTrue:ifFalse:, and conditional iteration of blocks, whileTrue: and whileFalse:.

The representation of conditions in the Smalltalk-80 system uses distinguished boolean objects named false and true. The first type of primitive control message provides for conditional selection of a block to be executed. This is similar to the IF . . . THEN . . . ELSE of ALGOL-like languages. The expression

queue isEmpty ifTrue: [index ← 0]
        ifFalse: [index ← queue next]

evaluates the expressions in the first block if the receiver is true and evaluates the expressions in the second block if the receiver is false. Two other forms of conditional selection provide only one alternative

queue isEmpty ifTrue: [index ← 0].
queue isEmpty ifFalse: [index ← queue next].

When ifTrue: is sent to false, it returns immediately without executing the block. When ifFalse: is sent to true, the block is not executed.

The second type of primitive control message repeatedly evaluates the expressions in a block as long as some condition holds. This is similar to the WHILE and UNTIL statements in ALGOL-like languages. This type of control message is a message to a block; the receiver, the block, evaluates the expressions it contains and determines whether or not to continue on the basis of the value of the last expression. The first form of this control message has selector whileTrue:. The method for whileTrue: repeatedly executes the argument block as long the receiver's value is true. For example,

[index < = limit] whileTrue: [self process: list at: index.
              index ← index + 1]

The binary message < = is understood by objects representing magnitudes. The value returned is the result of comparing whether the receiver is less than or equal to (< =) the argument.

The second conditional iteration message has selector whileFalse:. The method for whileFalse: repeatedly executes the argument block as long as the receiver's value is false. For example,

[queue isEmpty] whileFalse: [self process: queue next]

The messages whileTrue and whileFalse to a block provide a shorthand notation for messages of the form whileTrue: aBlock and whileFalse: aBlock, if the argument aBlock is an empty block.

Block arguments allow one or more of the variables inside the block to be given new values each time the block is executed. Instead of sending the block the message value, messages with selectors value: or value:value:, and so on, are sent to the block. The arguments of the value: messages are assigned to the block arguments (in order) before the block expressions are evaluated.

As an example, classes with indexed instance variables could implement a message with selector do: that takes a block as an argument and executes it once for every indexed variable. The block has a single block argument; the value of the appropriate indexed variable is passed to it for each execution. An example of the use of such a message is

list do: [:element | self process: element]

The message might be implemented as

do: aBlock | index |
   index ← 1.
   [index < = self size] whileTrue:
      [aBlock value: (self at: index).
        index ← index + 1]

Similar control messages can be implemented for any class. As an example, a simple repetition could be provided by a timesRepeat: aBlock message to instances of class Integer

timesRepeat: aBlock | index |
   index ← 1.
   [index < = self] whileTrue:
      [aBlock value.
        index ← index + 1]

Examples of implementing other control messages are given in L Peter Deutsch's article "Building Control Structures in the Smalltalk-80 System," on page 322.

The Smalltalk-80 System: Basic Classes

The Smalltalk-80 *language* provides a uniform syntax for retrieving objects, sending messages, and defining classes. The Smalltalk-80 *system* is a complete programming environment that includes many actual classes and instances. In support of the uniform syntax, this system includes class descriptions for Object, Class, Message, CompiledMethod, and Context, whose subclasses are BlockContext and MethodContext. Multiple independent processes are provided by classes ProcessorScheduler, Process, and Semaphore. The special object nil is the only instance of class UndefinedObject. These classes comprise the *kernel* Smalltalk-80 system.

The system also includes class descriptions to support basic data structures; these are numerical and collection classes. The class Number specifies the protocol appropriate for all numerical objects. Its subclasses provide specific representations of numbers. The subclasses are Float, Fraction, and Integer. For a variety of reasons, there are both SmallIntegers and LargeIntegers; of these, there are LargePositiveIntegers and LargeNegativeIntegers.

Class Collection specifies protocol appropriate to objects representing collections of objects. These include Bag, Set, OrderedCollection, LinkedList, MappedCollection, SortedCollection, and IndexedCollection. The latter provides protocol for objects with indexable instance variables. It has subclasses String and Array. Elements of a string are instances of class Character; bytes are stored in instances of ByteArray. A subclass of String is Symbol; a subclass of Set is Dictionary (a set of Associations).

Interval is a subclass of Collection with elements representing an arithmetic progression. Intervals can be created by sending the message to: or to:by: to Integer. So, the expressions 1 to: 5 by: 1 and 1 to: 5 each create a new Interval representing 1, 2, 3, 4, 5. As a Collection, Interval responds to the enumeration message do:. For example, in

(1 to: 5) do: [:index | anArray at: index put: index * 2]

the block argument index takes on successive values 1, 2, 3, 4, 5.

For programmer convenience, an Integer also responds to the messages to:do: and to:by:do:, allowing the parentheses in interval enumeration expressions to be omitted.

The ability to stream over indexed or ordered collections is provided by a hierarchy based on class Stream, including ReadStream, WriteStream, and ReadAndWriteStream. A file system, local or remote, is then implementable as a subclass of these kinds of Streams.

Since instances of the system classes described above are used in the implementation of all applications, an understanding of their message protocol is as necessary to understanding an implementation as an understanding of the language syntax. These system classes are fully described in the forthcoming Smalltalk books.

In addition to the basic data-structure classes, the Smalltalk-80 system includes class descriptions to support interactive graphics (forms and images and image editors, text and text editors), networking, standard files, and hard-copy printing. A complete Smalltalk-80 system contains about sixty class definitions, not including a variety of windows or views, menus, scrollbars, and the metaclasses. Many of these are discussed in companion articles in this issue. (See Daniel H H Ingalls's "The Design Principles Behind Smalltalk," page 286, and Larry Tesler's "The Smalltalk Environment," page 90.)

The important thing to note is that each of these class descriptions is implemented in the Smalltalk-80 language itself. Each can be examined and modified by the programmer. Some of the class descriptions contain methods that reference primitive methods; only these methods are implemented in the machine language of the implementation machine. It is a fundamental part of the philosophy of the system design that the programmer have such complete access. In this way, system designers, such as members of the Xerox Learning Research Group, are able to build the next Smalltalk in the complete context of Smalltalk itself. ■

August 1981 © BYTE Publications Inc

References

1. Birtwistle, Graham; Ole-Johan Dahl; Bjorn Myhrhaug; and Kristen Nygaard. *Simula Begin*. Philadelphia: Auerbach, 1973.
2. Goldberg, Adele and Alan Kay, editors. *Smalltalk-72 Instructional Manual*. Xerox PARC technical report, March 1976 (out of print).
3. Goldberg, Adele; David Robson; and Daniel H H Ingalls. *Smalltalk-80: The Language and Its Implementation* and *Smalltalk-80: The Interactive Programming Environment*, 1981 (books forthcoming).
4. Ingalls, Daniel H H. "The Smalltalk-76 Programming System: Design and Implementation." In *Proceedings of the Principles of Programming Languages Symposium*, January 1978.
5. Kay, Alan. *The Reactive Engine*. Ph.D. Thesis, University of Utah, September, 1969 (University Microfilms).

Glossary

Editor's Note: *This glossary provides concise definitions for many of the keywords and concepts related to Smalltalk-80. These definitions will be most useful if you first read the introductory Smalltalk articles. . . . GW*

General Terminology

object	a package of information and descriptions of its manipulation
message	a specification of one of an object's manipulations
method	a procedure-like entity; the description of a sequence of actions to be taken when a message is received by an object
class	a description of one or more similar objects
instance	an object described by a particular class
method dictionary	a set of associations between message selectors and methods; included in each class description
metaclass	a class whose (single) instance is itself a class
subclass	a class that is created by sharing the description of another class, often modifying some aspects of that description

Syntax Terminology

message receiver	the object to be manipulated, according to a message
message sender	the object requesting a manipulation
message selector	a symbolic name that describes a desired manipulation of an object
message argument	one of the objects specified in a message that provides information needed so that a message receiver can be manipulated appropriately
unary message	a message without arguments
binary message	a message with a single argument and a selector that is one of a set of special single or double characters
keyword message	a message that has one or more arguments and a selector made up of a series of identifiers with trailing colons, one preceding each argument

block	a literal method; an object representing a sequence of actions to be taken at a later time, upon receiving an "evaluation" message (such as one with selector value or value:)

Semantics

instance variable	a variable that is information used to distinguish an instance from other instances of the same class
class variable	a variable shared by all instances of a class and the class itself
named variable	an instance variable that is given a name in the class of the instance; the name is used in methods of the class
indexed variable	an instance variable with no name, accessed by message only; referred to by an integer (an index)
global or pool variable	a variable shared by instances of several classes; a system example is Smalltalk, a dictionary that includes references to all the defined classes
temporary variable	a variable that exists only while the method in which it is declared is in the process of execution
pseudo-variable	a variable available in every method without special declaration, but whose value cannot be changed using an assignment. System examples are self, super and thisContext.
nil	a special object, the only instance of class UndefinedObject

Implementation Terminology

field	the memory space in which the value of an object's variable is stored
bytecode	a machine instruction for the virtual machine
object pointer	a reference to an object
reference count	of an object, is the number of objects that point to it (ie: that contain its object pointer)

Design Principles Behind Smalltalk

Daniel H H Ingalls
Learning Research Group
Xerox Palo Alto Research Center
3333 Coyote Hill Rd
Palo Alto CA 94304

The purpose of the Smalltalk project is to provide computer support for the creative spirit in everyone. Our work flows from a vision that includes a creative individual and the best computing hardware available. We have chosen to concentrate on two principal areas of research: a language of description (programming language) that serves as an interface between the models in the human mind and those in computing hardware, and a language of interaction (user interface) that matches the human communication system to that of the computer. Our work has followed a two- to four-year cycle that can be seen to parallel the scientific method:

●Build an application program within the current system (make an observation)
●Based on that experience, redesign the language (formulate a theory)
●Build a new system based on the new design (make a prediction that can be tested)

The Smalltalk-80 system marks our fifth time through this cycle. In this article, I present some of the general principles we have observed in the course of our work. While the presentation frequently touches on Smalltalk "motherhood," the principles themselves are more general and should prove useful in evaluating other systems and in guiding future work.

Just to get warmed up, I'll start with a principle that is more social than technical and that is largely responsible for the particular bias of the Smalltalk project:

Personal Mastery: *If a system is to serve the creative spirit, it must be entirely comprehensible to a single individual.*

The point here is that the human potential manifests itself in individuals. To realize this potential, we must provide a medium that can be mastered by a single individual. Any barrier that exists between the user and some part of the system will eventually be a barrier to creative expression. Any part of the system that cannot be changed or that is not sufficiently general is a likely source of impediment. If one part of the system works differently from all the rest, that part will require additional effort to control. Such an added burden may detract from the final result and will inhibit future endeavors in that area. We can thus infer a general principle of design:

Good Design: *A system should be built with a minimum set of unchangeable parts; those parts should be as general as possible; and all parts of the system should be held in a uniform framework.*

Language

In designing a language for use with computers, we do not have to look far to find helpful hints. Everything we know about how people think and communicate is applicable. The mechanisms of human thought and communication have been engineered for millions of years, and we should respect them as being of sound design. Moreover, since we must work with this design for the next million years, it will save time if we make our computer models compatible with the mind, rather than the other way around.

Figure 1 illustrates the principal components in our discussion. A person is presented as having a body and a mind. The body is the site of primary experience, and, in the context of this discussion, it is the physical channel through which the universe is perceived and through which intentions are carried out. Experience is recorded and processed in the mind. Creative thought (without going into its mechanism) can be viewed as the spontaneous appearance of information in the mind. Language is the key to that information:

Purpose of Language: *To provide a framework for communication.*

The interaction between two individuals is represented in figure 1 as two arcs. The solid arc represents explicit communication: the actual words and movements uttered and perceived. The dashed arc represents implicit communication: the shared culture and experience that form the context of the explicit communication. In human interaction, much of the actual communication is achieved through reference to the shared context, and human language is built around such allusion. This is the case with computers as well.

It is no coincidence that a computer can be viewed as one of the participants in figure 1. In this case, the "body" provides for visual display of information and for sensing input from a human user. The "mind" of a computer includes the internal memory and processing elements and their contents. Figure 1 shows that several different issues are involved in the design of a computer language:

Scope: *The design of a language for using computers must deal with internal models, external media, and the interaction between these in both the human and the computer.*

This fact is responsible for the difficulty of explaining Smalltalk to people who view computer languages in a more restricted sense. Smalltalk is not simply a better way of organizing procedures or a different technique for storage management. It is not just an extensible hierarchy of data types, or a graphical user interface. It is all of these things and anything else that is needed to support the interactions shown in figure 1.

Communicating Objects

The mind observes a vast universe of experience, both immediate and recorded. One can derive a sense of

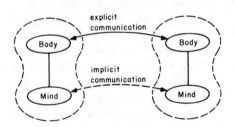

Figure 1: *The scope of language design. Communication between two people (or between one person and a computer) includes communication on two levels. Explicit communication includes the information that is transmitted in a given message. Implicit communication includes the relevant assumptions common to the two beings.*

oneness with the universe simply by letting this experience be, just as it is. However, if one wishes to participate, literally to *take a part*, in the universe, one must draw distinctions. In so doing one identifies an object in the universe, and simultaneously all the rest becomes not-that-object. Distinction by itself is a start, but the process of distinguishing does not get any easier. Every time you want to talk about "that chair over there," you have to repeat the entire process of distinguishing that chair. This is where the act of reference comes in: we can associate a unique identifier with an object, and, from that time on, only the mention of that identifier is necessary to refer to the original object.

We have said that a computer system should provide models that are compatible with those in the mind. Therefore:

Objects: *A computer language should support the concept of "object" and provide a uniform means for referring to the objects in its universe.*

The Smalltalk storage manager provides an object-oriented model of memory for the entire system. Uniform reference is achieved simply by associating a unique integer with every object in the system. This uniformity is important because it means that variables in the system can take on widely differing values and yet can be implemented as simple memory cells. Objects are created when expressions are evaluated, and they can then be passed around by uniform reference, so that no provision for their storage is necessary in the procedures that manipulate them. When all references to an object have disappeared from the system, the object itself vanishes, and its storage is reclaimed. Such behavior is essential to full support of the object metaphor:

Storage Management: *To be truly "object-oriented," a computer system must provide automatic storage management.*

A way to find out if a language is working well is to see if the programs look like they are doing what they are doing. If they are sprinkled with statements that relate to the management of storage, then their internal model is not well matched to that of humans. Can you imagine having to prepare someone for each thing you tell them or having to inform them when you are through with a given topic and that it can be forgotten?

Each object in our universe has a life of its own. Similarly, the brain provides for independent processing along with the storage of each mental object. This suggests a third principle for object-oriented design:

Messages: *Computing should be viewed as an intrinsic capability of objects that can be uniformly invoked by sending messages.*

Just as programs get messy if object storage is dealt with explicitly, control in the system becomes complicated if processing is performed extrinsically. Let us consider the process of adding 5 to a number. In most computer systems, the compiler figures out what kind of number it is and generates code to add 5 to it. This is not good enough for an object-oriented system because the exact kind of number cannot be determined by the compiler (more on this later). A possible solution is to call a general addition routine that examines the type of the arguments to determine the appropriate action. This is not a good approach because it means that this *critical* routine must be edited by novices who just want to experiment with their own class of numbers. It is also a poor design because intimate knowledge about the internals of objects is sprinkled throughout the system.

Smalltalk provides a much cleaner solution: it sends the *name* of the desired operation, along with any arguments, as a *message* to the number, with the understanding that the receiver knows best how to carry out the desired operation. Instead of a bit-grinding processor raping and plundering data structures, we have a universe of well-behaved objects that courteously ask each other to carry out their various desires. The transmission of messages is the only process that is carried on outside of objects and this is as it should be, since messages travel between objects. The principle of good design can be restated for languages:

Uniform Metaphor: *A language should be designed around a powerful metaphor that can be uniformly applied in all areas.*

Examples of success in this area ir clude LISP, which is built on tr model of linked structures; APL, which is built on the model of arrays; and Smalltalk, which is built on the model of communicating objects. In each case, large applications are viewed in the same way as the fundamental units from which the system is built. In Smalltalk especially, the interaction between the most primitive objects is viewed in the same way as the highest-level interaction between the computer and its user. Every object in Smalltalk, even a lowly integer, has a set of messages, a *protocol*, that defines the explicit communication to which that object can respond. Internally, objects may have local storage and access to other shared information which comprise the implicit context of all communication. For instance, the message + 5 (add five) carries an implicit assumption that the augend is the present value of the number receiving the message.

Organization

A uniform metaphor provides a framework in which complex systems can be built. Several related organizational principles contribute to the successful management of complexity. To begin with:

Modularity: *No component in a complex system should depend on the internal details of any other component.*

This principle is depicted in figure 2. If there are N components in a system, then there are roughly N-squared potential dependencies between them. If computer systems are ever to be of assistance in complex human tasks, they must be designed to minimize such interdependence. The message-sending metaphor provides modularity by decoupling the *intent* of a message (embodied in its name) from the *method* used by the recipient to carry out the intent. Structural information is similarly protected because all access to the internal state of an object is through this same message interface.

The complexity of a system can

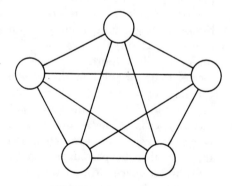

Figure 2: *System complexity. As the number of components in a system increases, the chances for unwanted interaction increase rapidly. Because of this, a computer language should be designed to minimize the possibilities of such interdependence.*

often be reduced by grouping similar components. Such grouping is achieved through data typing in conventional programming languages, and through *classes* in Smalltalk. A class describes other objects—their internal state, the message protocol they recognize, and the internal methods for responding to those messages. The objects so described are called *instances* of that class. Even classes themselves fit into this framework; they are just instances of class Class, which describes the appropriate protocol and implementation for object description:

Classification: *A language must provide a means for classifying similar objects, and for adding new classes of objects on equal footing with the kernel classes of the system.*

Classification is the objectification of *nessness*. In other words, when a human sees a chair, the experience is taken both literally as "that very thing" and abstractly as "that chair-like thing." Such abstraction results from the marvelous ability of the mind to merge "similar" experience, and this abstraction manifests itself as another object in the mind, the Platonic chair or chair*ness*.

Classes are the chief mechanism for extension in Smalltalk. For instance, a music system would be created by adding new classes that describe the representation and interaction protocol of Note, Melody, Score, Timbre, Player, and so on. The "equal footing" clause of the above principle is important because it insures that the system will be used as it was designed. In other words, a melody could be represented as an ad hoc collection of Integers representing pitch, duration, and other parameters, but if the language can handle Notes as easily as Integers, then the user will naturally describe a melody as a collection of Notes. At each stage of design, a human will naturally choose the most effective representation if the system provides for it. The principle of modularity has an interesting implication for the procedural components in a system:

Polymorphism: *A program should specify only the behavior of objects, not their representation.*

A conventional statement of this principle is that a program should never declare that a given object is a SmallInteger or a LargeInteger, but only that it responds to integer protocol. Such generic description is crucial to models of the real world. Consider an automobile traffic simulation. Many procedures in such a system will refer to the various vehicles involved. Suppose one wished to add, say, a street sweeper. Substantial amounts of computation (in the form of recompiling) and possible errors would be involved in making this simple extension if the code depended on the objects it manipulates. The message interface establishes an ideal framework for such extension. Provided that street sweepers support the same protocol as all other vehicles, no changes are needed to include them in the simulation:

Factoring: *Each independent component in a system should appear in only one place.*

There are many reasons for this principle. First of all, it saves time, effort, and space if additions to the system need only be made in one place. Second, users can more easily locate a component that satisfies a given need. Third, in the absence of proper factoring, problems arise in synchronizing changes and ensuring that all interdependent components are consistent. You can see that a failure in factoring amounts to a violation of modularity.

Smalltalk encourages well-factored designs through *inheritance*. Every class inherits behavior from its superclass. This inheritance extends through increasingly general classes, ultimately ending with class Object which describes the default behavior of all objects in the system. In our traffic simulation above, StreetSweeper (and all other vehicle classes) would be described as a subclass of a general Vehicle class, thus inheriting appropriate default behavior and avoiding repetition of the same concepts in many different places. Inheritance illustrates a further pragmatic benefit of factoring:

Leverage: *When a system is well factored, great leverage is available to users and implementers alike.*

Take the case of sorting an ordered collection of objects. In Smalltalk, the user would define a message called sort in the class OrderedCollection. When this has been done, all forms of ordered collections in the system will instantly acquire this new capability through inheritance. As an aside, it is worth noting that the same method can alphabetize text as well as sort numbers, since comparison protocol is recognized by the classes which support both text and numbers.

The benefits of structure for implementers are obvious. To begin with, there will be fewer primitives to implement. For instance, all graphics in Smalltalk are performed with a single primitive operation. With only one task to do, an implementer can bestow loving attention on every instruction, knowing that each small improvement in efficiency will be amplified throughout the system. It is natural to ask what set of primitive operations would be sufficient to support an entire computing system. The answer to this question is called a *virtual machine* specification:

Virtual Machine: *A virtual machine specification establishes a framework for the application of technology.*

The Smalltalk virtual machine establishes an object-oriented model for storage, a message-oriented model for processing, and a bitmap model for visual display of information. Through the use of microcode, and ultimately hardware, system performance can be improved dramatically without any compromise to the other virtues of the system.

User Interface

A user interface is simply a language in which most of the communication is visual. Because visual presentation overlaps heavily with established human culture, esthetics plays a very important role in this area. Since all capability of a computer system is ultimately delivered through the user interface, flexibility is also essential here. An enabling condition for adequate flexibility of a user interface can be stated as an object-oriented principle:

Reactive Principle: *Every component accessible to the user should be able to present itself in a meaningful way for observation and manipulation.*

This criterion is well supported by the model of communicating objects. By definition, each object provides an appropriate message protocol for interaction. This protocol is essentially a microlanguage particular to just that kind of object. At the level of the user interface, the appropriate language for each object on the screen is presented visually (as text, menus, pictures) and sensed through keyboard activity and the use of a pointing device.

It should be noted that operating systems seem to violate this principle. Here the programmer has to depart from an otherwise consistent framework of description, leave whatever context has been built up, and deal with an entirely different and usually very primitive environment. This need not be so:

Operating System: *An operating system is a collection of things that don't fit into a language. There shouldn't be one.*

Here are some examples of conventional operating system components that have been naturally incorporated into the Smalltalk language:

- Storage management—Entirely automatic. Objects are created by a message to their class and reclaimed when no further references to them exist. Expansion of the address space through virtual memory is similarly transparent.
- File system—Included in the normal framework through objects such as Files and Directories with message protocols that support file access.
- Display handling—The display is simply an instance of class Form, which is continually visible, and the graphical manipulation messages defined in that class are used to change the visible image.
- Keyboard input—The user input devices are similarly modeled as objects with appropriate messages for determining their state or reading their history as a sequence of events.
- Access to subsystems—Subsystems are naturally incorporated as independent objects within Smalltalk: there they can draw on the large

existing universe of description, and those that involve interaction with the user can participate as components in the user interface.
- Debugger—The state of the Smalltalk processor is accessible as an instance of class Process that owns a chain of stack frames. The debugger is just a Smalltalk subsystem that has access to manipulate the state of a suspended process. It should be noted that nearly the only run-time error that can occur in Smalltalk is for a message not to be recognized by its receiver.

Smalltalk has no "operating system" as such. The necessary primitive operations, such as reading a page from the disk, are incorporated as primitive methods in response to otherwise normal Smalltalk messages.

Future Work

As might be expected, work remains to be done on Smalltalk. The easiest part to describe is the continued application of the principles in this paper. For example, the Smalltalk-80 system falls short in its factoring because it supports only hierarchical inheritance. Future Smalltalk systems will generalize this model to arbitrary (multiple) inheritance. Also, message protocols have not been formalized. The organization provides for protocols,

but it is currently only a matter of style for protocols to be consistent from one class to another. This can be remedied easily by providing proper protocol objects that can be consistently shared. This will then allow formal typing of variables by protocol without losing the advantages of polymorphism.

The other remaining work is less easy to articulate. There are clearly other aspects to human thought that have not been addressed in this paper. These must be identified as metaphors that can complement the existing models of the language.

Sometimes the advance of computer systems seems depressingly slow. We forget that steam engines were high-tech to our grandparents. I am optimistic about the situation. Computer systems are, in fact, getting simpler and, as a result, more usable. I would like to close with a general principle which governs this process:

Natural Selection: *Languages and systems that are of sound design will persist, to be supplanted only by better ones.*

Even as the clock ticks, better and better computer support for the creative spirit is evolving. Help is on the way. ■

User-Oriented Descriptions of Smalltalk Systems

Trygve M H Reenskaug
Central Institute for Industrial Research
Blindern, Oslo 3
Norway

For many people, the workings of a computer remain a mystery. Just exactly what the computer does and how it does it is locked within the code of a computer language. The computer and the user understand two completely different languages. It is well known that only a few systems are designed and written so that they can be understood by the user. More than twenty years of experience has shown that a bad system design can never be hidden from the user, even by a masterfully devised user interface. A quality system, therefore, must be based on sound design that can be described in terms with which the user is familiar.

The Smalltalk system has been designed to handle a great variety of problems and solutions. It, therefore, provides the greatest possible flexibility for writing any kind of system a programmer may desire. While this flexibility is essential for experimenting, there is the potential for disastrous results if restrictions are not put on the system structures that are available to the application programmer.

This article shows how the basic metaphors of Smalltalk can be used to describe complex systems. Since this magazine is not yet distributed in a form readable by Smalltalk, we have to restrict ourselves to traditional written documentation. (Let it be a challenge to Smalltalk experimenters to convert this presentation into a graphic and dynamic one.)

The Smalltalk system user will most likely employ his system to organize the large amount of information that will be available to him,

> **More than twenty years of experience has shown us that a bad system design can never be hidden from the user, even by a masterfully devised user interface.**

such as reference materials in the form of market information, news services, and weather forecasts. Some data, such as travel information and bank transactions, may flow both to and from the owner. Other information, such as personal notes or material that is not yet ready for distribution, can remain private.

An individual's total information needs are very large and complex. His Smalltalk system, therefore, is also likely to be large and complex. The challenge to the Smalltalk experimenter is to find ways to structure systems so the user will not only understand how to use them, but also get an intuitive feel for their inner workings. In this way, the user can really be the master and the systems his faithful slaves.

An important part of any system is the software that controls the user's interaction with the information. Mastering the software is crucial to handling the information. With Smalltalk, software is just a special kind of information and is treated as any other information within the total system. It is available to the user in the usual manner.

A traditional way of describing software is through written documentation. Smalltalk provides more dynamic interfaces through the use of two-dimensional graphics and animation on the computer screen. Devising such interfaces is probably the greatest challenge in personal computing today, and it provides a rich field of endeavor for the interested experimenter.

System Descriptions

We can describe any application system in three different ways: *how it is used, its system structure,* and *its implementation:*

●*How it is used*—This is the least satisfactory type of description. The user operates the system through rote command sequences such as: *switch on the machine, type your password, hit button A, listen to your system saluting you by playing "Hail to the Chief."* Since 80% of all user manuals for electronic data processing systems are of this kind, we will not discuss them further here.

This level of understanding has been likened to walking around in a strange city following directions such as: "Go outside, turn right, walk straight ahead for four blocks, turn left . . . ." It is easy to get lost under such circumstances.

• *System structure*—With this type of description, the user has an intuition about the kinds of building blocks that make up the system, how they behave, and how they interact to form the complete system. We show that the basic Smalltalk metaphors of *objects* and *messages* are well suited to function as building blocks. The metaphors are simple and easy to understand; yet they permit construction of immensely powerful systems.

A basic system will have several thousand objects, and typical applications would contain many more.

Any Smalltalk system contains a large number of objects. A basic system will have several thousand objects, and typical applications would contain many more. The common software engineering device of *layering* becomes essential in making the whole thing manageable. In the description of a layer, essential function on that level is highlighted and inconsequential detail is relegated to lower levels. There is one absolute requirement of these simplified descriptions appearing on the different layers: *what is shown should be correct and complete as far as it goes.* This means that the structure of the description has to be a pure tree structure: the function of each module has to be limited to that module with *no hidden side effects upon the other modules.*

This level of understanding corresponds to the user having a street map of the system. He knows the major landmarks and the most important streets. This gives the user an intuition about the total structure and permits him tc find his way any-

where. It is almost impossible to get totally lost under these circumstances.

• *Implementation*—Descriptions at this level of understanding explain to the user how each individual object is built so that it behaves in the manner prescribed on the system structure level. Here he will find the third basic metaphor of Smalltalk, the *method.* A method is similar to a subroutine in other languages; it prescribes the actions to be taken by an object when it receives a message.

On all layers but the lowest, the behavior of an object is fairly complex, and we can think of it as composed of a number of *sub-objects* that are used to implement it. The purpose of the method is to enlist the aid of the sub-objects to implement the desired behavior. The user thus finds that the typical object is structured in much the same manner as his total system, and it consists of a number of sub-objects that send messages to each other. The description tool is recursive in that the same tool is used on all levels. This recursion description is probably the most powerful feature of Smalltalk. Once the user masters the few very general concepts, he can learn more and more about his system by simply using these concepts to dig deeper and deeper into the system layers. In addition, the user can modify and expand the system on any level by collecting new components out of the building blocks provided by the next level below it.

The user at this level now has an intuition of the overall layout of the city. He also has sub-maps of all the details and he knows how to read them. Depending on his personality, he may use these maps only when absolutely necessary, or he may use them to explore unknown territory. In contrast to the tourist, the Smalltalk user can even make modifications and new extensions to the city. The tools are there. The user decides if, when, and how he wants to use them.

Example of a System Description

The problem: Consider a small manufacturing company that has two

departments: sales and production. The responsibility of the sales department is to find customers for any product the company can make, to contact the production department to find out when the product can be delivered, and to sign a contract with the customer. The responsibility of the production department is to manufacture each product as cheaply as possible at a specified level of quality and to have it finished on the promised date. When the production department has manufactured the product, it is dispatched to the customer through the sales department.

The system: A natural way to map this into a Smalltalk system would be to represent each department as an object. The function of the Sales object would be to keep track of the state of each sale in the following sequence:

1. Fill in and send proposals
2. Reserve the necessary resources in production for the product
3. Send contracts and packing notes to the customer

The function of the Production object would be to:

1. Keep track of commitments
2. Schedule the manufacture of products
3. Help keep the product quality
4. Control the manufacturing process to get the products completed on time

It also seems reasonable to include a third kind of object in our system: Customer objects. The purpose of these objects would be to act as a receptacle for the messages being passed from the company to the customer and from the customer to the company. The various objects with a set of reasonable communication channels is shown in figure 1.

The overall processing of an order: The Smalltalk system would be programmed to reflect everything of importance that takes place during the processing of an order and to support its user on every step. The process that takes place inside the Smalltalk

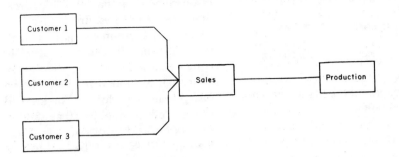

Figure 1: *A job-shop manufacturing company with its customers.*

system would, therefore, closely resemble the actual processing of an order. Let us assume the following real-life process, which is depicted in figure 2. A customer submits an intention to buy, a request for offer, to the company. The sales department books resources from the production department and returns an offer with the cost and delivery date to the customer. The customer answers with a purchase order. This is transcribed and passed from sales to production as a requisition. The product is manufactured in production, and a ready-note is sent to sales, which arranges for transport and sends packing notes to the customer.

In the Smalltalk system, the Sales object would help the user of the system in corresponding with the customer, in keeping track of progress, and in sending the required forms to the production department. The Production object would help the user in the planning and control of the manufacturing process.

In order to highlight the principles, we have made this a very simple system. The reader will have no difficulty in expanding it, for example, by adding an object for the accounting department that takes care of billing, an object for the warehouse that may or may not have the required product in stock, and so on. Also, figure 2 could probably be better documented on a Smalltalk computer by animating figure 1.

An Implementation Description

Let us inspect the Production object of figure 1 and see how it processes the message bookProductionFacilities: after:. When this message is received by the Production object, it consults its message dictionary to find the corresponding method. If the products were simple and the workshop small, the object could contain the current production plan directly and the method could go something like that

shown in listing 1.

One of the instance variables of the Production object is the table *productDuration* which contains the time it takes to manufacture various products. Looking at this table, we find the duration for a product. In this simple example, there is only one resource, and we find the first available time slot for the product by sending self the message findFreePeriod: after:. This corresponds to calling a local subroutine in other systems. We then reserve the resource for our product in that period. (These two steps could have been combined into one, but the separation gives us more flexibility in varying the planning algorithm if we wish to do so later.)

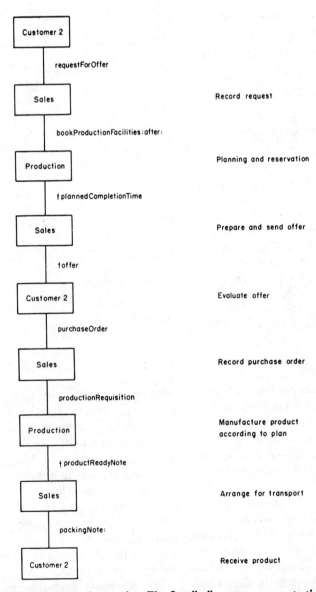

Figure 2: *The processing of an order. The Smalltalk system supports this processing through interaction with its owner in real-time.*

Listing 1: *Smalltalk method for the message* bookProductionFacilities:after:.

bookProductionFacilities: productType after: earliestStartTime

"Reserves production facilities for a new product of given type as soon as possible after the specified earliest starting time. Returns the planned completion time for the product."

```
| duration plannedStartTime |
duration ← productDuration at: productType.
plannedStartTime ← self findFreePeriod: duration after: earliestStartTime.
self reservePeriod: duration from: plannedStartTime.
↑ (plannedStartTime + duration)
```

Listing 2: *Alternate Smalltalk method for the message* bookProductionFacilities:after:.

bookProductionFacilities: productType after: earliestStartTime

"Reserves production facilities for a new product of given type as soon as possible after the specified earliest starting time. Returns the planned completion time for the product."

```
| productIdentification |
productIdentification ← jobManager defineProduct: productType.
jobManager schedule: productIdentification after: earliestStartTime.
↑ ( jobManager plannedCompletionTime: productIdentification).
```

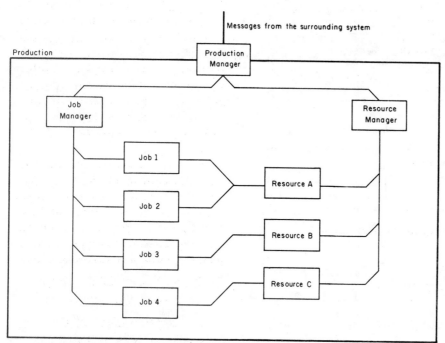

Figure 3: *The internals of the Production object.*

Lower-Level System Description

If the user wants more advanced aids for production control, the Production object would call upon the services of a subsystem of interconnected objects. A possible subsystem is shown in figure 3.

The entrance to the internals of the Production objects is through a Production Manager object; it is con-

nected to a Job Manager object and a Resource Manager object.

The manufacturing of a product is split into a number of jobs. The available production facilities (people and machines) are split into a number of resources. Each job is to be performed by a single resource. A natural way to map this into a Smalltalk system is to represent each job by a Job object and each resource by a Resource object.

In this scheme, each Job object ensures that the job is performed by its

resource within the available time. Similarly, each Resource object ensures that its resource is used in an efficient manner, that there is sufficient time available for preventive maintenance, and that there are no unacceptable overloads. The method in the Production object that handles the bookProductionFacilities:after: message could now be written as shown in listing 2.

One of the instance variables of the Production Manager object is a pointer to the Job Manager object. By using that pointer as a communication channel, the Production Manager object passes most of the work on to the Job Manager object. First, the Job Manager is asked to define the new product. The Job Manager creates the Job objects (see figure 3), links them to the proper Resource objects, and returns an identification that is to be used for future references to the product. The Job Manager is then asked to schedule the product for manufacturing as soon as possible after the given date. Finally, the Job Manager is asked when the product will be completed, and this value is returned to the outside world (in this case, to the Sales object). The planning process in the Production subsystem that is shown in figure 4 is controlled by this method.

Definition of New Objects

The first task of the Job Manager object is to define the new object. It receives message defineProduct: when this is to be done. The corresponding method could be something like that shown in listing 3. We are referencing two instance variables of the Job Manager object in this method: productDescriptions and productionManager. productDescriptions is an ordered collection with one member for each product type. Each of these members contains a sequence of small objects with the class, duration, and resource type for each of the jobs that go into the manufacture of such a product. productionManager contains a pointer to the Production Manager object. The result of the product creation is put into a third instance variable, the productDic-

The planned completion time is returned to the sender, in this case the Sales object.

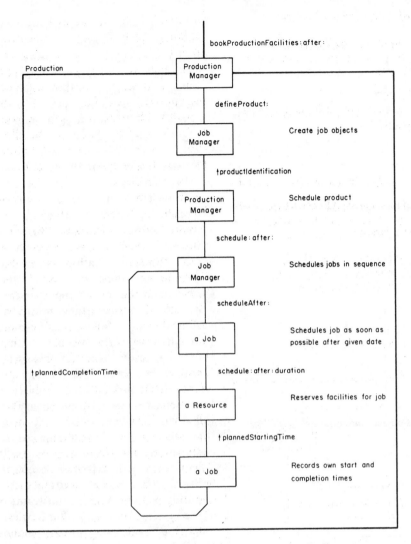

bookProductionFacilities : after :

Production

Production Manager	
Job Manager	Create job objects

defineProduct :

↑productIdentification

Production Manager	Schedule product

schedule : after :

Job Manager	Schedules jobs in sequence

scheduleAfter :

a Job	Schedules job as soon as possible after given date

↑plannedCompletionTime   schedule : after : duration

a Resource	Reserves facilities for job

↑plannedStartingTime

a Job	Records own start and completion times

Figure 4: *A simple planning algorithm implemented in a Smalltalk system.*

Listing 3: *Smalltalk method for the message* defineProduct:.

defineProduct: productType
```
   "To create a new product of given type. The corresponding Job objects are created
   and linked to their resource objects."
   |productIdentification jobDescriptions job jobList resourceObject |
   productIdentification ← self nextProductIdentification.
   jobDescriptions ← productDescriptions at: productType.
   jobList ← jobDescriptions collect:
      [ :description |
      job ← (description class) new.
      job duration: (description duration).
      resourceObject ← productionManager getResource: (description
      resourceType).
      job resource: resourceObject].
   productDictionary at: productIdentification put: jobList.
   ↑ productIdentification.
```

tionary. In this dictionary, each key is a product identification; the corresponding entry is the sequence of job objects for that product.

The first line of code gets a new, unique identification for the new product. Next, the list of job descriptions is retrieved from the productSpecification collection. We then build the sequence of Job objects by going systematically through the job descriptions. For each description, we create a new Job object of the given class, feed it its duration, and let it

connect itself to its Resource object. From figure 3, we see that there is no direct connection between the Job Manager object and the resources. We therefore have to go via the Production Manager object to get the pointer to the Resource object that we give to the new Job object.

We finally insert the new list of jobs into the productDictionary in the Production Manager object and return the product identification.

The Job Manager is built so that Job objects may belong to several different classes. The different Job objects created would all understand the same message protocols, but they would differ in their implementation. For example, a job might be: *wait for 24 hours while a resin glue is curing.* This does not need any resources, and the planning of such a job would be very simple—wait 24 hours. Another kind of job, such as pouring concrete, should not span a weekend, since joining old and new concrete could give weak spots in the product.

As is the case with Job objects, we often find that several objects share the same message protocols and process the messages with the same methods. Their only difference is that they appear in different places in the total system and that their instance

> **The Smalltalk user should be able to "open up" the application object on the screen to see its component parts and to find out how they work together.**

variables point to different objects (their states are different). Such objects are created by the same class object and are said to belong to the same class.

It would be very inefficient if each object of a class stored a replica of the message dictionary and all methods, and it would be extremely tiresome if we actually had to program each object by itself. We, therefore, use the

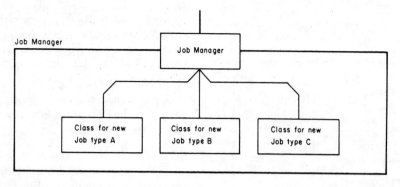

Figure 5: *Sub-objects in the Job Manager actually create the new Job objects.*

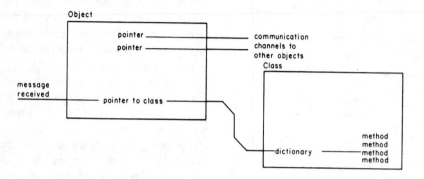

Figure 6: *All objects contain a pointer to a Class object that contains their message dictionary and methods.*

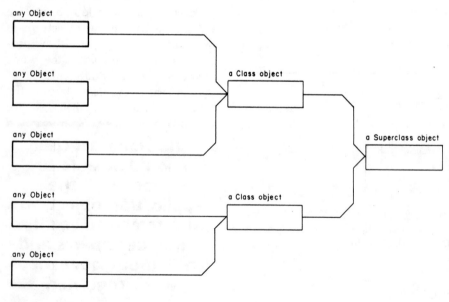

Figure 7: *The superclass-subclass chains of pointers. The user does not meet them unless he wants to become a real Smalltalk expert.*

concept of layering to let each and every object enlist the services of its class object in order to decode an incoming message and to select the proper method to process it. This mechanism is illustrated in figure 6. As in so many other parts of Smalltalk, we find a recursive argument.

Many classes are very similar; they differ only in the handling of a few messages. The different kinds of Job objects are a case in point. It seems reasonable to let a class object enlist the services of a superclass object whenever it is called upon to execute methods it shares with other classes. Many classes will then share the same

superclass; we get a tree-shaped class structure as shown in figure 7. Note that the purpose of this structure is convenience in programming and efficiency in implementation; it belongs on the lowest levels of the system hierarchy and is not part of the structure of the application system.

Future Experiments

When personal computing becomes sufficiently entertaining and interesting to become a widespread tool, the new user of a Smalltalk system is likely to begin by using its ready-made application systems for writing and illustrating documents, for designing aircraft wings, for doing homework, for searching through old court decisions, for composing music, or whatever. After a while, he may become curious as to how his system works. He should then be able to "open up" the application object on the screen to see its component parts and to find out how they work together. He could, for example, see something like figure 1 together with his usual user interface. By exercising the application commands, the computing process could be illustrated on the system diagram. Using Smalltalk to document itself in this manner should make it possible to make some novel and extremely powerful system description tools.

The next thing the user might want to do is to build new systems similar to the one he has been using. A *kit* of graphical building blocks would let the user compose a new system by editing the system diagram on the screen. While the Trip system (as described in reference 2) is not a proper kit, it could be a good source of ideas to the experimenter on building such systems.

Finally, the expert user would want to make his own kits. Even here, it is important that he sees only what he needs and that all unimportant details are suppressed. Since what is important in one context might be unimportant in another, and vice versa, the concepts of *filters* (see reference 1) will be an essential ingredient for the experimenter when he develops tools for these expert users.

Much experimenting needs to be

done before we learn how to make systems that are self-documenting on any level and that provide a smooth and stumble-free transition from one level to the next. It is hoped that the availability of Smalltalk will lead to great activity in this field, to the benefit of all future computer users.■

References

1. Goldberg, Adele and David Robson. "A Metaphor for User Interface Design." *Proceedings of the University of Hawaii Systems Science Symposium*, January 1979, Honolulu.
2. Gould, Laura and William Finzer. "A Study of TRIP: A Computer System for Animating Time-Rate-Distance Problems." *Proceedings of the IFIP World Conference on Computers in Education (WCCE-81)*, Lausanne, Switzerland, July 1981.
3. Ingalls, Daniel H H. "The Smalltalk-76 Programming System. Design and Implementation." *Conference Record of the Fifth Annual ACM Symposium on Principles of Programming Languages*, Tucson, Arizona, January 1978.

Experimental Prototyping in Smalltalk

Jim Diederich and Jack Milton
Mathematics Dept., University of California at Davis

Reprinted from *IEEE Software*, May 1987, pages 50–64. Copyright © 1987
by The Institute of Electrical and Electronics Engineers, Inc.

*Smalltalk promotes fearless programming.
Users can significantly alter an application —
even the system itself — without fearing
unrecoverable disasters.*

KEVIN REAGAN

Object-oriented programming is one of the central programming paradigms to emerge in this decade. The scope of its influence can be seen in the introduction of objects into numerous programming languages such as Loops, Objective-C, Object-Pascal, and Flavors, among others. Object-oriented concepts are also being incorporated into existing relational database technology. Database management systems now exist that are based on object-oriented principles, and one commercial version uses an extension of Smalltalk for its data definition and data manipulation languages. Additional uses and applications can be found in the proceedings of recent conferences.

Smalltalk is the principal object-oriented language. While a more complete discussion of Smalltalk's development is given in the so-called Green Book[1] and in the August 1981 issue of *Byte* magazine, it is important to note that Smalltalk is a descendent of Simula and has its origins at the Xerox Palo Alto Research Center in the early 1970s. It was developed by the Learning Research Group based largely on ideas of Alan Kay.

The language went through three major versions: Smalltalk-72, Smalltalk-76, and Smalltalk-80, which was first licensed for use in 1983. Commercial versions of Smalltalk are available on such workstations as the Tektronix 440X series, the Sun, and the IBM PC AT. Prerelease versions have been made available for the Apple Macintosh. An initial attempt at developing Smalltalk on minicomputers such as the Digital Equipment Corp. VAX line was judged unsuccessful in a multiuser environment. However, implementations for the MicroVAX are under development.

Smalltalk is more than just another programming language. It offers a completely new environment for software development. Many articles and books have been

IEEE SOFTWARE

written describing the features of the Smalltalk language and environment, but our primary objective is to convey just how *different* software development is in the Smalltalk system.

Our experience, based on our work in prototyping a database design system[2] over the past year suggests that Smalltalk goes well beyond facilitating programming. Indeed, it is an integral tool for promoting experimental prototyping. More explicitly, in our experiments we often made sweeping changes in the design system's architecture, generally with little reprogramming effort, and usually with the introduction of only simple bugs that were easily identified and fixed. To a large extent, our desire to try different approaches was significantly influenced by what we view as a new and emerging concept in programming.

Basic concepts

Two important aspects of the object definition in Smalltalk are encapsulation and hierarchy.

In encapsulation (or information-hiding), an object has its own data or local memory, called instance variables. An object also recognizes a set of procedures for manipulating its local memory. These procedures, called methods, are invoked by sending messages to the object.

Naturally, many objects will have the same type and will respond to the same messages. Consequently, objects are organized by a hierarchy of classes and subclasses. An object responds not only to messages defined for its class, but it can also inherit messages from all its superclasses.

Class definition. Figure 1 shows the definition of two classes, Person and Student. Person is a subclass of Object, which is the root class of all other classes. An instance of the class Person (an object from the class) will have local memory for its name, address, and birthDate. Student is a subclass of Person, and each instance of Student will inherit name, address, and birthDate, in addition to having instance variables college, class, major, currentCourses, and gpa.

Each instance variable will be an object, too, but it need not be bound to a particular object class. HonorsList is a class variable. Every method of the class Student will have access to (can read or change) the value of this variable.

(Note the naming conventions: Compound names have the first letter of each word capitalized except for the first word.

Encapsulation and hierarchy are two important aspects of object definition.

The case of the first letter of the first word depends on the use of the name. Thus an instance variable for a graduate student would be graduateStudent while a class or a class variable would be Graduate-Student.)

Messages. After creating the class Person, we can develop messages that can be sent to the class Person and to instances of the class. For example, the existing message, new, is inherited by the class Person from its superclass Object and will create an instance of Person. In Figure 2a, the temporary variable person is assigned (using the assignment symbol ←) and serves as a pointer to the object that is created as an instance of the class Person.

To give an instance a value for its name, we can create a message, name: aString, that can be sent to person, as Figure 2b shows. The object being sent the message, person in this case, is called the receiver of the message. Messages that have colon suffixes, such as name:, take an object as an argument, and those without colons do not.

A message can contain several parts, such as add:before:, which in this form, without arguments, is called a message selector. It can be used to add a new object before the current object in a list, as Figure 2c shows. Likewise, since Student is a subclass of Person, instances of Student can also be sent the message, name: 'Stefano'.

A subclass can also reimplement and thus override a message defined in its superclasses. For example, the message, passing, sent to a student might determine if the student's GPA is above 2.0. However, if we create a subclass GraduateStudent of Student, we can add a message also called passing for this subclass that instead determines if the GPA is above 3.0. Thus, if an instance of GraduateStudent is sent the message passing, the system looks to this class and finds the message with the 3.0 condition. Likewise, if an instance of Student is sent the message, the system uses the message with the 2.0 condition.

If we changed our minds and later wanted to use the same condition for both, we would delete the message for Graduate-

---

(a)	person ← Person new.
(b)	person name: 'Stefano'.
(c)	personList add: newName before: currentName.
(d)	name: aName name←aName.
(e)	name ↑name

Figure 2. (a) Creating an instance; (b) message modifying an instance variable; (c) message with two arguments; (d) method for the message name:; (e) method for the message name.

```
Object   subclass: #Person
    instance variables: ' name address birthDate '


Person   subclass: #Student
    instance variables: 'college class major currentCourses gpa '
        class variables: 'HonorsList '
```

Figure 1. Class definitions.

Student. Then whenever an instance of GraduateStudent is sent the message passing, the system first checks its class, and when the message is not found there, it goes up through the hierarchy to find and execute a message with that selector.

Methods. Messages are implemented in routines that are called methods. For example, the method for assigning the name of an instance of Person is quite simple, as Figure 2d shows. The first line of a method always gives the form of the message. In Figure 2d, name: is the message selector and aName is an argument. The remaining lines implement the method. In the second line the instance variable, name, of the message's receiver is assigned the value aName.

Similarly, Figure 2e shows the method for the message used to retrieve the person's name. Again, the first line of the method is the form of the message. In the second line, the instance variable, name, will be returned, as signified by the up arrow (↑), whenever the message, name, is sent to an instance of Person.

Every time a message is sent to an object, something is returned. The returned value may be significant or may merely inform the sender that a requested action is complete. This lets messages be concatenated. For example, person birthDate month, will return the month of person's birth since person birthDate returns a birthDate that has an instance variable month that is returned when the message month is sent.

Variables and scoping. To enforce the concept of encapsulation, there is only one way to modify an instance variable of an object — sending the object a message. Furthermore, if a variable appears in a

method, it can only be one of six types:
- an instance variable in the class of objects for which the method is defined,
- an argument of the message,
- a temporary variable local to the method,
- a class variable,
- a pool variable, or
- a global variable.

Class variables are shared by a class and its subclasses, pool variables are valid across designated classes, and global variables are shared by all classes.

In the method for name: in Figure 2d, name must be an instance variable because it is lowercase and it is in a method defined for instances of Person that have that instance variable. The variable, aName, is

> *To enforce the concept of encapsulation, there is only one way to modify an instance variable of an object.*

an argument of the message. There are no temporary or other types of variables in this method

Class, pool, and global variables are used sparingly. Thus, in practice, we have a very restricted type of lexical scoping. This strict information-hiding all but eliminates scoping-related problems, and names typically do not have to be modified to avoid naming conflicts.

For example, consider the method (in Figure 3) defined for instances of Person that when sent to a person, the receiver, switches its name with that of aPerson, the message's argument. Temporary variables, such as tempName in Figure 3, are declared by listing them in the vertical bars. They exist for the message's execution life. (Class and global variables are used for longer term storage and are not in the local memory of instances of the class.)

Note the various uses of name. In the first line of code, it is a message sent to aPerson to retrieve aPerson's name, and assigned to tempName. Because aPerson is

not the receiver of the message switchNamesWith:, the only way to retrieve its name is to send it the message, name.

The next use of name is as the argument of the message name: in the second line of code. In this case, because it is not declared a temporary variable, it must represent the instance variable of the message's receiver. In this line, the name of aPerson is modified to be the name of the receiver.

In the last line of code, name is the instance variable of the receiver and is changed to the name in tempName. The code in Figure 3 could have been written with different names for the message selectors, such as getName instead of name for retrieving a name and setName: instead of name: for storing a name.

We chose this example to illustrate the freedom permitted by the Smalltalk language; and this overloading of name presents no difficulty in understanding to the slightly experienced Smalltalk programmer.

There are some negative aspects to using getName and setName:. First,

    aPerson getName

is procedural in flavor while

    aPerson name

is more functional and has more of a natural-language flavor, which contributes to the readability of the code.

Second, it precludes the simple convention that messages with the same names as instance variables are used to retrieve their values, while those followed by a colon and argument are used to store the values. This convention makes remembering the message selectors for instance variables straightforward.

Control structures. Smalltalk control structures are also handled via the object-message paradigm. For example, a message, do: aBlock, can be sent to collections of various types to process each element. For example, the code in Figure 4a will process each student in classList. The argument of the block has a colon prefix, appears before the vertical bar, and is in turn instantiated to each of classList's elements.

```
switchNamesWith:   aPerson

|tempName|

tempName ←   aPerson name.
aPerson name: name.
name ← tempName.
```

Figure 3. A method in class Person.

The code following the bar is executed for each element in the list and illustrates the use of a conditional. The condition, an instance of the class Boolean, is enclosed in parentheses and is sent the message if-True:ifFalse:. Other conditional message selectors are ifTrue:, ifFalse:, and if-False:ifTrue:.

Understanding objects. When working with objects, an individual accustomed to non-object-oriented languages may experience some unanticipated difficulties. Most can easily be corrected once the symptoms are recognized.

For example, there is a tendency to take the object paradigm too literally and consider each appearance of an object as a unique object. Certainly in the real world, an object can only be in one place at a time. Suppose an instance of the class Card has the instance variables suit and rank. A hand is an Array that can hold as many as five cards, and a deck is an Ordered-Collection of 52 cards.

The code in Figure 4b will deal a card and place it at the first position in the hand. If you now inspect deck and hand using the inspector in Smalltalk (a tool for examining objects), you see that deck still contains the dealt card — and so does hand. A literal interpretation of object, that an object can only be in one place, would suggest to some that these are distinct cards. Unfortunately the inspector does not directly reveal whether they are distinct or not.

Assuming they are distinct might lead to an attempt to set the suit and rank of the card in the deck to nil to avoid redealing it, which will result in making the card in hand a blank card also. What in fact is occurring is that the assignment statement places a pointer in the variable aCard to the same card in both collections, deck and hand. Indeed, the card exists in one place, and aCard, deck, and hand merely provide alternative access structures that point to it.

In some cases, the problem is not so easily diagnosed, particularly when there are several layers of complexity such as when using the model-view-controller triad. Khoshafian and Copeland discuss different degrees of object identity.[3]

Fearless programming

While it is difficult to capture in an article the quite different sense of what it is like to work in an object-oriented language and environment, we will nevertheless try to present some sense of the flavor of prototyping in Smalltalk. What we would like to show, but can do so only partially, is that there is an undercurrent we characterize as fearless programming.

Fearless programming encourages experimentation with alternative approaches to algorithms, application programs, and system design without the fear of being caught up in a morass of detail that is too painful to sort out. Moreover, the system has a robust programming paradigm — the programmer can make bold changes to the system itself and, even after making significant errors, can often proceed through several different routes to recovery without harm.

In fact, fearless programming has played a large part in our development of new methods and faster algorithms for database normalization because it promotes experimentation. (We do not mean to imply that good design can be ignored or that good programming practices can be violated, for even Smalltalk methods can be created that have unanticipated side effects or fail to be coherent and properly modularized.)

Advantages. Naturally, the closer the constructs in a language are to the entities we deal with in the real world the less difficulty we encounter in translating the real-world problem into a program. Object orientation is a major step in this direction, since working with objects seems more natural than working with constructs found in standard languages.

For example, in a non-object-oriented language, if an element is retrieved from a list or an array, as in the assignment statement $x := array(5)$, then changes made to x are not reflected in the contents of array(5) and vice versa. This assignment in effect creates a duplicate element, and duplicates can easily lead to inconsistencies, since changes in one element are not automatically reflected in changes in the other.

This is not true when dealing with objects. If an object is retrieved from a list, any changes made in the object are reflected wherever the object is referenced. For instance, if aCard is a temporary variable and points at the object that is pointed at in the fifth position of hand via the statement aCard ← hand at: 5, subsequent changes to aCard are reflected in the object pointed at in the fifth position of hand.

Consider what happens if we want to group or sort the same collection of objects in different ways, perhaps for sequential access via an OrderedCollection and for direct access via a Dictionary. In this case, changes made to the objects are independent of the structures used to access them.

In standard languages, you would either have to create multiple lists, again leading to problems associated with duplication, or have to maintain multiple lists of pointers, which leads to more complex coding.

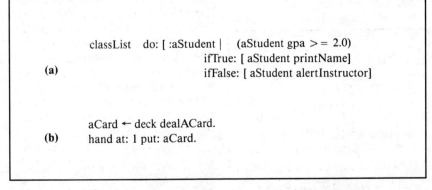

Figure 4. (a) Enumeration message do: and conditionals; (b) dealing a card.

(Duplicates can be made in Smalltalk, but they are not implicit and require sending one of the built-in messages for copying objects.)

The object-message paradigm and encapsulation tend to promote a more modular system because each message represents a module. This is desirable because smaller modules are easier to create and understand. In addition, there is also a tendency for each message to be a coherent unit because the very notion of sending messages focuses the development of each method on the semantic intent of the message.

And the reason the Smalltalk programmer can focus on the intent of each message — and is not tempted to embed additional functionality in messages — is that problems of interfacing modules, which are generally associated with bottom-up development, are essentially absent when working with objects and messages. (We view method creation as bottom-up and class creation as top-down).

One reason interfacing problems are minimal is that objects are generally passed as arguments in messages, and their instance variables do not explicitly appear. Consequently, changes in an object's structure have no implications for a vast majority of the messages in which they occur.

For example, in Figure 3, wholesale changes in the structure of the class Person, and even changes in the structure of its instance variable, name (the one of primary interest in the method), will have no effect whatsoever on the method for switchNamesWith:, and no changes are required in any other method in which this message selector appears.

Why? Because objects and their instance variables are not typed, and the binding of objects to instance variables occurs at runtime. Late binding promotes fearless programming because it lets the designer postpone typing and structural decisions not germane to the current state of the prototype.

It has been our experience that many methods will not require changes or recompilation as the prototype advances. Those that require recompilation are typically

small and require minimal time because compiling is incremental.

The existence of predefined object classes also contributes to this sense of fearless programming in that you have a wide selection of objects and messages to choose from, thus gaining a considerable head start in prototyping a system.

An additional advantage is that existing methods can be borrowed in a variety of ways. In some cases, the method can be directly copied to another class without change to its form or content. In other cases, the message will retain the same

---

Whatever problems arise and whatever morass you create tend to be at higher rather than lower levels of abstraction.

---

form — the message selectors and arguments remain unchanged, with only slight modifications required in the method. This often occurs when subclasses override messages.

And, as indicated in the discussion of Figure 3, this can be accomplished without fear of difficulties arising from scoping or naming considerations. Names do not have to be artificially modified to distinguish messages with the same selectors but can be used with different classes and subclasses.

Perhaps the most important contribution to fearless programming, apart from the environment, is that working with objects and messages has important analogs to working at the level of human cognition. Whatever problems arise and whatever morass you create tend to be at higher rather than lower levels of abstraction.

The use of messages conveys much about the semantics of operations on objects, reducing the need for documentation. (Other documentation requirements, including managing hierarchies and mes-

sages, are handled by the environment.) A great deal of clutter, unessential low-level detail, is eliminated from much of the code. This is, in part, due to the existence of predefined classes and messages.

For instance, there are various collection classes (including Set, Bag, Ordered-Collection, Array, and Dictionary) that respond to the same message, do: aBlock, to enumerate the objects of the collection and to operate on each in turn by executing the code in aBlock. Incrementing variables to process the collection is unnecessary. (Furthermore, these structures can be substituted for one another to improve performance in later stages of the prototype, often without any other changes in the code.)

In addition, objects are prepackaged bundles of parameters to be passed as arguments in messages and therefore tend to reduce the number of arguments present and to enhance the readability of the code.

Example. This example demonstrates these advantages. It is drawn from our work on relational databases but is simplified here. We will call a functional dependency a statement of the form $a \rightarrow b$ that we can read as "a implies b," as in propositional logic. It is possible that, given a collection F of functional dependencies, some dependencies are redundant.

Removing redundant dependencies from F is important in relational database design. For example, given the collection

$$F = \{ a \rightarrow b, b \rightarrow c, a \rightarrow c, b \rightarrow d, e \rightarrow c \}$$

the third functional dependency is redundant since it can be derived from the first and second using the transitivity rule:

if $a \rightarrow b$ and $b \rightarrow c$, then $a \rightarrow c$

There is a straightforward algorithm to determine if a functional dependency is redundant. As an illustration, to show that the functional dependency $f = (a \rightarrow c)$ is redundant, first form $F' = F - \{f\}$ (delete f from F).

Now pass through F' as many times as necessary to discover all attributes implied by the left side of f, $\{a\}$. All implied attributes, including a, are placed in a collection called closure, the closure of a with respect to F'.

In this example, closure = $\{a,b,c,d\}$ at the end of the passes over F'. If closure contains the right side of f, then f is redundant, which is true in this example, and it is deleted from F.

A natural starting point for developing an implementation to eliminate redundant functional dependencies is to define a class called FunctionalDependency. This class can be made a subclass of Object because no other class exists for which it would be a natural subclass.

It also seems appropriate to create two instance variables to represent the left and right sides (lhs and rhs) of the dependency. The declaration is

Object subclass: #FunctionalDependency
instance variables: ' lhs rhs '

The methods for new, lhs:, rhs:, lhs, and rhs can easily be coded to create an instance of FunctionalDependency and to set and retrieve the values of its instance variables, respectively. We store the set of functional dependencies F in a collection named SetOfFDs.

It is quite striking just how quickly and with such little code this and other algorithms can be implemented in Smalltalk.

Structural changes. Now suppose that, after having developed the algorithm outlined above, we believe it would be more efficient to mark a functional dependency f as inactive rather than to delete it from the SetOfFDs to form F' and then reinsert it into F if it is not redundant.

This can easily be achieved by adding a new instance variable, active, to the class FunctionalDependency. No other method defined on this class nor any other code in which functional dependencies are passed as arguments or sent existing messages need be changed to accommodate the addition of the new instance variable.

Consequently, a great deal of recompiling and relinking will be avoided. The changes will be isolated to modifying the method for the algorithm. This simply involves replacing statements for removing functional dependencies from SetOfFDs to form F' by statements for setting their instance variables active to false, testing whether a functional dependency was

active before using it in computing closure, and resetting active to true if the functional dependency is not redundant. At this stage, the method for eliminating redundant dependencies might look like the code in Figure 5.

The SetOfFDs in Figure 5 may be any of several predefined classes of collections in the Smalltalk system. Thus we can freely change the structure of the SetOfFDs to determine which gives the best performance. When this method is compiled, it is not necessary to have determined which class the SetOfFDs comes from because of the delayed binding.

Note that the functional dependencies in F above are not grouped by common left sides. Some algorithms require that they be grouped this way. One approach is to sort SetOfFDs according to their left sides. However, if the original set must be maintained (to allow, for example, direct access to functional dependencies if SetOfFDs is a dictionary), we can easily create collections using existing Smalltalk classes, denoted here as DepWithLHS(X), which will contain the dependencies with a common left side X.

But since we are working with functional dependencies as objects, if a functional dependency accessed from DepWithLHS(X) is made inactive, it will also be inactive if accessed from SetOfFDs. The change to the code in Figure 5 to accommodate the change in the algorithm is straightforward.

Also, we haven't yet written the method for computing closures, which is used in the second line of Figure 5 by sending the message closure to the left side of each functional dependency, closure ← eachfd lhs closure. As the code in Figure 5 is compiled, the system will notify the programmer and give an option to proceed and define the missing message later.

When developing our algorithms, we tried many approaches to computing closures. Some were conceptually similar but had different efficiencies, and others were conceptually new. In all cases, very little code had to be changed to accommodate the different versions of closure; clearly no changes were required for the code in Figure 5, and it was straightforward to borrow extensively from one version to the next.

While Smalltalk code may seem a bit strange because of unfamiliar naming conventions and syntax, it is generally true that after some initial difficulty it seems quite readable. Unessential details do not clutter the code, as Figure 5 shows. Only infrequently are lines needed to increment variables; parameters are not required for invoking routines, as they are hidden in the instance variables of the objects; and messages are simple, and their names reflect much of the semantics of what they do.

If a message is not understood by the programmer or reader of the code, it can be quickly examined. We do not mean to suggest that this cannot be accomplished in other languages, but it seems to occur more naturally in Smalltalk.

Conceptual changes. While implementing various types of closure in Smalltalk, we discovered a new approach to eliminating redundant functional dependencies. It involved deactivating all of the functional dependencies in a given DepWithLHS(X). As a result, we couldn't use the instance variable active to determine if a functional dependency was redundant.

One of the changes required to accommodate this was to introduce a new instance variable, redundant, for the class FunctionalDependency and to set its value

```
SetOfFDs     do: [:eachfd | eachfd active: false.
                  closure ← (eachfd   lhs) closure.
                  (closure includes: (eachfd    rhs))
                  ifFalse:[each fd active: true]].
```

Figure 5. Eliminating redundant dependencies.

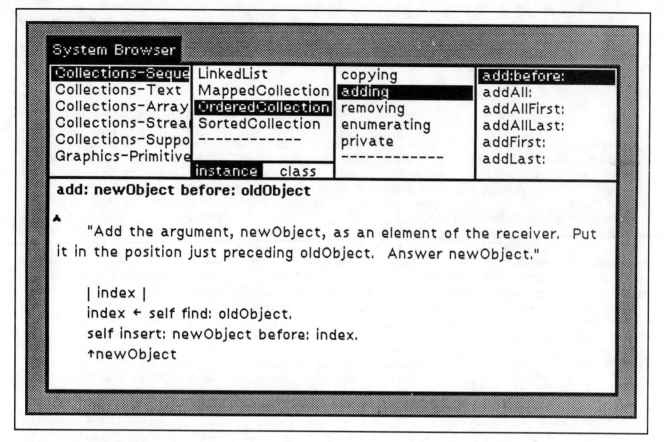

Figure 6. The system browser.

to true when a given functional dependency was discovered to be redundant. (For several reasons, we chose to save redundant dependencies rather than discard them.)

Though this is a small change, it nevertheless hints at how changes made at the conceptual level can be translated directly into messages and objects. This shows that the way we think about entities in an application can be translated directly into two fundamental aspects of an object, its attributes and its behavior. Of course, other parts of the code in other methods were affected by changing the semantics of the instance variable active. The Smalltalk environment provides the tools to work rapidly through the effects of these changes.

The Smalltalk system promotes trying alternatives. The time required to restructure objects, modify methods, create new methods, locate the effects of changes, and recompile the code to experiment with it, is much less of a factor in the cost/benefit ratio than you would incur if working with most standard languages.

Also, most changes occur at a high conceptual level, so it is more like working with changes in the specification than with changes in the code. However, we do not claim that Smalltalk is close to achieving the software engineering goal of directly compiling specifications.

Environment

While encapsulation and hierarchy form the basic foundations of the Smalltalk language, it is the rich environment that lets you work with its many classes, methods, and messages.

In Smalltalk, there are several window types available. These windows can be created, moved, reshaped, collapsed, and closed using a three-button mouse (some systems use a single-button mouse). Multiple, overlapping windows can be on the screen, and you can move from one window to the next to carry out different or related tasks.

Code can be modified and run from different kinds of windows, and application windows can be activated and deactivated. This is particularly useful if an error turns up while debugging an application and recovery from within the application is not possible.

The convenience of doing different things in the system quickly and efficiently also contributes significantly to fearless programming. You aren't caught up in the time-consuming cycle of doing something in edit mode, exiting and entering compile mode, exiting and entering run/debug mode, exiting and returning to edit mode to make changes. Tesler[4] has discussed the philosophy behind modeless environments and the early Smalltalk interface.

Organization. Because there is no single linear command list, beginners often wonder where the program is. Programming in Smalltalk is mainly adding new classes and messages, creating objects, and passing messages. Thus, being able to move around the system easily and to work with individual classes is critical to productive Smalltalk programming. The system classes are organized in a hierarchy with the class Object at the top, but you don't have to remember the exact hierarchy while programming because the interface provides a convenient organization method and access to the system classes through the system browser, shown in Figure 6.

The system browser window contains several panes, each with its own menu of actions. The second pane from the left along the top contains the name of classes, and the fourth pane contains message selectors. The first and third panes categorize similar types of classes and messages, respectively.

In Figure 6, the category of classes selected (indicated by reverse video) is Collections-Sequenceable. This class category contains classes linearly structured. One such class, OrderedCollection, is selected in the second pane.

The instance/class pair at the bottom of the second pane is a toggle. If instance is selected (as shown), what appears in the panes to the right and below will pertain to methods sent to instances of the class. If class is selected, it will pertain to methods sent to the class, which is also considered an object.

The various categories of messages that can be sent to instances of Ordered-Collection are shown in the third pane. Here, we have selected messages for adding objects to an ordered collection. The actual messages for adding are in the fourth pane with the message add: before: selected. The method for this message is shown in the large pane at the bottom of the browser window in Figure 6.

Using the browser. For the most part, the browser is used to create classes, create messages and methods, and to browse through the system. To indicate how these tools can be used to make changes, recall the example of working with the class FunctionalDependencies. There was a change in the semantics of the instance variable active when the instance variable redundant was added to the class. This required examining all the methods that might be affected, so we want to review all methods that modify or retrieve the instance variable active.

There are several ways to do this. One way is to select the class Functional-Dependency in the browser. We can then get a pop-up menu (Figure 7a) and select the item, inst var refs. Another pop-up menu appears (Figure 7b) that lists the instance variables for the class FunctionalDependency. By selecting the variable active, we get a window showing all methods where this instance variable appears (Figure 7c).

By examining each method, we see that the message active: modifies the value of the instance variable active and the mes-

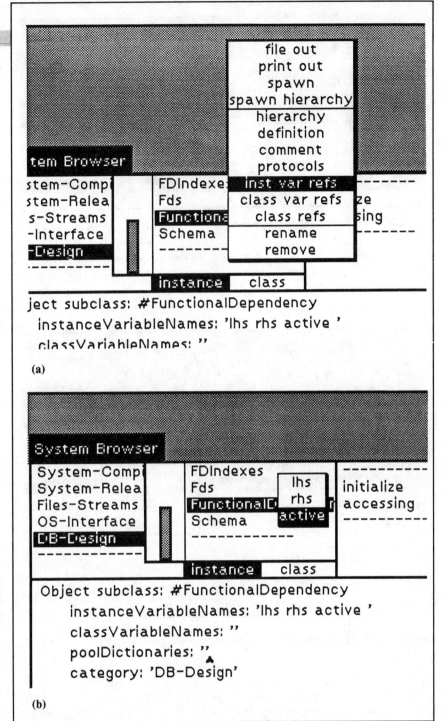

Figure 7. (a) Class pane menu; (b) instance variables.

sage active retrieves it. After selecting the method for active:, we can get a pop-up menu in the same window (we don't have to return to the browser) from which we can select an item, senders (see Figure 7d).

In this case, we are asking for all methods that use (send) the message active: in their code; the result is the window shown in Figure 8. By selecting each method, we can examine the code to see if

the change in active's semantics requires changes in the method. Whatever the changes may be, we can make them in this window (its top part is shown in Figure 8) and compile the code there.

Three items in the menu in Figure 7d — senders, implementers, and messages — can be very effective message tracers. Again, messages with the same name (but different functionality) might be imple-

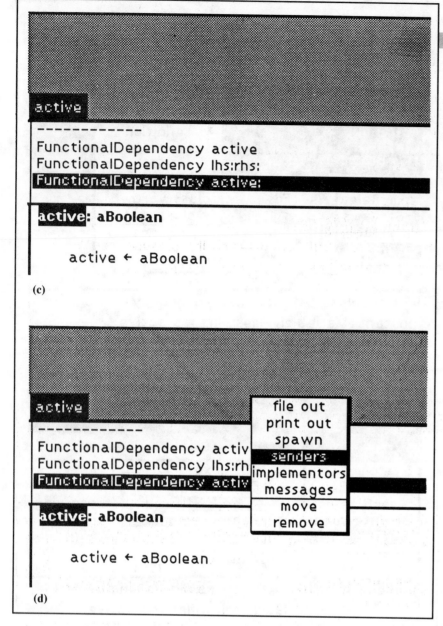

(c)

(d)

Figure 7. (c) Methods using active; (d) finding senders of active.

mented in different classes in the system, and a given method might use messages from other classes. The item, messages, can be selected directly from the menu in Figure 7d; it is also a menu option for the top pane in Figure 8. Selecting it will quickly get a menu of all messages in the selected method, as illustrated in Figure 9. If we select any of the messages in the menu in Figure 9, we will get another window of the type shown in Figure 8, which lists all classes where a message of that name is implemented. We can now select one class and inspect its method in the lower pane of the new window.

These facilities help the user browse through the system, as well as debug. In addition, the system has utilities to identify and correct syntactically and semantically incorrect code. The power of the complete tool collection contributes significantly to fearless programming.

Smalltalk source code is compiled into an intermediate form, called bytecodes, that is then interpreted. This compilation is done incrementally as new classes, messages, and the associated methods are defined. Code is displayed in the code pane of the browser and is compiled through the menu for that pane.

If the code contains a syntax error, an appropriate message is inserted into the code in reverse video. Because the message is in reverse video, it can easily be cut, the code can be corrected, and the method can be recompiled.

For browsing, a selection in the system browser's code pane, explain, is very helpful. You can select any token in a method, and the explain selection will indicate what type of token it is (class variable, global variable, name of a message, and so on) by inserting explanatory text in reverse video in the method display in the code pane.

Debugging. While changing the semantics of the instance variable active and introducing the new instance variable redundant, suppose we failed to initialize redundant to false when creating new instances of FunctionalDependency. This would lead to problems, which can be traced with the built-in debugger.

One approach is to place a halt in the code where the problems arise (in this case, the method for eliminating redundant dependencies) and to step through the code and examine the objects. When code is executed, a notifier will appear on the screen to indicate that a halt has been encountered. You have the option to proceed past the halt or to enter debug mode.

If you choose to debug, the window shown in Figure 10 appears, and the menu appearing over the top pane can be obtained. The top pane of the window contains the current activation stack — the list of messages leading to the halt. This list can be scrolled, and individual messages can be selected. Code for the selected message is displayed in the middle pane, and the bottom two entries in the top pane's pop-up menu can be used to run through a stepwise simulation of the program.

Selecting the item, step, executes the current selected message (redundant in Figure 10) and moves you to the next one (ifFalse:). Selecting the item, send, enters the method for the selected message, which then displays in the middle pane and can be treated the same way. The lower left pane contains instance variables of the message receiver displayed in the middle pane, and the lower right pane contains current values of all temporary variables in that method. The value of the loop variable, each, is an instance of class FunctionalDependency at this point.

You can inspect this object, as Figure 11 shows. The result is the window in Figure 12, where we have selected redundant,

```
Senders of active:
------------
Cover eliminateAttsandDeps
Cover eliminateRedundantDependencies
Cover linearEliminateRedundantDependencies:

eliminateRedundantDependencies

    self do: [:each | (each active )
                ifTrue: [each active: false.
                    (each rhs isSubsetOf: (each lhs closure: self))
                        ifFalse: [each active: true]]].
```

Figure 8. Senders of active:.

whose nil value shows in the right pane and reveals the problem that redundant was not initialized. Chapter 19 of the Orange Book[5] gives a more detailed description of the debugger.

There are other ways to invoke the debugger. For example, if a halt had not been placed in the code, a notifier would appear during execution upon test of the nil value of redundant. The notifier would indicate that a non-Boolean receiver had been encountered, and three options would be available:

(1) Set the value of the receiver to true and proceed with execution.

(2) Enter the debugger at the point of the problematic code.

(3) Stop the errant process simply by closing the debug window.

In the second case, the debugger window has the form of the one in Figure 10, and the programmer can proceed as above. The debugger is a particularly nice tool and certainly helps make runtime errors much more tolerable during program development. It can be very confusing to the beginner, however, as the depths of the code are explored with the option send. For example, a user who doesn't know how system-

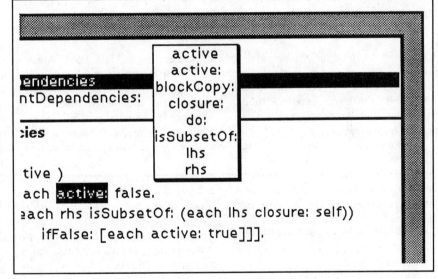

Figure 9. Messages in a method.

defined control structures are implemented could be confused by the system code when it is encountered.

Modifying Smalltalk. Fearless programming gives users confidence to attempt extensive changes in the system, even ones to the predefined classes. An example of

major restructuring from our database project would be too detailed to develop here, but we can give an example that has pervasive implications for the system.

We needed various ways of writing bitmaps of parts of the screen out to files, and the system did not already have all the necessary functionality. To capture bit-

```
Halt encountered.

[] in Cover>>eliminateRedundantDependen    full stack
Cover(OrderedCollection)>>do:                proceed
Cover>>eliminateRedundantDependencies        restart
UndefinedObject>>DoIt                        senders
                                             implementors
eliminateRedundantDependencies               messages
                                                step
self halt.                                      send


    self do: [:each | (each redundant)
                ifFalse: [each active: false.
                            (each rhs isSubsetOf: (each lhs closure: self))
                                ifTrue: [each redundant: true]
                                ifFalse: [each active: true]]].


self            |         | each       | ▲
firstIndex      |         |            |
lastIndex       |         |            |
```

Figure 10. The debugger.

maps with pop-up menus displayed at the time of capture, we had to deactivate the menus so they could be brought up on screen to have their picture taken without having the selected message sent when the button was released.

To achieve this, we added a class varia-

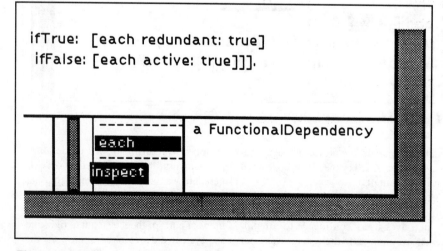

Figure 11. Inspecting a temporary variable.

ble, Active, to the class PopUpMenu, which governs pop-up menus, through which essentially all actions are initiated. If Active is true, all actions through menus will proceed as usual; if Active is false, a conditional placed in the code for sending menu messages returns a no-op value when

the mouse button is released, and the menu disappears with no action taken. We then defined a two-key sequence to toggle Active.

This change is very powerful because it covers the predominant means by which actions are taken in the system. This also makes it dangerous. It indeed led to several interesting debugging problems, two of which we will illustrate.

Fatal error. If the class variable Active is defined, but initialization to true or false is neglected, its default value will be nil. If anything is then executed through a pop-up menu, this nil value for Active will be encountered in the conditional code, and a notifier will appear. The menu for this notifier contains two options, proceed and debug, which would ordinarily function as described above.

In this case, however, using the middle button to generate the pop-up menu from which to choose an option would result in consultation of the same conditional code, which would again find that Active has the value nil. This would generate another notifier, which in turn would generate another notifier if we selected proceed or debug, and so on.

An attempt to close this window with the mouse and thus stop the process would also generate a notifier. The toggle mechanism could not now be used to set Active because that mechanism uses a conditional based on Active being true or false. Furthermore, you cannot shut down the system because a pop-up menu is also required to do so. The only choice in this case would be to abort the system itself.

To guard against major damage under such a condition, in fearless programming you take snapshots of the entire environment from time to time. After an abort, the system can immediately be recovered at the last snapshot, and all changes in the interim can be recovered from the changes file.

Avoiding a system abort. Our initial attempt to name the bitmaps we were capturing illustrates a serious problem that did not require a system abort. The capture was accomplished by executing code in a code pane of a window that produced a small window to type the name of the file to store the bitmap in, provided the value of Active is false. Unfortunately, when this code is executed, the naming window that automatically pops up uses an instance of PopUpMenu, which also finds that Active is false, and which therefore produces a new window asking that the naming window be named.

Unlike the previous example, the entire system functionality was not lost and there was a more elegant solution than a system abort. We can toggle the value of Active to true with the appropriate key, activate a system browser with a single click of the mouse, find the offending method in class PopUpMenu, change the code by deleting the conditional on Active, and recompile the method. When we return to the running application it will use the new, incrementally compiled code and stop asking for naming windows.

There will of course be several stray windows on the screen that will have to be closed, and there are various conditions in different versions of Smalltalk that might

prevent extrication from such a predicament without aborting the image. The permanent fix to this problem was relatively straightforward. The main point is that we changed the system during an application

run when our modifications cut too deep — and this ability contributes to the sense of fearless programming.

The environment in general — not just the debugger — has the tools needed to build, examine, modify, and test code. These tools are readily available and not limited or constrained by mode or context. Building, examining, modifying, and testing code are all related operations. While using the debugger, for instance, you aren't trapped in it. You can browse, modify code, and carry out a variety of tasks.

One measure of the Smalltalk environment's effectiveness is the extent to which hard copy is unnecessary during application development. Initially you use hard copy to sketch ideas and code, but as development proceeds your work becomes virtually paperless. The only reason for printing out code is to carry it away from the machine or for backup. Because we have always had to use printouts of various iterations of the code in other languages, we believe this to be a strong indication of the Smalltalk facilities' effectiveness.

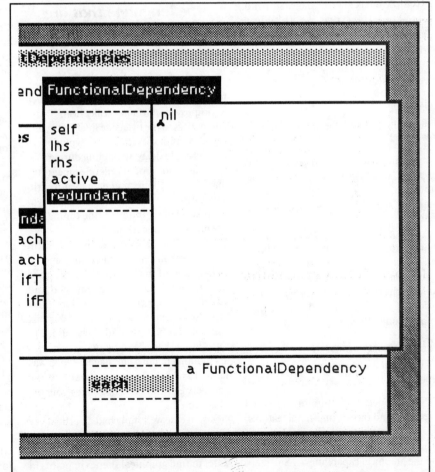

Figure 12. Viewing an object.

Other window types. In addition to the system browser and debugger windows, there are several other important window types. Code written in a workspace is not compiled into the system, so the workspace is generally used to try out existing messages, run applications, and develop and test new methods. A file list window is used to interact with the underlying file system.

Some versions of Smalltalk have windows to interact with modules written in other languages. Other windows, called system transcripts, let the system note that actions have been accomplished or special conditions have been encountered. Another window, called a system workspace, contains commonly needed code segments. A template for such segments can be modified in the system workspace and be executed on the spot.

For example, we might know that some class implements the message, suspend, but not know which one. We can activate a system workspace and locate the template

    Smalltalk browseAllImplementorsOf:
    #keywordSymbol

This can be easily edited to

    Smalltalk browseAllImplementersOf:
    #suspend

It can then be selected and executed, and the result will be a window such as that shown in Figure 8, which displays all methods that implement the message denoted by suspend.

Although Smalltalk provides excellent facilities to browse the structure of classes and objects and to examine their messages, it does not provide adequate facilities to examine the behavior of a complex application. Cunningham and Beck[6] have reported one effort to remedy this.

Misconceptions

Three Smalltalk areas are often misunderstood.

Performance. It is commonly believed that the abundance of high-level features, the uniform object-message implementation, the delayed binding of variable types, and the graphical capabilities of Smalltalk yield a system with poor overall performance.

In part, this can be attributed to the fact that the initial prerelease copies distributed by Xerox PARC to participating companies for refinement in the early 1980s were quite slow on different hardware implementations. It also did not help the performance image of Smalltalk that a major implementation on a VAX was particularly slow in a time-shared environment, and that the project thus limited its emphasis to implementations on workstations.[7] And it is well known that an absence of data typing and the lack of a global optimizing compiler typically exact heavy performance penalties.

We have found that there are nonenhanced commercial versions of the language that are quite fast.

Research is now under way to add performance enhancements to Smalltalk, such as improved garbage collection, faster alternatives to the bytecode interpreter, and typing facilities. With a data-typing facility, you could delay all binding during prototyping and product development for maximum flexibility and then identify critical sections and optimize, using data typing and other methods of fine tuning, for the mature application.

We have found, however, that even without such enhancements, there are commercial versions of the language that are quite fast. In particular, we implemented and tested database normalization algorithms in MProlog and Smalltalk on a Tektronix 4404 and found Smalltalk to be about 15 times faster than MProlog. After performance tuning in both languages, which was far more straightforward in Smalltalk, the gap between the two languages roughly quadrupled.

Just in case we simply had a particularly slow implementation of MProlog, we implemented and tested one set of procedures to find graphical shapes in points in the plane in C, Smalltalk, and MProlog — and the results were striking. The MProlog

program was about 80 times slower than the C program, but the Smalltalk program was a bit less than two times slower than the C program. The only performance enhancements we made were to correct obvious inefficiencies in the code.

For example, the Prolog program as originally published[8] was 500 times slower than the C program, and with a few rather obvious inefficiencies made for a rather unfair comparison. Some twiddling of the Prolog code eliminated a large amount of unnecessary backtracking and lowered the ratio to 80. We also ran the C program on a VAX 11/750, and the runtimes were within 15 percent of the runtimes on our workstation.

These limited tests certainly cannot even begin to characterize the performance of Smalltalk relative to MProlog and C, but they underscore what we had discovered: On our workstations, Smalltalk is very responsive during program development, and it performs quite well on the type of computation and data manipulation we are using.

The performance standard, which different versions of Smalltalk on different machines are measured by, is the language's performance on the Xerox Dorado, on which it is very fast. The Dorado is a descendant of the Xerox Alto and is a high-performance experimental microprogrammed personal computer with a microcycle time three times faster than the VAX 11/780.

There are commercially available workstations that run special Smalltalk as fast or faster than the Dorado. This performance is excellent and makes for an outstanding software prototyping environment. We would be willing to pay a far bigger performance penalty than we now pay in a language like C, for example, for the productivity gains we have achieved in Smalltalk.

Smalltalk provides system facilities to trace execution at varying degrees of granularity, to time code blocks, and to identify critical sections. There is a class named Benchmark that contains methods for micro and macro benchmarks to measure the relative efficiency of different bytecode interpreters.

Applications. Many commercial advertisements for Smalltalk characterize it as an artificial intelligence language. Indeed it may be excellent for a wide variety of artificial intelligence applications, and we are using it to create a production system for database design. However, it seems to be far more general-purpose, and it is not generally considered an artificial intelligence language by the artificial intelligence community.

The object-message paradigm provides a powerful general-purpose programming language. The graphical capabilities provide high-level primitives not only for the development of interfaces but for domains that need to use graphics. Built-in classes provide an excellent foundation for many applications.

A good example of built-in capabilities for other purposes is a set of classes that support discrete-event simulation. As a descendant of Simula, Smalltalk contains the basic mechanisms to support quasi-parallel processing, through the classes Process, ProcessorScheduler, and Semaphore. These allow process description and referencing, dynamically generated processes, and delimited and sequenced active phases of processes, with or without reference to the concept of system time.

Important capabilities are scheduling and executing processes of different priorities and easily suspending a process and resuming it later. Higher priority processes are executed before lower ones, and events with the same priority are handled on a first-come, first-served basis.

Part three of the so-called Blue Book[9] Smalltalk reference is devoted to discrete-event simulation. It develops the basic classes in addition to the built-in ones, and it develops several of the applications in Birtwistle's book[10] sufficiently to provide an excellent basis for simulation.

There are numerous significant errors in the simulation code in part three of the "corrected" first edition of the Blue Book, but these are being repaired and some of the code has been streamlined. One disadvantage of working with the simulation classes is that the debugger does not function well while tracing the suspension and resumption of processes. A simulation trace can be started in the debugger, but counts of active processes start to degrade, and certain debugger windows are not functional without coercion (such as hitting the abort key). For debugging complex and lengthy processes, the user cannot rely on the debugger.

Graphical paradigm. The basic paradigm for handling graphical applications in Smalltalk is through the model-view-controller triad. For the display of an object, the object itself is considered the model, the graphical layout is the view, and the coordination of user inputs to examine the model and the display is done through the controller.

Simple and complex nested views may be created and manipulated. Basic classes handle generic views and controllers, and the system interface itself is handled with the MVC, providing a rich set of tools serving as models for the programmer's development. Unfortunately, the promised and long-awaited tome from Xerox PARC on how to use the MVC has not been published, which leaves a hole in the documentation.

Coupled with the richness of the system, this makes learning to use the MVC a formidable task. Like the overall Smalltalk system itself, the MVC is rich and powerful, and this richness contributes to the initial learning difficulties.

Apparently grumbling about using the MVC is relatively common, and it is rumored that an alternative is sought. The concept of a pluggable view removes the need to build each application from scratch, but it certainly does not represent a radical departure from the MVC. Indeed, the Apple version of Smalltalk uses another Apple product, MacApp, heavily to build user interfaces in Smalltalk — a departure from using the MVC.

Thus, while Smalltalk contains a well-integrated set of graphical primitives, the beginning Smalltalk programmer should not expect to find a quick and easy path to developing graphical applications.

Learning experience

Smalltalk is not easy to learn, even if you have considerable experience with standard languages. The Blue Book and the Orange Book are excellent references, especially when coupled with the extensive on-line documentation — but they are not good textbooks.

The Blue Book deals mainly with features of the language, while the Orange Book deals with the environment. But the system is so rich and so well integrated that it is not easy to decompose the task of learning it into subtasks. It is like the classic chicken-and-egg situation — the rich set of tools can be used to overcome the complexity of the system, but at the same time you have to work with the system for some time before seeing how the tools can make a significant difference in working with the system.

We think learning Smalltalk is not like learning a language but like learning a culture. Over time, improvements in methods of learning the system should emerge, but the current paradigm involves intensive reading of both reference books, browsing the system on line, writing your own applications, and frequently moving from one reference or source to another. Fortunately, learning the system poses only a short-term disadvantage, but long-term productivity gains may be worth the initial investment.

Smalltalk promotes high productivity and reasonably low rework. While this may serve as a general characterization of fearless programming, there are some specific characteristics to consider in determining the extent to which a system promotes it. Briefly, fearless programming is:

• Referenceless. The system manages pointers to structures (objects in Smalltalk).

• Clutterless. The system abstracts out low-level detail.

• Typeless. Types need not be declared, so design decisions can be made flexibly.

• Modeless. Actions can be taken at will within the programming environment.

• Paperless. The system manages documentation, and the programmer does not rely on hard copy to examine the work.

Certainly for experimenting with algorithms, for rapid prototyping systems, and for developing programs that need highly interactive and graphical interfaces, you can expect a net gain in return for the investment of learning Smalltalk. One of the major advantages is that the object-message paradigm greatly helps conquer system complexity.

While the researcher interested in straightforward number-crunching may have little to gain in using Smalltalk, and while there may be other classes of users who find other languages and development environments much more suitable, we feel that programmers in many application areas would be well-served by the Smalltalk environment.

Moreover, the good performance of some commercial systems and the enhancements of Smalltalk under development suggest that Smalltalk may even have a future niche in scientific and real-time systems as well. Smalltalk promotes a good, new approach to programming. □

Acknowledgments

We'd like to express our appreciation for the many helpful comments by the referees.

References

1. Glenn Krasner, *Smalltalk-80: Bits of History, Words of Advice*, Addison-Wesley, Reading, Mass., 1983.

2. Jim Diederich and Jack Milton, "Oddessy: An Object-Oriented Database Design System," *Proc. Third Int'l Conf. Data Engineering*, Computer Society Press, Los Alamitos, Calif., 1987.

3. Setrag Khoshafian and George Copeland, "Object Identity," *Proc. First Ann. Conf. Object-Oriented Programming Systems, Languages, and Applications*, ACM, New York, 1986.

4. Larry Tesler, "The Smalltalk Environment," *Byte*, Aug. 1981, pp. 90-147.

5. Adele Goldberg, *Smalltalk-80: The Interactive Programming Environment*, Addison-Wesley, Reading, Mass., 1984.

6. Ward Cunningham and Kent Beck, "A Diagram for Object-Oriented Programs, *Proc. First Ann. Conf. Object-Oriented Programming Systems, Languages, and Applications*, ACM, New York, 1986.

7. David Patterson, "Smalltalk on a VAX," *Smalltalk-80 Newsletter*, Feb. 1984, pp 3-4 (available from Xerox Corp., Palo Alto, Calif.).

8. P.S.G. Swinson, "Prescriptive to Descriptive Programming: A Way Ahead for CAAD," *Proc. Logic Programming Workshop*, Architecture Dept., Univ. of Edinburgh, Scotland, 1980.

9. Adele Goldberg and David Robson, *Smalltalk-80: The Language and Its Implementation*, Addison-Wesley, Reading, Mass., 1983.

10. Graham Birtwistle, *A System for Discrete Event Modeling on Simula*, Macmillan, London, 1979.

Jack Milton is an associate professor of mathematics at the University of California at Davis. He is also an associate investigator on the Knowledge-Based Management Systems project at Stanford University and coordinates the Database Research Seminar there. His research interests include database design and object-oriented systems.

Milton did his undergraduate work at Swarthmore College and received a master's and a PhD in mathematics from Duke University. He is a member of ACM and the Computer Society of the IEEE.

Jim Diederich is an associate professor of mathematics at the University of California at Davis. His research interests include database design and object-oriented systems.

Diederich received a PhD in mathematics from the University of California at Riverside. His a member of ACM and the Computer Society of the IEEE.

The authors can be contacted at Math Dept., University of California, Davis, CA 95616.

96

Chapter 3: Object-Oriented Programming in Ada

Ada only partially supports the object-oriented philosophy. Ada's packages can be identified with classes. However, there is no mechanism for one package to inherit procedures from another. Nevertheless, the object-oriented point of view is very beneficial for Ada programmers. In this tutorial, we take the inclusive point of view and deem Ada and other languages that have a packaging construct but no inheritance mechanism to be "object-oriented."

Because of Ada's very careful development and the commitment to Ada by the U.S. Department of Defense, it is easy to argue that Ada is the most important object-oriented language.

An object type is usually implemented in Ada as a package. The package will contain a type definition and the procedures that operate on that type.

The paper by Richard A. Volz, Trevor N. Mudge, and David A. Gal, "Using Ada as a Programming Language for Robot-Based Manufacturing Cells," presents an example in Ada of a program for robot control. A manufacturing cell consists of a robot, an input conveyor, an output conveyor, a TV camera, and a machine for doing some work (for example a milling machine). The system includes an interface to a CAD database that includes things like the geometry of parts. The issue discussed in the paper is the development and management of the complex real-time software that controls the cell. The features of Ada can assist in achieving the usual design goals of such a system.

In the example four basic object types are defined:
- ROBOT: Provides the basic robot interface.
- POSITION: Provides data types for part and robot locations.
- CAD-MODEL: Provides CAD data base access.
- VISION: Provides an interface to the vision system.

The paper presents Ada package specifications for each of these object types.

Volz et al. consider whether or not generics could provide a variety of relatively specific and efficient vision systems at minimal programming cost. After weighing the benefits and the costs, they conclude that there is no clear benefit to the use of generics for this purpose. They discuss several other concerns they have in using Ada, but their final conclusion is that Ada works well for this kind of application.

The next paper, "Object-Based Computing and the Ada Programming Language," by G.D. Buzzard and T.N. Mudge is from the same group of researchers and considers a similar topic. It describes the concepts and goals of object-oriented computing and how they are implemented in Ada. A robot arm is used as an example of how an object can be implemented as an Ada package. The lack of support provided for protection of objects at run time and the lack of a unified abstraction mechanism in Ada are noted.

One interesting trade off that is discussed in this paper is that of whether or not to use a processor with an object-based architecture and/or an operating system that is object-based. Such architectures use some form of "capability addressing" scheme, which is expensive but support data security and program integrity in a dynamic environment. (See Volume 2, Chapter 5.) Ada was specifically designed not to require an object-oriented architecture. Therefore, the support Ada gives for object-oriented computing is static (i.e. made available in the language, but not mapped to the machine during compilation).

The major shortcoming of Ada in the area of protection mechanisms is that Ada provides an "all-or-none" approach to accessing the capabilities of a package. Buzzard and Mudge propose to remedy this by extending Ada to include package subtypes. Subtypes would permit access to a subset of the operations and types of a package. To implement this type of protection mechanism, support from the underlying hardware would be required.

Peter Wegner, in "On the Unification of Data and Program Abstraction in Ada," describes some differences between function-oriented and object-oriented programs, using Ada as the example language. Wegner views function-oriented programming as consisting of a process in which data is passed around among functions that perform some modification to it, and he views object-oriented programming as a process in which data and procedures are encapsulated in an object and the object receives requests to change the data. Thus, in object-oriented programming, the data that is changing is hidden from the user, whereas in function-oriented programming, the user sees the data and must pass the data around to the functions for processing.

Function-oriented programming is based on *data abstraction*, that is, an abstraction in which the type of an object and operations on objects of that type are provided in a capsule. The object itself is available to the user to pass to the operations. In Ada, data abstraction is provided by the package.

Object-oriented programming is based on *program abstraction*, that is, an abstraction in which an object and operations on that object are provided in a capsule. The object itself is not available to the user. In Ada, program abstraction can, in some instances, be provided by the generic package.

Wegner states that function-oriented programs are more easily verifiable than object-oriented programs, but object-oriented programs are better for users and provide a more realistic model of the real world. Therefore, we should consider the possibility of compiling object-oriented programs into their equivalent function-oriented counterparts for verification and optimization.

In Ada, packages are not ''first class'' entities because they cannot be assigned as values or passed as parameters. This limits the degree to which object-oriented programming can actually be practiced in Ada. Wegner proposes some changes to Ada that would remedy this. He suggests that such changes could be incorporated into a successor to Ada during the late 1980's. The changes proposed are similar to programming ideas already available in Smalltalk.

Additional material relevant to object-oriented programming in Ada can be found in Chapter 1 of Volume 2.

Additional References

D.G. Firesmith, ''Object-Oriented Development,'' *Proceedings, First International Conference on Ada Programming Language Applications for the NASA Space Station*, University of Houston--Clear Lake, Houston, Texas, 1986, pages D.4.1.1-D.4.1.11.

A brief description of object-oriented development using Ada. Includes a description of the subtasks necessary as the development proceeds and lessons learned from practical experience.

S. Nies, ''The Ada Object-Oriented Approach,'' *Proceedings, First International Conference on Ada Programming Language Applications for the NASA Space Station*, University of Houston--Clear Lake, Houston, Texas, 1986, pages D.4.5.1-D.4.5.2.

A description of the manner in which the object-oriented approach is being used during all phases of the life-cycle at Harris Corporation.

W.F. Appelbe and A.P. Ravn, ''Encapsulation Constructs in Systems Programming Languages,'' *ACM Transactions on Programming Languages and Systems*, Volume 6, Number 2, April 1984, pages 129-158.

Describes how Ada can be extended to conveniently implement the file system of the UNIX operating system. The extension is that of including the class concept from Smalltalk. The suitability of other languages, Pascal Plus, Modula-2, Mesa, and CLU, for implementing the file system is considered. The conclusion is that no existing high-level ''systems programming language'' provides sufficient encapsulation mechanisms (i.e., is not object-oriented enough) to permit a proper implementation of the file system. Smalltalk was not one of the languages considered.

M.W. Borger, ''Ada Software Design Issues,'' *Journal of Pascal, Ada and Modula-2*, Volume 4, Number 2, March/April 1985, pages 7-14.

Discusses the use of object-oriented design and many Ada features in the context of an implementation of a software utility.

R.A. Volz and T.N. Mudge, ''Robots are (Nothing More Than) Abstract Data Types,'' in *Proceedings of the SME Conference on Robotics Research*, Society of Manufacturing Engineers, Dearborn, Michigan, August 1984.

Using Ada as a Programming Language for Robot-Based Manufacturing Cells

RICHARD A. VOLZ, TREVOR N. MUDGE, AND DAVID A. GAL

Abstract—The Ada® programming language has been under development for the Department of Defense since 1976. Ada is intended as the Department of Defense's principal system implementation language. In particular, one of the primary aims of Ada has been to program real-time embedded systems. How Ada can be used to program a robot-based manufacturing cell, an example of a real-time embedded system is described in this paper. The computing issues in manufacturing cells are discussed with respect to Ada. Using an experimental manufacturing cell presently under construction as an example, a strategy for robot programming based on Ada is described. A case study of the software for the vision subsystem is used to illustrate a central feature of Ada: data abstraction. Additional important features of Ada for software management—program abstraction through generics and operator overloading, and multitasking—are also illustrated. The principal advantages and difficulties in using Ada for programming robot-based manufacturing cells are summarized based on the software issues described and the case study.

I. INTRODUCTION

WITH THE ADVENT of robot-based manufacturing cells, the need for a standard implementation language to program these cells has grown in importance. The present practice of designing new robot languages for nearly every new robot may satisfy the particular programming needs of each robot, but it is counterproductive from the standpoint of developing integrated manufacturing cell technology. Standardization is clearly needed. Moreover, the current high-level languages used to implement the real-time requirements of manufacturing systems lack some of the language tools, such as data abstraction, that facilitate programming in the large. Indeed, even the most sophisticated robot, numerically controlled (NC) machine tool, and related "manufacturing systems" programming languages presently in commercial use support neither data abstraction nor other features appropriate for large-scale programming [14], [28]. They are, therefore, unsuitable at the cell integration level. However, the Department of Defense's (DOD's) future system implementation language, Ada,® is an attempt to provide language constructs that can overcome most of these shortcomings.

Ada was originally developed at the instigation of the DOD [10] for programming embedded systems. Examples of embedded systems are, to quote one of the designers of

Manuscript received September 15, 1983; revised March 27, 1984. This work was supported in part by the Zimmer Foundation and in part by the Air Force Office of Scientific Research under contract F49620-82-C-0089.

The authors are with the Robot Systems Division, Center for Robotics and Integrated Manufacturing, Department of Electrical and Computer Engineering, University of Michigan, Ann Arbor, MI 48109.

® A registered trademark of the Department of Defense.

the language, "those for process control, missile guidance or even the sequencing of a dishwasher" ([2], p. vii). We would add to that list robot-based manufacturing cells. Ada is based on Pascal. However, significant extensions make it the first practical language to bring together important features that include data abstraction, separate compilation, multitasking, exception handling, encapsulation, and program abstraction through generics and operator overloading. These extensions make Ada particularly appealing for programming large-scale real-time embedded systems—a situation characteristic of robot-based manufacturing cells. Though fully validated compilers have only recently become commercially available, DOD's strong support of the language guarantees a large-scale presence in the future. This therefore warrants a serious inquiry into the feasibility of using Ada as a standard implementation language for manufacturing cells.

This paper describes an initial effort at using Ada as the basis for programming part of a manufacturing cell, specifically a robot, an interface to a vision sensor, and an interface to a computer-aided design (CAD) system. The system exploits the features of data abstraction, separate compilation, multitasking, exception handling, encapsulation, operator overloading, and generics found in the language; it expands on work summarized in [30]. Some of the principal computing issues involved in programming such a system are identified and discussed vis-à-vis the use of Ada. Much of the discussion is based on the example of the vision subsystem developed and the limitations and improvements encountered in the process. Section II discusses computing issues in manufacturing cells and how they relate to Ada. Section III describes appropriate features of Ada and a strategy for using Ada. Section IV illustrates one of the central features of Ada, data abstraction, by examining the development of the vision subsystem software. Section V discusses how program abstraction in the form of generics and operator overloading can be used to manage program development. Section VI discusses how multitasking can be used. Section VII summarizes the experience to date and notes both important advantages of using Ada and areas of concern where more work is needed.

II. COMPUTING ISSUES IN MANUFACTURING CELLS

To illustrate some of the computing problems that arise in flexible manufacturing cells, consider the simple cell shown in Fig. 1, major portions of which are presently

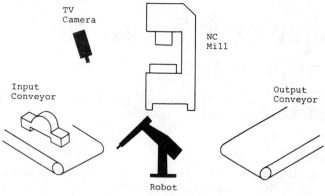

Fig. 1. Manufacturing cell.

under development in the Robot Research Laboratory at the University of Michigan. This cell is a simple machine loading/unloading system consisting of a process machine (an NC milling machine for this example); an input conveyor; a camera and associated machine vision system to sense incoming parts; a robot for loading, unloading, and tool changes; and an output conveyor. The incoming stock may arrive randomly oriented and must be located and identified by a machine vision system using the camera before being grasped by the robot. This example is conceptually relatively straightforward and, in fact, omits some additional features one might realistically expect such as post-machining inspection and adaptive control of the machining process. It is sufficient, however, for illustrating the principal points to be discussed.

The above example can also be used to illustrate a related activity that we believe will be of great importance in the future and that impinges on the current paper: the use of CAD information for driving cell operations. Our goal is for the cell to be able to manufacture any part within some reasonable class without human intervention. In other words, the cell will be able to automatically adapt to a particular type of part once the part has been identified by the vision system. In addition, in contrast to present practice, there will be no loss of production time due to training either the robot or the machine vision system [15], [12], [24]. Information to allow the vision system to identify a part and to allow the rest of the cell to perform the appropriate operations on the part is derived from a CAD database. Therefore, it is a prerequisite that all the parts to be handled by the cell have been designed via a CAD system.

The computer system that manages this cell must interact with a variety of devices and with at least one level of external computer system. The complexity of the resultant system, the interaction with real-time devices, and the interaction with the external computer system create the principal computing problem. A hierarchical computer system for controlling the cell is shown in Fig. 2[1]. A central cell control computer manages the overall behavior of the cell and handles communications with the CAD database

---

[1] Similar hierarchical structures have been proposed by several authors, e.g., Albus [1] and Wisnosky [34].

(in the cell being developed this is a multiprocessor version of Intel's iAPX432). Dedicated microcomputers function as attached processors to the cell controller and interface with the various physical process machines and sensors in the cell (in the cell being developed these are typically Intel 8086 based microcomputers). Even if all the necessary algorithms were known, which is far from the case [17], there are significant computing issues remaining:

- the development and management of the complex real-time software system to control the cell;
- the extraction of information from the CAD system to assist cell operations;
- the architecture of the computer system (hardware and software) to support the cell;
- the computational speed to meet the real-time requirements.

This paper primarily addresses the first of these points. The second point is beyond the scope of this paper although it does impinge upon the case study that we present. Research into the use of CAD information for cell operations, beyond automatic production of NC tool programs, is still in its infancy. Some early work in this area can be found in [4], [5], [33]. The last two issues are also beyond the scope of this paper; more on them can be found in [19], [20], [21], [29].

The software aspect of robot cell control itself encompasses a number of issues. Among the more important are

- the management of large complex software systems;
- the efficiency of code produced for real-time applications;
- interprocess communication and task synchronization;
- portability;
- program debugging, particularly the real-time aspects.

The first of these issues becomes more important when one considers complex systems with sophisticated sensors and several robots rather than a single dumb robot. Such systems will be much more common in the future, and the need to manage the ensuing software complexity will be correspondingly greater. The proven way of dealing with complexity in any system, software or otherwise, is to partition it into subsystems whose complexity is manageable. This partitioning is important not only in the design phase but also for system maintenance, where, in the case of embedded systems, it has been shown that often over 70 percent of the lifetime cost of large embedded software goes into software maintenance [7].

The second of these issues, computation speed, is a function not only of the underlying hardware but also of the efficiency of the code emitted by the translator. Several software techniques have evolved for dealing with this issue, two of the most important being code optimization and in-line code substitution. The first will almost certainly be developed for any translator used widely by the military or industry. The second can be particularly important when data abstraction causes a large number of procedure

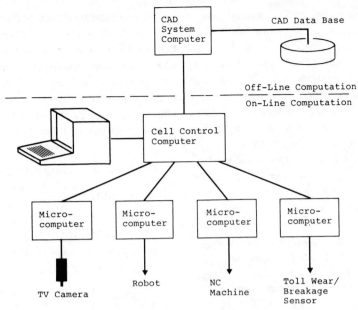

Fig. 2. Cell control.

calls (as it does in Ada). Nevertheless, the effectiveness of these, particularly for a language as large as Ada, is a matter of serious concern.

The third of these issues, interprocess communication and task synchronization, arises out of a need to support a multiprocessing system (see Fig. 2). Communication and synchronization are required in various multiprocessing situations: among tasks executing on the same processor, between a central control process and a dedicated attached processor controlling some sensor or robot joint, and among tasks executing on separate general purpose processors. Ideally, a robot programming language should support communication and synchronization mechanisms.

The fourth of these issues, portability among different robots and computer systems, is one of the principal difficulties with most robot programming languages. Little has been done to address this problem. It is most important that future language efforts not be made heavily machine dependent.

Finally, the fifth issue, program debugging, is complicated by the real-time aspect [31]. Reconstructing real-time events to track down errors is usually difficult and often impossible because of the irreproducibility of the external real-time events. Further, due to the fact that the physical movement of the devices under computer control can be very slow (at least compared to computer speeds), painfully long debug times can result. Unfortunately, the debugging issue cannot be ignored because the occurrence of an error that cannot be halted in midstream can be both dangerous and expensive.

The features present in Ada permit many of these issues to be addressed. The following section sketches a general way in which Ada can be tailored for expressing robot, sensor, and CAD operations.

III. ADA FOR CELL PROGRAMMING

Ada has been expressly designed to facilitate the deve opment and maintenance of large software systems throug.. partitioning. Separate compilation allows a team of cell designers to work concurrently on the development of separate subsystems. It also allows subsystems to be easily modified without affecting the rest of the system—an important feature for maintaining the system. Ada relies on data and program abstraction to simplify the construction of subsystem interfaces. Further, Ada provides multi-tasking and timing constructs, essential ingredients in manufacturing cells where there are typically several computation tasks that need to be performed in real time.

In this section we describe in a general way the important features of Ada and a strategy that can be used for developing a robot and sensor programming system based on the use of Ada. The design goals of Ada directly address most of the issues raised above, and these will be discussed in the context of their use for the programming system. The strategy and example described are based on the experimental system being implemented at the University of Michigan. The system will be used as an experimental vehicle for testing algorithms linking CAD to robot and sensor operation and for testing object-based architectures (see below) for robot/sensor systems. As of this writing, a vision system, a robot system, and algorithms for CAD-based vision training and determination of grip positions are functional. (The example below will illustrate some of these features while indicating the use of Ada.)

A. Features of Ada

The underlying philosophy of Ada is centered upon the use of *objects* for program design. An object is a data structure[2] having a unique identifier and an associated set of functions and procedures that can operate on it [22]. These "operators" are the only allowed means of manipulating the object. A number of advantages follow from this "object-based" programming methodology. Objects and their associated functions and procedures form natural boundaries along which to subdivide systems. In addition, because the structure of a data type is hidden from all but its associated operators, changes to the structure have a limited impact greatly simplifying program modification and maintenance. In effect, the data type can be abstracted and known only through operations performed on it. Thus, object-based programming provides a way to implement data abstraction, which, as a result of work in programming language design during the 1970's, has emerged as a major organizational concept in programming languages [27]. Several experimental programming languages have been implemented that were designed containing features to support abstract data types, but, with the possible exception of Modula-2 [32] and Concurrent Pascal [6], Ada is the first that is likely to see widespread use.

Ada provides a construct called a *package* that allows the programmer to encapsulate objects and their associated functions and procedures. In addition, it has *private* types and *limited private* types that further restrict encapsulation so that objects thus typed, while visible to program parts, can only be manipulated through procedure and function references. Together these features permit the programmer to hide data structure implementation and create abstract data types. The package definition consists of two parts, a *specification* part and a *body*. The specification part introduces the data types, variables and procedures visible to the user of the package. The body contains the implementation of the package and may be accessed only by the mechanism stated in the package specification.

Program abstraction is possible through the use of *generic* packages and subprograms, and operator overloading. These are a step in the direction of polymorphic function implementation [13], [18], and they allow, among other things, operations to be defined over a set of data types, thus providing a broader use of objects. An example is given in a later section. As shall be discussed further, the object and package concepts address the management and portability of complex software.

Ada also provides a *task* construct, which is a means of dividing a program into logically concurrent operations with possible synchronization between them [27]. In addition to forming the basis for real-time operations, tasks also provide a means of increasing processing efficiency in a parallel processor environment. Syntactically, tasks bear a resemblance to packages in the sense that they both have a specification part and a body. However, the specification part of a task is used solely to declare the synchronization points or *entry* points to the task—the entry points indicate where messages are received/transmitted by a task.

---

[2] The meaning of the term "object" is not universally agreed upon; our usage is fairly narrow. See [26] for a discussion of various viewpoints.

The program and data abstraction capabilities of Ada can give rise to a large number of procedure calls that in turn add processing overhead to the program. Ada provides an *inline pragma* (a compiler directive that expands the subroutine source code in-line wherever called), thus eliminating some of the entry/exit overhead associated with procedure calls. The effectiveness of the pragma has not been widely tested as yet.

B. A Strategy for Using Ada

Manufacturing cell or robot programming based upon Ada depends upon three central ideas:

1) the use of Ada's extensibility;
2) the use of Ada's data and program abstraction;
3) the use of Ada's real-time multitasking capabilities.

The use of Ada for programming manufacturing cells begins with the definition of *objects* for the various physical and logical components in the cell and the interfaces to these objects. Among these are the problem oriented primitives one would like to have in a robot language. These objects are embedded in Ada packages. Various mechanisms can be easily implemented to (nearly) automatically make these objects available to the programmer. The robot programmer can then use these objects and interfaces as though they were part of the language specification.

To provide a concrete illustration of the use of Ada as the system implementation language for cell programming, a system consisting of a robot, a vision sensor and a link to a CAD data base (e.g., part of the system shown in Figs. 1 and 2) is considered in a simplified manner. Four basic object types are defined in this illustration:

- ROBOT — Provides the basic robot interface.
- POSITION — Provides a set of data abstractions for part and robot locations.
- CAD-MODEL — Provides CAD data base access.
- VISION — Provides an interface to the vision subsystem.

Each of these basic objects is associated with an Ada package. A view of a portion of the main programs and the specification for each of these basic objects gives an introduction to the object oriented design approach.

Fig. 3 shows a portion of a sample main program. The action part of the example shown is to find a part on the input conveyor, move the robot to it and pick it up. It is assumed that the set of parts that could potentially appear on the conveyor are assigned to the variable SET-OF-PARTS. As mentioned earlier, the cell automatically reprograms itself to handle any one of the set once it has been identified by the vision subsystem. The names of the parts are assigned to SET-OF-PARTS from a terminal (see Fig. 2). This information is transmitted to procedure MAIN by a command interpreter (not shown). Details such as following a particular speed profile or the handling of exceptions

```
with TEXT_IO;                                    -- Make the procedures, functions
with POSITION; use POSITION;                     -- and data types defined in the named
with CAD_MODEL; use CAD_MODEL;                   -- packages available to create a robot
with VISION; use VISION;                         -- environment for the programmer.
with ROBOT; use ROBOT;

procedure MAIN is

    N: INTEGER;                                  -- Number in set of parts.

begin

    GET(N);                                      --Input from terminal.
    declare

        •
        •

        SET_OF_PARTS: PART_SET (1..N);           -- Set of parts that could potentially
                                                 -- appear on the conveyor.
        X: PART;                                 -- Data about the part found (6).
        TARGET_LOC, PICK: FRAME;                 -- Coordinate frames for the part
                                                 -- and its grasp point (4).

        •
        •

    begin

        CALIBRATE;                               -- Calibrate the robot before starting (7).
            •

        SET_SPEED (FAST);                        -- Set robot speed fast for motion
                                                 -- to approach point (7).
        X:= FIND (DECISION_TREE (SET_OF_PARTS)); -- Find and identify the part (5,6).
        PICK:= PICK_APP_POINT (X.NAME, X.STABLE_POS);  -- Approach point from CAD d/base (5).
        TARGET_LOC:= X.LOCATION * PICK;          -- Express approach point
                                                 -- in world coordinates (4).
        MOVE (TARGET_LOC);                       -- Move to approach point (7).
        SET_SPEED (SLOW);                        -- Set robot speed slow for final
                                                 -- motion to grasp point (7).
        PICK:= PICK_POINT (X. NAME, X.STABLE_POS);  -- Get grasp point from CAD database (5).
                                                 -- Put in world coordinates (4).
        TARGET_LOC:= X. LOCATION * PICK;         -- Move to grasp point (7).
        MOVE (TARGET_LOC);                       -- Grasp part (7).
        CLOSE_GRIP;
    end;

end MAIN;
```

Fig. 3. Outline of the main program controlling the robot.

are omitted since they would not tend to obscure the example. It is assumed that the geometry of the part is available in a CAD database and that off-line utilities are available to provide recognition information to the vision system (see next section) and the location on the part where it can be picked up (the grasp points are defined in a local coordinate system of the part itself). Such utilities are, in fact, under development and nearly complete [33].

The first part of this example identifies Ada packages that provide data types and services to the main program. The *with* and *use* clauses are the mechanism by which the robot environment is made available. (In the program parts shown, words in lower case bold are Ada key words. The upper case words are user-defined, or predefined, package, function, procedure, type or variable names.) The *with* clause tells the compiler that the programmer intends to use data types, procedures, and functions defined in the package named after the *with*. The *use* clause tells the compiler that the programmer wishes to reference the data types, procedures and functions defined in the package named after the *use* by the names given in the package

definition without including the name of the package as a qualifier. In general, however, the user might not even have to enter these *with* and *use* clauses directly. The *use* and *with* clauses could be placed in a program template with which the user begins. Alternatively an *include pragma* could be added to the compiler that would read a file of *with* and *use* clauses and include them in the program. In this way an environment of data types, and primitive operations tailored to a specific application, in this case robots, could be provided to the user.

The second half of the main program shows the use of the data types and functions provided by the Ada packages for the simple operation described above. The syntax used is similar to that found in several robot languages and the type and variable names are sufficiently mnemonic that one can follow the intent of the program with minimal reference to the supporting packages (see below). Note that comments are introduced by a preceding--and they can be placed anywhere in the text stream. In addition, the comments in Fig. 3 include one or two numbers in parentheses that are the figure numbers of relevant packages.

```
package POSITION is

    type COORD is new FLOAT;
    type ANGLE is new FLOAT;
    -- COORD and ANGLE are declared "new" floating point types.
    -- This way they will not be confused with other FLOAT's.

    type FRAME is private;
    -- FRAME is the representation of one coordinate system in terms of another.

    function BUILD_FRAME(X,Y,Z: in COORD; R,S,T: in ANGLE) return FRAME;
    -- Allows FRAME's to be constructed from lower level primitives. Necessary
    -- since FRAME is private and its structure cannot be directly accessed.

    function "*" ( A, B : in FRAME ) return FRAME;
    -- This function expresses the coordinate frame represented by B in
    -- terms of the one in which A is represented, i.e., it is a transformation.

    procedure UNBUILD_FRAME(A: in FRAME; X,Y,Z: out COORD; R,S,T: out ANGLE );
    -- Complement of BUILD_FRAME.

private
    type FRAME is array (1..4,1..4) of FLOAT; -- A 4×4 homogeneous transformation.
end POSITION;
```

Fig. 4.   Package specification for coordinate frames and related operations.

```
with POSITION; use POSITION;

package CAD_MODEL is
    type PART_ID is private;
    type D_INFO is private;
    type DECISION_INFO is access D_INFO;
    type PART_SET is array (INTEGER range <>) of PART_ID;
    type STABLE_POSITION is private;
    type S_POS_SET is array (INTEGER range <> ) of STABLE_POSITION;
    function DECISION_TREE (S: in PART_SET) return DECISION_INFO;
    function STABLE_POS_SET (PART_NAME: in PART_ID) return S_POS_SET;
    function PICK_POINT (PART_NAME: in PART_ID;
            STABLE_POS: in STABLE_POSITION) return FRAME;
    function PICK_APP_POINT (PART_NAME: in PART_ID;
            STABLE_POS: in STABLE_POSITION) return FRAME;

private

    type PART_ID is new STRING (1..8);
                                    -- Eight character part identifier.
    type STABLE_POSITION is new INTEGER;
                                    -- Index of stable positions.

    type D_INFO is                  -- Node in binary tree.
        record
            VALUE: FLOAT;
            LLINK: DECISION_INFO;
            RLINK: DECISION_INFO;
        end record;
end CAD_MODEL;
```

Fig. 5.   Package specifications for CAD_MODEL.

FIND is a procedure in the VISION package that finds and identifies the part on the input conveyor and returns the part's name, a 4 × 4 homogenous transformation giving the location of a coordinate frame for the part in terms of the robot's world coordinates and an index of which stable position the part was found in. These three items of data are stored as components of a record X.

PICK_APP_POINT and PICK_POINT are functions that return (from the CAD database or utilities acting upon it) 4 × 4 homogeneous transformations that express the approach and grasp points in terms of the coordinate frame for the part. The "*" has been overloaded (see below) to mean multiplication of 4 × 4 matrices so that the result is the transformation of the appropriate point in terms of the

world coordinates of the robot. TARGET LOC holds this transformation and is the argument of the MOVE procedure that actually causes robot motion.

Partial specifications for the packages referenced in Fig. 3 are given in Figs. 4–7.

The POSITION package defines the type FRAME to be a 4 × 4 matrix for use as a homogeneous transformation (Fig. 4). This type is intended to be used to represent various coordinate systems that will occur during the programming of a robot task in terms of other coordinate systems. While the 4 × 4 homogeneous matrix representation is most common for coordinate systems, it is not the only possibility. The POSITION package simply provides a standard interface to the programmers. The implementa-

```
with POSITION; use POSITION;
with CAD_MODEL; use CAD_MODEL;

package VISION is

    type PART is
       record
           NAME: PART_ID;
           LOCATION: FRAME;
           STABLE_POS: STABLE_POSITION;
       end record;

    function FIND (D_J: in DECISION_INFO) return PART;
    -- Identifies the part, its location and the position it is in.

end VISION;
```

Fig. 6. Package specification for VISION.

```
with POSITION; use POSITION;

package ROBOT is

    SLOW: constant := 0.1;          -- Fine motion speed.
    FAST: constant := 1.0;          -- Approach speed.
    subtype SPEED is FLOAT range SLOW..FAST;
                                    -- Bound speed for safety check.
    procedure CALIBRATE;            -- Calibrate the robot arm prior to use.
    procedure MOVE(DESTINATION: in FRAME);
                                    -- Move to a point given by applying
                                    -- the transform represented by FRAME.

    procedure OPEN_GRIP;
    procedure CLOSE_GRIP;
    procedure SET_SPEED (SPD: in SPEED);

end ROBOT;
```

Fig. 7. Package specification for ROBOT.

tion can be changed, even placed in special hardware, without the robot programmer having to change any code. The use of the attribute *private* means that the programmer cannot use any knowledge of how the data types is to be implemented. The function definition "*" gives meaning to the operation* in the context of two variables of type FRAME. This process is called overloading of the operator*. The implementation of the function (not shown) will implement a multiplication of two 4×4 matrices. The special structure of the homogeneous transformation might be taken into account in the implementation, but this is of no concern to the programmer, who need only be concerned with using the function.

The package CAD_MODEL provides an interface to the off-line CAD system (Fig. 5). This kind of package is not part of standard robot systems, but is an important part of our research on integrating robot programming and CAD. Several kinds of information can be derived from the CAD system. The vision system (see next section) calculates a set of features (area, perimeter, number of holes, etc.) from the image of the part being identified and uses a decision tree calculated from the set of parts which might be present to identify the part. Normally, the decision tree is obtained by on-line training of the vision system. However, the decision tree can be precalculated from the part description in the CAD data base and stored for use by the programming system. Similarly, grasp points for the parts can be precalculated [33].

The functions of CAD_MODEL access the database holding the required values, and the data types defined provide the views of the data required by other packages. PART_ID and PART_SET provide data types for identifying one or a set of part(s). Each part will typically have a set of stable positions in which it may lie. These may also be determined off-line from the CAD database. The example shows the stable position identified by an integer index, though since the type is private this fact may not be used by the rest of the program. The stable position is part of the information returned by the VISION system and is used by PICK_APP_POINT and PICK_POINT to determine the relative position of the approach and grasp points of the part. The function STABLE_POS_SET returns the set of stable positions in which a given part may be found. DECISION_TREE returns the decision information that is used by VISION as the basis for distinguishing elements of a set of parts from one another. The decision information is a binary tree pointed to by a variable of access type DECISION.

The VISION package provides the interface to the vision subsystem (Fig. 6). It uses the data types and interfaces provided by CAD_MODEL. The type PART that it defines has three components: the name of the part, a coordinate frame giving its location in terms of the world coordinates, and the stable position in which it was found. The function FIND causes a picture to be taken and returns a variable of type PART giving the pertinent information about the object found.

Finally, the ROBOT package provides a simple interface to the robot (Fig. 7). The intended operation should be obvious from the procedure names chosen.

One principal advantage of this system is its modularity and extensibility. If a new sensing or algorithmic capability is added, one need only insert a new package for it, insert the appropriate *use* and *with* clauses to make the addition available to the user, and recompile the system. If one wishes to make the program available to run with a different robot (of sufficient physical capabilities to handle the problem) only the package ROBOT need be changed. A standardization of the package interface specification, then, could lead to ready availability of ROBOT packages for a wide variety of robots and a much easier porting of programs from one robot to another.

IV. DATA ABSTRACTION

In the previous section the use of the separate compilation and the package facilities of Ada to create a robot programming environment were illustrated. In this and the next section the use of Ada is viewed from a different perspective: that of incorporating modern software concepts such as data and program abstraction into the robot programming environment. If properly used these features can bring several additional advantages to the robot programming system, including

- clearer conceptualization of the problem being programmed;
- better data security and avoidance of side effects;
- easier modification of the implementation;
- better maintainability and readability of the code.

These advantages, of course, are not intrinsic to Ada, but may be achieved to varying degrees in different languages by good programmers. However, Ada does provide the mechanism to make their use convenient. As robot programs become larger and encompass more of the manufacturing cell, these advantages will rise sharply in importance.

To provide a more detailed study of the use of Ada data and programming abstraction for cell control, a case study of one subsystem of the cell, the CAD-based vision system, is explored.

A. Overview of the Vision System

The vision subsystem was developed to allow recognition of nonoverlapping parts in our experimental manufacturing cell. It was not intended to produce new algorithms for computer vision, nor was it intended to be a simple transliteration of an existing vision system into Ada code. Rather, the goals of the vision subsystem were to implement the Stanford Research Institute (SRI) vision algorithms, taking advantage of the facilities provided in the Ada programming language to explore both the use of Ada and the use of CAD information to replace the vision training phase.

The SRI vision algorithms are described in [12] (for additional important concepts see [9], [11]. They are in-

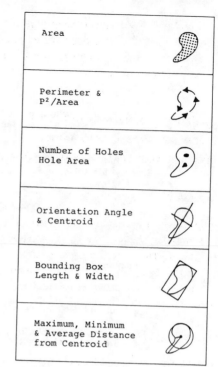

Fig. 8. Typical silhouette features.

tended to classify nonoverlapping parts represented as dark silhouettes against a light background. The image used is a matrix of binary valued pixels. The vision algorithms compute a set of features from the silhouettes. These include area, A; perimeter, P, and P^2/A; number of holes and hole area; position of centroid and its angle of orientation with respect to the field of view; bounding box length and width; maximum, minimum and average distance of the perimeter from centroid (see Fig. 8). A subset of the features (determined by the specific vision task at hand) are used to classify the parts viewed. The type of visual recognition that the SRI system is capable of is clearly very restricted. However, the system represents a judicious mix of well-understood techniques that are versatile enough for many industrial applications and that can be easily implemented in a small, rugged low-cost package. Indeed, systems based upon these techniques are now being produced by several vendors.

The connection of the vision system to the skeleton robot programming environment actually requires more detail than illustrated in Section III. The *with* clause must be expanded to include other packages that are referenced by the function of VISION. Fig. 6 is to be modified to

    with CAD_MODEL; **use** CAD_MODEL

    with ANALYZE; **use** ANALYZE;

    package VISION is

        ⋮

    end VISION.

The package ANALYZE provides the procedures and functions that calculate the features of the part to be recognized.

Actually, there are several levels of hierarchical decomposition within ANALYZE. It references three packages that are collectively responsible for determining the features of the object. Its specification begins

```
package ANALYZE is
        procedure SCANLINE_ENCODER ( . . . );
        procedure CONNECTIVITY_ANALYSIS ( . . . );
        procedure FINAL_FEATURE_CALCULATIONS ( . . . );
                 ⋮
        end ANALYZE.
```

The implementation (not shown) of FIND in VISION uses SCANLINE_ENCODER, CONNECTIVITY_ANALYSIS and FINAL_FEATURE_CALCULATIONS to determine the part features needed to use the decision tree. The following discussion will show how Ada has been employed to achieve the benefits of modern software concepts.

B. Ada-Based Implementation of Feature Extraction

1) Operation Overview: ANALYZE operates on a binary matrix of pixels that forms the image. The image is processed in raster scan order (one row at a time). Each raster scanline is converted from a row of light and dark

IMAGE	— — The camera's 256 × 256 pixel image.
ENCODED_SCANLINE	— — Expanded run length encoding of a scanline which includes the values needed to calculate the first and second moments, etc.
INTERMEDIATE_FEATURE_VECTOR	— — Values accumulated from the ENCODED_SCANLINE's.
PERIMETER	— — Contains all the exterior pixels for a given part (hole).
FINAL_FEATURE_VECTOR	— — Scalar values for each feature of each part and hole in the scene.

pixels to a smaller sequence of "runs" of contiguous pixels of a particular color. For example, the center scanline depicted in Fig. 9 has three runs of 3 (dark), 4 (light), and 4 (dark). Thus, the scanline can be "run length encoded" by the sequence 3-4-4 with one additional bit to indicate that the first run is dark. Dark runs are interpreted as belonging to a nonoverlapping part, while light runs are considered empty space surrounding the part or holes in the part.

Next, consecutive scanlines are analyzed for connectivity, overlapping dark runs and overlapping light runs are linked to form parts and holes respectively. The consecutive scanlines of Fig. 9 are linked into three regions: two potential parts separated by a gap or hole. As part of the linking or region growing operation, the number of pixels in each region (area), and the first and second moments of each region are calculated. This is accomplished by adding the values for each scanline to partial sums being accumulated in an intermediate feature (hole) vector. In addition, a list of the perimeter pixels of each part (hole) is

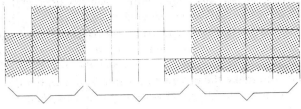

Fig. 9. Scanlines of pixels.

maintained. Thus, when all the runs for a part (hole) have been linked together the intermediate feature vector and perimeter list contain the information that is needed to calculate the final feature values for each part.

2) Object-Based Modularization: Program modularization using Ada objects is based upon creating an access module for each data structure that must be used by all procedures or functions referencing the data objects. Fig. 10 shows the relation of the data entities, the access modules and the routines provided by ANALYZE. The double headed hollow arrows indicate module access to data structures. These modules are the only ones that need to know the implementation details of the data structure. The data structures (see the right column of Fig. 10) operated on by the feature extraction program are as follows:

The operation of the feature calculation can be viewed, as follows: SCANLINE_ENCODER (SLE) obtains lines one at a time from the IMAGE module and encodes them, and, through the SCANLINE module stores the encoded scanlines. The scanlines are next accessed by CONNECTIVITY_ANALYSIS (CNA) that performs analysis of connected regions. CNA processing of one scanline can be done concurrently with the generation of the encodings of the scanline by SLE. The operation of FINAL_FEATURE_CALCULATION (FFC) can be similarly overlapped with that of CNA. The clear conceptualization afforded by this view of the operation exposes the fact that logically the above three subprograms can be considered to be operating in a pipelined fashion. In Section VI it will be shown how this logical pipelining could be translated into actual pipelining using Ada tasking.

By way of contrast, Fig. 11 shows a counterpart of Fig. 10 that would be typical of the more common control-based approach in which the program is based upon the flow of

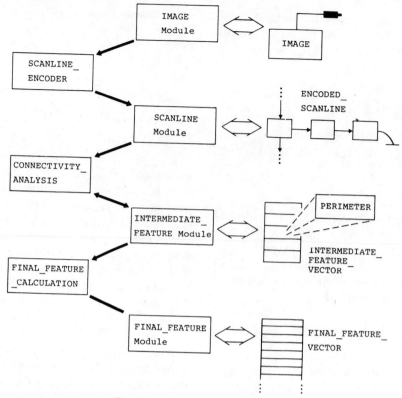

Fig. 10. Object-based modularization.

control. The more convoluted diagram obscures the conceptual simplicity apparent in the object-based approach. The procedures and functions in this case directly access the data structures they need. Data security is thus violated and possibility of spreading the effects of programming errors is increased (unwanted side effects).

3) Modification and Maintainability of the Program: The maintainability of the program is also substantially enhanced by the use of object-based modularization in Ada. The separation of the specification and implementation parts of a package provides a localization in procedure implementation changes. Both data structure and code changes are simplified. When modifications are required to the data structure, the only code that must be modified is in the local modules that have exclusive access to the data. For example, it is unimportant for the program to know the actual implementation of the IMAGE module, as long as there is a means of finding the coordinates where the image changes from light to dark and dark to light. The specification for the IMAGE package appears as

modules used have similar simplicity and mnemonic association with the required data access functions.

The above capability was used to considerable advantage during the debugging of the system. In actual operation, LOAD_NEW_IMAGE causes a GE-TN2500 camera to load an image into a frame grabber; an attached processor then translates the resulting matrix into a run length encoding and transfers the encoded image to the iAPX432. The vision system was ready for debugging, however, before the frame grabber was completed. To debug the system a simple package substitution was made: the IMAGE module access routines were changed to request column and row information from an operator's terminal. This proved to be an effective way to debug the system.

C. Objects in Ada

Object-based programs are rather difficult to implement in traditional block structured high-level languages. For example, data structures that must be accessed by separate

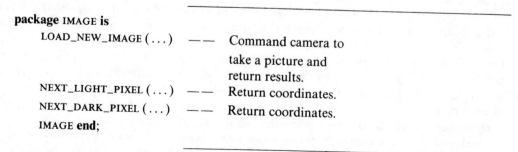

```
package IMAGE is
    LOAD_NEW_IMAGE ( . . . )    — —   Command camera to
                                        take a picture and
                                        return results.
    NEXT_LIGHT_PIXEL ( . . . )  — —   Return coordinates.
    NEXT_DARK_PIXEL ( . . . )   — —   Return coordinates.
    IMAGE end;
```

which clearly has the needed access functions. The other   blocks must be visible to at least one block within which

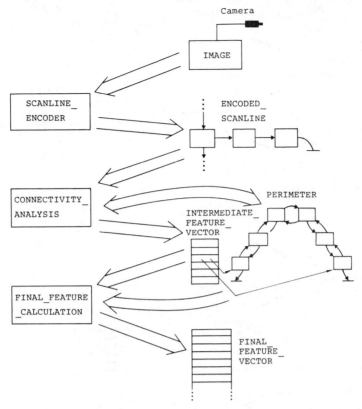

Fig. 11. Typical control-based modularization.

the separate blocks are nested. This leaves open the possibility of other nested blocks having unintended access to the data structures. In less restrictive languages memory locations can be made available to the subprograms that need access to them; however, this again raises the question of undesirable accessibility. In contrast, objects in Ada can be encapsulated with the package construct. Controlled access to the object is defined by the specification part of the package that formally defines visibility and scope rules for variable data objects and subprograms, and creates a visible environment for both the package body and any modules outside the package that need to manipulate objects in the package. Therefore, the specification is the construct that facilitates abstraction and permits easy implementation of abstract data types. The package body completes the code for each procedure and function in the package specification. The body and any modules that reference the package can be compiled separately from the specification, as long as they are able to recreate the environment of the specification section during their own compilation. In this way strong static-semantic checking can be achieved concurrently with separate compilation.

V. PROGRAM ABSTRACTION

A major objective of software management is in the ability to reuse algorithms that have been implemented previously. However, an undesirable attribute of strongly typed languages is the inability of type independent operations to be used on a variety of conflicting data types. Ada allows one to write a form of subroutine or package, (called generic subroutines or packages) in which the data-types manipulated are formal parameters. The Ada source code is then expanded, as necessary, to implement the desired subroutine or package for each data type desired. The expansion process, called instantiation, is similar to macroexpansion.

Generics are not limited, however, to operations which are independent of the data types involved. Though not as flexible as polymorphic functions [18], Ada generics can adjust for broad classes of objects by use of the *with* clause [10] and by passing functions as parameters during instantiation. In this way operations which are specific to the data type given as a generic formal parameter can be inherited. For example, if the FRAME type of the package POSITION were used as an argument to a generic procedure, the "*" would inherit the meaning of matrix multiply.

The concept of generics raises several interesting questions. One is whether a generic robot package can be defined and instantiated for specific instances of different robots. To test this on a limited scale, the use of generics in the vision system was examined. Contemporary vision systems [3], [15] utilize a list of nearly forty features which could be useful in distinguishing parts from one other, inspecting parts or guiding specific assembly operations. Most vision systems calculate subsets of four to twelve features from this list. Because of the limited amount of time, no vision system calculates the entire list at run-time. Selection of the proper subset is, therefore, crucial for an efficient solution. Furthermore, different applications require different subsets.

```
generic
        type FEATURES is (<>);                          --enumeration of desired features
    package FINAL_FEATURES is
        type FEATURE_VECTOR is array (FEATURES) of FLOAT;
    end FINAL_FEATURES:

--Next we define the generic feature calculation procedure

generic

        type FEATURES is (<>);                          --enumeration of desired features
        type FINAL_FEATURE_VECTOR is private;
        type INTERM_VECTOR is private;
        with function FEAT_CALC_1 (INTERM: in INTERM_VECTOR) return FLOAT;
                        •
                        •
        with function FEAT_CALC_N (INTERM: in INTERM_VECTOR) return FLOAT;

    procedure FINAL_FEAT_CALC(IMFV: in INTERM_VECTOR; FFCV: out FINAL_FEATURE_VECTOR);
    procedure FINAL_FEAT_CALC(IMFV: in INTERM_VECTOR; FFCV: out FINAL_FEATURE_VECTOR) is

        INDEX: FEATURES;                                --index into FINAL_FEATURE_VECTOR

    begin
        INDEX := FEATURES'FIRST;
        FFCV (INDEX) := FEAT_CALC_1 (IMFV);
                •
                •
        INDEX := FEATURES'SUCC(INDEX);
        FFCV(INDEX) := FEAT_CALC_N(IMFV);
    end FINAL_FEAT_CALC;

--Next,we show a sample instantiation of final feature calculation

    type DESIRED_FEATURES is (FEAT1, .. , FEATN);

    package FINAL is new FINAL_FEATURES(DESIRED_FEATURES); --This creates a package
                                                --with the desired feature vector.

    procedure FINAL_FEATURE_CALCULATION is new FINAL_FEAT_CALC(
        DESIRED_FEATURES,           --This now exists from the above subtype.
        FINAL.FEATURE_VECTOR,       --This exists from the above package instantiation.
        INTERMEDIATE_FEATURE_VECTOR,--This is defined elsewhere in the vision system.
        FEATURE_CALC1,              --This must be previously defined.
                •
                •
        FEATURE_CALCN);             --This  must be previously defined.

--Actual performance of the feature calculations occurs upon the following call assuming
--X and Y suitably declared earlier

        FINAL_FEATURE_CALCULATION(X,Y);
```

Fig. 12.

To obtain a vision system that could be easily adapted to a variety of vision tasks, a library of routines to calculate all features from an INTERMEDIATE_FEATURE_VECTOR could be established. (See Fig. 10 to relate module names to ensuing discussion.) Next, a generic FINAL_FEATURE_CAL-CULATION procedure could be written in which the FINAL_FEATURE_VECTOR is defined only in terms of the number of features desired. This is illustrated in Fig. 12. The generic procedure is called FINAL_FEAT_CALC. Its operation is expressed primarily in terms of a set of individual feature calculation functions generically called FEAT_CALC,..., FEAT_CALC_N. To create an actual instance of FINAL_FEAT_CALC that can be used to calculate a final feature vector, one must identify the set of features desired (accomplished by type DESIRED_FEATURES in the example) and supply actual objects for the generic parameters of FINAL_FEAT_CALC. FEATURE_CALC_1,···, FEATURE_CALC_N in the example, must be separately prepared. The instantiation creates an actual procedure FINAL_FEATURE

_CALCULATION that can be used to calculate the final feature vector. The point, of course, is that one can create different final feature calculations procedures by supplying different feature calculation functions.

While it was originally envisioned that through the use of generics a variety of relatively specific and efficient vision systems could be produced at a minimal programming cost, it is not clear that a great deal could be gained. One still must write all of the individual routines for feature calculation. Generics simply provides one way of incorporating the specific set to be used. Moreover, the example of Fig. 12 requires advance knowledge of the number of features to be used and is not amenable to use of a loop construct in implementation. These two restrictions might be eliminated by implementing the feature calculation routines as tasks and making one of the generic parameters to FINAL_FEAT_CALC a record whose components contain access pointers to the individual feature tasks. The record could have a discriminant stating the

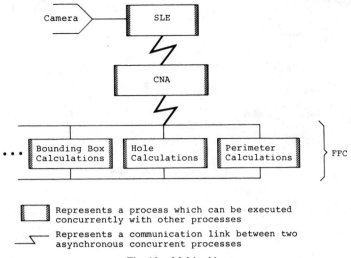

Fig. 13. Multitasking.

number of components. However, it hardly seems worth the extra complexity. The use of generics, then, to build a specially tailored vision system does not seem to offer as much as originally anticipated.

VI. MULTITASKING

The cell control computer (the iAPX432) in our experimental cell has a multiprocessor architecture that automatically provides parallel computation for multiple concurrent processes. Coupled with Ada's explicit multiprocessing through the task construct, it is possible to easily speed up some computation through parallel processing. This is illustrated for the vision system.

Again, using the ANALYZE package as an example, consider the processing of the three subprograms for scanline encoding (SLE), connectivity analysis (CNA), and final feature calculation (FFC). The clear conceptualization of Fig. 10 suggests that the calculation can be pipelined, and through tasking and multiprocessing, can be converted to parallel computations. Instead of waiting for all of the scanlines to be entirely encoded, CNA can begin after SLE has processed a single scanline. While CNA is processing one line of data, SLE can generate the next encoded scanline. A similar process can take place between CNA and FFC. Thus, conceptually each of the three tasks can be considered to be executing in a loop: fetching information from the previous task and sending information to the following task (see Fig. 13).

This pipelining can show a substantial reduction in processing time. With pipelining the processing time has a lower time bound equal to the time to process a single data item by all the tasks (filling the pipeline up) plus the time for the slowest task to work on $k - 1$ data items where k is the total number of data items processed. Let $T(k)$ be the time to run a program on k data records without multitasking, and let $MT(k)$ be the time to run the same program (now composed of n tasks, $P1, \cdots, Pn$) with multitasking, then

$$MT(k) = \text{time}(P1 + P2 + \ldots + Pn)$$

$$+ (k - 1)*\text{time}(\max(P1, P2, \cdots, Pn)) \leq T(k)$$

assuming sufficient processors are available. This, of course, is an ideal situation that assumes uniformity in the processing of data items and little or no overhead to manage the extra processors. Nevertheless, programs that cycle through large data sets on systems with enough processors should gravitate to this lower bound.

Transmission overhead is incurred with every transaction from the attached processor. This transmission overhead can also be overlapped with the operation of the SLE task, effectively hiding the overhead.

The calculations in the third task, the final feature calculations (FFC), conveniently separate into independent subtasks such as bounding box calculations, hole calculations, perimeter calculations, etc., all requiring the same input, the INTERMEDIATE_FEATURE_VECTOR, and all outputting to unique locations in the FINAL_FEATURE_VECTOR. These independent calculations can be grouped into parallel subtasks within the FFC task. The parent task (FFC) merely passes chunks of work to each subtask and waits for them to finish (see Fig. 12). Processing time for the tasks is bounded by the time necessary to process a data item through the longest subtask. In other words

$$MT(k) = \text{time}(\max(P1, P2, P3, \cdots, Pn)) \leq T(k)$$

where $P1, \cdots, Pn$ are the n tasks than can run in parallel. Again this is an ideal situation, but processing using this technique should reflect significant speed up provided the necessary processors are available.

The structure of an example Ada procedure corresponding to Fig. 13 that illustrates the pipeline and parallel computations possible is shown in Fig. 14.

```
procedure SLE is

    task CNA is
        entry START;
    end CNA;

    task FFC is
        entry START;
    end FFC;

    task body CNA is
    begin
        loop
            accept START;

            -- perform connectivity analysis on one line;

            FFC.START;
        end loop;
    end CNA;

    task body FFC is

    begin
        loop
            accept START;

            declare

                task FC1;

                task FCN;

                task body FC1 is
                begin
                    --perform feature calculation update on one line of data
                end FC1;

                task body FCN is
                begin
                    --perform feature calculation update on one line of data
                end FCN;
            begin
                --just let the feature tasks run in parallel
            end;
        end loop;
    end FFC;

begin -- SLE

    loop  -- until done
        -- perform one line  of scan line encoding analysis
        CNA.START;
    end loop;
end SLE;
```

Fig. 14.

VII. SUMMARY AND CONCLUSION

The future development of automated manufacturing cells will be increasingly linked to the integration of cell components amongst themselves and with higher level computer aided engineering functions. This integration will depend upon increasingly complex and sophisticated computer systems. The DOD language, Ada, was developed specifically for large complex real-time embedded software systems. This paper has outlined its use as the basis for developing manufacturing cell software and illustrated this with the implementation of a computer vision module via Ada. Five issues in robot cell software were identified at the beginning of the paper: complexity, code efficiency, communication and synchronization, portability, and debugging. Our experience to date has touched upon a majority, but not all, of these issues. The following paragraphs summarize our experience and conclusions about them.

From the view points of managing complex software, providing an application specific programming environment to the user, and achieving language standardization, Ada provides a number of advantages. These include the following.

- The use of data abstraction and operator overloading to create well modularized application specific code helps usability, readability and maintainability.
- The resulting application package can create a reasonable application specific environment.
- The resulting application package can create a reasonable application specific environment.
- The strong type checking significantly aids debugging.
- The separate compilation features in conjunction with the other features above aids flexibility and helps portability.
- The expressive power of the language is excellent.

These advantages are not surprising. They are exactly what computer scientists have been predicting for several years. Having these capabilities widely available in a standardized language, however, is very significant. Indeed, it is this standardization of Ada that can greatly aid in standardizing application specific "languages" and giving them portability. The portability can be inherited, to a large measure, from Ada.

Generics, on the other hand, while of great use in dealing with common data structures over different primitive data types, was of less utility than originally expected in the application specific uses for which it was examined. It is possible to instantiate an application specific vision module, as shown above. Similarly, one could conceive of using generics to manage the production of code for different robots—just instantiate the code for the robot you want from some generic package. However, since in both the vision case and in the multiple robot case, the controlling algorithms are different, one would have to pass in to the generic package (as parameters) the functions that perform the calculations specific to a given instantiation. While feasible, this eliminates much of the advantage to using generics. The resulting principle advantage would be an enforcement of a standard way of dealing with all features in the vision system or all robots in a multiple robot situation.

There are also a number of concerns which have arisen which either are a detraction to some users or bear further investigation:

- The heavy use of data abstractions creates additional procedure calls and corresponding overhead which can cause difficulty in a real-time environment.
- Strong typing can get in the way of what one wants to do.
- How usable will Ada really be, even with good environment creation through special packages, to the noncomputer professional?
- The debugging of robot programs requires close interaction with the programmer. It is not clear this can happen with Ada.
- The integration of systems involving multiple processors does not permit Ada communication and synchronization mechanisms to be fully utilized.

The use of the *inline* pragma was tested in our implementation of the vision system. By using *inline* for the most frequently used low level routines the computation time was reduced by a factor of nearly four. This must not be taken too seriously, however. The architecture of the iAPX 432 makes it particularly susceptible to inefficiency on context switching. Thus, the inline improvements in our experiments are probably much greater than will be obtained in general. Further investigation on the effectiveness of the expansion should be carried out. Also, the Ada *inline* pragma causes all invocations of a procedure to be expanded, while for memory management purposes, the programmer might find it more convenient to be able to selectively expand procedure calls.

The strong typing argument has raged for some time and is not specific to robot or manufacturing cell applications We believe that as the size and complexity of a software project increase so does the importance of using strong typing.

We do not ever expect to see robots on manufacturing cells programmed in Ada by shop floor personnel. We expect that as more complex arrangements of robots, sensors, and other machines are built, and as better links with computer-aided engineering and computer-aided design databases are forged, shop floor personnel will cease to "program" robots. Rather, they will interact with a program to identify what is to be done next or which option to choose in responding to an exception. The actual programming will be done in a more generic fashion by a person who has a good mix of manufacturing and computer engineering/science in his/her background. A person with this type of training should be able to deal with a "roboticized Ada."

The debugging issue is one that requires considerable additional research. All Ada implementations in progress are based on a compile translation while almost all robot programming languages are based on interpretive translation. From the point of view of the programmer, however, the robot program may be a separately prepared and debugged entity. What is really necessary is a fast interactive translate/debug system. This does not preclude compile translation, particularly if used in conjunction with a simulator [8], [16], [23].

Interprocess communication has been investigated in two contexts, the multitasking version of the vision system described in the previous section and attached processors for low level vision and robot control. The effectiveness of the former depends upon multiple processors with the capability to automatically pick up tasks and execute them as they are created. The latter did not really use the synchronization mechanisms of Ada; the communication was necessarily handled through low-level I/O drivers. This points to a major limitation in nearly all approaches to the integration of multiple smart devices, the need to deal with all devices via explicit I/O and program the devices in (often) different languages (PL/M and assembly language in our case). Often the processes with which one wants to communicate or synchronize exist on separate processors and the language communication and synchronization mechanisms do not extend across machine boundaries. Consequently we feel there is a strong need for a system integration language that can extend across machine boundaries. Whether or not Ada is suitable for such extensions is currently under investigation.

Recent programming language research has yielded a number of new concepts which will aid the program development process. A number of these are incorporated into Ada. Future languages will undoubtedly encompass more of these concepts. However, at present, the considerable resources being put into the Ada effort by the DOD coupled with its orientation toward real-time embedded systems makes us believe it will be a significant factor in the future. While we are not yet prepared to state that Ada is the answer to robot and manufacturing cell programming, we have been pleased with it so far and feel further investigation is warranted.

REFERENCES

[1] J. S. Albus, Charles R. McLean, Anthony J. Barbera, and M. L. Fitzgerald, "Hierarchical control for robots in an automated factory," in *Proc. 13th Int. Symp. Industrial Robots and Robots*, vol. 7, Apr. 1983, pp. 13–43.

[2] J. G. P. Barnes, *Programming in Ada*. London, England: Addison-Wesley, 1982.

[3] H. G. Barrow and J.M. Tenenbaum, "Computation vision," Artificial Intelligence Center, Stanford Research Institute, vol. 69, May 1981, no. 5, pp. 572—95.

[4] E. W. Baumann, "Model based vision and the MCL language," in *Proc. IEEE Syst. Man, Cybern. Conf.*, Oct. 1981, pp. 433–438.

[5] E. W. Baumann, "CAD model input for robotic sensory systems," in *Proc. Autofact IV*, Nov. 1982.

[6] P. Brinch Hansen, *The Architecture of Concurrent Programs*. Englewood Cliffs, NJ: Prentice-Hall, 1977.

[7] J. D. Cooper, June 17–18, 1982, "Why a DoD standard programming language," in *Proc. Ada Conf.*, Boston, MA and Washington, D.C., June 28–29, 1982, pp. 1–6.

[8] Ruediger Dillmann, "A graphical emulation system for robot design and program testing," in *Proc. 13th Int. Symp. Industrial Robots and Robot 7,*" Apr. 1983, *pp. 7-1-7-15.*

[9] R. Duda, J. Kremers, and D. Nitzan, "Automatic part classification," Stanford Research Institute, Menlo Park, CA, Fifth Rep., SRI Project 4391, Jan. 1976, pp. 7–22.

[10] *Ada* Programming Language (ANSI/MIL-STD-1815A), Washington, DC 20301: Ada Joint Program Office, Department of Defense, OUSD(R & E), Jan. 1983.

[11] R. Duda and D. Nitzan, "Error analysis for automatic part recognition," 5th Rep., NSF Grant G138100X1, SRI Project 4391, Stanford Research Institute, Menlo Park, CA, Jan. 1976, pp. 65–81.

[12] G. J. Gleason, "Vision module development," 9th Rep., NSF Grants APR75-13074 and DAR78-27128, SRI Projects 4391 and 8487, Stanford Research Institute, Menlo Park, CA, Aug. 1979, pp. 9–16.

[13] D. I. Good and W. D. Young, "Generics and verification in Ada," *Sigplan Notices*, vol. 15, Nov. 1980, pp. 123–127.

[14] W. A. Gruver, B. I. Soroka, J. J. Craig, and T. L. Turner, "Evaluation of commercially available robot programming languages," *Proc. 13th Int. Symp. Industrial Robots & Robots 7*, Apr. 1983, pp. 12-58–12-68.

[15] J. W. Hill, "Survey of commercial vision systems," *Industrial Automation Group*, May 1980.

[16] S. J. Kretch, "Robotic animation," *Robots VI Conf.*, Mar. 1982, (not in Proceedings: see McDonnell Douglas Automation Co., St. Louis, MO.).

[17] T. Lozano-Perez, "Robot programming," Artificial Intelligence Lab, MIT, Cambridge, MA, Dec. 1982, A.I. memo no. 698, pp. 56.

[18] R. Milner, "Theory of type polymorphism in programming," *Comput. and Syst. Sci.*, vol. 17, pp. 348–375, 1978.

[19] T. N. Mudge, "Special purpose VLSI processors for industrial robotics," in *Proc. IEEE Computer Society's 5th Int. Computer Software & Application Conf.*, Nov. 1981, pp. 270–271.

[20] T. N. Mudge, R. A. Volz, and D. E. Atkins, "Hardware/software transparency in robotics through object level design," in *Proc. Soc. Photo-optical Instrumentation Engineers Technical Symp. West*, SPIE 360, Aug. 1982, pp. 216–223.

[21] E. I. Organick, M. P. Maloney, D. Klass, and G. Lindstrom, "Transparent interface between software and hardware versions of Ada compilation units," Univ. Utah Rep. UTEC-83-030, Dept. Computer Science, Univ. Utah, June, 1983, 19 pp.

[22] E. I. Organick, "A Programmer's View of the Intel 432 System", Intel Corp., Santa Clara, CA, 1982.

[23] Alan de Pennington, M. Susan Bloor, and Mazin Balila "Geometric modelling: A contribution towards intelligent robots," in *Proc. 13th Int. Symp. Industrial Robots and Robots 7*, Apr. 1983, pp. 7-35-7-54.

[24] W. A. Perkins, A Computer Vision System that Learns to Inspect Parts, General Motors Research Laboratories, research publication GMR-3650, June 1981.

[25] E. S. Roberts, A. Evans, Jr., C. R. Morgan, and E. M. Clarke, "Task management in Ada—A critical evaluation for real-time multiprocessors," *Software—Practice and Experience*, vol. 11, pp. 1019–1051, 1981.

[26] T. Rentsch, "Object oriented programming," *Sigplan Notices*, vol. 17, no. 9, pp. 51–57, Sept. 1982.

[27] M. Shaw, "The impact of abstraction concerns on modular programming languages," *Proc. IEEE*, vol. 68, no. 9, pp. 1119–1130, Sept. 1980.

[28] K. G. Shin, A Comparative Study of Robot Programming Languages, Center for Robotics and Integrated Manufacturing, Univ. of Michigan, Ann Arbor, MI rep. RSD-TR-17-82, Nov. 1982, pp. 50.

[29] J. L. Turney and T. N. Mudge, "VLSI implementation of a numerical processor for robotics," in *Proc. 27th Int. Instrumentation Symp.*, Indianapolis, IN, Apr. 1981, pp. 169–175; also presented at the Instrument Society of America Anaheim Conf., Anaheim, MI, Oct. 1981.

[30] R. A.Volz, T. N. Mudge, and D. A. Gal, "Using Ada as a robot system programming language," in *Proc. 13th Int. Symp. Industrial Robots & Robots 7*, Apr. 1983, pp. 12-42–12-57.

[31] R. A. Volz and R. E. Richardson, *CRASH User's Manual*, Dept. Electrical and Computer Engineering Rep., Univ. of Michigan, Ann Arbor, MI, Aug. 1977.

[32] N. Wirth, *Programming in Modula-2*, 2nd ed. Berlin, Germany: Springer-Verlag, 1982.

[33] J. Wolter, T. C. Woo, and R. A. Volz, "Gripping position for 3D objects," in *Proc. 1982 Meeting of the Industry Applications Soc.*, Oct. 1982, pp. 1309–1314.

[34] Dennis E. Wisnosky, "Computer integrated manufacturing: The Air Force ICAM approach," SME/CASA tech. paper M581-953, 1981.

Object-Based Computing and the Ada Programming Language

G. D. Buzzard and T. N. Mudge
University of Michigan

Reprinted from *Computer*, March 1985, pages 11–19. Copyright © 1985 by
The Institute of Electrical and Electronics Engineers, Inc.

Developments in several areas of computer science and engineering have coalesced during the past several years into a systems design methodology known as object-based computing. The primary benefit of this methodology is that it raises the level of abstraction available in the design process. Among the events that have encouraged the development of object-based computing are:

(1) advances in programming language design, such as program decomposition criteria and abstraction mechanisms;

(2) advances in operating systems design, particularly those which address data integrity and program security; and

(3) advances in computer architecture that allow direct hardware support for many operating system and language concepts.

Object-based computing is characterized by the extensive use of abstraction. Resources such as data, logical or physical devices, and, in some systems, program segments, may be represented by *abstract types*. Instances of abstract types form the objects in object-based computing. These objects are manipulated exclusively by operations that are encapsulated in a protective environment commonly referred to as a *type manager* or *protection domain*.

This work was supported in part by the Air Force Office of Scientific Research under contract F49620-82-C-0089 and a Kodak Fellowship.

The first step in an object-based design philosophy is the identification of appropriate objects. The second step is the determination of operations on those objects. For example, consider a part-sorting system. The objects in such a system may include a camera, a robot, a frame (describing position), a set of parts, and bins to receive the parts. For robot objects, the set of available operations may include:

- INITIALIZE_ARM(robot_id)
- MOVE(robot_id, frame)
- OPEN(robot_id)
- CLOSE(robot_id)
- GET_FRAME(robot_id)

Each operation takes as a parameter *robot_id,* which uniquely identifies individual instances of the type robot, allowing a number of different robots to be used in the system. All instances of the same type share some common behavioral characteristics—in this case, the set of operations that is applicable to all robots.

Much of the growing interest in object-based computing is attributable to the Department of Defense's commitment to the Ada language project. Although Ada (DoD's proposed standard system implementation language for embedded systems) may not fit all definitions of an object-based language, it does incorporate key concepts. We will explain several concepts that are central to object-based computing and the extent to which they are supported by the Ada programming language. As part of the discussion, examples are given that have been drawn from our use of Ada in programming a robot-based manufacturing cell. [1,2]

Object-based computing concepts apply to both hardware and software systems. In software systems, the term object-based describes software environments that incorporate the concepts of data abstraction, [3] program abstraction, [4] and protection domains. [5] Objects are represented as individually addressable entities that uniquely identify their own contents as well as the operations that may be performed on them. In the case of the robot object type, users have the ability to address specific robot objects individually and to manipulate their contents in a protected manner through operations, such as MOVE, that are explicitly defined for use on robot objects. Users need not be concerned with such details as object representation.

There are two major goals in developing object-based software. The first is to reduce the total life-cycle software cost by increasing programmer productivity and reducing maintenance costs. The second goal is to implement software systems that resist both accidental and malicious corruption attempts. Protection domains, which are described in the next section, are used to achieve the latter goal. As will be shown, support for both of these goals is provided by the Ada language.

Reductions of total life-cycle software costs in Ada are aided by the abstraction mechanisms provided in the language. The high level of abstraction that can be attained helps to increase programmer productivity by permitting the construction of generalized, reusable software units such as the robot controller described earlier. Also, once the interfaces to the abstractions are defined, program development for the implementation of each abstraction can proceed independently and in parallel, since the implementation details remain hidden (abstracted) from the view of the rest of the system. Abstraction aids software maintainability as well, by containing the effect of all changes, except those involving the interfaces, within the module housing the abstraction.

In hardware, the term object-based refers to the architectural support provided for the abstractions mentioned above. An essential goal in the development of such systems is to provide an efficient execution environment for the software system. Among the commercially available computer systems that provide support for object-based computing are the IBM System/38, [6] the Intel iAPX 432, [7] and the Plessy

---

The Ada language provides constructs to support both data and program abstraction, as well as protection domains.

PP250. [8] Many of the ideas incorporated in the commercial systems were based on the results of several university projects (a good history of this work is given in Levy [9]). The most recent of these projects include Cm* [10] C.mmp, [11] and CAP. [12] A common thread running through all of these machines is the use of capability addressing techniques to implement secure protection domains, which can then be appropriately structured to provide data, program, and device abstractions.

Object-oriented machines are particularly well suited to applications that have stringent requirements for data security and program integrity in a dynamic environment. The high degree of abstraction provided by these machines also facilitates the interconnection of several processors into tightly coupled multiprocessor systems and/or distributed networks. For example, through the use of process/processor abstraction, Intel has achieved software-transparent multiprocessing in their iAPX 432 system. As a further example, Cm* combines both tightly coupled multiprocessing and distributed networking concepts in one system.

As might be expected, the advantages of an object-oriented architec-

ture are not achieved without cost. Present systems rely on some form of capability addressing. In current implementations, these addressing mechanisms greatly increase the address generation and translation times, even when translation "look-aside" and caching schemes are employed. The manipulation of capabilities is also expensive. For example, to copy a capability requires 10 memory references on Cm*, [13] and between two and 12, depending on the addressing mode used, on the iAPX 432.

The Ada language was specifically designed not to require an object-oriented architecture. Virtually all of the support for object-based computing in Ada is static. For example, the type checking required by the Ada language specification may be performed at compile time. Hence, much of the burden for providing error detection and security is placed on the program development system. While this arrangement allows Ada to be targeted for existing "conventional" machines, it also places some restrictions on the flexibility of the language.

Concepts in object-based computing

As noted earlier, abstraction plays a central role in object-based computing. The Ada language provides constructs to support both data and program abstraction, as well as protection domains. Of the two forms of abstraction, data abstraction is the most widely used and understood.

Data abstraction. This term refers to a programming style in which instances of abstract data types are manipulated by operations that are exclusively encapsulated within the protective environment of protection domains. In a definition borrowed from Shaw, [3] an abstract type is defined as a program unit characterized by the following visibility properties:

- *Visible outside of the module containing the type definition*: the name of the type and the names and semantic specifications of all visible operations (procedures and functions) that are permitted to use the representation of the type. Some languages (e.g., Ada) also include formal specifications of the values that variables of this type may assume, and of the properties of these operations.

- *Not visible outside of the module containing the type definition*: the representation of the type in terms of built-in data types or other defined types, the bodies of the visible routines, and hidden routines that may be called only from within the module.

The constructs for implementing abstract data types in Ada are "packages" and "private" (hidden) types.[14] The Ada package effectively places a wall around a group of declarations and permits access only to those declarations that are intended to be visible. Packages actually come in two parts, the specification and the body. The package specification formally specifies the abstract data type and its interface to the outside world, along with other information that may be necessary to enforce type consistency across compilation boundaries (Ada supports the notion of programs that comprise several separate compilation units). The body of the package contains the hidden implementation details.

Consider, for example, the Ada package ROBOT, whose specification is shown in Figure 1. This package can be used to abstract (hide) the implementation details of the type ROBOT_ARM, which has a physical device (a robot arm) associated with it. The operations available for manipulating this device, and even its existence, will be hidden by the abstraction (during program development, the physical robot arm may be represented by simulation code). Thus the applications programmer is freed from having to consider anything other than generating the code necessary to control the actions of an abstract device—the robot arm. Furthermore, the complete logical description of this abstract device is provided by the

package specification, which is delimited by "**package** ROBOT **is**" and "**end** ROBOT;". (Ada reserved words are shown in bold, while user-defined and predefined package names, procedure names, function names, types, and variables are shown in upper case.)

The types defined in the package specification are as follows:

- ROBOT_ARM—the abstracted data type;
- ARM_MODEL—an enumeration type listing all of the robot arm models recognized by this system (two common robot models are shown, ASEA and PUMA); and
- FRAME—a 4×4 matrix that represents a homogeneous transformation. It represents the position and orientation of the hand of the robot arm by indicating the matrix necessary to transform the coordinate system of the base of the arm to the coordinate system in the hand.

The procedures are as follows:

- INITIALIZE_ARM—initializes an instance of the type ROBOT_ARM and moves the arm to a known starting position. The output of the procedure is of type ROBOT_ARM, and the input is of type ARM_MODEL.
- MOVE—takes as input a ROBOT_ARM and a FRAME and moves the arm and its hand to the position and orientation corresponding to the transformation given by FRAME. The updated arm is output, and its "hidden" state is changed to reflect its new position and orientation.
- OPEN and CLOSE control the arm's gripper;
- GET_FRAME is a function that provides controlled access to the hidden state, returning a value of type FRAME.

As noted earlier, the abstracted data type is ROBOT_ARM. It is the intent of the package ROBOT that this type be known only through the subprograms (procedures and functions) mentioned above and declared in the

```
package ROBOT is
   type ROBOT__ARM is limited private;
   type ARM__MODEL is (ASEA, PUMA, . . .);
   type FRAME is array (1..4, 1..4) of FLOAT;

   procedure INITIALIZE__ARM (X: out
      ROBOT __ARM; KIND: in ARM__MODEL);
   procedure MOVE (X: in out ROBOT__ARM;
      DESTINATION: in FRAME);
   procedure OPEN (X: in out ROBOT__ARM);
   procedure CLOSE (X: in out ROBOT__ARM);
   function GET__FRAME (X: ROBOT__ARM)
      return FRAME;

private--not visible
   type ROBOT__ARM is record
      • -- Complete record contains
      • -- component of type FRAME
      • -- and ARM__MODEL
end ROBOT;
```

Figure 1. Specification for the package ROBOT.

visible part of the package specification. The visible or public part of the package specification extends up to the reserved word "private." Hidden from public view within the package body are all of the other procedures, functions, and data structures that are necessary to effect movement of the physical robot arm and to update its representative data structure.

The fact that the type ROBOT_ARM is declared to be "limited private," and that its definition is given in the private part of the package specification, means that while subprograms in packages external to ROBOT may possess an object of the type ROBOT_ARM, they cannot use it in any way other than as a parameter to pass to one of the routines defined in the visible part of the ROBOT package specification. Even tests for equality between two objects of type ROBOT_ARM are not allowed outside of the ROBOT package. Hence, possibilities for programming errors that directly affect the ROBOT_ARM are restricted to the domain defined by the package ROBOT. Moreover, since assignments to limited private types are also not allowed outside of their defining domain, the possibility of having inconsistent representations for the same robot arm (e.g., the logical data structure not reflecting the correct location of the physical robot) is eliminated.

In order to use the ROBOT package, the user program must first create instances of the necessary types in its declarative part, as follows:

```
RBT:     ROBOT.ROBOT__ARM;
ARM:     ROBOT.ARM__MODEL
            : = ASEA;
TRANS:   ROBOT.FRAME;
```

Notice the use of explicit qualification ("ROBOT.") to name the defining domain for the types ROBOT_ARM, ARM_MODEL, and FRAME. This terminology informs the compiler that, for instance, the variable RBT is to be of type ROBOT_ARM, which is defined in the package ROBOT.

In the user program, subprograms from the ROBOT package to initialize and move a robot may be invoked as follows:

```
ROBOT.INITIALIZE__ARM(RBT, ARM);
  • -- compute a value for TRANS,
  • -- the homogeneous transform
  • -- describing
  • -- the movement required.
ROBOT.MOVE(RBT, TRANS);
```

The first parameter for both of the procedure calls, RBT, provides the logical representation of the robot that is to be manipulated. The second parameter of INITIALIZE_ARM specifies that RBT be the logical representation of an ASEA robot. The only way that any operations on the data structure RBT may be performed is by passing it as a parameter to a subprogram that appears in the visible part of the package ROBOT. Even though the user program has full access to the type FRAME, which is a component (not shown) of the limited private type ROBOT_ARM, it still may not directly manipulate the FRAME component of ROBOT_ARM. That is, external packages are prevented from directly manipulating components of hidden record types (private or limited private), regardless of the visibility of the components' types. The data structures, excluding those that are explicitly declared private or limited private, along with the procedures and functions that appear in the public part of the package specification, are directly available for

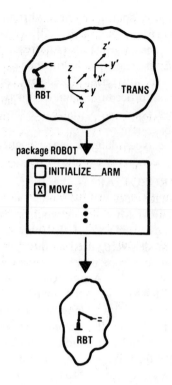

Figure 2. Logical view of data abstraction.

use by packages external to ROBOT. Figure 2 provides a logical conceptualization of how the package ROBOT is used to move an instance of an ASEA robot. The same "black box" package can also be used to move any other valid instance of ROBOT_ARM.

Through the use of packages and private types, the Ada language provides easy-to-use constructs to support data abstraction. As we have seen, data abstraction is a powerful tool for both program development and error confinement. However, it is not the only form of abstraction provided by the Ada language. Program abstraction provides a different and, in some senses, a more powerful conceptual view.

Program abstraction. Programs and subprograms provide another common level of abstraction. Program abstraction enables operations on implicit objects. In addition to hiding the representation of and access to an object, the object's existence is also hidden. The result is a more com-

plete form of hiding and, usually, a more concise interface than data abstraction.

Program abstraction in Ada is realized through generic package or subprogram instantiation. Ada allows the declaration of generic program units that serve as templates for packages or subprograms from which actual pakcages or subprograms can be obtained. Generic program units may have actual parameters that provide instantiation-specific details of the template. These parameters can be data objects, types, or subprograms. Thus, the parameter associations allow generic units to do the following: directly manipulate data objects provided by the user; create and manage data structures or logical devices corresponding to an arbitrary type supplied by the user; and use abstract, instantiation-dependent subprograms made available by the user.

Through their types, the formal parameters specify the expectations that the generic unit makes about the actual parameters that will be supplied by the user of the generic unit at instantiation time. For example, a generic package that manages stacks might have a formal data object parameter of type POSITIVE that indicates the maximum size of the stack. This formal parameter will be matched by any actual parameter whose value at instantiation time is an integer greater than or equal to one. The same generic package may also have a formal type pàrameter of type private that allows the user to specify the type of elements that are to be handled by the instantiation of the stack package. This formal parameter will be matched by any actual parameter for which, at least, the (in)equality tests and assignment are defined; these are the only operations allowed on data objects whose types are private.

Generic formal subprogram parameters, when used, allow the user to provide—or select from a library— subprograms for use within the generic unit. In the case of a generic terminal handler, for instance, subprogram parameters for SEND and RECEIVE procedures would free the programmer from having to accommodate the differing communication protocols that exist for various terminal types. Matching rules for generic formal subprogram parameters are similar to those for nongeneric subprogram parameters. In effect, the generic formal parameters provide a written "contract" between the writer of the generic template and the writer of any program that is designed to use this template. The terms of this contract are rigidly enforced by the type-checking facilities present in the compiler.

Generic units allow a higher level of abstraction than data abstraction, because the abstracted data type may be completely hidden within an instance of the generic package body. The hidden data structure is accessed through internal package variables that are nonlocal to the subprograms within the package. Manipulation of the data structure occurs as a controlled side effect—strictly contained within the package body—of the requested operation. Thus generic units support a programming style in which the specified (visible) operations either directly or indirectly transform a hidden internal state that depends only on past operations applied to the initial state of the system.

The ROBOT package example is repeated in Figure 3 using program abstraction techniques. The external packages are no longer required to supply the type ROBOT_ARM for each operation that they invoke on the arm. Instead, the packages specify the element of the enumeration type ARM_MODEL that corresponds to the arm that they wish to use when they instantiate the generic package ROBOT (the generic package extends from the keyword **generic** to **end** ROBOT;). The generic template is filled in based on the value of the generic formal parameter ARM at the time of instantiation. Hence, the statements:

```
package RBT__ASEA is new ROBOT(ASEA);
package RBT__PUMA is new ROBOT(PUMA);
```

would create instances of the package ROBOT specifically for an ASEA robot and a PUMA robot, respectively. A new instance of the package would be created for each robot in the target system. Recall that in data abstraction, only one instance of the package existed. The logical view of a system consisting of one ASEA robot and one PUMA robot is illustrated in Figure 4.

Implementations for both program and data abstraction require that certain procedure bodies contain conditionally executed code segments to account for the differences between the

```
type ARM__MODEL is (ASEA, PUMA, . . . );
    •
    •
    •
generic
    ARM: ARM__MODEL;
package ROBOT is
    type FRAME is array (1..4, 1..4) of FLOAT;
    procedure MOVE (DESTINATION: in FRAME);
    procedure OPEN;
    procedure CLOSE;
    function GET__FRAME return FRAME;
end ROBOT;
```

Figure 3. Specification for the generic package ROBOT.

numbers of links and the type of joints used in the different robots, and to allow individual robots to communicate with their respective device drivers. An alternative solution available in program abstraction is to add subprogram parameters to the formal part of the generic package. The actual subprograms, which could be made available to the applications programmer in the form of a library, would provide the necessary abstractions for manipulating their corresponding devices. The user would then select the appropriate set of actual parameters for each specific generic instantiation.

The biggest difference between data and program abstraction lies in the program unit that possesses the instance of the abstracted data type. In data abstraction, the type is possessed by a program unit that is external to the unit that manages the type; hence, the unit that manages the type is commonly referred to as an external type manager. In program abstraction, the type is maintained within the unit that manages it; hence, the managing unit is commonly referred to as an internal type manager. External type managers

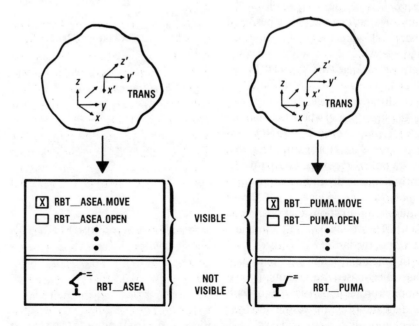

Figure 4. Logical view of program abstraction.

119

support a functional programming style in which the type to be manipulated is passed as a parameter to a subprogram that performs its operation without side effects.

The chief advantage of this programming style is that it can be modeled more readily using well-known mathematical techniques, thus opening up greater possiblilities for correctness proof methods. In Ada, it is also the case that data objects created at run-time by the dynamic instantiation of types can be handled by external type managers, whereas the instantiation of internal type managers and the creation of their enclosed data objects is static—that is, it must occur at compile time. It can be argued, however, that internal type managers provide a much more realistic model of the real-world objects that the computer program is meant to manipulate, and that the protection against errors both at run-time and during program development is much greater. Non-generic packages may also function as internal type managers. However, in doing so, generality is lost, since the abstraction would be available for only one instance.

Intel has provided a powerful extention to the Ada language for the iAPX 432 processor that allows the programming of dynamic internal type managers. This has been accomplished by allowing packages to be types, and hence, allowing them to assume assignable values. For example, we could define a package type ROBOT (Figure 5), create instances of ROBOT for each different physical robot·(Figure 6), declare an array whose elements are instances of the package type ROBOT, and then, during program execution, assign values (package bodies) to the array elements depending upon which robots we use (see Figure 7). The procedures and functions that operate on ROBOTS are invoked in the manner shown in the last line of Figure 7.

In Smalltalk, a language that takes the object-based programming philosophy further than Ada, the concepts of data and program abstraction have been rationalized so that objects are all treated alike, regardless of whether the objects represent program modules or data structures.[15] It has been proposed that these concepts be merged together in Ada as well.[4,16] In fact, Intel has already taken an initial step in this direction with their "package type" extension to the Ada language mentioned above.[17] Extensions such as package types and those described in Wegner[4] and Jessop[16] combine the dynamic flexibility of data abstraction with the conceptual and protection benefits of program abstraction, resulting in a powerful universal abstraction mechanism. The availability of such a mechanism relieves the software designer of the restrictive choice between adopting a program-oriented or data-oriented software design methodology—a choice that must occur very early in the design process.

Protection domains. Protection domains, and the inherent security that they provide, constitute another key concept. The basis for secure, error-tolerant execution environments lies in the principle of system closure.[5] This principle states that the effects of all operations on a closed system shall re-

```
package type ROBOT is
    type FRAME is array (1..4, 1..4) of FLOAT;
    procedure MOVE (DESTINATION: in FRAME);
    procedure OPEN;
    procedure CLOSE;
    function GET__FRAME return FRAME;
end ROBOT;
```

Figure 5. A package type.

```
package RBT__ASEA is constant ROBOT;
package body RBT__ASEA is
    •
    •
    •
end RBT__ASEA;

package RBT__PUMA is constant ROBOT;
package body RBT__PUMA is
    •
    •
    •
end RBT__PUMA;
```

Figure 6. Instances of package types.

main strictly within that system. One common construct used for providing system closure is the protection domain.[18] Briefly stated, a protection domain is an environment or context that defines the set of access rights and operations that are currently available to a specific user for objects contained within the domain. The concepts embodied in protection domains are similar to those underlying Ada packages.

Protection domain schemes generally provide facilities for error confinement, error detection and categorization, reconfiguration, and restarting. Error confinement and security strategies generally involve both process isolation and resource control. The basic premise of process isolation is that processes are given only the capabilities necessary to complete their required tasks. By implication, any interactions with external objects (e.g., sending messages to other processes) must be strictly formalized and controlled. Resource control refers to the binding of physical resource units to computational objects. Examples include the binding of processes to processors, or the assignment of memory to currently executing contexts.

These controls ensure that when the resource units are released or preempted, all of the information contained within the unit is returned to a null state. Information is thus prevented from "leaking" out of a protection domain, even if it is left in an area that eventually becomes accessible to other users. Error confinement also aids the program debugging process, since bugs will be located in modules where errors are detected. Program maintenance benefits as well, since the protection domain defines the maximal set of modules that can be affected by modifying the system. Error detection and categorization involves dynamic checking for object type inconsistencies and access constraint violations during procedure execution. The categorization of detected errors can then be used to aid in restoring the system to a known state. Reconfiguration facilities attempt to restore the system to an operable state by removing the failed component—hardware or software. If the reconfiguration attempt is successful, the system is restarted.

Perhaps the most elegant mechanism for implementing protection domains is capability addressing. While much can be done at compile time in languages such as Ada to enforce the concept of protection domains, there

```
declare
    type ROBOT__ARRAY is array (1 . . LAST)
      of ROBOT;
    ROBOTS: ROBOT__ARRAY;
    NEW__POSITION: FRAME;

begin
    case ARM is
        when ASEA   = >
            ROBOTS(I) : = RBT__ASEA;
        when PUMA   = >
            ROBOTS(I) : = RBT__PUMA;
            •
            •
            •
    end case;

    ROBOTS(I).MOVE(NEW__POSITION);
        •
        •
        •
```

Figure 7. Assignment of package type.

are many cases where the dynamic enforcement of access rights provided by capability addressing is useful. As an example, consider a system in which it is desirable to grant different rights (perhaps the ability to invoke a different set of operations) to the various users of a given object based on information presented at run-time. Capability addressing permits users to dynamically determine whether they have indeed been granted the right to perform a requested operation. Determinations such as this are not possible at compile time. Compile-time protection enforcement also lacks the ability to support the detection of and recovery from access failures in the run-time system.

A capability can be thought of as the name of an object. An object cannot be accessed—nor its existence determined—unless its name is known. The capability also contains the access rights to the object (e.g., read, write, or capability copy rights; see Figure 8). The only subsequent modification allowed outside of the domain in which the capability is defined is the restriction of these rights. Capabilities are created along with their respective

objects. The initial control of the capability, and hence of the object, belongs solely to the defining domain. Consider the case of a user—**package USER** in Figure 8—that selects the package ROBOT of Figure 1 in a system employing capability addressing. The defining domain for a variable of type ROBOT_ARM is ROBOT. In the case of pass-by-reference parameter association, the rights of the capability given to the instantiating context are restricted to "copy" because ROBOT_ARM is a limited private type. Within the defining domain, the capabilities may be amplified as needed. For example, a variable of type ROBOT_ARM is passed as a parameter to both the MOVE and GET_ FRAME procedures. In the case of MOVE, ROBOT_ARM is a parameter of mode **in out,** requiring both read and write rights. In case of GET_FRAME, ROBOT_ARM is an **in** parameter, and thus requires only read rights.

The use of capabilities is not dependent on the particular method of parameter association used. Rather, in the case of paramaters passed by reference, the capability is amplified at the

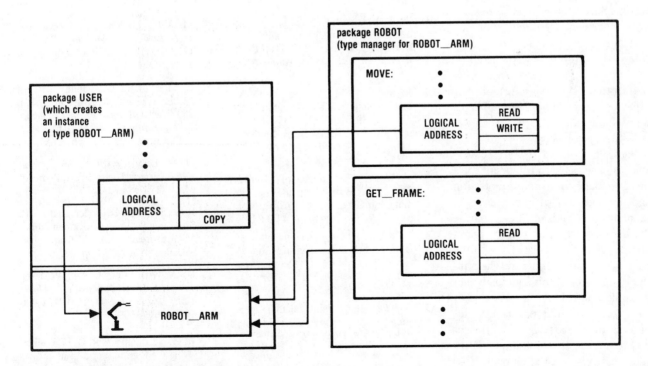

Figure 8. Capabilities and protection domains.

subprogram interface to allow the appropriate access rights. This is permitted because amplification occurs within the defining domain for the parameter type. In the case of parameters passed by value, the new instance of the parameter type is created with the appropriate access rights, and the parameter values are then copied—again, this is permitted since it also occurs within the defining domain.

Though the Ada language specifically avoids any mention of capability addressing, constructs that support many of the concepts embodied in protection domains are provided. They include packages and private types, and their associated compile-time type checking and exception handlers. The latter permit users to detect and categorize errors, and to reconfigure and restart the system. Protection domain concepts such as the control of information "leakage" lie below what is normally considered to be the language level. The major shortcoming of Ada with respect to support for protection domains lies in the fact that all users of objects external to the defining domain are treated equally. That is, Ada provides an "all or none" type of protection mechanism. A possible extension to Ada that would address this problem is to allow both package types and subtypes. Package subtypes would permit access to a discrete subset of the operations and types that are found in the visible part of the package specification,[16] in effect creating a limited form of capability that would be applicable only to Ada package objects.

Package subtypes strike a reasonable balance between the desire for a fine granularity of dynamic protection and the high cost of implementing a capability mechanism. They also have the desirable characteristic of maintaining semantic consistency with the existing language definition. The principal limitation of this solution is that dynamic control of the visibility of package types/subtypes is not addressed. In this case, the most efficient way to address this limitation and ensure security is to require support from the underlying hardware.

Ada provides good support for both data and program abstraction. However, in an effort to allow Ada to be used efficiently on existing machines with conventional architectures, the language has been designed to require little dynamic checking. This effect is most noticeable in the limited support provided for protection domains and the lack of a unified abstraction mechanism that would include features such as package types. However, these features are usually not required in the application area for which Ada was primarily targeted—embedded systems. Current embedded systems typically have many static attributes: configurations are not modified at run-time; program implementations are not changed; and devices are not taken on- and off-line. Hence, within its intended application area, the Ada language is suitable for object-based computing on conventional architectures. □

References

1. R. A. Volz and T. N. Mudge, "Robots are (Nothing More Than) Abstract Data Types," *Proc. SME Conference on Robotics Research,* Aug. 1984.

2. R. A. Volz, T. N. Mudge, and D. A. Gal, "Using Ada as a Programming Language for Robot-based Manufacturing Cells," *IEEE Trans. Systems, Man, and Cybernetics,* Nov./Dec. 1984 (to appear).

3. M. Shaw, "The Impact of Abstraction Concerns on Modular Programming Languages," *Proc. IEEE,* Vol. 68, No. 9, Sept. 1980, pp. 1119-1130.

4. P. Wegner, "On the Unification of Data and Program Abstraction in Ada," *10th Annual ACM Symp. Principles of Programming Languages,* Jan. 1983, pp. 256-264.

5. P. J. Denning, "Fault Tolerant Operating Systems," *Computing Surveys,* Vol. 8, No. 4, Dec. 1976, pp. 359-389.

6. *IBM System/38 Functional Concepts Manual,* GA21-9330-1, IBM Corporation, Rochester, Minn., 1982.

7. *iAPX 432 General Data Processor Architecture Ref. Manual,* Rev. 3, 171860-003, Intel Corporation, Santa Clara, Calif., 1983.

8. D. M. England, "Capability Concept Mechanism and Structure in System 250," *Int'l Workshop on Protection in Operating Systems,* IRIA, Rocquencourt, Aug. 1974, pp. 63-82.

9. H. M. Levy, *Capability-based Computer Systems,* Digital Press, Bedford, Mass., 1983.

10. R. J. Swan, S. H. Fuller, and D. P. Siewiorek, "Cm*: A Modular Multi-Microprocessor," *AFIPS Conf. Proc.* Vol. 46, 1977, NCC, pp. 637-643.

11. W. A. Wulf and C. G. Bell, "C.mmp—A Multi-Mini-Processor," *AFIPS Conf. Proc.,* Vol. 41, Part II, FJCC 1972, pp. 765-777.

12. R. H. Needham and R. D. H. Walker, "The CAP computer and its protection system," *ACM Sixth Symp. Operating System Principles,* 1977.

13. A. K. Jones and E. F. Gehringer, eds., "The Cm* Multiprocessor Project: A Research Review," Carnegie-Mellon University Report CMU-CS-80-131, Department of Computer Science, July 1980.

14. J. G. P. Barnes, *Programming in Ada,* 2nd ed., Addison-Wesley, London, 1984.

15. A. Goldberg and D. Robson, *Smalltalk-80: The Language and its Implementation,* Addison-Wesley, Reading, Mass., 1983.

16. W. H. Jessop, "Ada Packages and Distributed Systems,"*Sigplan Notices,* Vol. 17, No. 2, Feb. 1982, pp. 28-36.

17. *Reference Manual for the Intel 432 Extensions to Ada,*172283-001, Intel Corporation, Santa Clara, Calif., 1981.

18. T. A. Linden, "Operating System Structures to Support Security and Reliable Software," *Comp. Surveys,* Vol. 8, No. 4, Dec. 1976, pp. 409-445.

Gregory D. Buzzard received the BS and MS degrees in electrical engineering from the University of Michigan, Ann Arbor, in 1981 and 1982, respectively. He is currently pursuing the PhD in electrical engineering in the area of architectural support for inter-task communication in distributed systems.

Buzzard is a Kodak Fellow and a member of the University's Robotics Research Laboratory. He is also a member of Eta Kappa Nu, Tau Beta Pi, ACM and the IEEE Computer Society.

Trevor Mudge received the BSc degree in cybernetics from the University of Reading, England, in 1969, and the MS and PhD degrees in computer science from the University of Illinois, Urbana, in 1973 and 1977, respectively. He has been with the Department of Electrical Engineering and Computer Science at the University of Michigan since 1977 and currently holds the rank of associate professor. His research interests include computer architecture, programming languages, VLSI design, and computer vision.

Questions concerning this article can be addressed to the authors at the Center for Robotics and Integrated Manufacturing, University of Michigan, 2514 E. Engineering Bldg., Ann Arbor, MI 48109.

On the Unification of Data
and Program Abstraction in Ada

Peter Wegner

Department of Computer Science
Brown University
Box 1910
Providence, RI 02912

Abstract Ada is rich in the variety of its abstraction mechanisms. It has both a data abstraction mechanism (packages with private data types) that supports a functional programming style and a program abstraction mechanism (generic program units) that supports an object-oriented program style. Tradeoffs between data and program abstraction are examined and it is pointed out that Ada discourages program abstraction because program units are not first-class objects. It is shown how program units could be made into first-class objects by introducing closures as values for functions and records with function components as values for packages. Further unification by allowing types to be first-class objects conflicts with the requirement of compile-time type invariance. The relaxation of this requirement in a manner that preserves type consistency is examined and leads to a notion of value for types as tuples of operations. It is suggested in the conclusion that our understanding of abstraction for object-oriented languages and of other language design, implementation, and environment issues will have progressed sufficiently by 1985 to warrant the design of a successor to Ada by the late 1980s.

Structured Entities

Records in Ada are a mechanism for defining structures with data components, while packages are a mechanism for defining structures with both program and data components. The similarity of the declaration and instantiation mechanism for records and packages is illustrated below for a record type and a generic package with identical components.

Example 1: Record Types and Generic Packages

```
type PERSON_RECORD is    -- type declaration
  record
    HEIGHT, WEIGHT: FLOAT;
    MARRIED: BOOLEAN;
    CHILDREN: INTEGER;
  end record;

R: PERSON_RECORD;        -- object declaration
```

This work was supported in part by ONR contract N00014-78C-0656.

"On the Unification of Data and Program Abstraction in Ada" by P. Wegner from *Proceedings of the 10th Annual ACM Symposium on Principles of Programming Languages*, 1983, pages 256–264. Copyright 1983, Association for Computing Machinery, Inc., reprinted by permission.

```
generic                  -- generic package declaration
package PERSON_PACKAGE is
  HEIGHT, WEIGHT: FLOAT;
  MARRIED: BOOLEAN;
  CHILDREN: INTEGER;
end

package P is new PERSON_PACKAGE;    -- instantiation
```

The object declaration mechanism for creating a record object R of the type PERSON_RECORD is similar to the generic instantiation mechanism for instantiating a package P of the type PERSON_PACKAGE. This similarity is emphasized by making the record object R and the package P have components of identical name and type. It is further underlined by the fact that both records and packages use the dot notation for component accessing.

Example 2: Component Accessing for Objects and Packages

```
R.HEIGHT := R.HEIGHT + 1;
P.HEIGHT := P.HEIGHT + 1;
```

In spite of these similarities, record objects and packages in Ada have very different properties, as illustrated by the following tabular comparison:

Example 3: Attributes of Record Objects and Packages

	have a type
	are "created" by declarations
	components must be typed objects
record	may be values of variables
objects	may be passed as a parameter
	may be component of a record or array
	may be component of a list (access value)
	have a visible specification
	may be "created" by generic instantiation
	components include types, program units
packages	cannot be values of variables
	cannot be passed as a parameter
	may have generic parameters
	may have a hidden body

Records may be assigned and passed as parameters and may occur as components of arrays and records. Packages are not typed objects and cannot be assigned or passed as parameters or appear as components of structured objects. However, packages may have richer components and more powerful forms of parameterization than records. Record components are restricted to be typed objects while package components may include types, subprogram specifications and package specifications. Record parameterization is restricted to discriminants of a discrete type. Generic packages have a compile-time parameterization mechanism richer than that for subprograms which allows types and subprograms to be generic parameters.

Let's examine the nature of the notion of type. A type has type-dependent attributes such as integers and type-independent attributes such as declaration, parameter passing and assignment applicable to all types. Specific types of a programming language are generally defined in terms of type-dependent attributes. Type-independent attributes are not considered to be part of the type definition but part of the language definition. Their specification is distributed in other parts of a language manual, such as the section on assignment, parameter passing, etc. However, in examining the nature of the notion of type we must concentrate on type-independent attributes. The attributes mentioned in example 3 are all type-independent.

In its attempt to be conservative (safe) Ada has not permitted packages (or subprograms) to be declared or passed as parameters, or to have other attributes of types. The mechanisms and attributes for declaring and instantiating typed objects and program units are entirely separate. However, attributes such as declaration, instantiation, having components, being components of structures, having parameters, or being passed as parameters do not depend on whether an entity is a data or a program structure. Even the property of being assignable as the value of a variable can be extended from typed objects to program units if the proper notion of the value of a variable is introduced, as is the case in languages like Russell [4] or ML [2].

We shall explore mechanisms for the unification of typed objects and program units. Before doing so, however, some of the ways in which dual language mechanisms for data and program abstraction give rise to complexity in current Ada will be examined.

Data and Program Abstraction

Abstraction is concerned with specifying relevant attributes of a class of objects, situations or processes and ignoring (hiding) irrelevant attributes. Different forms of abstraction are concerned with different ways of specifying relevant attributes and hiding irrelevant attributes. We are concerned with providing users of an abstraction with operations on a data object while hiding its data representation. Ada provides two abstraction mechanisms for hiding data representations that are respectively related to the type and generic mechanisms.

(1) Data abstraction which provides the user with a "private" (hidden) type and operations on objects of the type.

(2) Program abstraction which provides operations on an object whose representation and identity is hidden from the user. Program abstraction provides a stronger form of hiding than data abstraction since the identity as well as the representation of the object is hidden from the user.

Queues will be used as a running example to illustrate language design and programming methodology issues which arise in comparing data and program abstraction mechanisms. Queues may be abstractly defined by a set of operations such as **APPEND** and **REMOVE** which capture the first-in first-out behavior of queue elements. They may be realized in Ada either as packages with private types which allow the user to create queue objects and operate upon them using package operations, or as generic packages whose instantiations contain queue operations in the interface specification.

Example 4: Data Versus Object Abstraction

```
package QP is              -- QP is an abstract data type
  type QUEUE is private;
  operations on queue
private
  -- representation of queue
  -- hidden from user but visible to the compiler
end QP;


P,Q:QUEUE;                 -- object declaration


generic                    -- QG is a generic package
  -- generic formal parameters
package QG is
  operations on queue
end QG;


package R is new QG(actual-parameters);   -- instantiation
```

The package **QP** is a data abstraction whose operations are shared by objects P,Q of the type **QUEUE** created by users of the package. The generic package **QG** represents an entirely different view of queue abstractions, identifying the queue with a set of operations and eliminating the need for a queue type with an identity separate from that of the operations. Creation of objects which share a set of operations is replaced by creation of packages which determine a set of operations. Generic packages are program abstractions since they determine a template for a package rather than for a data object.

Queue data objects such as P may have values assignable to other variables Q of the same type and may be passed as parameters of procedures. The package instance R provides the user with queue operations but cannot be assigned or passed as a parameter. On the other hand, generic packages may have type parameters so that queues of integers and of messages can be instantiated from the same generic template. The generic package has a more powerful instantiation mechanism than the abstract data type but less powerful facilities for manipulating instances.

The above tradeoffs between data and as program abstraction are determined by language-imposed properties of Ada rather than by intrinsic differences between methods of abstraction. The proposed unification of objects and program units would eliminate artificial restrictions such as the inability to pass packages as parameters or to parameterize types, and would allow the use of abstract entities as values and parameters independently of idiosyncratic language restrictions.

The full specification for **QP** includes procedures for appending and removing queue elements, functions for testing if the queue is full or empty, and exceptions which are raised when the user attempts to append to a full queue or remove from an empty queue.

Example 5: Hiding the Representation of Queues

```
package QP is
  type QUEUE(MAX: NATURAL := 100) is limited private;

  procedure APPEND(Q: in out QUEUE; E: in INTEGER);
  procedure REMOVE(Q: in out QUEUE; E: out INTEGER);
  function IS_FULL(Q: in QUEUE) return BOOLEAN;
  function IS_EMPTY(Q: in QUEUE) return BOOLEAN;
  FULL, EMPTY: exception;

private
  type QUEUE( MAX: NATURAL := 100) is
    record
      FIRST, LAST: INTEGER := 1;
      COUNT: INTEGER := 0;
      ELEMENTS: array(1..MAX) of INTEGER;
    end record;
end QP;

package body QP is
  -- bodies of APPEND, REMOVE, IS_FULL, IS_EMPTY
end;

P: QUEUE(50);
```

The corresponding generic package has a simpler interface than the abstract data type because the type name need not be specified and the data structure for queues is buried in the body of the package.

Example 6: A Package which is a Queue

```
generic
  type ELEMENT is private;
  SIZE: INTEGER := 100;
package QG is
  procedure APPEND(E: in ELEMENT);
  procedure REMOVE(E: out ELEMENT);
  function IS_FULL return BOOLEAN;
  function IS_EMPTY return BOOLEAN;
  FULL, EMPTY: exception;
end QG;

package body QG is
  -- contains local definition of queue data structure
  -- and the bodies of package operations
  -- which have side effects on the queue
  -- through non-local variables
end QG;

package Q is new QG(INTEGER, 50);
```

Generic packages not only have a simpler interface. They also have a simpler calling sequence, since the queue is a local data structure of the generic queue package and an explicit parameter of abstract data type operations.

Example 7: Comparison of User Calls

```
Q.APPEND(E);        -- call of APPEND in generic package
QP.APPEND(Q,E);     -- call of APPEND in abstract data type
```

Simpler interfaces and simpler user calling sequences are two intrinsic advantages of generic instantiation over data abstraction. This simplicity must be balanced against the fact that APPEND and REMOVE procedures of the generic abstraction achieve simplicity of the interface through hidden side effects on the local queue data structure. We shall see below that generic abstraction represents an object-oriented programming style while data abstraction represents a functional programming style. Comparison of these two programming styles for this particular example provides insight into general tradeoffs between functional and object-oriented programming.

Functional versus Object-Oriented Programming

Abstract data types require users to create queue objects, to manage storage for queue objects, and to pass them as parameters to queue operations. Generic packages represent a higher level of abstraction because they completely hide the queue data structure in the body of the package and implement shared access to the hidden data structure by non-local variables of queue operations whose side effects are strictly contained within the package body.

Example 8: Parameters versus Shared Data Structures

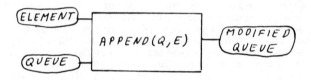

a) Abstract Data Types and Functional Programming

b) Generic Abstraction and Object-Oriented Programming

Abstract data types conceptually realize APPEND by passing the queue and the element to the procedure and returning the modified queue as a result. Generic abstractions share the queue data structure among package operations using non-local variables (such as Q above) as the sharing mechanism. Abstract data types support a "functional programming" style using functions that have no side effects, while generic abstraction supports an "object oriented" programming style in which queue operations transform a hidden internal state that depends on the history of the operations applied to the initial state of the queue.

Functional programming has the advantage that programs are mathematically tractable and more easily verifiable. There are no restrictions on the order of evaluation, and lazy evaluation that delays evaluation until its value is needed can be performed. Object-oriented programming achieves greater abstraction by hiding the data as an internal state, may provide a more realistic model of real world objects (which often hide an updatable internal state under a deceptively simple interface). Moreover, object abstractions can be more efficiently implemented on a Von Neumann machine than corresponding function abstractions.

Since object-oriented programming is better for users and for executing on a computer the user language and machine language should probably be object-oriented. Since functional programs are better for verification and optimization, we should consider compiling object-oriented source programs into equivalent functional programs for verification and optimization, and then transforming them back into an object-oriented form for execution. The equivalence between functional programs of the form 8a) and object-oriented programs of the form 8b) holds only under very restricted conditions in the absence of sharing. But the attempt to explore such equivalence could lead to insights concerning the conditions under which object-oriented programming is equivalent to functional programming.

The proposed transformation from high-level object-oriented programs to lower level functional programs suggests that mathematical notation should be regarded as an assembly language suitable for automating proofs and performing optimization rather than a high-level language appropriate for modelling real-world problems. This accords with the fact that complete mathematical rigor may obscure fundamental concepts by excessive attention to detail.

The queue example illustrates that functional programming achieves its simplicity by greatly increasing the volume of parametric information (messages) when functions are called and when values are returned. This extra information must be managed in the environment of the function, so that simplicity at one level is achieved by "irresponsibly" passing the buck to the next level. This contrasts with the object-oriented (generic) approach where state information is carefully managed within the abstraction itself and full responsibility is exercised over accessing and sharing the local data.

The essence of packages is their ability to define a local data structure (an internal state) that is shared by non-local variables of its subprograms. Program abstraction encourages the use of subprograms with non-local variables within packages. This violation of the accepted wisdom that functions should not have side effects or non-local variables must be balanced against the fact that such variables not only increase efficiency but increase the level of abstraction by allowing side effects on the local state.

Side effects have traditionally been considered harmful. The present discussion illustrates that side effects are a necessary mechanism for information hiding. They allow a subprogram to have effects that are hidden from the user which change the "internal" system state and affect the future behavior of the system.

Controlled side effects that affect future system behavior are desirable and natural in many practical situations. Depositing money in a bank account is an example of a transaction in which a side effect that affects future behavior of the system is desired. Flexibility of human behavior is possible only because past experiences have side effects that affect future behavior. Pure functions are constrained to have the same behavior every time they are called with given inputs, while functions with controlled side effects can can cause desired changes in a local environment and adapt their behavior to changing circumstances.

The partition between parameters and non-local variables in a subprogram thus reflects a desirable partition between external communication for interaction with its users and internal communication with other components of a subsystem that provide a desired service for the user.

Programmers designing large programs with many hundreds of modules must choose between data and program abstraction as a basis for module design. In current Ada instances of data abstractions may be manipulated as first-class objects while generic instances may be used but not manipulated. The designers of Ada clearly envisaged data abstraction to be the primary abstraction mechanism. However, abstractions consisting of a collection of operation without an associated type appear to be simpler and higher-level than data abstractions. The fact that programmers are penalized in defining such abstractions is certainly undesirable. However, in fairness to Ada it should be pointed out that the ability to define such abstractions at all is an improvement over previous languages.

The Hybrid Status of Tasks

Tasks in Ada have a hybrid status in that they are both program units and typed objects. They are program units in the sense that they have separate specifications and bodies. However, they may be declared as types from which objects are created by object declarations. A task type QUEUE with a body common to all objects of the task type, and an associated object declaration Q of the type QUEUE can be specified as follows:

Example 9: Task Types and Task Objects

```
task type QUEUE is       -- task type specification
  entry APPEND(E: in INTEGER);
  entry REMOVE(E: out INTEGER);
end;

task body Q is ...

Q: QUEUE;                -- task object of the type queue
```

Tasks can specify only entry points in their interface and cannot directly support "concurrent data abstractions" which export a type to users. Queues (buffers) shared by concurrently executing tasks are realized by "object-oriented" abstractions with a shared state in the task body. This is appropriate since sharing of the queue buffer by the competing tasks is generally the appropriate semantics, and simulation of such sharing by an an abstract data type that relies on passing the queue data structure from users to the queueing task and returning the modified queue to the user would be difficult.

Objects of a task type may be passed as parameters and appear as components of structured objects and as elements of lists. However they are not "first-class" objects because they do not have values which can be tested for equality or assigned as values of task variables. Moreover, they are not "first-class" program units for the following reasons:

(1) Task specifications may specify only entry points while package specifications may specify a wide variety of computational resources.

(2) Tasks cannot be made generic or have generic parameters. The type mechanism rather than the generic mechanism is used to define task templates so that objects created from the template can be passed as parameters.

In order to achieve the effect of generic parameters for tasks it is necessary to embed them in a package.

127

Example 10: Embedding Tasks in Generic Packages

```
generic
  type ELEMENT is private;
package QG is
  task QT is
    entry APPEND(E: in ELEMENT);
    entry REMOVE(E: out ELEMENT);
  end;
end;

package Q is new QG(INTEGER);
```

The instance **Q** of the generic package **QG** contains a task for concurrently appending and removing elements from a queue whose data structure is defined local to the task body (in the associated package body). This construction is clearly clumsy and reflects the fact that tasks were not designed to be general user interfaces. The user interface for concurrent queues can be better modelled by packages containing procedure calls to **APPEND** and **REMOVE** which result in concurrent calls to a task whose specification and body is defined entirely within the package body.

The dual status of tasks as both objects and program units reflects the fact that the language designers first conceived of tasks as program units, and then allowed them to be typed objects so that they could be dynamically created, passed as parameters, and appear as components of lists and structures. This has strange consequences such as the fact that a subprogram can be passed as a parameter only if it is defined to be concurrent. The task construct is unsatisfactory because it contravenes the esthetics of the language design and because tasks are second-class entities, both as objects and as program units. One of the consequences of the second-class status of tasks is that they cannot compete with packages as vehicles for interface specification and may require a package interface as in the above example.

Thus we see that the duality between objects and program units in Ada leads to design complications when introducing new language constructs which have both program and data attributes.

Program Units as First-Class Objects

Packages in Ada provide a collection of resources to users of the package which are specified in the package specification and implemented in the package body.

Example 11: Structure of Package Specifications

```
package KITCHEN_SINK is
  resource 1            -- resources may include
  resource 2            -- subprograms
  ...                   -- types
  resource N            -- variables (typed objects)
end KITCHEN_SINK;       -- packages, tasks, exceptions

package body KITCHEN_SINK is
  implementation of resources
end
```

The resources provided by a package may in general include subprograms, types, typed objects, packages, tasks and exceptions. The set of resources permitted in a package may well be richer than is necessary for good programming style. In particular, variables (typed objects) should perhaps be excluded from the package interface. This would allow a package to be viewed consistently as an entity with a hidden internal state rather than as an entity whose state is partly hidden in the package body and partly visible in typed variables of the package specification. However the view of packages as a collection of operations on a shared hidden data structure is narrower than that of packages as an arbitrary collection of resources, and the question of whether the narrower view significantly restricts expressive power needs further study.

Packages are an "object-oriented" language construct in the sense that they may be used to define objects whose behavior is characterized by a set of operations on a common hidden data structure. However packages are not "first-class" objects in the sense that they cannot be assigned as values of variables, cannot be passed as parameters, and cannot appear as components of structures or lists. This inconsistency between declarative power and manipulation ability for packages is a basic flaw of Ada. It has caused extensive debate concerning the degree to which Ada is an object-oriented language.

The design decision to make packages "second-class" objects was made because it was felt that design and implementation of packages as as first-class objects was beyond the state of the art. However, advances in our understanding of object-oriented language design and implementation in the last decade provide a basis for designing an integrated Ada-like object-oriented language in which language constructs such as packages are first-class objects.

The key to unification of records and packages is making functions into first-class objects. Let's assume that we have a notion of "value" for functions, so that functions can be assigned, passed as a parameter, returned as a function value, and be a component of a record or array. Package values may then be defined in terms of function values as records with function-valued components.

In the example below we introduce the neutral keyword "tuple" to denote a structure with components and indicate that records may be viewed as tuples of field names and packages may be viewed as tuples of resource specifications.

Example 12: Record and Package Values

```
tuple (field1, field2, ..., fieldN);
  -- a record value is a tuple of fields

tuple (resource1, resource2, ..., resourceN);
  -- a package value is a tuple of resources
```

Record and package types may be uniformly defined in terms of functions which return a tuple as their value. A functional specification of record and package types in an Ada-style syntax is given below:

Example 13: Record and Package Types

a) Record Tuples

type RTYPE is   -- function that produces tuple of fields
 tuple (field1, field2, ... , fieldN);

R: RTYPE;   -- call function RTYPE, assign value to R

b) Package Tuples

type PTYPE is -- function that produces tuple of resources
 use (body of package) in
  tuple (resource1, resource2, ... , resourceN);

P: PTYPE;   -- call function PTYPE, assign value to P

Both records and packages are defined above as tuples whose components may be accessed by selectors. In the case of records the action when a component has been selected is always access to a named field. In the case of packages the action is determined by a programmer-defined specification in the package body that may involve manipulation of a hidden local data structure. The action for record components such as **R.field1** is determined by the system while the action for package components such as **P.resource1** may be specified by the programmer. The role of the package body is to allow the programmer to define the actions to be performed when components of the package specification are selected. A record may be viewed as a degenerate package specification with an empty body that causes components to have a default system-defined interpretation in terms of read and write operations.

Now that we have seen how subprogram values may be used in defining package values, we shall review how subprogram values may be defined in terms of closures. A closure consists of a representation of the subprogram body together with an environment specification for interpreting its non-local variables. The closure of a subprogram **APPEND** with a non-local variable that refers to a shared queue data structure has the following form:

Example 14: Format for Subprogram Closures

closure
 = (subprogram body, identifier-value pairs)
 = (body of APPEND, <"Q", pointer to queue>)

The generic package of example 8 has the following form in our notation:

Example 15: Generic Queue Type

type QG is
 use(APPEND, REMOVE, initialized queue) in
  tuple (specification of QG);

Q: QG;   -- creates instance of QG called Q

Elaboration of the declaration **Q: QG;** causes a "value" for the package **Q** to be created consisting of an initially empty queue data structure and closures of package procedures such as **APPEND** and **REMOVE** with bindings of their non-local variables to the local queue data structure. Calls such as **Q.APPEND(E);** by the user append the element E to the queue specified by the binding of non-local variables of **Q.APPEND.**

Closures allow non-local variables in a subprogram definition to be statically bound to the environment in which the subprogram declaration is elaborated so that they are independent of the environment in which the subprogram is executed. They provide an operational model for subprogram values that may be used as a basis for designing abstract machines for languages having subprograms as first-class values. An extended abstract machine for languages with packages as first-class values may then be defined using the definition of packages in terms of subprogram closures. The ability to define a simple abstract machine which embodies the operational semantics of languages we are trying to design is a key to simplicity of the associated programming language.

The interdependence of resources in a package is reflected in the fact that the collection of closures representing package resources refer to shared resources hidden from the user and accessible only to resources within the package. The operational model of hiding and sharing in terms of an interdependent collection of closures deserves further study and may come to play a central role as a semantic foundation for object-oriented programming. Once the basic model is understood, variants that allow access control, adding and deleting resources, multiple views that share the same hidden resources, and concurrent and distributed processing for hidden resources may be considered.

Ada permits the specification and body of subprograms and packages to be separately compiled. The operational implications of separate compilation will be briefly considered. Separate compilation for packages requires that the specification contain sufficient information for the user to write synactically correct calls on package resources and for the compiler to check the type-correctness of such calls. Separately compiled bodies may be indicated in our notation as follows:

Example 16: Package Types with Separate Bodies

type QG is
 separate (body of QG) in
  tuple (specification of QG);

Q: QG;

Separate compilation of bodies requires careful partitioning between the information needed to invoke resources of a package and that needed during execution of such resources. Once this separation is understood the provision of separate compilation facilities is straightforward. There may however be tradeoffs between information and efficiency. One such tradeoff arises in connection with the Ada requirement that the data representation for private data types be included in the specification. This information belongs logically in the package body since it is an implementation detail. It was included in the package specification because it was felt by the designers that the compiler needed this information to make compile-time decisions about storage allocation. This dilemma arises because abstract data types require storage for user-created abstract data objects to be managed in the user environment, and does not arise at all for object-oriented abstractions which remove this burden from the user.

The term "entity" will be used to refer to the extended notion of type resulting from the unification of types and program units. The set of attributes permitted for entities should be a union of those associated with types and program units in current Ada.

Example 17: Attributes of Entities

	has a type which determines operations
	is created by declarations
	may have components
	may be components (of arrays, records)
attributes	may be access values (of lists)
of	may have parameters
entities	may be parameters, returned as values
	may be assigned as values of variables
	may be tested for equality
	may have a hidden body

The proposed unification requires a generalization of the notion of value so that subprograms have closures as their values and package values are tuples of resources whose interpretation is determined by the package body. This generalization of the notion of value requires partial abandonment of the activation-record-stack run-time environment, and might result in a penalty in execution-time efficiency. But with careful design of the run-time environment and hardware-supported garbage collection these penalties would be acceptable. It is expected that object-oriented computers of the future will have built-in on-the-fly garbage collection that will greatly reduce the execution-time penalty of having a heap. Moreover, the user who uses only values that do not violate the stack discipline would be able to run as efficiently as in current Ada.

The proposed changes would result in an "object-oriented language" with the notion of entities with values playing a central semantic role. The language would be simpler because redundant concepts and mechanisms would disappear and confusing non-uniformities in abstraction parameterization and accessing for data and program structures would be eliminated. Some of the proposed features are currently present in languages like Algol 68 [3] (procedure values), Lisp (attribute lists for defining objects), Russell [4] (careful analysis of notion of type), and Smalltalk [5] (modules are first-class objects). The proposed language would be an Ada-like language just as Ada is a Pascal-like language, but would reflect the state of the art in 1985 rather than 1975. It would reflect our increased understanding of modular programming, recent work on object-oriented languages and architectures, and the lessons we have learned in developing Ada.

Types as First-Class Objects

The domain of applicability of type-independent operations can be extended from data objects to program units by making program units into first-class values. It is tempting to extend the domain even further by making types into first-class values and permitting parameter passing, assignment, and other operations for types. This requires careful analysis of the notion of value for types. Tradeoffs between reliability, efficiency, and readability of languages with compile-time type invariance, and expressiveness resulting from run-time variability of types will be examined.

Strong typing in Ada restricts the compile-time variability of types and conflicts with the treatment of types as first-class objects which can be manipulated at run time. We shall examine the restrictions on the run-time variability of types imposed by Ada, and consider relaxing these restrictions so that types may have some of the run-time variability enjoyed by objects. The mechanisms for preserving type consistency when run-time variability for

types is introduced suggests that type values be tuples of operators as proposed by Demers and Donahue for Russell [4].

Ada requires all occurrences of a type-valued expression to be manifest at compile time. This implies that assignment to type-valued variables and run-time passing of type-valued parameters must be prohibited. However, Ada allows generic abstractions to have compile-time type parameters subject to the restriction that actual parameters of a generic instantiation are determinable at compile time. A generic queue type QG with a generic type parameter (for queue elements) whose actual parameter value is specified at generic instantiation time is illustrated below:

Example 18: Generic Type Parameters

```
type QG (formal type parameter) is
   use (body of QG) in
      tuple (specification of QG);

Q: QG (actual type (compile-time constant));
```

Generic bodies may contain identifiers associated with different types for different instantiations. But all type variability is resolved at compile time during generic instantiation. Instantiation is conceptually a macro expansion with substitution of the actual parameter for all instances of the formal parameter in the "expanded" generic body. Expansions for different actual types result in different overloading of the operators and subprograms for the generic type in the body of QG that are automatically taken care of by the overloading rules of Ada (which cause compile-time substitution of different code for different overloadings of an operator). Thus overloading of APPEND for queues of integers and queues of messages is realized by different subprograms in the compiled program. Generics allow the programmer to write generic definitions with type variables and objects of variable type but are designed so that all type variability may be resolved at compile time by the overloading mechanism. Overloaded operators and subprograms applicable to objects of a given generic type are implicit formal parameters of the generic body that are bound to specific actual parameters at compile time determined by the actual type parameter supplied at generic instantiation time.

Run-time type variability for Ada could be introduced in one of the following ways:

(1) Changing the semantics of generics so that instantiation is at execution time rather than at compile-time and actual type parameters are allowed to be variables.

(2) Allowing the types of subprogram parameters to be variables that are bound at the time of subprogram call.

Execution-time generic instantiation would require resolution of overloaded operators and subprograms to be performed when the actual type is supplied during execution, or even later at the time that operators are used. Instantiation could consist of execution-time macro expansion of object code for the particular overloading of operators or of simply noting the type and using it in subsequent interpretive execution of overloaded operators. Type consistency is guaranteed either way because the system knows the operators for each type and ensures the right execution-time overloading for operators of the generic body.

Subprograms with type variables may be illustrated by a SORT procedure which has an array parameter whose elements have a variable type **T2** and is supplied with a "<" operator that compares elements of the type **T2** and returns a Boolean result.

Example 19: Type Variability in Procedures

procedure SORT(X: array (T1) of T2; with "<"(T2,T2)BOOL);

Explicitly supplied operators such as "<" allow a programmer-defined meaning to be associated with operations on the type **T2**, either because none exists or because the programmer wishes to redefine the meaning. Implicitly supplied operators such as assignment for elements being sorted are assumed to have a default meaning for all element types **T2**. In general each variable type may have both implicitly overloaded operators whose overloading is supplied by default by the system and explicitly overloaded operators supplied by the programmer.

The above examples illustrate that type consistency in a strongly typed language may be maintained by supplying operators on objects with the type along with the type itself at the time the type value is bound. Such operators may be supplied either explicitly by the programmer or implicitly by the system. The need for such operators demonstrates that the operators are effectively part of the "value" associated with a type.

Abandoning strong typing altogether leads to "typeless" languages such as the lambda calculus, Lisp, or Snobol 4, in which types of variables are not known at compile time. Languages like SNOBOL 4, which combine typelessness for variables with a notion of type for values, are type-consistent in the sense that execution time checks guarantee that only legitimate operators can be applied to values of variables. The type is part of the value and a run-time type check causes dynamic selection among overloadings of an operator.

Variant records provide a mechanism for selective typelessness that allows the programmer to defer type checking to run-time for selective variables. Variant records in Ada have a discriminant field that identifies the current variant and provide different code segments for operating on different variants of the type. Tests are provided to allow programmer-defined checks for type consistency, but these tests could in principle be backed up by system-defined checking for consistency of the tag field of a variant record with the operations to be applied to the data.

We have indicated a number of options on the spectrum between manifest compile-time type specification and complete typelessness. Type variability was found to be closely coupled to mechanisms for binding operators for a given type to specific operations. Compile-time type resolution for generic instances in Ada is closely coupled to compile-time binding of overloaded operators, while run-time type variation requires run-time binding of operators. Operators are effectively additional parameters of type varying modules that are bound when the type is bound.

Type consistency of type-varying modules can be assured if we associate new values with all operators on objects of a given type every time the type changes. This effectively identifies the "value" of a given type with the tuple of all operators on objects of the type. If we systematically update this value every time the type changes then type consistency is automatically maintained no matter how much run-time type variability is introduced. From this point of view strong typing is seen to be a syntactic requirement for textual type invariance that is completely orthogonal to the requirement of type consistency.

The identification of the type value with the tuple of its operations allows types to be treated as first-class values and allows unification of the notion of type with that of records and packages as a tuple of resources. This approach has been taken by Demers and Donahue in advocating and implementing the principle of type completeness for the language Russell [4]. The present discussion indicates how completeness consistency can be approached starting from strongly-typed languages such as Ada. Strong typing may be seen as a requirement for restricting textual variability of types that is orthogonal to type consistency. Abandoning strong typing may result in severe problems of execution-time efficiency and program readability and is not necessarily recommended for higher-level languages. However, the notion of type and package values as tuples with similar structure is attractive. Moreover, the conceptual introduction of types as first-class values decouples considerations of textual type invariance from considerations of type consistency, thereby allowing a more flexible approach to the design of type systems for higher-level languages.

Comparison with CLU

CLU [6] is a programming language whose type mechanism supports both program and data abstraction. It is instructive to compare clusters (the abstraction mechanism of CLU) with the data abstraction and generic type mechanisms of Ada.

Clusters are types. Instances of a cluster are introduced by declarations. Instances of clusters are first-class objects (they can be passed as parameters and be components of structures). But a cluster is semantically like a package with a set of operations on a private data type. Declaration of an instance is conceptually like generic instantiation, since declarations create an instance of the complete cluster rather than just of the data type. The cluster data type may be thought of as the value attribute of the cluster. It may be initialized by a "create" operation and then updated by operators that modify the value.

CLU allows clusters to have generic parameters, but breaks down the process of supplying actual parameters and creating instances of the cluster into two steps. This simplifies create operations for clusters. It permits the declaration of both clusters and data types to be modeled by parameterless operations with similar syntax and semantics.

CLU, like Lisp, distinguishes between binding a variable to a conceptually preexisting object (CLU assignment) and changing the state of a preexisting object. Its notion of assignment is very different from the Ada notion of assignment which causes a copy of an object to be placed into a "container" associated with the variable. The CLU and Lisp mechanisms for binding values to variables provide a cleaner basis for associating first-class values with arbitrary objects than the mechanisms of Pascal and Ada.

The work on guardians [7], which is an evolution of the work on CLU for distributed processes, explicitly introduces two kinds of modules whose mechanisms for communication are respectively governed by message passing and shared variables. Guardians, which represent complete nodes of a distributed network, can communicate with each other only by message passing, while modules within a given guardian can communicate through shared variables or parameters. Any successor to Ada should contain both abstraction mechanisms for concurrently executable modules which can communicate only by message passing and submodules which can communicate by shared variables or parameters.

CLU provides a model for the unification of program and data abstraction in the presence of strong typing that is a good reference point for the unification of objects and program units in Ada. Lisp, ML, and Russell provide additional models. The successor of Ada should try to combine the Ada approach to separation between interface specifications and module bodies with mechanisms in the above languages for the unification of values, functions, structures, and types.

Conclusion

The duality between objects and program units in Ada is a source of unnecessary complexity which could be eliminated by replacing these separate but redundant notions by a single notion (entity) having both object and program attributes. This duality gives rise to complexity at the level of programming methodology which forces the user to make artificial choices between data and program abstractions. It gives rise to complexity at the level of language design because the designer is forced to choose between a commitment to a program view or data view of a language construct or, as in the case of Ada tasks, to violate the duality between objects and program units that lies at the core of the language design. A unified mechanism for handling objects and program units would not merely result in a simpler language with a smaller number of "orthogonal" concepts. It would remove the need for an artificial and premature commitment to program-oriented or data-oriented views at the level of programming methodology or language design. The development of a uniform mechanism for abstraction and of a consistent mechanism for types are important issues in designing a successor to Ada. This paper is not intended to provide definitive solutions but to stimulate further discussion.

The designers of Ada were asked (as part of the rules of the Ada design competition) to choose between a complex language (PL/I or Algol 68) and a simple language (Pascal) as a starting point for Ada. The alternative of building outwards from a "simple" Pascal framework was chosen over that of scaling down and modifying the more complex Algol 68 or PL/I frameworks. In designing a successor to Ada we could similarly start with a complex language such as Ada itself or with a simpler language such as CLU, Russell or ML. Choice of Ada as a starting point could result in a simpler, more powerful language easily learned by Ada programmers, while choice of a simple language would allow us to start from sound principles and a simple abstract machine and add required semantic features and syntactic sugaring in a way that is consistent with the basic model. Clearly the answer is to combine the two approaches so that the understanding of language structure in the research community can be combined with the understanding of problem-solving requirements accumulated during the design of Ada. It is not too early to start thinking about the redesign of Ada, making use of the suggestions in this paper and of advances in hardware and language design and implementation technology in the 1980s [8]. The period between now and 1985 could be used for research and requirements analysis, with the objective of producing a new language design by 1987 and of completing an implementation of the new language by 1990. Experience gained in the design and implementation of current Ada will prove extremely useful. Current Ada may be viewed as a "rapid" prototype for the proposed successor.

We conclude that a strongly-typed Ada-like language with first-class values for data objects, program units, and types is desirable and feasible. The principles of design depend on a uniform notion of value that permits type-independent operations such as assignment, parameter passing, and component selection to be uniformly performed for all entities, and on the development of a simple abstract machine and an architecture that pemits efficient implementation of the abstract machine. The present paper complements fundamental research in this area on languages which derive from the lambda calculus by showing how notions of value and structure developed for such languages can be used to simplify, unify and model the constructs of Ada.

Acknowledgements

The author is indebted to David McQueen and Luca Cardelli for showing how generic package abstractions could be realized in ML by functions which return records with functional components, to Alessandro Giacalone for implementing closures in statically scoped Lisp, and to Alan Demers for clarifying the notion of types as first-class values represented by tuples of operators.

References

(1) Reference Manual for the Ada Programming Language, US Department of Defense, July 1980, GPO 008-000-00354-8.

(2) Gordon M., Milner R., Morris L., Newey M., and Wadsworth C., A Metalanguage (ML) for Interactive Proof in LCF, Proc 5th POPL Symposium, January 1978.

(3) Van Wijngaarden et al, Revised Report on the Algorithmic Language Algol 68, Numer. Math., Feb 1975.

(4) Demers. A. and Donahue J., "Type Completeness" as a Language Principle, Proc 7th POPL Symposium, January 1980.

(5) Smalltalk Issue, Byte, August 1981.

(6) Liskov B. Snyder A., Atkinson R., and Schaffert C., Abstraction Mechanisms in CLU, CACM August 1977.

(7) Liskov B. and Scheifler R., Guardians and Actions: Linguistic Support for Robust Distributed Programs, Proc 9th POPL Conference, Jan 1982.

(8) Wegner P., Emperors, Generals, and Programmers, ACM Forum, CACM February 1982.

Chapter 4: Object-Oriented Programming in Other Languages

Although Smalltalk and Ada are the most important languages related to object-oriented programming, there have been many other languages built that support objects or which add object-oriented features to existing languages. Some of these languages are considered in this chapter.

Descriptions of some of the more well-known object-oriented languages and pointers to the literature are included in the references.

In the first paper, "History and Goals of Modula-2," Niklaus Wirth describes the forces that led to the development of Modula-2. Modula-2 is an extension of Pascal that includes the *module*, a device for encapsulating procedures and data; however, like Ada, it has no inheritance mechanism. Modula-2 is an outgrowth of two earlier languages: Modula and Mesa. Modula is an earlier language of Wirth's. Mesa is a language created at Xerox PARC and is a predecessor of Smalltalk.

Modules are very similar to packages in Ada. Wirth has found through his experience that providing the module facility was one thing, and using it wisely was something else. One rule is to make the interface between modules as "thin" as possible. Another is that a typical good use of a module is as the collection of routines that operate on a set of data. Thus we see the basic idea of object coming up again.

In "Modular Programming in C: An Approach and an Example," Kalyan Dutta explains how object-oriented programming can in part be incorporated into ordinary C, a language not designed with objects in mind. The approach uses available tools in C from a different perspective than usual. In particular, functions and variables can be hidden from other parts of the software system by declaring them "static" in the language. Other objects can be made public by declaring them "extern." An example of this usage is presented in the paper.

This paper reminds one of the way in which structured programming was incorporated into every language, even assembly language, no matter how unstructured they were to begin with. Is it a good idea to take a new concept like structured programming or object-oriented programming and force it to somehow fit into whatever language you are working with? It's a hard question to answer because of the trade offs involved. On the one hand, when a new concept comes along, that is an improvement over the former way of doing things, it is important to incorporate it into your work. On the other, some very strange constructs can creep into our

programming when we force a language to do things for which it was not designed. A way around the dilemma in the past has been to invent some higher level language, say a program design language, that has the features we want, do the real programming in this language, and then hand (or machine) translate it into whatever language is forced upon us. We have seen, for example, Ada design language being used for many projects that have no intention of actually using Ada for the final program.

In object-oriented programming, some important skills are to think of your program as being made up of objects and to choose these objects in a natural way. Fortunately, these skills are independent of the language in which you must program. Select an object-oriented language if you can, otherwise, think in objects and map your thoughts, the best you can into the programming language.

Brad J. Cox, in "Message/Object Programming: An Evolutionary Change in Programming Technology," describes the operator/operand model of programming and notes a major oversight: Operators and their operands are usually very closely coupled together, not independent. He also describes the ideas of classes, messages, encapsulation, and inheritance (borrowed from Smalltalk) and how they are made available in "Objective-C," an extension of C for object-oriented programming.

The approach of the paper is a fine example of the ideas presented above. A higher level language incorporating the needed concepts has been created above C. This higher level language, Objective-C, can be used as the vehicle for programming and then machine translated to C.

The paper is an excellent overview of the ideas of object-oriented programming and how they can be incorporated into conventional languages.

In "Object-Oriented Languages for the Macintosh," Kurt Schmucker describes the current status (as of August 1986) of object-oriented languages for the Apple Macintosh. The languages described are Smalltalk, Object Pascal, Neon, ExperCommonLisp, Objective-C, Object Assembler, and Object Logo. Because so many languages are available and because an excellent object-oriented user interface is available (see "MacApp: An Application Framework," in Chapter 2 of Volume 2), the Macintosh is an ideal computer for object-oriented applications.

The paper by Daniel G. Bobrow, Kenneth Kahn, Gregor Kiczales, Larry Masinter, Mark Stefik, and Frank Zdybel,

"CommonLoops: Merging Lisp and Object-Oriented Programming," describes an extension to Common Lisp which supports object-oriented programming. The extension is called CommonLoops because it draws upon Loops (Lisp Object-Oriented Programming System), an earlier language that added objects to Lisp. CommonLoops attempts to achieve its capabilities by modifying Common Lisp constructs in as graceful a way as possible. CommonLoops is intended to provide a small efficient kernel in which other, more capable, object-oriented languages can be implemented.

Some of the capabilities of the language follow.

A method is a procedure that is run when a particular message is sent to a particular type of object. CommonLoops extends Lisp's function call to include messages by interpreting the form "(foo a b)" in a way such that the particular function invoked depends on the identifier "foo" as well as the type of a and the type of b. Methods are defined by using a new defining form, *defmethod*, which is upward compatible with Lisp's usual defining form, *defun*. An example of the use of defmethod is

(defmethod move ((b block) x y) ...)

Here, move is being defined only for calls in which the first argument has type "block."

CommonLoops allows a kind of inheritance to be achieved by extending the syntax of defstruct to include a list of structures. For example, if one defines

(defstruct (titled-window (:include (window titled-thing))))

then the structure titled-window inherits all the features of window and titled-thing. The inheritance mechanism allows functions defined for one structure to be inherited by another. For example, if move is defined for windows, then it is automatically also available for titled-windows.

The CommonLoops effort addresses the problem of incorporating Smalltalk-style object-based programming in another language. Extensions to the language were found to be necessary. Extrapolating, it seems that any serious attempt to add the important object-oriented capabilities to an existing language will require extensions.

The final paper, "Object-Oriented Programming: Themes and Variations," by Mark Stefik and Daniel G. Bobrow, describes object-oriented languages from the point of view of the Artificial Intelligence community. The languages considered are Smalltalk, Loops, CommonLoops, Flavors, Object Lisp, KEE, and STROBE. Much of the article is concerned with comparing how the various fundamental object-oriented ideas are implemented in these languages. The themes considered include message sending, classes, instances, metaclasses, inheritance, multiple inheritance, method specialization, method combination, composite objects, and perspectives. The article is an excellent overview of current important ideas in object-oriented programming.

References

Actor

An object-oriented programming language available from The Whitewater Group, 906 University Place, Evanston, IL 60201.

A.P. Bernat, "Actor Goes on Stage," *AI Expert*, Volume 2, Number 3, March 1987, pages 40-44.

The design goals for Actor were to improve upon Smalltalk by making a language that
- is easier to learn for traditional programmers;
- requires a smaller amount of memory;
- is faster.

In Bernat's opinion, these goals were met.

C.B. Duff, "Designing an Efficient Language," *Byte*, Volume 11, Number 8, August 1986, pages 211-224.

A description of the rationale for developing Actor. This article is reproduced in Chapter 3 of Volume 2.

C++

An object-oriented extension of C that was developed at AT&T Bell Laboratories.

B. Stroustrup, *The C++ Programming Language*, Addison-Wesley, Reading, Massachusetts, 1986.

The definitive reference and guide to the C++ programming language. Written by its inventor.

B. Stroustrup, "An Overview of C++," *Object-Oriented Programming Workshop*, June 9-13, 1986, *SIGPLAN Notices*, ACM, Inc., New York, New York, Volume 21, Number 10, October 1986, pages 7-18.

G.M. Vose, "Review of *The C++ Programming Language*," *Byte*, Volume 11, Number 8, August 1986, pages 63-68.

CommonLoops

An effort to add the major ideas of object-oriented programming to Common Lisp in as straightforward a way as possible.

D.G. Bobrow, K. Kahn, G. Kiczales, L. Masinter, M. Stefik, and F. Zdybel, "CommonLoops: Merging Lisp and Object-Oriented Programming," *OOPSLA'86, SIGPLAN Notices*, ACM, Inc., New York, New York, Volume 21, Number 11, November 1986, pages 17-29.

Reproduced in this chapter.

M. Stefik and D.G. Bobrow, "Object-Oriented Programming: Themes and Variations," *The AI Magazine*, Volume 6, Number 4, Winter 1986, pages 40-62.

Reproduced in this chapter.

CommonObjects

An object-oriented extension of Common Lisp that was developed at Hewlett-Packard during 1983-1985.

A. Snyder, "CommonObjects: An Overview," *Object-Oriented Programming Workshop*, June 9-13, 1986, *SIGPLAN Notices*, ACM, Inc., New York, New York, Volume 21, Number 10, October 1986, pages 19-28.

Concurrent Prolog

Developed in Japan in about 1982. The major ideas of object-oriented programming are expressible in the language even though it was not developed with this in mind.

E. Shapiro and A. Takeuchi, "Object Oriented Programming in Concurrent Prolog," *New Generation Computing*, Volume 1, 1983, pages 25-48.

Flavors

The east coast version of object-oriented Lisp. Available primarily on Symbolics Lisp machines.

D.A. Moon, "Object-Oriented Programming with Flavors," *OOPSLA'86, SIGPLAN Notices*, ACM, Inc., New York, New York, Volume 21, Number 11, November 1986, pages 1-8.

A short description of what it is like to use Flavors.

Symbolics Common Lisp: Language Concepts, Symbolics Corporation, Cambridge, Massachusetts, August 1986, pages 47-54 and 353-474.

The definitive guide to Flavors.

M. Stefik and D.G. Bobrow, "Object-Oriented Programming: Themes and Variations," *The AI Magazine*, Volume 6, Number 4, Winter 1986, pages 40-62.

Reproduced in this chapter.

Loops

The west coast version of object-oriented Lisp.

D.G. Bobrow and M. Stefik, *The Loops Manual*, Xerox Corp., Palo Alto, Calif., 1983.

M. Stefik and D.G. Bobrow, "Object-Oriented Programming: Themes and Variations," *The AI Magazine*, Volume 6, Number 4, Winter 1986, pages 40-62.

Reproduced in this chapter.

ModPascal

An object-oriented extension of Pascal that was developed at the University of Kaiserslautern.

W.G. Olthoff, "Augmentation of Object-Oriented Programming by Concepts of Abstract Data Type Theory: The ModPascal Experience," *OOPSLA'86, SIGPLAN Notices*, ACM, Inc., New York, New York, Volume 21, Number 11, November 1986, pages 429-443.

Modula-2

Byte, Volume 9, Number 8, August 1984.

This issue of *Byte* has four articles devoted to Modula-2 in addition to the article by Wirth, which is reprinted in this chapter.

N. Wirth, "Modula: A Language for Modular Programming," *Software—Practice and Experience*, Volume 7, Number 1, January-February 1977, pages 3-35.

N. Wirth, "Design and Implementation of Modula," *Software—Practice and Experience*, Volume 7, Number 1, January-February 1977, pages 67-84.

N. Wirth, *Programming in Modula-2*, 3rd edition, Springer-Verlag, New York, New York, 1985.

A. Wegmann, "Object-Oriented Programming Using Modula-2," *Journal of Pascal, Ada and Modula-2*, Volume 5, Number 3, May/June 1986, pages 5-17.

Oaklisp

An object-oriented dialect of Lisp strongly based on the Scheme philosophy. In Oaklisp, types are first class objects in the sense that functions are first class objects in Scheme. Oaklisp runs on the Macintosh.

K.J. Lang and B.A. Pearlmutter, "Oaklisp: An Object-Oriented Scheme with First Class Types," *OOPSLA'86, SIGPLAN Notices*, ACM, Inc., New York, New York, Volume 21, Number 11, November 1986, pages 30-37.

Object Pascal

An object-oriented extension of Pascal, which was designed jointly by Niklaus Wirth and a team from Apple.

L. Tesler, "Object Pascal Report," *Structured Language World*, Volume 9, Number 3, 1985, pages 10-14.

K.J. Schmucker, "Object-Oriented Languages for the Macintosh," *Byte*, Volume 11, Number 8, August 1986, pages 177-185.

Reprinted in this chapter.

Objective-C

A machine-independent object-oriented extension of C developed by Brad Cox's Productivity Products International and first shipped in 1983. It is machine-independent because it comes as a compiler for converting Objective-C into C. It is available for IBM PCs, VAXs, and many other machines.

B.J. Cox, *Object-Oriented Programming An Evolutionary Approach*, Addison-Wesley, Reading, Massachusetts, 1986.

K.J. Schmucker, "Object-Oriented Languages for the Macintosh," *Byte*, Volume 11, Number 8, August 1986, pages 177-185.

Reprinted in this chapter.

Object-Oriented Forth

An extension of Forth that provides features similar to the package construct in Ada.

D. Pountain, "Object-Oriented Forth," *Byte*, Volume 11, Number 8, August 1986, pages 227-233.

Orient84/K

An object-oriented concurrent programming language that was developed at Keio University in 1984. Every object can run concurrently. The language syntax and semantics are based on those of Prolog and Smalltalk.

Y. Ishiwkawa and M. Tokor, "A Concurrent Object-Oriented Knowledge Representation Language Orient84/K: Its Features and Implementation," *OOPSLA'86, SIGPLAN Notices*, ACM, Inc., New York, New York, Volume 21, Number 11, November 1986, pages 232-241.

Simula

O.-J. Dahl and K. Nygaard, "Simula: An Algol-Based Simulation Language," *Communications of the ACM*, Volume 9, Number 9, September 1966, pages 671-678.

This is a description of the first object-oriented language by two of its inventors. Simula contains features that facilitate the programming of models of real-world processes (i.e., simulations). In the real world there are entities, such as people, that carry information and act upon it. To model this, Simula incorporates the concept of *process*: something that is a data carrier and can execute actions. In later languages, this became known as an object.

G.M. Birtwistle, O.-J. Dahl, B. Myhrhaug, and K. Nygaard, *Simula Begin*, Studentlitteratur, Lund, Sweden, 1979.

This is the programming manual for Simula.

M.P. Papazoglou, P.I. Georgiadis, and D.G. Maritsas, "An Outline of the Programming Language Simula," *Computer Languages*, Volume 9, Number 2, 1984, pages 107-131.

SPOOL

SPOOL (LOOPS backwards?) is an object-oriented extension to Prolog, which was developed at IBM Japan in about 1985.

K. Fukunaga and S.-I. Hirose, "An Experience with a Prolog-based Object-Oriented Language," *OOPSLA'86, SIGPLAN Notices*, ACM, Inc., New York, New York, Volume 21, Number 11, November 1986, pages 224-231.

Trellis/Owl

An object-based language that includes multiple inheritance and compile-time type checking. It was developed at Digital Equipment Corporation between 1982 and 1986.

C. Schaffert, T. Cooper, B. Bullis, M. Kilian, and C. Wilpolt, "An Introduction to Trellis/Owl" *OOPSLA'86, SIGPLAN Notices*, ACM, Inc., New York, New York, Volume 21, Number 11, November 1986, pages 9-16.

Vulcan

Although Concurrent Prolog can cleanly build objects, the notation for doing so is verbose and awkward. Vulcan is a preprocessor for Concurrent Prolog, which allows the use of more traditional notation for object-oriented constructs.

K. Kahn, E.D. Tribble, M.S. Miller, and D.G. Bobrow, "Objects in Concurrent Logic Programming Languages," *OOPSLA'86, SIGPLAN Notices*, ACM, Inc., New York, New York, Volume 21, Number 11, November 1986, pages 242-257.

Language Design

D.M. Harland, *Polymorphic Programming Languages*, Ellis Horwood, Chichester, England, 1984.

This book describes the state of the art in designing polymorphic programming languages and develops POLY, a particular polymorphic language. It gives a comparison of POLY with object-oriented languages, including Smalltalk.

HISTORY AND GOALS OF MODULA-2

BY NIKLAUS WIRTH

The module comes of age

BY 1977 THE concept of high-level language, and with it Pascal, had gained popularity. To a major degree this was due to the recognition that mastering the art of programming is based on the understanding of its underlying concepts, and that therefore it is essential to use a notation that displays the concepts in a lucid manner and emphasizes the need for orderly structures. Equally widespread, however, was the belief that the price for this gain in structure and lucidity was unduly high, and that it was well worth paying it in the classroom but not in the competitive world of industry. This amounted to nothing less than the relegation of modern programming tools to the world of ivory towers and toys.

Naturally, this claim was more than a belief; it could be proven. Even worse: it didn't have to be proven, it was evident. The same algorithm expressed in FORTRAN would run twice as fast as when expressed in Pascal or PL/I. And it was widely known that a clever programmer using an assembler could even enlarge this factor. In the same vein, the code generated by a high-level language compiler was considerably larger than the one constructed by the clever coder at a lower level.

The numbers, although measured, proven, and therefore true, were based on a misunderstanding caused by many people's inability to distinguish between a programming language and its implementation. A programming language is a *formalism* suitable for expressing algorithms and data structures, based on a concise and formal definition of its constructs and their meaning. (From this it follows that the term *language* is actually most unfortunate and misleading.) An *implementation* is a mechanism for the interpretation of programs expressed in the formalism. I am afraid that even today many professionals, including teachers and writers, fail to make this fundamental distinction.

I was then fully aware that the claimed loss in effectiveness was not inherent in

•••
Dr. Niklaus Wirth is head of the Department of Computer Science at ETH (the Swiss Federal Institute of Technology) Institut für Informatik (8092 Zürich, Switzerland). He developed several programming languages, including Pascal and Modula-2, and the Lilith personal computer, and has received the IEEE Emanuel R. Piore Award for outstanding achievement in the field of information processing.

the concept of the high-level, structured language, but in the inadequacy of the present implementations. Consequently, in our efforts to develop a compiler for Pascal we paid much attention to achieving an efficient compiler, i.e., a compiler that compiled fast and also generated dense and effective code. Eventually, our second Pascal compiler for the CDC Cyber computer, completed in 1974, generated code whose efficiency was genuinely comparable with that of a good FORTRAN compiler.

Ironically, however, the breakthrough of Pascal did not come from our valiant efforts to measure up to FORTRAN production compilers. It rather came from our so-called portable Pascal p-compiler, where efficiency was a very minor concern. In San Diego, Ken Bowles had the insight and courage to write p-code interpreters for various microprocessors that had just appeared on the market with loud fanfare. He introduced Pascal to the world of computer users and fans, where the efficiency of the programming process was often much more relevant than that of the resulting programs. Even more important, these users were seldom compelled to remain

Modula-2 grew out of Pascal and incorporates a few major and some minor improvements.

compatible with their past; they were less likely to adhere to the widespread misconception that their software libraries were so valuable, merely because their development had cost so much.

The success of Pascal implementations for microcomputers, however, has not eliminated the value of good compilers. To the contrary, it has increased the motivation to produce high-quality implementations.

THE PROJECT LILITH

An implementation does not consist of the compiler alone but includes the interpreting computer. Our efforts in constructing a good Pascal implementation were bounded by the suitability of the target computer. In fact, we spent a large amount of energy to conceal and make up for the inadequacy of the underlying computer. We had learned a lot about compiler design, but I also recognized that a truly satisfactory design would have to encompass programming language, compiler, and computer, all properly matched.

My visit to the Xerox Palo Alto Research Center (PARC) in 1976/1977, and my confrontation with its powerful personal workstation, the Alto, provided the incentive to undertake a new research project encompassing all these aspects. I was intrigued by the Alto's singularly simple design concept and the resulting flexibility for the programmer. Thus, I embarked on learning about hardware design and, upon returning to Switzerland, started the project that resulted in the computer Lilith, a personal workstation based on a powerful processor (Am 2901), a bit-mapped display, a mouse as input device, and an architecture tailored to the needs of a compiler. With a staff of six part-time assistants this seemed to be an overly ambitious goal, a project almost certainly doomed to failure. Nevertheless, after two years, two prototypes of Lilith were operational,

together with a compiler, an operating system, an advanced full-screen mouse-driven text editor, an interactive line-drawing editor, and elementary utility programs.

Apart from the motivation and competence of the team members, the feasibility of the ambitious task rested on three fixed constraints that I had postulated at the start: (1) we would implement a *single language*, and all software would be written in that language, without exception whatsoever; (2) the operating system would be designed for a *single user*, thus avoiding difficult problems of scheduling, protection, resource management, and accounting; (3) the computer would have a *single processor*, powerful enough to execute programs and to perform the raster operations on the displayed bit map.

Indeed, considering that Lilith was to be a personal workstation, there were no advantages to be gained by deviating from these constraints, in spite of widespread popular trends to develop multiprocessor, multilanguage, multiuser systems.

The first constraint required a language equally suitable for expressing algorithms on a high level of abstraction and for expressing operations directly accessing machine facilities, equally suitable for formulating a database system as for programming a disk driver. Evidently, Pascal was not capable enough, and I did not favor the common escape of embellishing it with a few "desirable extensions." Modula, a small language that I had designed in the preceding years to experiment with the concepts of multiprogramming, clearly did not suffice either. But it featured a facility to partition programs into modules with explicitly specified interfaces. This was precisely the facility needed to allow the introduction of so-called low-level facilities in the high-level language, because it allowed you to encapsulate them and to constrain their dangerousness to clearly delineated parts of a program. Hence, the choice for the new language was Pascal, augmented by the module and a few other facilities, and regularized by a more systematic syntax. Thus was born Modula-2.

MODULA-2

The language was defined in 1978 (10 years after Pascal) and implemented by

L. Geissmann, S.E. Knudsen, and C. Jacobi on the PDP-11. Its small store of available memory (28,000 16-bit words or 56K bytes) caused many obstacles and was the reason for the first compiler's five-pass structure. In the summer of 1979, the compiler was completed, and at the same time, the first Lilith prototype became operational. The operating system Medos-2 had been constructed by S.E. Knudsen concurrently, and together with the compiler it was transported from the PDP-11 to Lilith within three weeks. This was in itself an encouraging feat in software engineering and proof of Modula-2's usefulness as a system-implementation language. After a year's in-house use, I published the report on Modula-2 and we released the Modula-2 compiler to interested parties (March 1980). The defining report is included in the tutorial book *Programming in Modula-2* (N. Wirth, New York: Springer-Verlag, 1982) which I prepared up to the camera-ready stage with the aid of Lilith and a document-formatting system that I programmed, of course, in Modula-2.

As mentioned already, Modula-2 grew out of Pascal and incorporates a few major and a fair number of minor improvements. The single most outstanding added facility is the module structure. Basically, this facility allows you to partition programs into units with relatively well-defined interfaces. More specifically, it allows you to control the visibility of declared objects and to hide them from places where they better remain unknown. Since it plays such an important role, we shall now look briefly into the history of Modula-2's development.

Although the principle of information hiding was much discussed in the early 1970s, it is perhaps Modula's merit to place it consistently into the framework of a clearly defined language. To the best of my knowledge, it was David Parnas who first coined the expression *information hiding*. Both Tony Hoare and Per Brinch Hansen gave it form by connecting it to the class facility of the programming language Simula. This is essentially, in terms of Pascal, a record type; the set of instantiations of this type forms what Simula terminology calls a *class*. In contrast to Pascal records, the Simula class allows you to associate procedures with the data represented by the field identifiers. Hoare and Brinch Hansen then postulated that while the names of the procedures would normally be visible, those of the data would remain hidden except within the associated procedures. This feature was implemented in Brinch Hansen's Concurrent Pascal and embodied the principle of information hiding, which in the meantime (1975) had been promoted to that of *data abstraction*. The example in listing 1 serves to exemplify the issue: we use a liberal Pascal notation ("N" is a constant):

In a program using this class (type), one might declare variables

q0,q1: queue

and thereafter access them by statements like

q0.put(13.7)   q1.get(v)

but statements like "q0.n := 237" or "q1.in := q0.out," which evidently interfere with the presented implementation of the abstraction of a queue, would be disallowed. More importantly, they would be prevented by the compiler, which does not "see" the field identifiers "n," "in," and "out" that are hidden inside the class (record) declaration.

Unfortunately, these proposals intertwined several independent concepts like visibility, instantiation, indirection of access, concurrency, and mutual exclusion. Both authors had actually postulated these kinds of classes to embody areas of mutual exclusion in multiprocessing systems, and the facility became more widely known as a *monitor* (in which the HALT statements are re-placed by synchronization operations).

In the development of the experimental multiprogramming language Modula-1, I strived for clarity of concept and was convinced that a substantial disentangling of the various intertwined concepts was mandatory. Together with H. Sandmayr we found a possible solution in the structure then called module that would concern the aspect of visibility only. This, I believe, was the major breakthrough, because in all other languages the visibility issue had always remained intimately connected with that of existence. In particular, it was now possible to declare sets of static, global objects that were visible from selected parts of the program only. This is typically desirable to encapsulate certain permanent parts of a system (like device drivers, storage allocators, window handlers, etc.). I enhanced this module facility with so-called *import* and *export* lists that allow the explicit control of visibility across the "module wall" of each individual object. Furthermore, true to Algol and Pascal tradition, modules can be nested. An export now signifies the extension of visibility to the outside, and import signifies its extension to the inside (see figure 1).

SEPARATION OF SPECIFICATION AND IMPLEMENTATION

During my aforementioned stay at PARC in 1976, I became acquainted with the language Mesa, a Pascal offspring specifically designed to meet the needs of large system development. Mesa also incorporated an information-hiding feature. It also allowed you to encapsulate program parts into modules but lacked the ability to control the visibility of individual objects, and it entangled the facility once again with another feature, namely that of *separate compilation*, a facility of implementation. Its noteworthy contribution was the separation of the declarations of the exported objects from that of the ones to remain hidden. The former is called the *definition part*, the latter is the *implementation part*, which contains all those details that are relevant to the realization of the exported mechanisms, but not to their functional definition.

The combination of Mesa's module facility with split definition and implementation parts, and the (nestable) Modula-1 modules with controllable import and export resulted in Modula-2.

The facility of separate compilation posed some nontrivial problems. The key idea is that the compilation of a definition part results in a (compiled) symbol table (represented as a file). The file contains all information relevant to importers (clients) of that module. If, at a later time, another module imports objects from, say, modules M1 and M2, then the compiler accesses the previously generated symbol files of M1 and M2. Thus, the rules of type consistency are observed across module boundaries as well. This makes separate compilation genuinely helpful and safe, in contrast to *independent compilation* as known from assemblers and FORTRAN compilers, which is a misleading pitfall when used with high-level, data-typed languages.

It is noteworthy that Ada incorporates this form of module in almost identical form, although under the name *package*. We can attest that this is one of the more essential features of any system language because we have made extensive use of it for the last five years. Regrettably, Ada designers have failed to restrict separate compilability to global modules.

USING MODULES EFFECTIVELY

During the last five years, we have seen that postulating and providing a new facility is one thing, and learning to make good use of it is another. The more intricate and sophisticated a facility is, the smaller is the chance that it will be used wisely. In fact, finding the appropriate structure for the data and

Listing 1: *Sample queue routine in Pascal.*

```
TYPE queue =
RECORD n, in, out: INTEGER;
        (*n = no. of filled slots; initially 0*)
        buffer: ARRAY [0 .. N – 1] OF REAL;

        PROCEDURE Put(x:REAL);
        BEGIN IF n = N THEN HALT (*full*);
                buffer[in]:=x; in:=(in + 1)MOD N;n:=n + 1
        END;

        PROCEDURE get(VAR x: REAL);
        BEGIN if N = 0 THEN HALT (*empty*)
                x:=buffer[out]; out:=(out + 1) MOD N;n:= n – 1
        END
END
```

program is the key to successful programming. With the module we have added another level of granularity in program structuring. The difficulties of finding a good partitioning—I carefully avoid the word "optimal"—are cumulated at this level, because often the modules are the units that are constructed by different programmers. Their contracts, in fact, are the definition parts of their modules. The definition parts establish the interfaces, which constitute the first task in a system's design process. Lucky are those who hit a good solution at the outset, for any change affects all participants. If a definition module A has been changed in any way, then all modules that import A must be adapted (and at least be recompiled). This is not the case, however, if only the implementation part of A had been modified. Hence, a fair degree of decoupling is established. Extreme examples are the primary utility modules of an operating system, because they are used by virtually every program. The system may well be modified without hampering the users. However, the slightest change in a definition module will require the recompilation of all clients.

The first rule to be observed when you deal with modules is that the interfaces must be considered before implementations are attempted. The terser they are, the smaller the chance for mistakes and the need for changes. Interfaces should, by their very definition, be "thin."

A second observation is that a module usually hides a set of data and provides a set of operators to manipulate this data. By forcing the client to access this data via the offered procedures, the module's designer may guarantee that certain consistency conditions are always observed, i.e., always remain invariant. In the queue model shown in listing 1, it is guaranteed that the counter n truly reflects the number of elements contained in the buffer and that their order of coming out of the queue is the same as that of going in.

As a consequence, a module is typically chosen as the collection of routines that operate on a set of data, which can be seen by the client as an abstraction defined by the accessible set of procedures.

Often, a module is also chosen as the collection of procedures that constitute a level of abstraction of data that is residing elsewhere. For example, a module containing a set of input and output routines such as

ReadInteger(f,x) and WriteReal(f,x)

will allow you to think in terms of the abstract concept of a sequence of integers and real numbers, and to ignore the details of its implementation in terms of bits, bytes, buffers, files, disk sectors, etc.

Consequently, such a module is chosen in order to establish a new level of abstraction. The success of such an abstraction crucially depends on its rigorous definition and your willingness to genuinely ignore its implementation. Please don't misunderstand! I do not say to remain ignorant of its implementations, but rather only use an implementation's properties that are defined in terms of the abstraction. To cite a well-known example: if you think in terms of integers, it does not make sense to ask for the value of an integer's last bit, even if you know that it is represented as a sequence of bits. Instead you should ask whether the integer is odd.

COMPUTERS, LANGUAGES, AND COMMERCIALISM

It is precisely the ability to think in terms of proper abstractions that is the hallmark of a competent programmer. Even more, he or she is expected to be able to jump from one level to another without mixing them up. A structured language is enormously helpful in this endeavor, but it does not do it for you. It is like with a horse: you may guide it to the water, but it has to do the drinking itself. I am afraid that this simple truth is in stark contrast to the numerous lulling advertisements being published in such abundance. They cleverly reinforce themselves with slogans like *Switching to Pascal solves all your (programming) problems* and *Our Computer speaks Pascal*, and, in fact, represent nothing more than an extremely aggressive sales campaign.

Sooner or later, people will, through

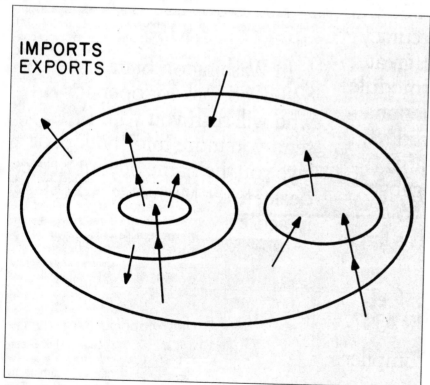

IMPORTS EXPORTS

Figure 1: *Crucial to the structure of Modula-2 is the concept of the module, which may be nested inside other modules. Within each module, the visibility of objects to other modules may be controlled via the IMPORT and EXPORT functions.*

harsh experiences, realize that they have become victims of slogans and fads, and that owning the best of tools is worthless unless that tool is thoroughly understood. I am afraid that the modern trend of overselling can become counterproductive. I have seen progressive teachers proudly offering their students the chance to learn structured Pascal, and I quickly realized that the students had no inkling of what structure meant. And I have seen professional programmers proudly present Pascal programs abounding with neatly indented structures, comments (for documentation, of course), and lots of procedures and sophisticated data types. Upon closer inspection, however, the baroque nomenclatures and structures revealed themselves as deadweight. Sometimes, redesigning these programs led to drastic, even tenfold, reduction in their size and complexity. I sadly realized that a high-level programming language could not only be used to design beautiful programs with much less effort, but also to hide incompetence underneath an impressive coating of glamour and frills. The analogy to literature became all too evident. We must do our best to avoid the misuse of modern programming languages for the selling of lousy contents through enticing packaging. Style may be essential to achieve a good design, but ultimately it is the design, and not the style, that counts.

Let me emphasize the point: neither owning a computer nor programming in a modern language will itself solve any problems, not even yours. But it may be instrumental. Predominantly, I have noticed, more effort is spent on obtaining those instrumental tools than on mastering them. And this is a grave mistake. Perhaps the most effective precaution against it is this rule: Know what the tool is to achieve and what you are going to use it for before you acquire it. This holds for language as well as computers—the more sophisticated it is, the more effort you will need for its mastery, the bigger will be the chance for its misuse, but, presumably, the higher the ultimate reward. I hope that this reward is not only measured in terms of problems solved and dollars earned, but also in the learners' satisfaction of having gained understanding, ability, and genuine insight. ■

Modular programming in C :
an approach and an example

Kalyan Dutta
Lockheed Palo Alto Research Laboratory

Unlike ADA or Modula-2, the programming language C is not inherently modular. But by exploiting certain features of the language it is possible to build modular design into C programs. This has advantages in large programming projects where source code will be written by many programmers, or in applications calling for a collection of syntactically identical interconnected modules.

The approach suggested here is not as ambitious as in Stroustrup[1982], requiring a change to the C compiler; rather, standard C (Kernighan & Ritchie[1978]) is used. This is more in keeping with the work of Boyd[1983, 1984].

1. The problem

Normally, in a collection of C source files (modules), defined functions are external objects; their names are known globally. This places the burden of avoiding duplicate function names upon the programmer(s). There is also in C a great temptation to declare a large number of variables external for purposes of inter-module communication. The problem is that these variables are also globally defined, and care must be taken to make them unique.

What is needed is a mechanism for hiding objects (variables or functions), i.e., for declaring objects as being private, and for making public only those objects that are required to be accessed by other modules.

2. A solution

Functions and variables that are declared "static" in C have just the desired property; they are invisible to other program modules. To quote from Kernighan & Ritchie[1978, Sec.4.6] :

"In C, "static" connotes not only permanence but also a degree of what might be called "privacy." ... external static objects (variables or functions) are known only within the source file in which they appear, and their names do not interfere with variables or functions of the same name in other files.

Reprinted with permission from *SIGPLAN Notices*, Volume 20, Number 3, March 1985, pages 9-15. Copyright © 1985 by Kalyan Dutta.

External static variables and functions provide a way to conceal data objects and any internal routines that manipulate them so that other routines and data can not conflict even inadvertently."

3. An approach

To emphasize the approach used, let us introduce two synonyms for the C keywords "static" and "extern". These synonyms are

```
#define PRIVATE static
#define PUBLIC  extern
```

These synonyms would commonly be part of a header file to be included in each source module, and processed by the C compiler preprocessor.

Adhering now to the convention that each globally defined object (variable or function) must be declared PRIVATE or PUBLIC*, we see that PRIVATE objects are entirely local to the defining module, while PUBLIC objects may be referenced in other modules. Of course, all objects in a module, whether PRIVATE or PUBLIC, must still be uniquely defined.

This simple approach to module-level object hiding allows the programmer to use arbitrary PRIVATE object naming and to ensure that only those objects that must be are made PUBLIC.

To delve further into the matter we need an example. Let us look at a programming example in which the use of a large number of identical modules is appropriate.

4. An example

A menu structure can be implemented as a collection of menu nodes connected as a directed graph. Each menu node has the following attributes: a set of menu "keys" and an action associated with each "key". By allowing the associated action to include the invocation of a new menu node, we see that arbitrarily complex menu structures can be thus defined.

Consider an implementation that will accept a simple description of such a menu "tree" and will automatically generate the associated menu traversal program.

---

* Normally not explicitly used in C programs, the "storage class specifier" extern is the default class, (Kernighan & Ritchie[1978], Appendix A, C Reference Manual); however, all defined functions may be so declared explicitly, including the entry routine main.

The key observation here is that every menu node is syntactically identical with every other node. Therefore all we need is a single node processing module that will serve as a template for each node in the menu structure.

We will consider the simple example of a such a menu structure consisting of just two distinct menu nodes. The complete module listing for each menu node is given below. They are shown side by side to emphasize their similarity.

```
Oct 29 12:09 1984  nodel.c Page 1


#include        "menu.h"

/* references to other menu nodes */

PUBLIC  int     node2();

/* references to private node functions */

PRIVATE doit() {
        fprintf(stdout,"nodel: pop\n");
        return 1;
}
PRIVATE init() {
        fprintf(stdout,"calling nodel\n");
}
PRIVATE wrapup() {
        fprintf(stdout,"leaving nodel\n");
}

/* keys associated with this node */

PRIVATE Keypad  keys[] = {
        "exit_ndl",     doit,
        "call_nd2",     node2,
        "nodelnop",     NULL,
        NULL,           NULL
};

/* definition of this node as a module */

PUBLIC  MODULE(nodel,init,keys,wrapup)
```

```
Oct 29 12:09 1984  node2.c Page 1


#include        "menu.h"

/* references to other menu nodes */

PUBLIC  int     nodel();

/* references to private node functions */

PRIVATE doit() {
        fprintf(stdout,"node2: pop\n");
        return 1;
}
PRIVATE endit() {
        fprintf(stdout,"node2: double pop\n");
        return 2;
}
PRIVATE init() {
        fprintf(stdout,"calling node2\n");
}
PRIVATE wrapup() {
        fprintf(stdout,"leaving node2\n");
}

/* keys associated with this node */

PRIVATE Keypad  keys[] = {
        "dbl_jump",     endit,
        "sngl_jmp",     doit,
        "call_ndl",     nodel,
        "node2nop",     NULL,
        NULL,           NULL
};

/* definition of this node as a module */

PUBLIC  MODULE(node2,init,keys,wrapup)
```

Note that the syntactic organization of both menu nodes is the same, but that similarly named routines have different actions in the two nodes. The specification for each menu module can be broken up into four logical sections :

1)   The PUBLIC names of other menu nodes pointed to by this node
2)   a set of functions PRIVATE to this node
3)   the PRIVATE keypad associated with this node, and
4)   the declaration of this node as a PUBLIC module.

A keypad is declared as an array of pairs of keys (each distinguished here by its own key legend) and associated functions.

At each node, one action associated with a key may be to do nothing, or to call a PRIVATEly defined function (e.g. doit). Although these functions may be multiply defined, the modularity convention adopted here allows each reference to be correctly resolved.

Another action attached to a key may be to call up another node, PUBLICly defined. Here node1 may call up node2, and vice versa.* All of the structure of the menu graph arises solely as a result of such calls; no other structure is imposed by the menu generation program. (In this instance although only two nodes are defined, the resulting menu structure is arbitrarily deep.)

In this example the names of two functions (init and wrapup) form part of the definition of each node as a module. These functions are called upon first entering a node, and just prior to leaving it, respectively. These function definitions are not essential but simply emphasize the uniformity of design. One or both of these definitions may be omitted, with the C keyword NULL replacing the name in the module definition.

The structure of a keypad and the definition of a MODULE declaration (as well as the synonyms for PUBLIC and PRIVATE) are to be found in the header file menu.h :

```
Oct 29 12:09 1984   menu.h Page 1


#include        <stdio.h>

#define PRIVATE static
#define PUBLIC  extern

typedef struct  Keypad {
        char    *legend;
        int     (*ifunc)();
} Keypad, *Keyptr;

#define MODULE(name,init,keys,wrapup) name() \
        { return _workwith(init,keys,wrapup); }
```

The declaration of each node as a module is thus resolved as an implicit reference to the PUBLIC function _workwith, with the keypad for that node as an argument.

With this organization, the menu traversal routine itself is quite simple; it works with the set of keys in one node at a time, and maintains a linked list of keys organized as a stack as it traverses nodes. Here is the PUBLIC function _workwith :

---

* There is no difficulty with circular referencing here if we consider each invocation to call up a fresh instance of a node.

```
#include        "menu.h"

typedef struct  Stack   {
        short   level;
        char    *name;
        union   {
                int     (*ptr)();
        } u;
        struct  Stack   *next;
} Stack;

PUBLIC  int     _workwith(init,keys,wrapup)
int     (*init)();
Keyptr  keys;
int     (*wrapup)();
{
        char    input[20];
        int     status;
        Stack   *sp;
        Stack   *lookup();
        Stack   *install();
        Stack   *mkfree();

        if (init) (*init)();
        install(keys);
        display();

        while (fscanf(stdin,"%s",input)&&(sp=lookup(input))) {
                if (sp->u.ptr) {
                        if (status=(*(sp->u.ptr))()) {
                                mkfree();
                                if (wrapup) (*wrapup)();
                                return --status;
                        }
                        display();
                }
        }
        mkfree();
        if (wrapup) (*wrapup)();
        return NULL;
}

PUBLIC  main()
{
        fprintf(stdout,"menu exit status %d\n",nodel());
}
```

Within its loop, _workwith compares a string read at the standard input with one of the keys in the current node and exe- cutes the associated function. No match results in an exit from the node.   Also included is a facility for effecting multiple levels of return from a node by using a nonzero return value.

The stack itself is PRIVATE to _workwith, as are the func- tions install and mkfree which respectively place on the stack and remove all keys for a node. The PRIVATE function lookup finds a key in the current node.

In accord with our modular approach, these and other support routines are declared PRIVATE and thus hidden from the menu modules themselves. They are listed at the end of this note.

5. Conclusions

Modular programming is possible in C by using certain programming approaches. These approaches are useful in large programs and in certain inherently modular problems where module-level object hiding results in uniform module designs.

6. References

S.Boyd, "Modular C", ACM SIGPLAN Notices, V18, 1983.

S.Boyd, "Free and bound generics: two techniques for abstract data types in modular C", ACM SIGPLAN Notices, v19, 1984.

B.W.Kernighan & D.M.Ritchie, "The C Programming Language", Prentice-Hall, 1978.

B.Stroustrup, "Classes: an abstract data type facility for the C language", ACM SIGPLAN Notices, v17, 1982.

7. Implementation Details

```
Oct 29 13:43 1984   menu.c Page 2

*/

PRIVATE int      level = -1;
PRIVATE Stack    *s_list = 0;

PRIVATE Stack    *install(key)
Keyptr  key;
{
        int      i;
        Stack    *s_new;
        Stack    *lookup();
        char     *emalloc();

        level++;
        for (i=0; key[i].legend; i++) {

                if (lookup(key[i].legend))
                        fprintf(stderr,"install: dup. key legend %s\n",
                                key[i].legend);

                s_new = (Stack *)emalloc(sizeof(Stack));
                strcpy((s_new->name
                        =emalloc(strlen(key[i].legend)+1)),key[i].legend);
                s_new->u.ptr = key[i].ifunc;
                s_new->level = level;
                s_new->next = s_list;
                s_list = s_new;
        }
        return s_list;
}

PRIVATE char     *emalloc(n)
unsigned n;
{
        char     *p;
        char     *malloc();

        if ((p=malloc(n))==NULL) fprintf(stderr,"out of memory\n");

        return p;
}
```

```
*/

PRIVATE Stack   *lookup(legend)
char    *legend;
{
        Stack   *sp;

        for (sp=s_list; sp!=(Stack *)0, sp->level==level; sp=sp->next)
                if (!strncmp(sp->name,legend,strlen(legend))) return sp;

        return NULL;
}

PRIVATE display()
{
        Stack   *sp;
        int     i;

        for (i=0; i<level; i++) fprintf(stdout,"    ");
        fprintf(stdout," ----------\n");
        for (sp=s_list; sp!=(Stack *)0, sp->level==level; sp=sp->next) {
                for (i=0; i<level; i++) fprintf(stdout,"    ");
                fprintf(stdout,"| %s |\n",sp->name);
        }
        for (i=0; i<level; i++) fprintf(stdout,"    ");
        fprintf(stdout," ----------\n");
}

PRIVATE Stack   *mkfree()
{
        Stack   *sp;

        while ((sp=s_list)->level==level) {
                s_list = s_list->next;
                free(sp->name);
                free(sp);
        }
        level--;
        return s_list;
}
```

Message/Object Programming: An Evolutionary Change in Programming Technology

Brad J. Cox

Productivity Products, Inc.

Message/Object
An Evolutionary Change

Brad J. Cox,

Reprinted from *IEEE Software*, January 1984, pages 50–61. Copyright ©
1984 by The Institute of Electrical and Electronics Engineers, Inc.

**Could a marriage of the
message/object model, a la
Smalltalk-80, and the
operator/operand model,
a la Unix, improve the lot of
both users and programmers?
Stay tuned...**

This article is a tutorial on the object-oriented programming style used in Smalltalk-80 and a personal history of the reasons that led me to pursue this style within conventional languages such as C. It addresses the questions:

- What is message/object programming?
- How does it differ from conventional programming?
- What can be gained by adopting it?
- How can it be achieved through software *evolution,* as opposed to revolution?

The concurrency problem

Programming tools have become increasingly important as software costs have continued to rise. This has led to the development of sophisticated programming environments, such as Unix, Smalltalk-80, Interlisp, and Ada. These programming environments emphasize solitary tools, which serve the individual computer user; they place only moderate emphasis on coordination tools, which help individuals cooperate toward a common goal.

Brooks has pointed out the importance of coordination in determining programmer productivity. His book, *The Mythical Manmonth,* [1] emphasized the need for tools that increase organizational, as well as individual, productivity. But coordination tools are difficult. They deal with group behavior, so they must deal with concurrency. This raises problems for which our sequentially organized computers and our con-

cepts, tools, and methodologies are notoriously ill suited. We still lack the conceptual foundations that would allow coordination tools to be deployed as routinely as solitary tools, since concurrency must be handled with the ad hoc, expensive, and unsatisfactory techniques we now use in building distributed operating systems, for example.

Toward more malleable software. This article addresses a smaller problem that appears solvable today; the building of systems malleable enough to keep up with organizations' propensity for creating, transporting, and manipulating a tremendous variety of data types.

This is done by adding a thin layer of object-oriented structure on top of conventional hardware, languages, and operating systems. This layer addresses several problems peculiar to coordination tools, particularly by providing the ability to share arbitrary objects in the way we now share files. It allows programmers to define new data types and install them in working systems, often without changing the rest of the system. And it provides ways to move arbitrary data types across address-space barriers among organizational participants.

Object-oriented programming replaces conventional operator/operand concepts with new ones—messages/objects. Objects are private data, and the operations supported on that data and messages are a request for an object to perform one of its operations.

Programming:
in Programming Technology

Productivity Products International

This produces more malleable software—software that supports change, reusability, and enhancement—because the decision of how a command will be implemented is not made by the environment of the operation, but by the object that performs it. Objects encapsulate a data type inside the set of procedures, which understands how to manipulate that data type, so operator/operand dependencies are encapsulated inside the objects. This grants systems greater independence from the objects they contain. For example, new data types can often be added to existing systems without changing working code.

Coordination tools need intimate, up-to-date knowledge of schedules, concurrency, participants, roles, protocols, and the organization's way of doing business. Malleability is not only desirable, it's crucial; coordination tools must quickly track changes in the organization they support.

The message/object model represents only a small step toward this new class of applications, because malleability alone is not enough—new concepts are also needed for handling concurrency. But it does address the need to dynamically create, manipulate, and move arbitrary data types among organizational participants.

The goal. The goal of message/object programming is the same as that of conventional software tools: its purpose is to transfer work *from* the user *to* the machine. However, its contributions and costs are permanently and intimately integrated inside the target code. So its effects are felt not just while programs are being built, but while they are being used. And they continue to apply when old modules are reused in new applications or when new objects must be added to old applications.

The phrase "object-oriented programming" has been used for a bewildering range of concepts—everything from programming languages that just provide abstract data types (Simula and its derivatives, such as Ada) to powerful data description languages (the so-called knowledge representation languages). I will not survey the meanings of "object-oriented programming" in these many contexts; in this article, only Smalltalk-80 meanings apply.[2,3]

Evolution or revolution? Object-oriented programming can be considered either revolutionary or evolutionary, depending on the degree to which access to conventional programming techniques is retained.

Pure object-oriented languages such as Smalltalk-80 represent the revolutionary approach and provide the advantage of conceptual simplicity. The programmer works in a computational environment that contains only objects, so the break with the past is clean and crisp.

This article, however, proposes an *evolutionary* approach—adding object-oriented concepts on top of conventional languages. A number of these hybrid languages exist today, including Objective-C,* OOPC,[4] Flavors, and Clascal.** These languages do not offer the conceptual

> A thin layer of object-oriented structure, added on top of contentional hardware, languages, and operating systems, can address several problems peculiar to coordination tools.

consistency of Smalltalk-80, but they do have one considerable advantage: They can often be used for production programming, where pure languages like Smalltalk are usually unacceptable. Smalltalk-80 eliminates conventional operators and operands in favor of dynamically bound objects, so there is no recourse when conventional programming techniques are needed.

Hybrid languages just add a new power tool to the programmer's kit, a tool that can be picked up when it fits the task at hand or set aside when conventional techniques are sufficient. Since they retain conventional languages as a substrate, efficiency can be outstanding. And older tools, programs, and databases can be integrated into new, object-oriented environments with the ease of calling a subroutine.

*Objective-C is a commercial precompiler that adds Smalltalk-80 encapsulation, inheritance, classes, messages, and objects to the C language.

**Clascal is a modified front end to the Pascal compiler used to develop *Lisa.* It provides object-oriented semantics similar, but not identical, to those of Smalltalk-80.

The operator/operand model often leads to program structures radically different from the structure of the problem domain.

The message/object model decouples the environment from the data types it contains.

The operator/operand model

We are taught very early that computers do *operations* on *operands*, and this computational model is preserved through everything we learn subsequently. Once we know that larger operators can be built out of stored sequences of operators, our progress as programmers becomes a matter of increasing the number of different operators we know—text editors, command languages, machine languages, linkers, debuggers, high-level languages, subroutine libraries, application packages, and so forth. We think of the computer as two disjoint compartments, one containing operators and the other operands, and we express our intentions by selecting what operators are to be applied and to what operands in what order.

I call this conventional model of computation the operator/operand model (see Figure 1).

This model applies at every level. At the machine level, we deal with instructions and data; at the language level, expressions and variables; at the library level, subroutines and arguments; and at the command language level, programs and files. The implementation changes at each level, but the concepts remain the same:

(1) Operators are active and make some predetermined change to whatever operand is supplied them.

(2) Operands are passive and change only when affected by some operator.

(3) The *environment* determines what operators are to be applied to what operands in what order.

The term environment stands for whatever determines what happens next. It encompasses the computer user, his input device, and the programs running on his behalf. When the environment applies an operator to an operand—for example, the Fortran operator *sqrt* to the operand *x*—it holds three distinct responsibilities:

(1) *Time:* The environment is responsible for controlling the progression of events in time. For example, a second operator is to be applied just after the first one has finished.

(2) *Space:* The environment is responsible for controlling the movement of computational objects through computational space. For example, the operand will be found within, and the result delivered to, the environment's address space.

(3) *Operator/operand interdependencies:* The environment is responsible for ensuring that the operands meet the data type assumptions made by the operator. For example, since *sqrt* assumes a floating-point argument, the environment is responsible for ensuring that *x* is a floating-point number.

The message/object model does not change the first two responsibilities, but they will need to be reexamined when truly concurrent systems are considered.

The new model does, however, alter the third responsibility; the ramifications of this change are the main topic of this article.

A major oversight. The operator/operand model treats operators and operands as if they were independent. But in practice, operators place strong restrictions on the types of operands they handle correctly. For example, operators like text editors depend on their operands being text files. The operator/operand model provides no way to record this dependence, so the environment must

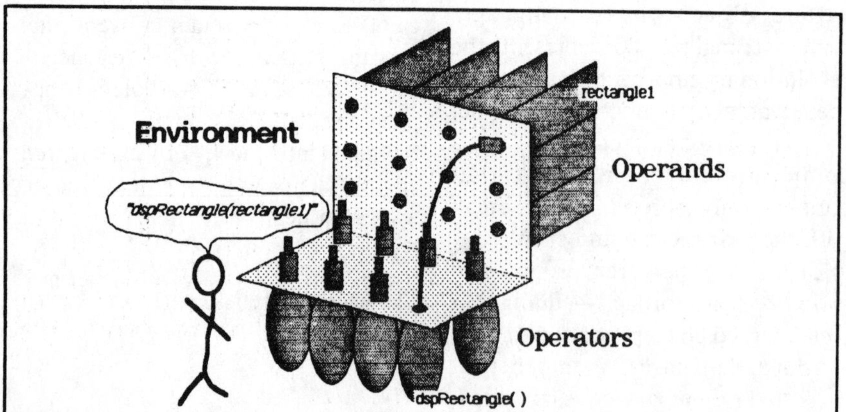

Figure 1. The operator/operand model.

take on the task of remembering the type requirements of the operators and the data type of the operands. This is a major oversight in the conceptual model we use to design, control, and understand computer systems.

Imagine what would happen if electricians used this model to design electrical systems. If they treated electrical operators (power sources) and operands (power sinks) independently, the user would be responsible for remembering the pairs that carry high-voltage power for the air conditioner and those carrying low-voltage signals for the telephone. Our buildings would be wired top to bottom with standard, interchangeable plugs and sockets, requiring us to keep wiring manuals close at hand just to avoid electrocution!

Yet in computing, we've grown accustomed to handling this type of knowledge manually and give it little thought until we're called on to explain to a novice why text editors should not be run on binary files, compilers on grocery lists, or file deletion commands on messages in an electronic mailbox.

Under the message/object approach, by contrast, objects record their type (class) explicitly. This record is used at runtime to determine the set of operations that can be performed on objects of this class. The old operator/operand concepts remain intact, but they are submerged within a thin layer of new structure that records what operations are valid for what operands. This extra structure is analogous to the incompatible plugs and sockets that have made electrical power a safe, dependable resource.

The message/object model

The message/object model decouples the environment from the data types it contains by moving responsibility for operator/operand interdependencies out of implicit storage in the environment and into explicit storage in data structures called classes.

Classes. Classes collect their operators in a table that associates each operator with a name that suggests its meaning without revealing its implementation. The instances of that class—the objects—are like conventional operands, but they record their type explicitly by identifying their class in some standard manner (see Figure 2).

The unit of modularity in a message/object system is the class, so programmers speak of developing classes rather than programs or modules. Each class defines a table of procedures, called *methods* or *behaviors,* and declares the data variables that comprise its instances. Space for these variables is held in *objects.* An object is some private memory and the set of operations provided by its class.

Messages. The environment manipulates objects by selecting an object and telling it what to do. The object decides how to carry out its assignment by selecting the message implementation in the table of messages its class supports. This is generally called "sending the object a message," an unfortunate phrase that now seems too entrenched to change. The word message suggests that objects are concurrent actors that communicate asynchronously, when it actually refers to a conventional function call, modified along lines having nothing to do with concurrency. The common opinion that object-oriented programming is somehow a natural for distributed processing is often based on little more than the misleading use of the world message. (For a more ambitious interpretation of object-oriented programming in which messages *are* used for concurrency, see Yanezawa and Hewitt.[5]).

Although operators and messages are identical with respect to concurrency, they differ with respect to where implementation decisions are recorded. With the operator/operand model, the environment must tell the machine how each command should be implemented, doing this by naming a specific piece of executable code appropriate to the data type at hand. The environment is therefore dependent on the set of operator/operand pairs known at the time it was built.

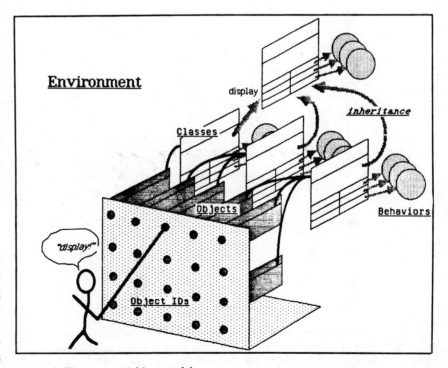

Figure 2. The message/object model.

By contrast, the environment in the message/object model is responsible only for deciding what should be done; the object decides how to do it. Type dependencies cannot spread through the system, since they become permanently encapsulated within classes.

These benefits don't necessarily apply to every language that claims to be object-oriented, only to those that bind commands to implementations dynamically at runtime. For example, Simula and its many derivatives[6] are based on static binding. All data types are declared explicitly in the environment and the compiler translates all commands to implementations at compile time. There's no runtime overhead, but the type declarations in the environment make it explicitly dependent on the types known when it was developed. Without dynamic binding, there is no new assurance that programs can work correctly regardless of the data type supplied.

Objects and conventional languages

The message/object model involves objects, classes, messages, and implementations, all of which can easily be built from concepts found in most conventional programming languages. Class structures and their dispatch tables can be built either manually, with data initialization statements, or by automating the job with such tools as Objective-C, OOPC, or Clascal.

Objects are blocks of memory, allocated from a heap, that identify their class in some standard way. Messaging can be implemented with a conventional subroutine—the messaging routine—that converts commands to implementations via a dispatch table in the class structures.

Conventional languages already provide ways to define new operators and operands, and this is retained intact. But a thin skin of added structure transforms this support into ways of defining classes and methods.

Encapsulation

Unix and Smalltalk-80 are both software development environments of comparable age; both contain compilers, editors, debuggers, networking software, etc. So what accounts for the fact that Smalltalk was written in a tenth as many lines of code?

Part of the reason is different functionality; Unix provides more languages, but Smalltalk provides more graphics. And there are at least two other plausible reasons for this dramatic reduction in code bulk: encapsulation and inheritance (Figure 3).

The following example shows how encapsulation reduces code bulk. It involves building a container that accumulates two types selected arbitrarily by the user—point and rectangle, for example—and then prints the ensemble. We assume that printing functions for each type, prnPoint( ) and prnRectangle( ), are defined elsewhere.

Containment is easily implemented in C by means of an array of pointers. But to print the contained items correctly, there must be a way to determine the type held in each slot at runtime. A typical solution involves testing the type explicitly (see Figure 4.)

Since the user has a hand in determining the type of data stored in each slot, this problem cannot be solved with static binding. The problem *requires* dynamic binding, so the programmer has added it with hand-tools—conditional expressions. The switch expression fulfills the environment's responsibility for ensuring that the printing functions are called with the correct data type as arguments. But the case labels have made the container useless for holding other kinds of contents. The operator/operand model makes the environment responsible for managing data type dependencies, so environmental code like the container cannot be reusable. It must be changed whenever new data types are added.

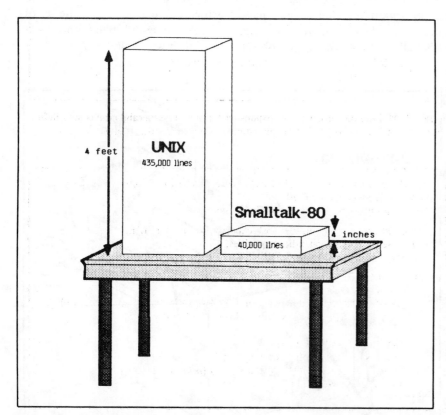

Figure 3. Unix and Smalltalk compared on the basis of code bulk. The latest release of Unix, from the University of California, Berkeley, contains 435,000 lines of source; Smalltalk-80 contains only 40,000 lines.

Containment really should be reusable, since it appears so often in programming. Expression tree nodes, electronic mailboxes, screen windows, directories, buffers, and files are just containers for different data types. Yet each must be designed, coded, and tested individually, and code to support each occupies space in high-speed memory and contributes to the bulk that complicates software maintenance. This is efficiency?

This problem is avoided by making the objects responsible for choosing implementations for their own commands. For example, the container would be expressed in Objective-C as

for ($i = 0$; $i < $ MAX; $i + +$)
    [slot[i] print];

The outer brackets delimit a message expression, which commands the object in the ith slot to print itself. Rectangles implement print by running prnRectangle( ), and points implement print with prnPoint( ). The container no longer needs to probe its contents to learn their type, so it can be reused to hold any data type that supports a print command. Dynamic binding is provided with power tools, and the way is then clear to deploy an additional reusability tool—inheritance—for customizing the generic container for more specialized uses, such as Mailbox, Expression, or Desk.

Inheritance

Inheritance is a technique that allows new classes to be built on top of older, less specialized classes instead of being rewritten from scratch. Classes are created by first inheriting all the variables and behaviors defined by some more primitive class and then adding increasingly specialized variables and behaviors. In other words, programmers create new classes out of old ones by specifying how the new ones differ.

As a technique for organizing information, inheritance is common in everyday experience. When I say, "That dog is a Yorkshire terrier," you immediately understand not only that it has the long hair, small size, color, and temperament of its breed, but also that it holds other characteristics shared by all dogs. Dogs, in turn, inherit the characteristics of larger, less specialized classes, such as mammals, mammals inherit characteristics of vertebrates, and so forth. To describe an object, I state its class, and the listener automatically uses inheritance to derive its general properties by tracing an inheritance tree from one specific instance at the end of a branch back toward primitive concepts at the root.

In the message/object model, inheritance organizes the body of operators and operands and their interdependencies. The message/object model is a way of capturing operator/operand dependencies at their source (the programmer) and storing them explicitly inside the system; inheritance is a way of organizing this information for ready reference.

For example, the Objective-C class library contains a class called "Array" that supports the storage and retrieval of a fixed number of objects by index. Figure 5 shows how a container class can be written by inheriting the work that went into building the array class.

This file states that containers differ from arrays by having one additional instance variable called firstEmptySlot, in addition to any variables declared by Array and its superclasses. The superclass of Array is Object. Object declares the instance variable "isa," which every object inherits to record its class. These variables are concatenated to define the memory layout of con-

```
for (i = 0; i < MAX; i+ +) {
    p = slot[i];            /* Load the pointer in the ith slot into p*/
    switch (p - >kind) {    /* Test the type of the ith slot */
    case POINT:             /* Print a point */
        prnPoint(p); break;
    case RECTANGLE:         /* Print a rectangle */
        prnRectangle(p); break;
    default:                /* unexpected type */
        error( );
    }
```

Figure 4. Making the environment responsible for operator/operand type compatibility produces environmental code like this container, which is not reusable.

```
/# Holds a fixed number of objects and prints them on demand.
#define DEFAULTSIZE 10
= Container:Array { short firstEmptySlot; }

/# Build an empty container with capacity DEFAULTSIZE.
/#     Send new: to get other capacities.
+ new { return [self new:DEFAULTSIZE]; }

/# Put anObject in my first empty slot. Warn of overflows.
- add:anObject {
    if (firstEmptySlot > = capacity) return [self error:"container is full"];
    else return [self At:firstEmptySlot + + Put:anObject];
}
/# Print myself and my contents.
- print { short n; printf("Container = {");
    for (n = 0; n < firstEmptySlot; n + +) [[self At:n] print];
    printf("}"); return self;
}
```

Figure 5. An Objective-C source file defining a simplified container. This implementation begins by inheriting tested code in the Array class and then describes how containers differ from arrays.

tainer instances. For example, the default container produced by sending a "new" message to the container factor is shown in Figure 6.

The rest of the file defines (1) a list of behaviors for a factory that builds container instances and (2) a list of behaviors for the instances themselves. The two sets are distinguished by leading + or − tokens and are added to the behaviors inherited from the superclass. The ID of the container factory is published in the global variable "Container." It can be instructed to create new container instances.

Each method declares a message *selector*, which can have formal arguments, and an *implementation*. Each compares to a C function definition, except that the code is entered in a dispatch table to be called indirectly via messaging, not directly by name. For example, the last method declares that each container instance will recognize a print message; implemented by using an At: method (inherited from Array) to access the *n*th element of the array; and sending object a print message, just as before.

With the Smalltalk-80 scheme, variables are inherited statically at compile time. For example, Objective-C implements the C conditional expression if

if (firstEmptySlot >= capacity)...

by treating the two instance variables as offsets from the object base address delivered in the (hidden) formal argument self. This argument is automatically provided to all methods to identify the object receiving the message:

if (self − >firstEmptySlot> =
   self − >capacity) . . .

Conversely, behaviors (code) are inherited dynamically during messaging. Each class structure contains a dispatch table associating the name and implementation for each method defined in that class. When a message is directed at any instance, the messaging logic finds the class by following a link from the instance. It then searches the dispatch table to find an implementation for the name requested in the message. If this search fails, the behavior is inherited by continuing the search through each of the more primitive classes between the given one and the root of the inheritance tree.

The power of this simple scheme is remarkable. The inheritance tree is rooted on the most generic class, Object. By definition, all objects inherit the variables and behaviors defined there. For example, Object declares the isa variable upon which the messaging logic relies for determining the class of any object, and this guarantees that every object in the system will have a valid isa variable.

The Object class defines a set of generic behaviors that are inherited by every object in the system. These primitive behaviors know about only the "isa" variable; but since "isa" identifies the class structure, this is sufficient to provide a surprising number of capabilities for literally every object. For example, a piece of environmental code can immediately assume that any object has sufficient behavior to reply its class ID, reply the set of messages it supports, test whether the object is an instance of some specific class, and so forth.

To illustrate, suppose we decide to have all objects recognize the abstract operation print. We would start by defining a print method in the Object class. Although this code can reference only the "isa" vari-

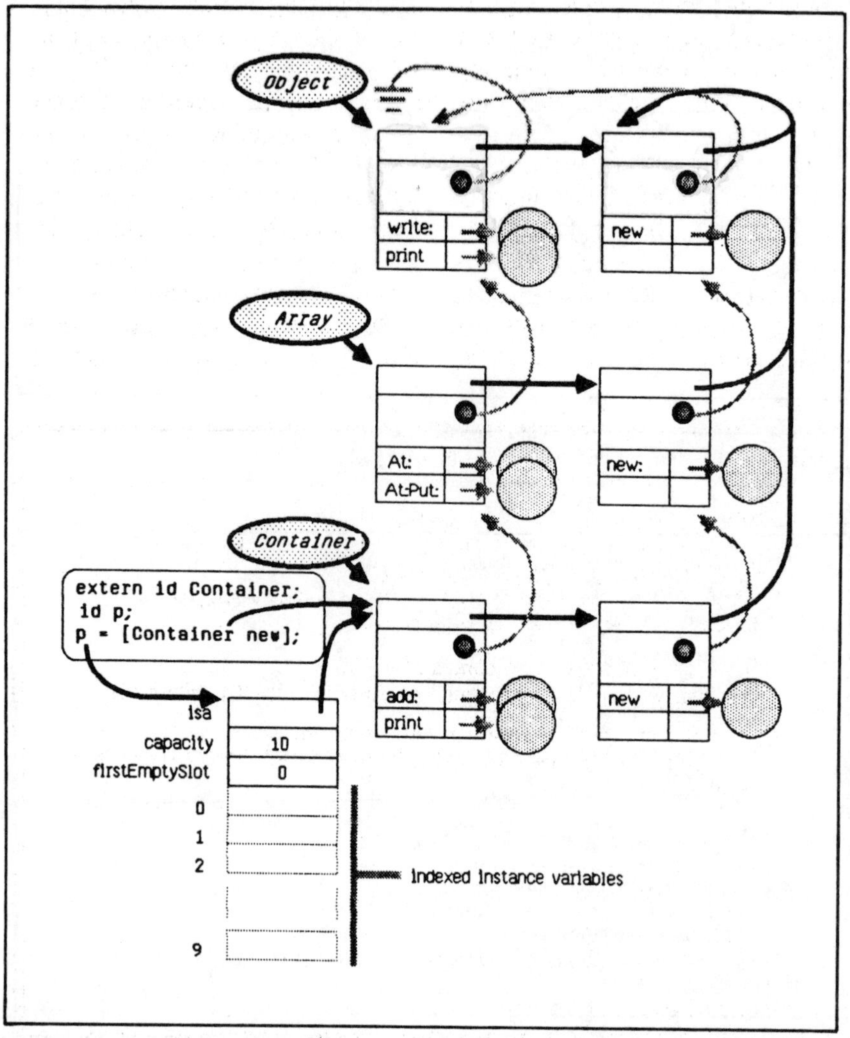

Figure 6. A container, fresh from its factory, and the full class structures that support it.

able, this provides enough information to support a nonspecialized printing capability (a labeled octal dump) by determining the object's class and, from that, the class name and the size of the object. Since every object automatically inherits this behavior, the environment can assume that any object it encounters can respond to the print message.

Specialized classes build on the generic classes they inherit by appending specialized states and behaviors, which often override existing generic behaviors. Say, for example, we want instances of a TextString class to be printed as text rather than octal numbers. We'd accomplish this by defining a specialized print command inside the new class that overrides the primitive one in Object. This done, TextStrings will be specially printed.

Notice that a new data type has just been integrated into an existing system without changing working code.

Automatic object save/restore

A remarkable amount of effort is spent hand coding the logic for moving structured data between memory and I/O devices. Many applications involve parsing input data, processing it, and then reconstituting the data on the output stream. This I/O code is often more time consuming to develop and test than the processing logic, and it must be continually adjusted as data structures evolve during development.

Objective-C provides an automatic way of moving complete graphs of objects between memory and I/O devices by elaborating on the print idea described above. A write routine is defined in the Object class. It works like print, except that it uses typing information captured by the compiler and preserved in the class structures to treat each instance variable appropriately.

The output file represents the contents of each variable of every object in the graph. Object references (edges of the graph) are represented in the file as record numbers. A read method is also provided; it interprets the format produced by write. The two routines work together; a write command to any object in an arbitrary graph of objects generates a file that read can use to regenerate that graph.

Since this is defined in the Object class, every object automatically inherits the ability to save itself in a form that allows it to be mailed to other users for integration into their environments. This is one example of how electronic mail can be extended to carry arbitrary data types. Or, more generally, it is one way of moving arbitrary objects across arbitrary computing barriers.

To illustrate, the program in Figure 7 builds a container, puts a number of points and rectangles in it, and prints the ensemble. Next, it tells the container to write itself to a file and then reloads the container and its contents from the file, printing the new instance.

The Objective-C compiler uses this save/restore capability to maintain a small database, which makes the inheritance hierarchy available across multiple invocations of the compiler and keeps track of selector codes and method return types. The code to support this database was not hand-crafted, but was instead inherited from the Object class. The savings in development time were incalculable, since compiler data structures could be changed at will without complicated I/O code updates.

Objects as models

A large class of computer applications parallel some physical or conceptual process. Traditional data processing applications model the financial state of a company; newsroom automation software models the flow of stories through a newsroom; a compiler's expression tree models the syntactic structure of the program being compiled; and so forth.

Objects are natural metaphors for model building in that each is a capsule of state and behavior, a virtual machine that can be used as a computer-based executable instance of a corresponding entity in the user's problem domain. This potential for close correspondence between computer and problem domains can be useful in building inexpensive, understandable systems.

The operator/operand model often leads to program structures

```
main( ) { FILE *fd, *fopen( ); id p;
    extern id Container, Point, Rectangle, AscFiler; /# Import factory, ids

    /# Build a container, load it, and print
    p = [Container new:10];    /#Build a container of capacity = 10
    [p add:[Point x:15 y:20]];   /# Add a point
    [p add:[Rectangle x:15 y:25 dx:5 dy:7]]; /# Add a rectangle
    [p print]; printf("\n");   /# Print the lot

    /# Save the container and contents in a file
    [AscFiler write:p To:fd = fopen("container.io", "w")]; fclose(fd);

    /# Reload the container and contents and print again
    p = [AscFiler readFrom:fd = fopen("container.io", "r")]; fclose(fd);
    [p print]; printf("\n");
}
---Runtime results---
Container = {(10,20) (15,25)*(5,7) }
Container = {(10,20) (15,25)*(5,7) }

---Contents of container.io---
48{#Container s10 s2 @2 @3 @0 @0 @0 @0 @0 @0 @0 @0 }
8{#Point s10 s20 }
12{#Rectangle s15 s25 s5 s7 }
```

Figure 7. A driver routine to put the Container class through its paces. It also demonstrates automatic object save/restore.

radically different from the structure of the problem domain. The two current schools of software design, functional decomposition and data decomposition, offer the designer a choice between mapping the problem domain into a set of operators (functions) or a set of operands (data).

Many applications can be designed by straightforwardly examining the problem domain, identifying the objects found there and their behaviors, and deciding how to implement each behavior in the computer.

By contrast, object-oriented design treats functions and data as two indivisible aspects of objects in the problem domain. Many applications can be designed by straightforwardly examining the problem domain, identifying the objects found there and their behaviors, and deciding how to implement each behavior in the computer. As a result, the designer is not forced to restate his problem in computer-domain terms, where everything must be either an operator or an operand.

However, problem domains often involve concurrency, and messaging provides no new leverage for expressing concurrent problems. While messaging could, of course, be redefined to allow the sender and receiver to run concurrently, this seems no more fruitful than proposing that all subroutine calls release the called routine to compute concurrently. No, as far as concurrency is concerned, it seems more useful to consider message/object programming in the same light as Fortran, Lisp, or assembly language with respect to concurrency. They're all sequential languages, but they can all be used to build higher level constructs that exhibit concurrency. Concurrent models, operating systems, and coor-

dination tools can be built from such lower level objects as processes, queues, and semaphores, just as we've been doing all along.

The screen application generator experience

In 1981, I was in a research team responsible for designing and building an advanced programming environment. "Buy the best and build the rest" was our motto. We concentrated on constructing new tools that might deliver order-of-magnitude impact, and bought the more traditional ones (compilers, debuggers, editors, configuration managers, etc.).

At that time, we were experimenting with ideas for adding a consistent user interface to the expected large number of tools. I got the notion that program generator technology might help, by generating parts of the user interface automatically. I set about building SAG (screen application generator), a program generator that translated screen descriptions into C programs that provided editing for arbitrarily complex screen forms. I took as its trial application the editing of travel expense vouchers, a task we were then doing manually—one that considerably inconvenienced everyone in our group.

Special-purpose languages are rather easy to build using Unix's compiler-building tools, which generated the parser and lexical scanner for the screen description language. The language was soon working, and I had a working prototype of the expense account in short order.

The expense accounting tool was an immediate hit, even though this early prototype had no ability to save transactions in files or produce hard copy. Why then the enthusiasm? SAG allowed the program to be designed to the needs of the user, rather than bow to the needs of the implementor. For example, arbitrary dependencies could be declared between fields; this ability allowed row and column totals to be updated as soon as the fields they depended on changed. The users saw this as a

significant convenience when balancing trip expenses against the amount advanced for the trip, particularly since trips often involved foreign currency complications. Inspired by the enthusiasm at the demonstration, I set out to add the missing I/O code.

That's when my troubles started. This part of the job took months

---

Even though the expense account tool was a success according to its users, I came to realize that my screen application generator notion had flopped.

—so long, in fact, that any savings from the generator were submerged in costs that were not reduced by the investment in building SAG. The problems arose because expense account records had to be stored in files between runs, without losing their internal structure (pointers). SAG's data structures were somewhat complex, so the logic to move them into files and retrieve them was complicated. The eventual solution involved an additional language that represented the structures on disk and another parser for interpreting this special-purpose language. And since Unix typesetting programs were used to print final copy for the accounting department, the parsing had to be reimplemented in a simpler fashion inside every postprocessor!

Even though the expense account tool was a success according to its users, I came to realize that my screen application generator notion had flopped. After all, its whole point was to test a new tool that should allow quality user interface programs to be built cheaply, yet it failed to help with the most time-consuming part of the task. My tool was no help for building the other operators needed for the expense transaction data type: printing, writing to disk, reading from disk, and typesetting.

We needed similar repertoires of operators for each of the numerous data types in the full-scale programming environment. The number of different programs to be written, documented, maintained, and taught grows with the *product* of the number of different data types multiplied by the number of operators for each data type. With only a 14-character Unix file name to distinguish them, how would anyone keep them all straight?

This led me to recognize that we should think of expense account transactions as a new data type, one analogous to those already provided at the machine level by the hardware designers, but defined by software rather than etched into silicon. We needed a way to build new data types analogous to paper forms, each holding a collection of data and exhibiting a repertoire of behaviors, such as the ability to display the data for editing, move it to a file for permanent storage, and send it to a printer for final copy.

The same idea could be extended to treat the entire computing environment as a large collection of abstract data types. Source programs, compiled programs, schedules, calendars, memos, unformatted documents, formatted documents, and so forth could all be treated as tangible objects that live inside the machine and flow between role-players in the programming project team just like paper objects flow through offices.

Object identifiers

One key decision has not been discussed: the scheme used for identifying objects. These IDs greatly influence the ultimate power and efficiency of any implementation of the object concept.

Smalltalk-80 and Objective-C both use IDs that are unique only within a personal address space. For example, Objective-C uses the object's memory address as its ID. Such

designs optimize efficiency while objects are in fast memory, but complicate moving them outside of this space, since the ID becomes meaningless when written to disk or transmitted to other role players in the organization. Laborious schemes, like Objective-C's automatic I/O mechanism, must be used to locate every such name and convert it into a form independent of addresses in memory.

The opposite extreme. But since messaging, allocation, and deallocation are the only operations supported on object IDs, local changes inside these three functions can support a move to the opposite extreme. For example, the IDs could be taken as globally unique numbers analogous to those used inside operating systems to identify shared files across a population of file system users. The messaging logic would include a test to spot messages to nonresident objects and to load them on demand. Doing this would make the allocation/deallocation logic messier, but the problems are analogous to those now being solved daily inside file systems. The main difficulty would be to provide a policy for resolving simultaneous update problems.

This scheme sacrifices some run-time efficiency (the residence test) in order to have the messaging routine dynamically load objects into private memory when they're needed there. All IDs now have global validity; if we make the further assumption that objects only store machine primitives and object IDs (i.e., no pointers), objects can be moved freely between memory and disk and among role players in the organization.

Far-reaching consequences. Since objects represent any data type, the consequences of the scheme described above are profound. Classes and the executable code they contain are objects, so they also become dynamically loadable and the need for linkers and loaders vanishes. Objects are automatically moved back

to disk when memory space runs short, so there's no longer any need for I/O routines to save information in files. And since objects are now shareable, moving arbitrary objects by electronic mail becomes as simple as posting the ID of the mailed object in the receiver's mailbox.

Of course, the ramifications of such schemes are so far-reaching that it becomes hard to predict how

---

Smalltalk-80 and Objective-C both use IDs that are unique only within a personal address space.

---

usable such a system would be. For one thing, this is a thinly disguised argument for replacing all memory pointers with pointers into a much larger shared address space. Efficiency could be extremely poor without special hardware support. The garbage collection problem, hard enough now inside fast memory, is moved onto disk where it might prove completely intractable—or fade to insignificance when huge, nonerasable memories like optical disks are applied. The usual barrier between memory and disk vanishes, so what is gained by discarding our linkers, loaders, and I/O routines could be lost in reliability if the whole disk becomes vulnerable to user error. And what is gained through better communications among organizational role players could be lost if the whole system becomes exposed to the mistakes of any individual. Even if these problems are solved, we've only moved the computing barrier outwards one notch, to encompass small groups that share a single CPU and a single object address space.

Although the message/object concept can provide a uniform conceptual framework for working with shared object systems, exploiting this potential is not a straightforward task, especially when dealing with hardware not optimized for message passing or global naming. Although objects could provide a single, uniform computational metaphor that spans all levels from CPU to file system, all known implementations compromise uniformity at some level. Smalltalk-80 exploited uniformity within a personal virtual memory space, but stopped short of the file system. Objective-C sacrificed uniformity at the language level, but retained much of C's computational efficiency. The Cola[7] command language supports objects at the file system level by relying on the Hydra operating system and its utilities to supply the lower levels.

Efficiency

Message/object programming seeks to remove work from the user and give it to the machine, so it trades machine cycles to gain the benefits described in this article.

It is, of course, quite difficult to estimate costs precisely because message/object programming is a concept that can be explored in many different implementations, each with very different cost factors. For example, we won't learn much by comparing C and Smalltalk-80 directly because the comparison would include not only the cost of the message/object model, but also the costs of Smalltalk-80's automatic garbage collection, interactive tool environment, and graphical user interface.

Comparing C and Objective-C could be more meaningful, since these languages are identical in these respects. But even this would be complicated by the fact that Objective-C is a hybrid of two languages of opposite philosophies, each designed for very different jobs. Programmers have considerable freedom to apply each tool to the job at which it excels. For example, a compiler developer would normally favor C constructs over message expressions within the lexical analyzer because this code requires maximum efficiency—C's forte—and little bulk and complexity. In the rest of the compiler, these factors flip in impor-

---

Message/object programming seeks to remove work from the user and give it to the machine.

---

tance, and the Smalltalk-80 coding style, with heavy use of message expressions, would be favored.

Comparing the speed of message expressions with function calls is one way to evaluate costs, if one keeps in mind that message expressions perform tests that function calls do not. In a real application like the Container example, the cost of this test would have to be charged against function calls whenever argument types could not be predicted at compile time.

Message speeds can be varied almost arbitrarily by trading space for speed. The slowest technique involves searching for the selector in the method dictionaries of a linked list of inherited classes. The fastest involves keeping a table of all methods in each class so that look ups can be done just by indexing this table. And various compromises are possible, such as holding the results of the full look up in caches of various capacities.

Objective-C supports each of these via a library of message routines. A cached implementation is the default; the indexed implementation can be enabled by calling a function that builds this table for classes the user feels are time critical. Table 1 compares messaging speed with subroutine call speeds using 10 classes (C0-C9) of 10 methods each (m0-m9). C0 inherits Object, C1 inherits C0, and so forth. All methods perform the same C instruction, return self. The effect of deep inheritance is gauged by sending a self message inherited from the Object class. The measurements in Table 1 were taken on a Fortune Systems 32:16 system, which is based on the Motorola 68000 microprocessor.

The ratios show that messaging can be from 2.67 to almost 70 times slower than an equivalent subroutine call for the slowest technique, though the extremes are limit cases rarely encountered in real applications. With the fastest technique, message times are constant at 2.03. Although not shown in the table, using a cache of 1000 gives message speeds of about 2.90.

These speeds can still be improved considerably, since the method dictionaries are searched by the straightforward linear search and both are coded in C; assembly language would be worthwhile in this small, heavily used subroutine.

The Smalltalk-80 user interface is radically different from what most programmers are accustomed to—so different that it has diverted attention away from other attributes that could be even more relevant to today's software crisis.

This article has shown that Smalltalk's dynamically bound message/

Table 1.
Messaging speed and subroutine call speed compared.

TEST	MICROSECONDS		RATIO	
	SEARCHED	INDEXED	SEARCHED	INDEXED
SUBROUTINE(i,i);	51	51	1.00	1.00
[C0 m0];	138	105	2.67	2.03
[C0 m9];	368	105	7.12	2.03
[C0 self];	891	105	17.24	2.03
[C9 m0];	138	105	2.67	2.03
[C9 m9];	368	105	7.12	2.03
[C9 self];	3483	105	67.37	2.03

IEEE SOFTWARE

object paradigm solves several key problems that can prevent us from building highly malleable, reusable software. Static binding requires all data types to be known at compile time. This makes environmental code explicitly dependent on the type of contents known when the code was developed—when new data types must be introduced, the change ripples throughout the environment. The late binding provided by messaging weakens this dependence so that environmental code can often be reused without change as new data types are added over time.

Objective-C demonstrates that late and early binding need not compete—conventional languages can often be extended with Smalltalk constructs to provide hybrid languages that have the strengths of both parents. Although these languages sacrifice the conceptual purity of Smalltalk, they do provide late-binding tools when and where they are most needed—today, on the workbench of the programmers who are struggling to keep large software systems up to date in a changing world. ∎

References

1. Fred Brooks, *The Mythical Man-month,* Addison-Wesley, New York, 1974.

2. *Byte,* Vol. 6, No. 8, Aug. 1981.

3. Goldberg and Robson, *Smalltalk-80, The Language and Its Implementation,* Addison-Wesley, New York, 1983.

4. Brad Cox, "The Object-Oriented Precompiler—Programming Smalltalk-80 Methods in C Languages," *ACM Sigplan Notices,* Vol. 18, No. 1, Jan. 1983, pp. 15-22.

5. A. Yanezawa and C. Hewitt, "Modeling Distributed Systems," *Proc. 5th Int'l Joint Conf. Artificial Intelligence,* Aug. 1977, pp 370-376.

6. Bjarne Stroustrup, "Classes: An Abstract Data Type Facility for the C Language," *ACM Sigplan Notices,* Vol. 17, No. 1, Jan. 1982, pp. 42-51.

7. Richard Snodgrass, "An Object-Oriented Command Language," *IEEE Trans. Software Engineering,* Vol. SE-9, No. 1, Jan. 1983, pp. 1-8.

Brad J. Cox, vice president of software development at Productivity Products International, manages the development of object-oriented languages and applications based on conventional languages and operating systems.

Cox received his BS degree from Furman University and his PhD in chemistry from the University of Chicago. He is a member of ACM and IEEE and has published several papers and articles on object-oriented programming. He is currently writing a book on the same topic.

His address is Productivity Products, Inc., 37 High Rock Rd., Sandy Hook, CT 06482; (203) 426-1875.

OBJECT-ORIENTED LANGUAGES FOR THE MACINTOSH

BY KURT J. SCHMUCKER

An overview of the languages and their capabilities

CURRENTLY, A LARGE NUMBER of object-oriented languages are available, and more are being designed and implemented every year. Some of these languages now on the market or in development are for the Apple Macintosh, an ideal computer for object-oriented languages because of its processing power and the nature of its user interface. In this article I will survey some of the Macintosh object-oriented languages. I will also present a table detailing each language's object-oriented characteristics, such as whether it can access the MacApp class library (see my article "MacApp: An Application Framework" on page 189) or whether it provides for class methods. After describing the languages, I will discuss the mechanics of programming with them on the Mac.

SMALLTALK

The Smalltalk language is the ancestor of all object-oriented languages. It was implemented on the Macintosh by Apple as part of an experiment to demonstrate Smalltalk's portability and debug the Smalltalk specification. Apple currently distributes Smalltalk for the Mac as an unsupported, low-cost product, but a fully supported and greatly enhanced version is expected soon. A fact sheet on Smalltalk and the other languages I describe in this article is presented in table 1.

Smalltalk has a message-sending syntax that often seems unusual to the novice object-oriented programmer, but it quickly becomes the natural way of doing things. Smalltalk syntax and the syntaxes of all the languages I discuss herein are shown in table 2.

New classes and methods are defined by editing standard templates in an interactive source-code browser. The class library for the Macintosh version of Smalltalk contains over 300 classes with special classes for accessing the Macintosh file system, the Macintosh Toolbox (including the QuickDraw routines), and the AppleTalk network added by Apple. Since Smalltalk has been described in previous BYTE articles and elsewhere, I will not elaborate on its language features.

OBJECT PASCAL

Object Pascal is Apple's second object-oriented extension of Pascal. (The first, Clascal, was only for the Lisa Office System and thus is no longer supported by Apple.) The syntax for Object Pascal was jointly designed by Apple's Clascal team and Niklaus Wirth, the designer of Pascal, who was invited to Apple's Cupertino headquarters specifically for this project. In addition to implementing Object Pascal on the Mac, Apple has put the Object Pascal specification in the public domain and encouraged others to implement compilers and interpreters for it. Several such developments are under way.

Object Pascal implements classes as an extension of

Kurt J. Schmucker, director of educational services for Productivity Products International (Severna Park Mall, H & R Block Office, 575 Richie Highway, Severna Park, MD 21146), teaches seminars on object-oriented programming. Kurt has written three books on computer science, including the forthcoming Object-oriented Programming for the Macintosh *(Hayden, 1986).*

Pascal's RECORD structure. In Pascal, records have only data as their component fields, but in Object Pascal, object types (as classes are called in Object Pascal) have data fields (instance variables) and method fields. Messages are sent using the same syntactic construct used in ordinary Pascal for field qualification—the period.

Thus, in Object Pascal, accessing an instance variable and accessing a method (that is, sending a message) are accomplished with the same syntax.

New classes are defined using one new compiler key-

Table 1: *Summary of object-oriented languages.*

		Smalltalk-80	Object Pascal	Neon	ExperCommonLISP	Objective-C	Object Assembler	Object Logo
General	Developer	Apple Computer	Apple Computer	Kriya Systems	Exper-Telligence	Productivity Products	Apple Computer	Coral Software
	Base language	None	Pascal	FORTH	LISP	C	68000 assembler	Logo & CommonLisp
	Current version	0.2	1.0	1.5	2.0	3.1	1.0	1.0
	Toolbox access	Yes, but difficult	Yes	Yes	Yes	Yes	Yes	Yes
	Supports 128K ROM	No	Yes	Yes	Yes	Yes	Yes	Yes
Object-oriented Information	Instance variables and instance methods	Yes	Yes	Yes	Yes	Yes	Yes	Yes
	Class variables	Yes	No	No	Yes	Yes, but cannot be inherited	No	Yes
	Class methods	Yes	No	No	Yes	Yes	No	Yes
	Multiple inheritance	No	No	No	No	No	No	Yes
	Unique instance methods	No	No	No	No	No	No	Yes
	Number of classes in class library	Approx. 300	Approx. 30	Approx. 40	Approx. 45 in ExperCaste	Approx. 25	Approx. 30	Approx. 30
	MacApp access	Yes	Yes	Planned	Planned	Planned	Yes	Planned
Summary	Greatest strength	compatible with other Smalltalks	simplicity of design	speed	object-oriented features; library size	portability to other machines	speed	uniform treatment of objects
	Greatest weakness	speed	limited object-oriented concepts (no class methods)	"unusual" syntax of FORTH	LISP still an "unusual" language	not a native compiler	limited object-oriented concepts (no class methods)	longer learning time for experienced object-oriented programmers
	Other	requires 1000K of RAM for serious work	supported by Apple Computer	numerous user groups, bimonthly newsletter	(note: not shipping at press time)	—	(note: not shipping at press time)	(note: not shipping at press time)

word, OBJECT. The basic schema is

```
TYPE
    ClassName = OBJECT (SuperclassName)
    < instance variable declarations >
    < method header definitions >
    END;
```

where < > denote optional portions of this schema. Methods are defined as ordinary Pascal procedures or functions that have been qualified with the name of the class:

```
PROCEDURE ClassName.ProcedureName(argumentList);
BEGIN
    .
    .
    .
END;
```

Object Pascal is a "bare bones" object-oriented language. It makes no provision for class methods, class variables, multiple inheritance, or metaclasses. These concepts were specifically excluded in an attempt to streamline the learning curve encountered by most novice object-oriented programmers.

The Object Pascal class library is MacApp.

NEON

The language Neon is, depending on your programming-language point of view, either an object-oriented extension to the FORTH language or an incisive and efficient implementation of Smalltalk as a threaded interpreted language. Regardless of which view you take, Neon is a remarkably concise language that nicely bridges the gap between the object-oriented languages (à la Smalltalk) and the threaded languages (à la FORTH). Neon was developed by Kriya Systems expressly for the Mac and was first shipped in 1984.

The basic Neon syntax shows its strong FORTH heritage: From the point of view of most of the other languages discussed in this article, Neon's syntax is backward. (To be fair, many programmers consider the Smalltalk syntax, which has the object precede the message, to be backward compared to the procedure call used in most languages, so perhaps Neon, with the message preceding the object, is one of the few object-oriented languages to get it right!)

New classes and methods are defined using special Neon compiler words that delimit class definitions (:CLASS and ;CLASS) and method definitions (:M and ;M). The basic schemas are

```
:CLASS ClassName <Super SuperClassName < n Indexed>
    <instance variable names >
    < method definitions >
;CLASS
```

and

```
:M Selector: < { named arguments \ local variables — results } >
    < method body >
;M
```

where < > denote optional portions of these schemas.

One of the most useful features of Neon is the provi-

sion for both named arguments and local variables in methods. Named arguments let you associate a name with the arguments placed on the stack prior to the invocation of the method and then simply refer to these arguments by name when you need them in the body of the method. Local variables let you declare and use temporary variables in the method body. Both features simplify the use of Neon compared to the complex stack manipulations often required in FORTH.

Neon allows you to choose between the efficiency of static binding and the flexibility of dynamic binding (called *early binding* and *late binding* in the Neon manual) on a message-by-message basis. Early binding will resolve at compile time a message sent to a given object into an invocation of a particular method in a particular class; late binding will leave this resolution until run time. The compile-time determination is made based on the declared classes for the reference variables. (Thus, Neon is like Object Pascal, which allows a reference variable to be declared of a certain class, and unlike Smalltalk, in which all object references are equal.) The Neon line Get: myInt will send the Get: message to the object referred to by myInt, with the resolution of that message determined at compile time by the declared class of myInt. The line Get: [myInt] will send the Get: message to the object referred to by myInt, with the resolution of that message determined at run time by the run-time class of myInt. Late binding can be used with any construct that generates an object reference, such as Get: [i at: myArray] to send the message Get: to the object referred to by the *i*th element of the array object myArray, with the resolution of that message determined at run time by the run-time class of the object stored at that element in the array.

The basic approach of the current Neon class library—unlike that of MacApp, which provides a completely functional application framework—is to "lift" the Toolbox data types to the level of classes. Accordingly, Neon has classes like Point, Window, Dialog, and Event, which provide a more functional set of building blocks than do the basic Toolbox data types and procedures for the Pascal or C

Table 2: *A comparison of the syntax of each language. The message,* msg, *with argument,* arg, *is sent to the object referenced by* obj.

Syntax	Language
obj msg: arg.	Smalltalk
obj.msg(arg);	Object Pascal
arg msg: obj	Neon
(obj 'msg <arg>)	ExperCommonLISP
[obj msg: arg];	Objective-C
MOVE.W arg(A6)₋(SP) MOVE.L obj(A6)₋(SP) MethCall msg	Object Assembler
tell :obj [msg "arg]	Object Logo

programmer, but not quite the type of building blocks that the MacApp classes provide for the Object Pascal programmer.

EXPERCOMMONLISP

The language ExperCommonLISP is one of the most comprehensive object-oriented languages for the Macintosh in that it implements all of the features of object-oriented languages (except unique instance methods), provides a set of classes that mirror the Toolbox data types, and, with the next release, will provide MacApp access. Exper-CommonLISP was developed by ExperTelligence expressly for the Mac. It was derived from the ExperLISP product available for the Mac since early 1985.

ExperCommonLISP syntax shows its strong LISP heritage: Message sending, setting object reference variables, accessing instance variables, and other object-oriented programming language features are accomplished with list functions.

(setq Triangle (send Object 'subclass)) defines a new subclass of Object, named Triangle, by sending the message subclass to the Object class. (setq tri1 (send Triangle 'New)) instantiates a new instance of the Triangle class and stores a reference to this new instance in the variable tri1. (send tri1 'height) sends the message height to the object referenced by tri1.

Actually, the definition of a new class in ExperCommonLISP can be much more detailed than this simple example shows. The full class-definition schema includes provisions for instance and class variables and instance and class methods.

Note: LISP users will observe that this schema uses terms like arg_lists rather than the traditional lambda-list style common to LISP. The lists are written here in a nonrigorous, informal notation. This is to make this explanation of ExperCommonLISP more understandable to those who do not have a reading knowledge of LISP.

```
(setq NewClass(CLASS (superclass₁ superclass₂...superclassₙ)
    (IVS (iv₁)(iv₂)...(ivₙ))
    (Methods      (method₁(arg_list)(body))
                  (method₂(arg_list)(body))



                  (methodₙ(arg_list)(body)))
    (CVS (iv₁)(iv₂)...(ivₙ))
    (Metamethods(method₁(arg_list)(body))
                  (method₂(arg_list)(body))



                  (methodₙ(arg_list)(body))))
```

where

• IVS is a keyword for the instance-variable-definition clause. Each portion of that clause names an instance variable and provides its initial value and attributes.
• Methods is a keyword for the method-definition clause. Each portion of that clause defines a message, its argument list, and the method that will be invoked when that message is received by an instance of this class.
• CVS is a keyword for the class-variable-definition clause. Like the instance-variable-definition clause, each portion of the CVS clause names an class variable and provides its initial value and attributes.
• Metamethods is a keyword for the class-method-definition clause. Each portion of that clause defines a class message, its argument list, and the class method that will be invoked when that message is received by the class object.

Even this detailed schema does not present a full picture of the facilities in ExperCommonLISP. As one example of a capability in ExperCommonLISP that is not exhibited by this schema and is not present in any of the other object-oriented languages discussed in this article, consider the more detailed format of the following instance-variable-definition clause: (IVS (instance-variable₁-definition) (instance-variable₂-definition)...(instance-variableₙ-definition)) where an instance-variable definition has the form (< instance-variable-name > < default-value-form > < set > < get >).

The keywords get and set specify whether the instance variable can be accessed from outside the object. If the keyword get is used, the variable can be read from outside; if the keyword set is used, the variable can be written. Thus, the degree of encapsulation can be set on a class-by-class basis, and within a class on an instance-variable-by-instance-variable basis. This is a much more flexible middle ground between the unrestricted access provided by Object Pascal and the total lack of access provided by Smalltalk.

The ExperCommonLISP class library includes a set of classes that "lift up" the Toolbox data types to the level of objects as well as the MacApp classes. As with Smalltalk, Neon, and Object Logo, this MacApp access is achieved by a reimplementation of the MacApp class functionality by ExperTelligence.

OBJECTIVE-C

Objective-C brings the basic notions of object-oriented programming to the C language in a manner that is machine-independent. This is accomplished by a compiler that accepts Objective-C source code and outputs an equivalent C source code. The resulting C source code can then be compiled for execution on the target machine. This has resulted in a language that can (and does) exist on both the IBM PC and the VAX-11/780 and on many machines in between. Objective-C was developed by

> *Perhaps the greatest strength of Objective-C is that it is available on a large number of machines.*

Productivity Products International (PPI) and first shipped in 1983.

The Objective-C language is a strict superset of the C language. The object-oriented extensions are achieved by adding a new expression type to the C language, the message expression. Syntactically, this message expression is delimited by brackets (see table 2). The message expression brackets can be distinguished from the standard-array subscripting brackets used in ordinary C by context. The internal message syntax is similar to that of Smalltalk; it even follows Smalltalk's syntax for keyword messages. This new expression type exists on an equal level with all C expressions. The result is that an Objective-C statement message expression can be used anywhere that an expression can be used in C. A sample statement that shows the resulting flexibility is: [Point x: foo( ) + 7 y: [box top]]. In this statement, the keyword message x:y: is being sent to the Point class. The first argument (of the x: portion) is the result of a function call and an addition (foo( ) + 7). The second argument (of the y: portion) is the result of sending the message top to the object referred to by box.

New classes are defined in a special class-description file of the following form:

```
= ClassName: SuperClassName (PhylaList) { Instance Variable Declarations }
+ ClassMethodName {Method Implementation}
- InstanceMethodName {Method Implementation}
= :
```

Only one class may be defined in any such file, although the number of class-method definitions and instance-method definitions may vary.

One object-oriented programming concept that is unique to Objective-C is *phyla*. Phyla in Objective-C are groups of classes, just as phyla in biology are higher-order organizations than the biological notion of a class. When you indicate that a new class belongs to a particular phylum, you are stating that this class will often be used together with the other classes in that phylum. When the Objective-C source code is compiled, this information is used to generate a more efficient method table structure.

The Objective-C class library consists of some 25 classes that implement collection classes, basic geometric notions, and standard data structures—all in a machine-independent way. The fact that the Objective-C language is available on a large number of machines and that its class library is machine-independent is perhaps its greatest strength. Productivity Products International coined the term "software-IC" to describe such a machine-independent class, although the term is now used to describe any well-designed class. (The concept of a software-IC has been described in "Software-ICs" by Lamar Ledbetter and Brad Cox, June 1985 BYTE.)

OBJECT ASSEMBLER

Object Assembler is a set of macros for the Motorola 68000 assembly language that provides easy access to the MacApp class library and to class-definition facilities. It is built on top of the macro assembly language provided by the Macintosh Programmer's Workshop assembler. Object Assembler was developed by Apple expressly for the Macintosh and it will be officially shipped late in 1986.

The Object Assembler macros let you define new classes, define method bodies, instantiate objects, easily reference instance variables by name, and invoke methods, including inherited ones. A few examples will demonstrate the use of these Object Assembler macros. The basic schema for defining a new class in Object Assembler, for example, is

```
MACRO
ObjectDef &TypeName,&Heritage,&FieldList,&MethodList
```

and an example of the use of this macro is:

```
ObjectDef Shape,Object,                \
        ((boundRect,8),                \
        (borderThickness,2),           \
        (color,2)),                    \
        ((Draw),                       \
        (MoveBy),                      \
        (Stretch))                     \

ObjectDef Arc,Shape,                   \
        ((startAngle,2),               \
        (arcAngle,2)),                 \
        ((Draw,OVERRIDE),              \
        (GetArea),                     \
        (SetArcAngle))                 \
```

(The backslash is required by the assembler when continuing a statement from one line to the next.)

Let me demonstrate defining a method and referencing an instance variable by name with some examples.

Defining a method:

Schema

```
        MACRO
        &ProcName ProcMethOf &TypeName

        MACRO
        EndMethod
```

Example

```
        Draw ProcMethOf Arc
        <code>
        EndMethod
```

Accessing an instance variable:

Schema

```
        MACRO
        ObjectWith &TypeName

        MACRO
        EndObjectWith
```

Example:

```
        ObjectWith Arc
        MOVE.L startAngle(A1), – (SP)
        PEA   boundRect(A1)
        EndObjectWith
```

In this example of accessing an instance variable, A1 must already be loaded with an arc object reference. The ObjectWith macro simply qualifies startAngle and boundRect for you. Note that the ProcMethOf (and the corresponding FuncMethOf) macros automatically invoke the

ObjectWith macro with the given class, making references to the instance variables of that class easy.

In terms of its object-oriented semantics, Object Assembler is just like Object Pascal. MacApp access is provided, as is access to any class implemented in Object Pascal. It also is possible to subclass Object Assembler classes in Object Pascal. No easy access is possible to classes implemented in other languages.

OBJECT LOGO

Object Logo is the most unusual object-oriented language for the Macintosh because it is implemented as a classless language—an object-oriented language in which there is no firm distinction between an instance object and a factory object (a class) that makes those instances. Object Logo was developed by Coral Software Corporation expressly for the Mac, and it is scheduled to be shipped in the summer of 1986.

In designing a language that has no distinction between classes and instances, Coral Software's programmers left out a concept that is commonly used in the implementation of object-oriented languages. Classes, after all, are really an implementation convenience—a way of economizing on the amounts of memory required to write object-oriented programs. From Coral's point of view, the conceptual issues in using an object-oriented language are more important than implementation efficiency concerns. By removing the class "artifact," Coral has designed a language in which all objects are treated uniformly, which it believes is easier to learn than traditional object-oriented languages.

There are a number of technical consequences of this philosophical decision to remove distinctions between classes and objects. In Object Logo, objects can be given instance variables and methods "on the fly" during an interactive session. You could, for example, create an object, give it two instance variables, then define a couple of methods, use those methods, clone the object (i.e., copy all relevant object information), *add some instance variables, remove some methods*, and then clone the object. In terms of the vocabulary I have developed up to this point, you have created an instance (from no template), redefined the structure of an instance while it existed, added new methods while it existed, and then used it as a factory to produce a new instance just like itself—all notions that don't make sense with the traditional object-oriented vocabulary. The problem isn't with the vocabulary. The problem is that many of the notions of object-oriented programming that we have spent so long acquiring just don't apply to Object Logo as well as they do to other languages. Consequently, Object Logo is somewhat harder to learn than the other object-oriented languages described in this article, *if* you are already familiar with other object-oriented languages. Object Logo requires that you unlearn some concepts about object-oriented programming and learn some new ones that don't fit in with your conceptual model of how objects, classes, messages, and methods interrelate. For example, Object Logo is the only language described in this article that provides for unique

instance methods—methods not associated with a data structure shared among objects with a similar format, but rather methods directly "attached" to objects. In Object Logo, such a concept is natural; in the other languages discussed here, it is most unusual.

Because conceptual simplicity was one of the major goals in the design of Object Logo, Object Logo adds only a few new primitives to the Logo language.

KINDOF anObject creates a new object which inherits from anObject. TALKTO anObject makes anObject the "current object." (At any time during the execution of an Object Logo interactive session, there is exactly one current object. All references to variables and procedures are resolved in the context of this current object.) HAVE word thing adds the instance variable word to the current object. The initial value of word, in the context of the current object, is thing. HOWTO procedureName adds the method procedureName to the current object. USUAL invokes the inherited method. (This is essentially equivalent to the Object Pascal INHERITED and to sending messages to super in Smalltalk.) And TELL anObject InstructionList executes a list of instructions in the context of anObject without making anObject.

Object Logo is one of the few languages in this article that implements multiple inheritance. In Object Logo, a subclass can invoke *all* methods for a message common to its immediate ancestors. This style differs considerably from that of Smalltalk. (For legal reasons, the version of Smalltalk for the Mac does not have multiple inheritance. This is the only major technical difference with other Smalltalk implementations.)

At the time of this writing, no comprehensive listing of the Object Logo class library was available. However, the plans for Object Logo class library include a complete reimplementation of the MacApp classes using their Logo primitives for accessing the Toolbox. Like Neon and ExperCommonLISP, this reimplementation will produce a semantically similar set of classes so that the MacApp programmer could move from Object Pascal or Neon to Object Logo with very little additional training about the MacApp class library.

PROGRAMMING WITH A MAC OBJECT-ORIENTED LANGUAGE

Object-oriented languages for the Macintosh can be divided into two sets—those that have interactive interpreters and those that don't. The languages with interactive interpreters—Smalltalk, Neon, ExperCommonLISP, and Object Logo—have self-contained development environments consisting of a text editor, an interpreter, a compiler (sometimes), and other application building tools. These development environments are generally in accordance with the Macintosh User Interface Standard. New classes are developed interactively with reasonably functional debugging facilities. When debugged, the new classes are loaded into a working image that then can be saved in a snapshot. Many such snapshots can be saved on disk, each representing a different development effort, a different project, and so on. Classes are used as incremental building blocks: As soon as a new class is defined, it is available for use. The results of developments in different images can be combined in a single image, usually by recompiling the source code versions of the new classes and methods. None of these languages can use procedures written in standard languages like Pascal or C, or classes written in other object-oriented languages, with the exception of ExperCommonLISP, which can access Pascal and C procedures.

In the languages that do not currently have interactive interpreters on the Macintosh—Object Pascal, Object Assembler, and Objective-C—classes are developed first (using a standard text editor) and compiled with the ap-propriate compilers. Then a main program using these classes is written, compiled, and linked with the classes. All of these languages can access procedures and functions written in either Pascal, C, or assembly language.

Most of these languages, whether compiled or interpreted, contain all the facilities to construct a stand-alone Macintosh application. For example, they have special routines to construct menus and to link the choice of a particular menu item with the execution of a certain method. Each of these object-oriented languages has its particular strengths and weaknesses as an implementation language depending on your application and background. ■

CommonLoops

Merging Lisp and Object-Oriented Programming

Daniel G. Bobrow, Kenneth Kahn, Gregor Kiczales,

Larry Masinter, Mark Stefik, and Frank Zdybel

Xerox Palo Alto Research Center

Palo Alto, California 94304

CommonLoops blends object-oriented programming smoothly and tightly with the procedure-oriented design of Lisp. Functions and methods are combined in a more general abstraction. Message passing is invoked via normal Lisp function call. Methods are viewed as partial descriptions of procedures. Lisp data types are integrated with object classes. With these integrations, it is easy to incrementally move a program between the procedure and object-oriented styles.

One of the most important properties of CommonLoops is its extensive use of meta-objects. We discuss three kinds of meta-objects: objects for classes, objects for methods, and objects for discriminators. We argue that these meta-objects make practical both efficient implementation and experimentation with new ideas for object-oriented programming.

CommonLoops' small kernel is powerful enough to implement the major object-oriented systems in use today.

Introduction

Over the last decade many systems have been written that add objects to Lisp (e.g., Flavors, Loops, ObjectLisp.) Each of these has attracted a group of users that recognize the benefits of message sending and specialization and have endorsed an object-oriented style. The object languages in these systems have been embedded in Lisp with different degrees of integration.

Lisp continues to be an important and powerful language for symbol manipulation and is widely used for programming in artificial intelligence applications. One of Lisp's interesting strengths is its ability to absorb other languages, that is, its use as a base for implementing experimental languages.

Within the procedure-oriented paradigm, Lisp provides an important approach for factoring programs that is different from common practice in object-oriented programming. In this paper we present the linguistic mechanisms that we have developed for integrating these styles. We argue that the unification results in something greater than the sum of the parts, that is, that the mechanisms needed for integrating object-oriented and procedure-oriented approaches give CommonLoops surprising strength.

We describe a smooth integration of these ideas that can work efficiently in Lisp systems implemented on a wide variety of machines. We chose the Common Lisp dialect as a base on which to build CommonLoops (a Common Lisp Object-Oriented Programming System). because Common Lisp is supported on almost all commercial Lisp workstations. A portable implementation of CommonLoops is available and is being used in many Common Lisp implementations.

With respect to Lisp, CommonLoops has tried to satisfy a number of different, sometimes conflicting goals:

Compatibility: CommonLoops is compatible with Lisp's functional programming style. Message sending uses the same syntax as function call. Method definition is an extension of Lisp function definition. This is described in section I. Object space is defined as a natural extension of the Common Lisp type space. This is described in section II. Integrated syntax and type spaces allow incremental conversion of programs from a functional to an object-oriented style.

Powerful base: CommonLoops is rich enough for building interesting applications without the need for higher level object languages. It also provides several desirable extensions to object-oriented programming. Method lookup can be based on the class of more than one argument (a "multi-method"). Behavior for an individual object can be specified.

Portability: CommonLoops provides a small kernel that is easy to integrate into Common Lisp

"CommonLoops: Merging Lisp and Object-Oriented Programming" by D.G. Bobrow, K. Kahn, G. Kiczales, L. Masinter, M. Stefik, and F. Zdybel from the *Proceedings of the Conference on Object-Oriented Programming Systems, Languages and Applications*, 1986, pages 17–29. Copyright 1986, Association for Computing Machinery, Inc., reprinted by permission.

implementations. CommonLoops is currently running in five different implementations of Common Lisp.

Flexibility: CommonLoops can be used to implement the major object languages in use today (e.g., Flavors, Smalltalk and Loops) as well as new languages like ObjectLisp. CommonLoops supports intercallability among objects from these different languages. The use of meta-objects in CommonLoops supports variations in object representation, method syntax, combination and optimization. This makes CommonLoops open-ended enough to support research and experimentation with future object and knowledge representation languages, while providing a base for standardization.

Efficiency: Using proven software techniques, described in section III, CommonLoops can run efficiently without special hardware support. This is important because Common Lisp runs on a wide variety of hardware bases.

I. Methods and Functions

In Lisp, functions are applied to arguments. The code that is run is determined only by the name of the function. The lisp form

```
(foo a b)
```

can be interpreted in terms of a function calling primitive, funcall as:

```
(funcall (function-specified-by 'foo)
         a b).
```

In object-oriented systems one "sends messages" to objects. The code that is run is determined by both the name of the message and the type (class) of the object. Methods defined for a particular selector are associated with a class. In the next section we will indicate how we merge the ideas of Lisp datatypes and object classes. The following message using selector sel:

```
(send a 'sel b)
```

can be interpreted as the function call:

```
(funcall
  (method-specified-by 'sel (type-of a))
  a b).
```

The collection of all methods defined for sel define the "generic" function for that selector. Which method is run when a generic function is invoked is determined by the type of the first argument. Thus a method is a partial description of a generic function restricted to objects of a particular type. With this understanding of

method invocation, we can reinterpret all standard Lisp calls:

```
(foo a b)
```

as meaning

```
(funcall
  (method-specified-by 'foo (type-of a))
  a b).
```

if there is a method defined for foo and (type-of a). Some of the ideas described here were independently invented and implemented in New Flavors [MoonKeene86]. Because of their similarity, we will contrast CommonLoops with New Flavors where appropriate. We adapted their term, generic function, to describe the collection of methods for a selector.

A method for move applicable only when the first argument is of type block is defined in CommonLoops as follows:

```
(defmeth move ((obj block) x y)
  <code for moving a block>)
```

The code for this method is added to the generic function for move, and is invoked for objects of type block, or any subtype. If there was an existing method for the same selector and type, defmeth replaces that method. To invoke this method, one simply writes:

```
(move block1 x-pos y-pos)
```

Given that block1 is of type block, the code above will be invoked. Other methods for move could be defined for first argument being a window, a sketch, etc. If more than one method is applicable (because of subclassing), the most specific method is used.

Default Methods

If one uses the defmeth form without specifying any type as in:

```
(defmeth move (thing x y)    ...)
```

this code is run when no more specific method of the generic function for move is applicable. When only such a default method is supplied, it is like defining an ordinary Lisp function. There is no speed penalty for using such default methods instead of functions.

The difference between defining a default method and defining an ordinary Lisp function is that the latter is not allowed to be augmented by specialized method definitions. This protects users from inadvertently overriding or specializing predefined functions where perhaps special compilation optimizations have been used. For example, in most Lisp implementations calls to the primitives car, cdr, and cons are compiled specially for efficiency. Specializing these functions could either have disastrous effect on system efficiency, or no effect on previously compiled code.

However, it is often useful to be able to define methods which specialize existing Lisp functions. To make the Lisp function print specializable, one uses:

```
(make-specializable 'print
                     '(thing stream))
```

This declares that the pre-existing lisp function print is to become the default method for the generic function, and that additional methods can be added.

Multi-Methods

CommonLoops extends Lisp's function call even further. It allows the method to be specified in terms of the types of any number of arguments to the form. It interprets the form:

```
(foo a b)
```

as

```
(funcall
 (method-specified-by 'foo
                       (type-of a)
                       (type-of b))
  a b).
```

Thus, unlike most other object-oriented schemes, CommonLoops allows method-lookup to be based on more that the class of the first argument. For example,

```
(defmeth insidep
    ((w window) (x integer) (y integer))
     ...)
```

defines the method for insidep when the first argument is a window and the second and third arguments are integers.

For any set of arguments, there may be several methods whose type specifications match. The most specific applicable method is called. Method specificity is determined by the specificity of the leftmost type specifiers which differ. However, as discussed below, other regimes can be implemented using the meta-objects facility.

Method and Discriminator Objects

In CommonLoops all the data-structures used to implement the system are objects. In particular, defining a method creates three objects, the *method*, the *discriminator* and the *discriminating-function*.

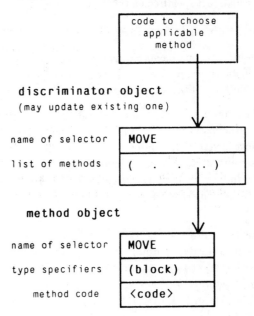

Figure 1: These three objects are used for interpretation of a call. The discriminating function is the code object that selects the method to be called. The discriminator object describes the generic function and is used to construct the discriminating function. It uses the information in the method object; the method object is also used in the compilation of the code for the specific method.

The method object represents the method being defined. The method object contains the type-specifiers and the code for the method. The discriminator object contains a list of all the methods defined on a particular selector. Hence, it describes the generic function. Together, the discriminator and all of its methods produce the discriminating function, a piece of Lisp code which is called when the selector is invoked to determine which method to call. Because the method-lookup and calling mechanisms are under control of the discriminator and method objects, specialized method-lookup and method-combination mechanisms can be implemented by defining new classes of discriminators and methods which specialize parts of the method-lookup protocol.

One such special class are methods which are specialized to individuals. By this we mean that some methods are applicable only if called with a specific object as argument. For example, this would allow a special-case for a connection to a particular host on a network for some period of time when special rerouting needs to be done. Standard protocol makes a method applicable to an individual more specific than any method just specified on types.

Method Combination

Frequently, when one specializes behavior for a given class of object, the desire is to add only a little behavior to the methods of the super-classes.

The primary mechanism for method combination in CommonLoops is `run-super` which is defined to run the most specific method matching the arguments of the current method that is more general than the method in which the `run-super` occurs. If there is no such method an error is signaled.

For example,
```
(defmeth move
  ((w bounded-window)
   (x integer)
   (y integer))
  (cond ((in-bounds-p w x y)
(run-super))
        (t ...   ;; move to closest point inside
         (run-super)))))
```

defines a method which specializes the `move` method on window so that it always moves in-bounds.

The `run-super` is essentially the mechanism of method combination found in Smalltalk, Loops, Director and Object-Lisp. It is both powerful and simple. It allows arbitrary combination of inherited code with current code using Lisp as the combination language.

Sometimes it is more useful to have a declarative means of specifying method combination. In Flavors, for example, `before` and `after` parts can be specified for any method, and these will be run before and after any directly specialized method without requiring any statement in the specialized method. `Before` and `after` parts can be attached any place in the inheritance chain, and are combined in a single method at definition time. In CommonLoops we implement this feature using a special discriminator object that indexes these parts and does the method combination. We have implemented in CommonLoops the interface for user defined method combination specified for New Flavors.

Method and discriminator objects are used to implement both `run-super` and the user defined method combination mechanism. This provides the flexibility of choosing either of the standard kinds of combination in use today. In addition, the existence of these meta-objects allows experimentation with other kinds of combination and invocation. We are currently looking at integrating logic programming into the CommonLoops framework. Logic programming requires specialized method and discriminator objects to combine method clauses using backtracking search.

Processing of method code

The code that implements a method is interpreted and compiled in a context in which the method object is available. The method can use information from the type-specifiers to optimize parts of the method body, or to provide special syntax within the body of the method to access the slots of arguments to the method. Because this processing is done using a defined protocol of messages to the method object, it can be extended by users.

II. Defining Classes

CommonLoops uses `defstruct` to define its classes, extending the syntax of the construct found in Common Lisp for defining composite structures.

```
(defstruct position
  (x-coord 0)
  (y-coord 0))
```

defines a class named `position`, and specifies that instances of that class should have two slots, `x-coord` and `y-coord`, each initialized to 0. As a side effect of defining this structure, `defstruct` also defines a function to make instances of type `position`, and functions `position-x-coord` and `position-y-coord` to access the slots of an instance. An updating form using `setf` and these access functions is used to change the values in the slots, e.g.:

```
(setf (position-x-coord i-1) 13)
```

In addition, `defstruct` can define an extension of a previously defined class.

```
(defstruct (3d-position
              (:include position))
  (z-coord 0))
```

The new structure is a subclass of the old, and includes all of its slots and may add slots of its own. Thus `3d-position` has slots `x-coord`, `y-coord`, and `z-coord`, and inherits all methods defined on `position`.

Meta-classes

In CommonLoops, as in Smalltalk, classes are themselves instances of other classes. These special classes are known as meta-classes. The figure below indicates the relationships of the classes defined above, and their meta-class structure-class.

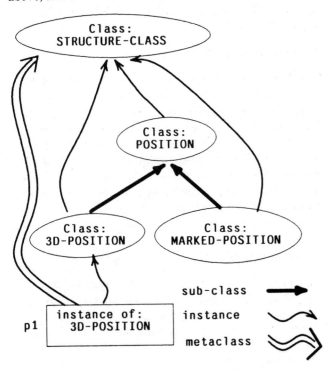

Figure 2: Three different relations are illustrated in this diagram. 3d-position and marked-position are both subclasses of position, and inherit its structure and behavior. p1 is an instance of 3d-position, the three position classes are instances of structure-class. We call structure-class the "meta-class" of p1, since it is the class of its class.

Meta-classes control the behavior of the class as a whole, and the class-related behavior of the instances such as initialization, as do Smalltalk meta-classes. In Flavors, the Flavors themselves are not instances of any Flavor, and hence their behavior is uniform.

In CommonLoops, meta-classes have important additional roles. A meta-class controls the interpretation of the defstruct form; it also controls the representation of instances of the class; it specifies the order of inheritance for classes; finally, it controls allocation and access to instance slots.

Interpreting the Defstruct Form

Because some meta-classes need to provide defstruct options not provided by other meta-classes, CommonLoops separates the interpretation of the defstruct form into two parts. In the first part, the defstruct is checked to make sure it conforms to basic defstruct syntax and the meta-class is determined

by looking for a :class option. Then expand-defstruct is called on the meta-class and the defstruct form. This allows the meta-class to process the defstruct form and interpret the options as it chooses.

Representation of Objects

Meta-classes control the representation of instances. Consider the following definitions of the class position:

```
(defstruct (position
            (:class structure-class))
  (x-coord 0)
  (y-coord 0))

(defstruct (position (:class class))
  (x-coord 0)
  (y-coord 0))
```

In the first definition, the structure-class meta-class is specified. An instance of position created using this definition will be represented as a linear block of storage with two data items. This very efficient in space. The second definition specifies the meta-class class which causes the instances to be represented in a more flexible way, with a level of indirection between a header and the storage for the data. This allows such an instance to track any changes in its class (adding or deleting intance variables) without users of the instance needing to do anything to update the instance. Automatic updating occurs when access to slots is requested. The instance can even change its class, and invisibly update its structure. Because the meta-class is responsible for the implementation of the instance, it is also responsible for access to slots of the instance. We return to this below.

Multiple inheritance

Many meta-classes allow multiple inheritance. These meta-classes extend the syntax of the :include defstruct option to allow a list of included classes. For example,

```
(defstruct
  (titled-window
    (:include (window titled-thing))))
```

defines a new-class, titled-window, which includes both window and titled-thing as super-classes. Under control of the meta-class, the new class will inherit slots from the super-classes. Although the usual inheritance for slots is to take the union of those specified in the included-classes, some meta-classes could signal an error if there were an overlap in names.

The class being defined is the root of a sub-lattice from which descriptions are inherited. The specified order of the included classes determines a local precedence among the classes. This is used as the basis of the precedence relation for specificity. The specificity of classes with respect to this new one is cached in the class as an ordered list that we call the *class precedence list*.

The meta-class determines the algorithm for computing the class precedence list from the local precedences. The algorithm used by the meta-class c l a s s is left to right, depth first up to joins, with the constraint that the local ordering of any local precedence list must be maintained. Except for the last constraint, this is the same as the algorithm used in Loops. The constraint is violated when a local precedence list contains C1 before C2, and C1 is somehow a super of C2. In this case, CommonLoops signals an error. This algorithm produces the same ordering as the one used in New Flavors.

for structures of CommonLisp, the built-in types, and the meta-class c l a s s designed to facilitate exploratory programming [Sheil]. The user can define a new meta-class to provide other functionality for a different object system. For example, with Gary Drescher, we have looked at defining a metaclass that supports ObjectLisp [Drescher] inheritance and behavior.

Slot-Options in Class

The representation of instances used by c l a s s allows three additional allocation strategies for slots in addition to the usual direct allocation of storage in the instance. These provide facilities that have been found useful in a number of object systems. In each case, the user of the class does not need to change the form of access to change the form of allocation.

A :c l a s s allocation specifies that the slot is stored only in the class; no storage is allocated for it in the instances. Thus, the slot is shared by all instances of the structure. Updating the value in one instance is seen by all. This option provides functionality similar

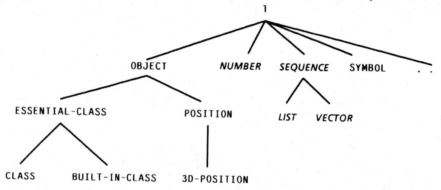

Figure 3. Classes in italics are instances of b u i l t - i n - c l a s s, *all others are instances of* c l a s s. t *is the super-class of everything in CommonLoops. It corresponds to the Common Lisp type specifier of the same name.* e s s e n t i a l - c l a s s *is a primitive class used to implement meta-classes. All meta-classes have* e s s e n t i a l - c l a s s *as a super-class. It defines default behavior which all metaclasses must have.*

Initial classes in CommonLoops.

CommonLoops uses the flexibility provided by meta-classes to define classes which correspond to the primitive Lisp types. These classes are part of the same class lattice as all other CommonLoops classes. Thus the Lisp data-type space is included in the CommonLoops class lattice. This means that methods can be defined on the Lisp built-in classes as well as on types defined by defstruct. This is a significant difference from New Flavors.

As shown in Figure 3, CommonLoops provides several pre-defined meta-classes which provide functionality

to class variables in Smalltalk and Loops, except that CommonLoops class variables share the same name space with instance variables.

A :d y n a m i c allocation specifies that storage for this slot should be allocated in the instance, but only when the slot is first used. If the first access is a fetch, then storage is allocated, the d e f a u l t - i n i t form is evaluated, the value is stored in the slot and returned. If the first access is a s e t f, then storage is allocated, the value is stored in the slot, and returned. This allows infrequently used slots to have initialization declarations, but take storage only if needed.

An allocation option of :none means that the slot should not exist in this instance. This is used to override inheritance of slots defined by a super class.

The meta-class class also allows objects to have slots that do not appear in the defstruct declaration. This gives objects their own property lists: this is analogous to Flavor's plist-mixin flavor. It differs from a plist-mixin in that there is uniform access to slots independent of whether they were declared.

III. CommonLoops Implementation

CommonLoops can be implemented efficiently, even on conventional machines. The most important cases for time-critical applications are well understood and have been implemented in several object-oriented systems.

Method Lookup.

Implementation of method lookup can be specialized with respect to four cases: where there is only one method defined for a particular selector, where the only method has no type specification, where all the methods have specifiers only on their first argument, and the general case.

Single Method: In this case there is only one non-default method defined on the selector. A static analysis of Loops and Flavors code shows that approximately 50% of the selectors fall in this category. In this case the method can be compiled with a type check to make sure it is applicable. The method-lookup time is only the time required to check the types of the arguments.

Default Method Only: This case is similar to the single method case except that the method has no type specifiers at all, so it is always applicable. In this case there is no type check required. It is implemented as a if it were defined as a function.

Classical Methods Only: When there are multiple methods, all of which only have type specifiers on their first argument the situation is the same as in Smalltalk and Flavors. We call this "classical" to stress its equivalence to classical object programming systems. On stock hardware this can be implemented using any of the proven method-lookup caching schemes. The cache can either be a global cache, a selector-specific cache, a callee cache, or a caller cache. Variations have been used in Smalltalk-80 systems [Krasner], Loops, and Flavors. On specialized hardware this can be implemented using the same mechanisms as in Flavors. A default method can easily be combined with a set of classical methods, calling it instead of a standard error.

Multiple Multi-Methods: In the remaining case, a selector has more than one method, and at least one of them has a type specifier on other than the first argument. A standard case might have type specifiers for the first two arguments, e.g. where the types for show could be

```
(square, display-stream)
(square, print-stream)
(circle, display-stream)
...
```

In our current implementation of multi-method invocation, we have implemented a straightforward extension of the caching techniques used for classical method lookup. We do not have enough experience with multi-methods to know what other common patterns should be optimized.

In classical object-oriented programming, this example could be handled by introducing a second level of message sending. Instead of having separate multi-methods for each case, one could (by convention) write two methods for each case. Thus, the show message for square would send a second message to the stream (show-square-on) that would embed the type information about square implicitly in the selector.

Multi-method lookup in CommonLoops is faster than multiple sequential method lookups. The overhead for doing lookup is the time of an extra function call (a call to the discriminator function which then calls the chosen method) plus the time of a type check for each specialized argument.

Slot access and Meta-classes

Slot access can be implemented in a variety of ways. The meta-class class uses a caching technique similar to that used in Smalltalk. The meta-class structure-class, because it does not allow multiple inheritance, can compile out the slot lookups in the standard way. Another meta-class could use the self-mapping-table technique used in Flavors.

We have also experimented with ways to compile out the cost of method lookup and slot lookup entirely. Having meta-classes and discriminator objects allows the specification of special ways of accomplishing a call to a selector when the types of some the arguments are known at compile-time. In certain cases the appropriate method can be determined at compile-time so that no method lookup need occur at run-time. The body of the method can even be compiled in-line.

Compilation of calls to accessor functions is a common case where in-line expansion works well. The resulting code can access the slot directly. Meta-classes which do this kind of optimization are useful in production versions of applications where the time to change a program vs. program execution speed tradeoffs can be pushed completely towards execution speed.

Flexibility to use different slot-access or method-lookup schemes based on the meta-class is an important feature of CommonLoops. Efficiency is a matter of tradeoffs. Object systems without meta-classes must choose one set of tradeoffs and implement it as well as possible. Then, users have to live with it. In CommonLoops, several different sets of tradeoffs can be implemented as well as allowing users to choose which set of tradeoffs is appropriate for a given situation.

IV. CommonLoops and other Systems

In this section we consider several important object-oriented languages. All of these languages have been influential in the design of CommonLoops, and we try to note similarities and differences. A general overview of features of object languages and multiparadigm systems can be found in [StefikBobrow86]

Loops

Loops [BobrowStefik83] is a multi-paradigm system for knowledge programming implemented in Interlisp-D. It is integrated into the interactive environment provided by Interlisp-D. It also provides special environmental capabilities, such as class browsers and object inspectors. The design of CommonLoops draws on our experience with Loops, but is a major departure from it.

CommonLoops provides new functionality but also introduces many minor incompatibilities and lacks some functionality of Loops as discussed below. Features of Loops such as composite-objects that are appropriately implemented in terms of the CommonLoops kernel are not discussed. Modifying Loops to run on top of CommonLoops will require a substantial programming effort.

Class variables. Loops supports the notion of class variables that are accessed via special functions.

CommonLoops provides class variables which provide nearly equivalent functionality. There are not, however, different name spaces for instance variables and class variables as there are in Loops. We now believe that the advantages for modifiability of a program outweigh the advantages of multiple name spaces.

Default values. Loops supports the notion of a default value which at slot access time finds the default value in the class or the super classes of the class. CommonLoops provides init-forms in slot-descriptions that specify how to compute the default value at creation time. The essential difference is that in Loops an instance tracks the slot description until given a local value while CommonLoops always gives a local value at creation time. The Loops behavior can be implemented in CommonLoops using annotated values as described in the section on open design questions. In our experience, initial values are satisfactory for most of the applications of default values.

Slot properties. In Loops a slot can have named properties in addition to a value. This provides a convenient way to store more information about a value without interfering with access of the value. This can be supported using annotated values.

Active values. In Loops a value can be active, so that specified functions can be run when a slot containing an active value is accessed. CommonLoops can provide comparable capabilities, as discussed below in the section on open design questions.

Smalltalk-80 System

The Smalltalk-80 system [GoldbergRobson] is both an object-oriented programming language and a vertically integrated programming environment that is uniformly object structured. The strength and importance of the Smalltalk-80 system rests not only with its object-oriented programming style, but also in the careful engineering of the set of kernel classes and their behavior that define the Smalltalk-80 image.

In terms of its provisions for class definition, name lookup, method discrimination, and method combination CommonLoops can be viewed as a superset of Smalltalk-80, with some notable exceptions:

The Smalltalk-80 virtual machine directly supports only single superclass inheritance. Nevertheless, additional inheritance schemes can be implemented (by changing the manner in which new classes are defined) and multiple superclass inheritance is included as part of the standard Smalltalk-80 environment. It operates substantially the same as in CommonLoops, except that multiply inherited methods for the same selector must be redefined at the common subclass, or else an error will result when the method is invoked. This Smalltalk-80 feature is inconvenient for mixin classes that specialize standard methods as used in Flavors and Loops.

The Smalltalk-80 multiple inheritance scheme provides an explicit scheme for method combination: objects can send messages to themselves in a way that specifies from which superclass method lookup is to proceed. This is done by composing the name of the superclass with the selector, e.g. an instance of ReadWriteStream may send itself the message ReadStream next to indicate that the ReadStream superclass is to supply the method. This explicitness can cause problems because methods build in as constants information about the class hierarchy, which may change.

Classes and meta-classes bear the same relationship to each other and there is some overlap of function in both systems. However, there are some significant differences in functionality. Instances of all Smalltalk classes (except for the compiled method class) are realized in terms of just three basic implementations: pointer objects, word objects, and byte objects. The class definition directly determines which implementation is to be used. By convention in Smalltalk each class has a unique meta-class.

In Smalltalk enumerating the instances of a class is intended to be computationally bearable (just how bearable depends on implementation dependent factors, e.g. whether and how virtual memory is implemented.) As a result, Smalltalk classes can broadcast to their instances. This makes them extensional, as well as intensional, characterizations of sets of objects. Since even integers have a class in CommonLoops, it is not generally useful to enumerate all instances of every class. It is straightforward in CommonLoops to implement a meta-class that allows a class to keep a list of instances it has created.

In the Smalltalk-80 system, one can find all references to an most types of objects. It is even possible to interchange all the references to an object with all the references to some other object, regardless of their respective classes. In effect, the two objects exchange identities. This operation is inexpensive if the object memory indirects references via an object table, which is the standard practice. This capability enables, among other things, cheap re-sizing of instances of

variable length classes. In CommonLoops, instances of classes created by the meta-class class can easily modify their contents and class pointers to achieve the same functionality.

Smalltalk provides class variables, which are shared by all the instances of a class and its subclasses, and pool variables, which are shared by all instances of some set of classes and their subclasses. The effect of class variables is directly achieved in CommonLoops through the :allocation class slot option. The effect of Smalltalk's pool variables can be achieved through the expedient of defining a common superclass among the classes to be "pooled", which contributes nothing but a shared slot.

Smalltalk differs more fundamentally from CommonLoops in that Smalltalk objects are encapsulated, and control primitives are based upon message passing. In Smalltalk, unlike CommonLoops, only methods of an object can access and update the state directly (this is not strictly true, but the operations provided for breaking encapsulation are viewed as just that, and used primarily for building debuggers, viewers etc.). All other methods must send messages.

Conditionals, iteration, and the like in Smalltalk are done via message passing, and contexts (stack frames) are first class objects. CommonLoops relies upon the Common Lisp control constructs which in general are special forms and cannot be specialized.

New Flavors

CommonLoops is practically a superset of New Flavors. CommonLoops and Flavors share the notion of generic function. In developing CommonLoops we have included the Flavors mechanism for user-defined method combination.

The New Flavors algorithm for computing class-precedence is a refinement of the old Flavors algorithm which solves problems found in old Flavors, Loops and earlier versions of CommonLoops. We have described our equivalent to the New Flavors algorithm.

To be entirely compatible with New Flavors, CommonLoops would need to provide some syntactic support for the mechanisms for defining classes and methods. Machine dependent support is also necessary (and easily added) to provide the performance on microcoded machines.

The important difference between CommonLoops and New Flavors is the existence of meta-objects in

CommonLoops. Meta-objects make CommonLoops much more extensible. Meta-objects allow experimentation with other kinds of object systems. They allow CommonLoops to treat primitive Lisp types as classes. Methods can be defined on those types, and the standard CommonLoops mechanisms for accessing the slots of a structure can be used to access the fields of primitive Lisp objects.

Other Object languages

ObjectLisp [Drescher] also integrates objects and Lisp. Unlike CommonLoops, ObjectLisp distinguishes fundamentally between Lisp types and ObjectLisp objects. This means that one cannot define methods on existing types. Another difference is that ObjectLisp supports only classical methods.

T shares with CommonLoops the common syntax for message sending and function call. Like ObjectLisp, T supports only classical methods and there is no integration of Lisp types with objects. [ReesAdams]

IV. Open design questions

In this section we present some extensions to CommonLoops which seem attractive, and which suggest directions for future research.

Complex type specifiers

Extending CommonLoops to handle more complex type specifiers is attractive. The simplest extension is to allow logical combinations of the simpler type specifiers, for example

```
(or block window)
```

Another extension would be to allow an arbitrary predicate to be used. Yet another extension would allow specification based on the number of arguments.

The problem occurs when there are ambiguities about which method to use. For example, which of the two:

```
(or block window) (or block house)
```

is more specific with respect to block.

For this reason, we have chosen to disallow method type-specifiers which cannot be ordered by specificity in the kernel of CommonLoops. A user who wants to add such methods to CommonLoops can do so by defining a special method class and using the method-lookup protocol to specify different method-lookup rules.

We believe that handling incomplete type specifiers and the possible resolutions (backtracing, unification, production system rules) is a fertile area for language design and research, and perhaps a foundation for a graceful merger of Lisp, Prolog and production systems.

Structural versus Procedural Views of Objects

The object-oriented programming community is split on the issue of whether the specification or interface description of a class of objects should be strictly procedural, or whether it should be split into procedural and structural parts. In the procedural view an object is defined by its message protocols. As a matter of principle, programs that interact with an object should make no assumptions about the internal representations of the object. A procedural view of a complex number is defined in terms its response to messages such as x, y, rho, theta, plus, print etc. CommonLoops continues the Common Lisp convention by usually generating access methods for structural components.

A description which includes a structural description could include the fact that x, y, rho, and theta are structural components of a complex number, that is, these named pieces are intended to have memory-cell semantics. Notice that the structural description need not be isomorphic with the implementation structure. For example, a complex number may be implemented as a pair x and y, with rho and theta computed.

Those that favor including a structural description argue that language forms should support this way of thinking. In CommonLoops, a uniform procedure ref is available to access structural parts by name, e.g.
```
(ref some-complex 'theta),
```
instead requiring the use of an access function for each
```
(complex-number-theta some-complex).
```
Use of the ref form allows one to write code that can iterate through the slots of a structure, for example, as in a comparison routine. Also, in CommonLoops, the developmental meta-class supports slots in instances that are not declared in the class. The ref form provides a uniform way of accessing both declared and undeclared slots. The ref form has some advantages with respect to expressivity.
```
(ref x y)
```
is equivalent to the wordier
```
(funcall
  (find-accessor-function
    (class-of x)
    y)
  x y).
```
A ref form is also generally an appropriate first argument for setf, unlike funcall, because ref is used with memory-cell semantics.

A shortcoming with a structural description is that sometimes one wants procedures to be invoked upon access to a structural component. A way to achieve this within the structural framework uses annotated values as described below.

Annotated Values --- Views and Implementations

Access-oriented programming is one of the popular features of Loops and several frame languages such as KEE, UNITS, and STROBE. The merits of this feature are often confounded with the merits of its various implementations. In this section, we try to separate these issues, and indicate alternative implementations available in CommonLoops.

In access-oriented programming, fetching from or storing in an object can cause user-defined operations to be invoked. *Procedural annotations (or active values)* associate objects with slots so that methods are invoked when values are fetched and stored. It is also useful to associate other information with a slot in addition to its value. *Structural (or property) annotations* associate arbitrary extendible property lists with a value in an object. Collectively these kinds of annotations are called annotated values. These annotations can be installed on slots and can be nested recursively.

Annotated values reify the notion of storage cell and are a valuable abstraction for organizing programs. Structural annotations can be used for in-core documentation. They are also used for attaching records for different purposes. For example, such annotations can record histories of changes, dependencies on other slots, or degrees of belief. Procedural annotations can be used as interfaces between programs that compute and programs that monitor those computations. For example, they can represent probes that connect slots in a simulation program to viewers and gauges in a display program.

Annotated values are conveniently represented as objects, and must satisfy a number of criteria for efficiency of operation and non-interference [Stefik]. When multiple annotations are installed on the same value, the access operations must compose in the same order as the nesting. Annotated values can be implemented in different ways that optimize performance depending on the expected patterns of common use.

One implementation of annotated values in CommonLoops would require the slot-access primitives of the meta-class check whether the value is an active value object. The active value check can be made fast if the active value objects are wrapped in a unique data type. This technique for implementing active values has been sucessfully in Loops. Hardware or microcode support of this fast check would allow the use of annotated values in ordinary Lisp structures (e.g. in cons-cells), greatly extending the utility of this abstraction.

Alternatively, a procedural implementation of annotated values could be built upon the ability in CommonLoops to specialize methods with respect to individuals. For those slots for which a special action is desired upon access, one can define methods for those accessors and objects that do the special action.

CommonLoops is capable of supporting either implementation. In addition, we believe that it is appropriate in CommonLoops to provide meta-classes that can support annotated values according to the needs of optimization. If active values are to be attached and detached frequently, checking dynamically for annotated values may be preferable to changing the discriminator frequently. If probes are usually installed only once, then one may prefer the lower overhead of the procedural implementation. If access to properties is relatively rare compared with the access to values, then differentiating property access at compile-time might be preferred.

It is useful to be able to view a program that uses annotations in terms of that abstraction, rather than in implementation terms. The issue of supporting views of programs is discussed more generally in the next section.

Programming Environment Support

Programming environments must provide computational support for particular views (or perspectives) of programs [BobrowStefik86]. A view is said to support a particular programming abstraction when the elements of the view are in the terminology of the abstraction and the operations possible within that viewer are those appropriate for the abstraction.

For example, a viewer that supports the view of a program in terms of annotated values would show annotated values, not methods or wrappers that make up their implementation. The installation and nesting of annotated values are the appropriate actions available in the viewer.

Another important and popular view of object-oriented programs is that classes are defined by their slots and methods. While program listings often show structure and methods separated, it is useful to view such programs as organized in terms of classes with access to slot and method descriptions. CommonLoops viewers in definition groups [Bobrow] also provide access to any multi-method from all of its associated classes. Thus, CommonLoops supports the classical view with appropriate extensions.

Views of classes can be organized around semantic categories, as in the standard Smalltalk-80 browser, or around a graph of the class inheritance lattice of some portion of the system, as in Loops, and Commonloops. In the latter case, certain operations become natural to perform directly through the lattice browser -- for example, promoting methods or slots to more general classes, or changing the inheritance structure. Changing the name of a slot or selector through a browser can invoke analysis routines that can find and change all occurrences of the name in code.

Viewers on CommonLoops also support a procedural abstraction. For example, they provide static browsers of program calling structure, where each discriminator is considered as a single function. However, through these browsers, one can get access to individual method definitions from the corresponding discriminator.

To provide viable support for programming with an abstraction, the viewers must be integrated with the debugging system. For example, to support a view of program in terms of methods, it should not be necessary to understand how methods are implemented or to refer to methods created automatically by the system. Rather, debugging should use the same terms that the programmer uses in writing the program.

V. Summary and Conclusions

Over the last ten years many systems have been written that add object-oriented programming to Lisp (e.g., Flavors, Loops, Object-LISP.) Each of these has attracted a group of users that recognize the benefits of message sending and specialization and have endorsed the object-oriented style. The object-languages in these systems have been embedded in Lisp with different degrees of integration.

Interest in object-oriented programming has also been spurred by work in expert systems. Several knowledge programming systems (ABE, ART, KEE, Strobe, UNITS, etc.) have emerged. These systems have included variations and extensions on object-oriented programming and tools for creating knowledge bases in terms of objects. As research continues, additional knowledge programming systems will emerge. Each of these will have their advocates and perhaps their niche in the range of applications and computer architectures. All of these systems can benefit from an object-oriented base that is efficient and extensible.

The creation of a good base involves both theoretical language design and engineering concerns. CommonLoops has attempted to respond to several kinds of pressure on the design of such a system.

The applications community wants to use a system for its work. The language must be suitable for state-of-the-art applications and systems that they build on top of it. The language must have an efficient implementation. It is an advantage if the language is a graceful extension of Common Lisp because existing code and existing programming skills can be preserved.

Vendors share these interests. They want their systems to provide a suitable base for a large fraction of the applications. They want the kernel of the language to be lean, easy to maintain, and efficient; they want the kernel to be principled and free of idiosyncratic features with no enduring value beyond their history. Vendors don't want to implement multiple versions of object languages, gratuitously different and incompatible.

The research community has somewhat different interests. Like the application community, it needs to be able to share code, but it is concerned with being able to try out other ways of doing things. New ideas for languages come out of the experience of the research community. To build higher level languages, the base must provide mechanisms for open-ended experimentation.

CommonLoops has responded to these pressures by providing a base for experimentation through the use of meta-objects, while capturing in its kernel the ability to implement the features of current object-oriented systems. By integrating classes with the Lisp type system, and using a syntax for method invocation that is identical to Lisp function call, CommonLoops makes possible a smooth and incremental transition from using only the functional paradigm for user code to using the object paradigm. As a portable system implemented in a widely available base, it allows users the choice of hardware and environments, and a road to the future.

Acknowledgments

Many people read early drafts of this paper, helped us to sharpen the ideas and present them more coherently. Thanks to Eric Benson, John Seely Brown, Margaret Butler, Johan de Kleer, Peter Deutsch, Richard Gabriel, Stanley Lanning, Henry Lieberman, Mark S. Miller, Sanjay Mittal, Randy Trigg, Bill van Melle, Daniel Weld, and Jon L. White.

References

[Bobrow] Bobrow, D. G., Fogelsong, D. J., Miller, M. S., *Definition Groups, Making Sources First Class Objects,* ISL Report, Xerox PARC, 1986

[BobrowStefik83] Bobrow, Daniel G., Stefik, Mark. *The Loops Manual*, Intelligent Systems Laboratory, Xerox Corporation, 1983

[BobrowStefik86] Bobrow, Daniel G. and Stefik, Mark. "Perspectives on Artificial Intelligence Programming", *Science* V231, No 4741, p 951 February 28, 1986

[Drescher] *ObjectLISP User Manual*, LMI, 1000 Massachusetts Avenue, Cambridge, MA 02138.

[GoldbergRobson] A. Goldberg and D. Robson. *Smalltalk-80: The Language and its Implementation.* Addison-Wesley, Reading, MA 1983.

[MoonKeene86] Moon, D., Keene, S, *New Flavors.* ACM 1986 OOPSLA Conference

[Krasner] Glenn Krasner, Ed. *Smalltalk-80: Bits of History, Words of Advice.* Addison-Wesley, Reading, MA, 1983.

[ReesAdams] Rees, , J. A. and Adams, N. I. T: a dialect of Lisp or, lamda: the ultimate software tool, ACM Symposium on Lisp and Functional Programming, 1982

[Sheil] Sheil, B. "Power Tools for Programmers", in Barstow, D. et al (editor) *Interactive Programming Environments*, McGraw Hill, 1984

[Steele] Steele, G.L. *Common Lisp: the language.* Digital Press.1984.

[StefikBobrow86] Stefik, M., Bobrow, D.G. Object-oriented Programming: Themes and Variations. *AI Magazine* **6:4**, Winter 1986.

[Stefik] Stefik, M., Bobrow, D.G., Kahn, K. Integrating access-oriented programming into a multi-paradigm environment, *IEEE Software*, 1986.

Object-Oriented Programming: Themes and Variations

Mark Stefik & Daniel G. Bobrow

Intelligent Systems Laboratory, Xerox Palo Alto Research Center, 3333 Coyote Hill Road, Palo Alto, California 94304

Many of the ideas behind object-oriented programming have roots going back to SIMULA (Dahl & Nygaard, 1966). The first substantial interactive, display-based implementation was the SMALLTALK language (Goldberg & Robson, 1983). The object-oriented style has often been advocated for simulation programs, systems programming, graphics, and AI programming. The history of ideas has some additional threads including work on message passing as in ACTORS (Lieberman, 1981), and multiple inheritance as in FLAVORS (Weinreb & Moon, 1981). It is also related to a line of work in AI on the theory of frames (Minsky, 1975) and their implementation in knowledge representation languages such as KRL (Bobrow & Winograd, 1977), KEE (Fikes & Kehler, 1985), FRL (Goldstein & Roberts, 1977) and UNITS (Stefik, 1979).

One might expect from this long history that by now there would be agreement on the fundamental principles of object-oriented programming. As it turns out, the programming language community is still actively experimenting. Extreme languages can be found which share the description "object-oriented" but very little else. For example, there are object-oriented operating systems that use a much more general notion of message sending than in most of the languages described here.

This article is an introduction to the basic ideas of programming with objects. A map of the field is naturally drawn from where one stands. Most of the examples will be from the authors' own system, Loops (Bobrow & Stefik, 1981), and we will describe other object languages from that vantage point. We have not tried to be complete in our survey; there are probably fifty or more object-oriented programming languages now in use, mostly with very limited distribution. We have selected ones we know that are widely used for applications in artificial intelligence or have a particularly interesting variation of an issue under discussion. For pedagogical purposes we begin with a white lie. We introduce message sending and specialization as the most fundamental concepts of object-oriented programming. Then, we will return to fundamentals and see why some object languages don't have message sending, and others don't have specialization.

Thanks to Ken Kahn and Mark Miller who were especially generous with their time and ideas as we prepared this article for publication. Thanks also to Sanjay Mittal and Stanley Lanning who read earlier drafts and who contributed to the design and implementation of Loops. Ken Kahn, Gregor Kiczales, Larry Masinter, and Frank Zdybel helped broaden our understanding of the variations in object-oriented languages as we worked together on the design of CommonLoops. Much of the discussion in this paper was inspired by the electronic dialog of the members of the Object-oriented Subcommittee for Common Lisp.

Special thanks to John Seely Brown and Lynn Conway, who encouraged our work on Loops, and helped us to develop larger visions while we slogged through the bits. Thanks also to Bill Spencer and George Pake for maintaining the kind of intellectual environment at PARC that has allowed many different projects in language design to flourish.

Abstract

Over the past few years object-oriented programming languages have become popular in the artificial intelligence community, often as add-ons to Lisp. This is an introduction to the concepts of object-oriented programming based on our experience of them in Loops, and secondarily a survey of some of the important variations and open issues that are being explored and debated among users of different dialects.

Reprinted with permission from *The AI Magazine*, Volume 6, Number 4, Winter 1986, pages 40–62. Copyright © 1984 and 1985 by Xerox Corporation.

Basic Concepts of Object-Oriented Programming

The term object-oriented programming has been used to mean different things, but one thing these languages have in common is *objects*. Objects are entities that combine the properties of procedures and data since they perform computations and save local state. Uniform use of objects contrasts with the use of separate procedures and data in conventional programming.

All of the action in object-oriented programming comes from sending messages between objects. Message sending is a form of indirect procedure call. Instead of naming a procedure to perform an operation on an object, one sends the object a message. A selector in the message specifies the kind of operation. Objects respond to messages using their own procedures (called "methods") for performing operations.

Message sending supports an important principle in programming: *data abstraction*. The principle is that calling programs should not make assumptions about the implementation and internal representations of *data types* that they use. Its purpose is to make it possible to change underlying implementations without changing the calling programs. A data type is implemented by choosing a representation for values and writing a procedure for each operation. A language supports *data abstraction* when it has a mechanism for bundling together all of the procedures for a data type. In object-oriented programming the class represents the data type and the values are its instance variables; the operations are methods the class responds to.

Messages are usually designed in sets to define a uniform interface to objects that provide a facility. Such a set of related messages is called a *protocol*. For example, a protocol for manipulating icons on a display screen could include messages for creating images of icons, moving them, expanding them, shrinking them, and deleting them. When a message protocol is designed for a class, it should be made general enough to allow alternative implementations.

There is additional leverage for building systems when the protocols are *standardized*. This leverage comes from *polymorphism*. In general the term polymorphism means "having or assuming different forms," but in the context of object-oriented programming, it refers to the capability for different classes of objects to respond to exactly the same protocols. Protocols enable a program to treat uniformly objects that arise from different classes. Protocols extend the notion of *modularity* (reusable and modifiable pieces as enabled by data-abstracted subroutines) to *polymorphism* (interchangeable pieces as enabled by message sending).

After message sending, the second major idea in object-oriented programming is specialization. Specialization is a technique that uses class inheritance to elide information. Inheritance enables the easy creation of objects that are *almost like* other objects with a few incremental changes. Inheritance reduces the need to specify redundant information and simplifies updating and modification, since information can be entered and changed in one place.

We have observed in our applications of Loops that changes to the inheritance network are very common in program reorganization. Programmers often create new classes and reorganize their classes as they understand the opportunities for factoring parts of their programs. The Loops programming environment facilitates such changes with an interactive graphics *browser* for adding and deleting classes, renaming classes, splitting classes, and rerouting inheritance paths in the lattice.

Specialization and message sending *synergize* to support program extensions that preserve important invariants. Polymorphism extends downwards in the inheritance network because subclasses inherit protocols. Instances of a new subclass follow exactly the same protocols as the parent class, until local specialized methods are defined. Splitting a class, renaming a class, or adding a new class along an inheritance path *does not affect simple message sending* unless a new method is introduced. Similarly, deleting a class does not affect message sending if the deleted class does not have a local method involved in the protocol. Together, messsage sending and specialization provide a robust framework for extending and modifying programs.

Fundamentals Revisited

Object languages differ, even in the fundamentals. We next consider object languages that do not have message sending, and one that does not have specialization.

Variations on Message Sending.   When object languages are embedded in Lisp, the simplest approach to providing message sending is to define a form for message sending such as:

```
(send object selector arg1 arg2 ...)
```

However, some language designers find the use of two distinct forms of procedure call to be unaesthetic and a violation of data abstraction: a programmer is forced to be aware of whether the subsystem is implemented in terms of objects, that is, whether one should invoke methods or functions.

An alternative is to unify procedure call with message sending. Various approaches to this have been proposed. The T (Rees & Meehan, 1984) programming language unifies message sending and procedure calling by using the standard Lisp syntax for invoking either methods or functions. For example, (display obj x y) could be used either to invoke the display method associated with obj, or to invoke the display lisp function. A name conflict resulting in ambiguity is an error.

CommonLoops (Bobrow, Kan, Kiezales, Masinter, Stefik, & Zdybel, 1985) takes this unification another step.

Lisp function call syntax is the only procedure calling mechanism, but ordinary Lisp functions can be extended by methods to be applied when the arguments satisfy certain restrictions. In Lisp, functions are applied to arguments. The code that is run is determined by the name of the function. The Lisp form (foo a b) can be viewed as:

(funcall (function-specified-by 'foo) a b).

Sending a message (send a foo b) in object-oriented programing can be viewed as equivalent to the invocation of:

(funcall (method-specified-by 'foo (type-of a)) a b).

The code that is run is determined by both the name of the message, foo, and the type of the object, a. A method is invoked only if its arguments match the specifications. In this scheme a method with no type specifications in its arguments is applied if no other method matches. These methods are equivalent to ordinary functions, when there are no other methods for that selector. From the point of view of the caller, there is no difference between calling a function and invoking a method.

CommonLoops extends the notion of method by introducing the notion of "multi-methods" to Common Lisp. It interprets the form (foo a b ...) as:

(funcall (method-specified-by 'foo (type-of a)

(type-of b)...) a b ...).

The familiar methods of "classical" object-oriented programming are a special case where the type (class) of only the first argument is used. Thus there is a continuum of definition from simple functions to those whose arguments are fully specified, and the user need not be aware of whether there are multiple implementations that depend on the types of the arguments. For any set of arguments to a selector, there can be several methods whose type specifications match. The most specific applicable method is invoked.

A variation among object oriented languages is whether the method lookup procedure is "built-in." In the languages we have described here, there is a standard mechanism for interpreting messages — with the selector always used as a key to the method. In Actors, the message is itself an object that the receiver processes however it wishes. This allows other possibilities such as pattern matching on the message form. It also allows "message plumbing" where the receiver forwards the entire message to one or more other objects. Splitting streams to allow one output to go to two sources is a simple example of the use of this feature.

Variations on Specialization.

Specialization as we have introduced it so far is a way to arrange classes so that they can inherit methods and protocols from other classes. This is a special case of a more general concept: the concept is that objects need to handle some messages themselves, and to pass along to other objects those messages that they don't handle.

In actor languages (Lieberman, 1981) this notion is called "delegation" and it is used for those programming situations where inheritance would be used in most other object languages. Delegation is more general than specialization, because an actor can delegate a message to an arbitrary other object rather than being confined to the paths of a hierarchy or class lattice.

If delegation was used in its full generality for most situations in actor programming, the specifications of delegation could become quite verbose and the advantages of abstraction hierarchies would be lost. Actor programs would be quite difficult to debug. In practice, there are programming cliches in these languages that emulate the usual forms of inheritance from more conventional object languages, and macros for language support. However, since there is no standardization on the type of inheritance, it makes it more difficult for a reader of the code to understand what will happen.

Classes and Instances

In most object languages objects are divided into two major categories: classes and instances. A class is a description of one or more similar objects. In comparison with procedural programming languages, classes correspond to types. For example, if "number" is a type (class), then "4" is an instance. In an object language, *Apple* would be a class, and *apple-1* and *apple-2* would be instances of that class. Classes participate in the inheritance lattice directly; instances participate indirectly through their classes. Classes and instances have a declarative structure that is defined in terms of object variables for storing state, and methods for responding to messages.

Even in these fundamentals, object languages differ. Some object languages do not distinguish between classes and instances. At least one object language does not provide a declarative structure for objects at all. Some languages do not distinguish methods from variable structure. Languages also differ in the extent to which variables can be annotated.

Themes

We begin be describing classes and instances as they are conceived in Loops. We will then consider some variations.

What's in a Class?   A class in Loops is a description of one or more similar objects. For example, the class *Apple* provides a description for making instances, such as *apple-1* and *apple-2*. Although we usually reserve the term instance to refer to objects that are not classes, even classes are instances of a class (usually the one named *Class*). Every object in Loops is an instance of exactly one class.

GLOSSARY FOR OBJECT-ORIENTED PROGRAMMING

class. A class is a description of one or more similar objects. For example, the class *Apple*, is a description of the structure and behavior of instances, such as *apple-1* and *apple-2*. Loops and Smalltalk classes describe the instance variables, class variables, and methods of their instances as well as the position of the class in the inheritance lattice.

class inheritance. When a class is placed in the class lattice, it inherits variables and methods from its superclasses. This means that any variable that is defined higher in the class lattice will also appear in instances of this class. If a variable is defined in more than one place, the overriding value is determined by the inheritance order. The inheritance order is depth-first up to joins, and left-to-right in the list of superclasses.

class variable. A class variable is a variable stored in the class whose value is shared by all instances of the class. Compare with *instance variable*.

composite object. A group of interconnected objects that are instantiated together, a recursive extension of the notion of object. A composite is defined by a template that describes the subobjects and their connections.

data abstraction. The principle that programs should not make assumptions about implementations and internal representations. A *data type* is characterized by operations on its values. In object-oriented programming the operations are methods of a class. The class represents the data type and the values are its instances.

default value. A value for an instance variable that has not been set explicitly in the instance. The default value is found in the class, and tracks that value until it is changed in the instance. This contrasts with initial values.

delegation. A technique for forwarding a message off to be handled by another object.

initial value. A value for an instance variable that is computed and installed in the instance at object creation. Different systems provide initial values and/or default values.

instance. The term "instance" is used in two ways. The phrase "instance of" describes the relation between an object and and its class. The methods and structure of an instance are determined by its class. All objects in Loops (including classes) are instances of some class. The noun "instance" refers to objects that are not classes.

instantiate. To make a new instance of a class.

instance variable. Instance variables (sometimes called slots) are variables for which local storage is available in instances. This contrasts with class variables, which have storage only in the class. In some languages instance variables can have optional properties.

lattice. In this document we are using "lattice" as a directed graph without cycles. In Loops, the inheritance network is arranged in a lattice. A lattice is more general than a tree because it admits more than one parent. Like a tree, a lattice rules out the possibility that a class can (even indirectly) have itself as a superclass.

metaclass. This term is used in two ways: as a relationship applied to an instance, it refers to the class of the instance's class; as a noun it refers to a class all of whose instances are classes.

message. The specification of an operation to be performed on an object. Similar to a procedure call, except that the operation to be performed is named indirectly through a *selector* whose interpretation is determined by the class of the object, rather than a procedure name with a single interpretation.

method. The function that implements the response when a message is sent to an object. In Loops, a class associates *selectors* with methods.

mixin. A class designed to augment the description of its subclasses in a multiple inheritance lattice. For example, the mixin *NamedObject* allocates an instance variable for holding an object's name, and connects the value of that variable to the object symbol table.

object. The primitive element of object-oriented programming. Objects combine the attributes of procedures and data. Objects store data in variables, and respond to messages by carrying out procedures (methods).

perspective. A form of composite object interpreted as different views on the same conceptual entity. For example, one might represent the concept for "Joe" in terms of *JoeAsAMan, JoeAsAGolfer, JoeAsAWelder, JoeAsAFather*. One can access any of these by view name from each of the others.

polymorphism. The capability for different classes of objects to respond to exactly the same protocols. Protocols enable a program to treat uniformly objects that arise from different classes. A critical feature is that even when the same message is sent from the same place in code, it can invoke different methods.

protocol. A standardized set of messages for implementing something. Two classes which implement the same set of messages are said to follow the same protocol.

slot. See instance variable

specialization. The process of modifying a generic thing for a specific use.

subclass. A class that is lower in the inheritance lattice than a given class.

super class. A class that is higher in the inheritance lattice than a given class.

Figure 1 shows an example of a class in Loops. A class definition is organized in several parts a class name, a metaclass, super classes, variables, and methods. The metaclass part names the metaclass (*Class* in this case) and uses a property list for storing documentation. A *metaclass* describes operations on this class viewed as a Loops object. The super class part (supers) locates a class in the inheritance network. The other parts of a class definition describe the places for specifying data storage and procedures.

Truck

MetaClass Class

    EditedBy *(*dgb "29-Feb-85 4:32)*

    doc*(**This sample class illustrates the syntax of classes in Loops.*

        Commentary is inserted in a standard property in the class.
—*e.g. Trucks are . . .)*

Supers (Vehicle CargoCarrier)

Class Variables

    tankCapacity 79 doc*(*gallons of diesel)*

Instance Variables

    owner PIE *doc(*owner of truck)*

    highway 66 *doc(*Route number of the highway.)*

    milePost 0 *doc(*location on the highway)*

    direction East *doc(*One of North, East, South, or West.)*

    cargoList NL *doc(*List of cargo descriptions.)*

    totalWeight 0 *doc(*Current weight of cargo in tons.)*

Methods

    Drive Truck.Drive *doc(*Moves the vehicle in the simulation)*

    Park Truck.Park *doc(*Parks the truck in a double space.)*

    Display Truck.Display *doc(*Draws the truck in the display.)*

The class, called *Truck,* inherits variables and methods from both of its super classes *(Vehicle and CargoCarrier).* The form of the definition here shows the additions and substitutions to inherited information. In this example a value for the class variable *tankCapacity* is introduced, and six instance variables *(highway, milePost, direction, cargoList, and totalWeight)* are defined, along with their default values. The Methods declaration names the procedures (Interlisp functions) that implement the methods. For example, *Truck.Drive* is the name of a function that implements the *Drive* method for instances of *Truck.*

Example of a Class Definition in Loops.

Figure 1.

Variables in objects are used for storing state. Loops supports two kinds of variables: class variables and instance variables. Class variables are used to hold information shared by all instances of the class. Instance vari-

ables contain the information specific to a particular instance. Both kinds of variables have names, values, and other properties. We call the instance variable part of a class definition the *instance variable description*, because it specifies the names and default values of variables to be created in instances of the class. It acts as a template to guide the creation of instances. For example, the class *Point* might specify two instance variables, x and y with default values of 0, and a class variable associated with all points, *lastSelectedPoint*. Each instance of *Point* would have its own x and y instance variables, but all of the instances would use the same *lastSelectedPoint* class variable; any changes made to the value of *lastSelectedPoint* would be seen by all of the instances. Default values are the values that would be fetched from the instance variables if the variables have not been assigned values particular to the instance. As motivated by Smalltalk, Loops also has indexed instance variables, thus allowing some instances to behave like dynamically allocable arrays.

A class specifies the behavior of its instances in terms of their response to *messages*. A message is made of arguments and a *selector*. The class associates a selector (*e.g.,* the selector "Drive" in Figure 1.) with a *method*, a procedure to respond to the message. When a message is sent to an instance, its response is determined by using the selector to find the method in a symbol table in the class. The method is located in the symbol table and then executed. Since all instances of a class share the same methods, any difference in response by two instances is determined by a difference in the values of their instance variables.

What's in an Instance? Most objects in a Loops program are instances (that is, not classes). For example, in a traffic simulation program there may be one class named *Truck* and hundreds of instances of it representing trucks on the highways of a simulation world. All of these truck instances respond to the same messages, and share the class variables defined in the class *Truck*. What each instance holds privately are the values and properties of its instance variables, and perhaps an object name. The variables of an instance are initialized with a special token indicating to the Loops access functions that the variables have not been locally set yet. Figure 2 shows an example of an instance object.

Instantiation and Metaclasses. The term *metaclass* is used in two ways: as a relationship applied to an instance, it refers to the class of the instance's class; as a noun it refers to a class all of whose instances are classes. The internal implementation of an instance is determined by its metaclass.

For example, to create a new instance of the class *MacTruck* a *New* message is sent to *MacTruck*. This creates a data structure representing the truck with space for all of the instance variables. The method for creating the

Figure 2 (left box)

Automobile-1

Class Automobile

InstanceVariables

highway 66

milePost 38

direction East

driver Sanjay

fuel ?

...

Instances have local storage for their instance variables. If no local value has been set yet, default values for instance variables are obtained from the class. In this example, the "?" in the value place for the instance variable *fuel* indicates that the actual value is to be obtained by lookup from the class *Automobile*. Methods and class variables are not shown since they are accessed through the class.

**Instance of an Automobile
in a Traffic Simulation Model.
Figure 2.**

Figure 3 (right box)

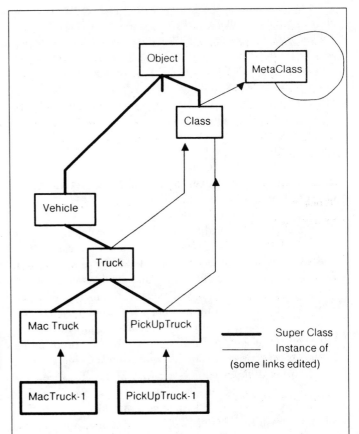

Super Class
Instance of
(some links edited)

Instantiation is the process of making a new object. In Loops, this process begins when a *New* message is sent to a class. In this figure, the instance *MacTruck-1* is created by sending a *New* message to *MacTruck*. The line between *MacTruck-1* and *MacTruck* indicates the instance-of relationship between the instance and its class. Similarly, a class like *PickUpTruck* is created by sending a *New* message to *Class*. The line between *PickUpTruck* and *Class* indicates the instance-of relationship between the class *PickUpTruck* and its metaclass *Class*. Every object has an instance-of relationship with exactly one class. *Class* and *MetaClass* are called metaclasses, since all of their "instances" are classes. Another important metaclass is *AbstractClass* (not shown). *AbstractClass* is the metaClass for classes not meant to be instantiated (*e.g.*, like Vehicle).

Instantiation.

Figure 3.

---

data structure is found in *MacTruck's* metaclass—*Class*. To create a new class (*e.g.*, the class *PickUpTruck*, an instance of the class *Class*), a New message is sent to *Class*. The method for creating and installing the data structure is found in the metaclass of *Class* called *MetaClass*. The *New* method creates a data structure for the new class, with space for class variables, instance variable description, and a method lookup table. The new class is also installed in the inheritance network. Figure 3 illustrates this process of instantiation.

AbstractClass is an example of a useful metaclass in Loops. It is used for classes that are placeholders in the inheritance network that it would not make sense to instantiate. For example, its response to a *New* message is to cause an error. Other metaclasses can be created for representing some classes of objects as specialized LISP records and data structures.

Classes and Instances, Revisited.

The distinction between classes and instances is usual in object languages. In applications where instances greatly outnumber classes, a different internal representation allows economies of storage in representation. It also provides a natural boundary for display of inheritance, and hence helps to limit the visual clutter in presentations of the inheritance network.

The object language of KEE (Fikes & Kehler, 1985) does not provide distinct representations for classes and instances. All objects, or "units," as they are called in KEE, have the same status. Any object can be given "member"

slots which will be inherited by instances of this object. Proponents of this more uniform approach have argued that for many applications, the distinction does little work and that it just adds unnecessary complications. Similarly there is no such distinction in actor languages (Lieberman, 1981). Inheritance of variables in these languges is generally replaced by a copying operation. ThingLab (Borning, 1979), a constraint driven object language used prototypes rather than classes to drive object creation, and specialization was simply instantiation followed by editing.

In Object Lisp (Drescher, 1985), the declarative structures conventionally associated with classes are dispensed with. Objects are simply binding environments, that is, "closures." An operation is provided for creating and nesting these environments. Object variables are Lisp variables bound within an object environment; methods are function names bound within such an environment. To get the effect of message sending, one "ASKS" for a given form to be evaluated in the dynamic scope of a given object. Nested environments are used to achieve the layered "inheritance" effect of specialization. Use of an "ASKS" form, however, precludes the unification of message-sending and procedure call that is now appearing in other object languages.

Not all object languages have metaclasses. Since Flavors are not objects, instances of Flavors have no metaclasses. All Flavor instances are implemented the same way: as vectors. Loops uses metaclasses to allow variations in implementation for different classes. For example, some objects provide a level of indirection to their variable storage, allowing updating of the object if there are changes in its class definition. Smalltalk-80 has metaclasses, and uses them primarily to allow differential initialization at object creation time. CommonLoops (Bobrow, *et al.*, 1985) makes more extensive use of metaclasses than Loops, using them as a sort of "escape mechanism" for bringing flexibility to representation and notations of objects.

Another difference in systems is whether instance variables of an object can be accessed from other than a method of the object. Proponents of this strict *encapsulation*, as in Smalltalk, base their argument on limiting knowledge of the internal representation of an object, making the locus of responsibility for any problems with the object state well-bounded. A counter argument is that encapsulation can be done by convention. Loops allows direct access to object variables to support a knowledge representation style of programming. This is particularly useful, for example, in writing programs that compare two objects.

Not all object languages provide property annotations for variables. In Smalltalk, Flavors, and Object Lisp, variables have values and nothing more. However, languages intended primarily for knowledge engineering applications tend to support annotations. For example, KEE, STROBE (Smith, 1983), and Loops, which are all direct descendants of the Units Package, have this. Annotations are useful for storing auxiliary information such as dependency records, documentation, histories of past values, constraints, and certainty information.

In Loops, the approach to annotating variables has evolved over time. In its most recent incarnation, property annotations have been unified with a means for triggering procedure call on variable access (active values) (Stefik, Bobrow, & Kahn, 1986). These annotations are contained in objects and it is possible to annotate annotations recursively.

The distinction between class variables and instance variables varies across object languages. Smalltalk makes the same distinction as Loops (and was the source of the idea for the Loops developers). Flavors does not have class variables. KEE provides *own* and *member* declarations for slots, serving essentially the same purposes as the distinction between class and instance variables. CommonLoops provides primitives for describing when, how, and where storage is allocated for variables. From these primitives, the important notions of class variables can be defined, except that they share the same name space as other object variables.

Most object languages treat variables and methods as distinct kinds of things: Variables are for storage and methods are for procedures. This distinction is blurred somewhat by active values in Loops, which make it possible to annotate the value of a variable in any object so that access will trigger a procedure. The distinction is blurred also in languages like KEE, STROBE, and the Units Package in which methods are procedure names stored in instance variables (which they call slots). In these languages there is an additional kind of message sending: sending a message to a slot. For specified kinds of messages, the value returned can be just the value of the slot.

Another important extension in the Units Package, KEE, and STROBE is that slots are annotated by datatypes. The datatype distinguishes the kind of data being kept in the slot, be it an integer, a list, a procedure, or something defined for an application. An object representing the datatype provides specialized methods for such operations as printing, editing, displaying, and matching. These datatype methods are activated when a slot message is not handled by a procedure attached to the slot itself. The form of message forwarding and representation of datatypes as objects provides another opportunity for factoring and sharing information. Thus, what all slots of a given type share, independent of where they occur, is characterized by methods in the corresponding datatype object.

Inheritance

Inheritance is the concept in object languages that is used to define objects that are almost like other objects. Mechanisms like this are important because they make it possible to declare that certain specifications are shared by multiple parts of a program. Inheritance helps to keep programs shorter and more tightly organized. The concepts of inheritance arise in all object languages, whether they are based on specialization or delegation and copying.

We begin with the simplest model of inheritance, hierarchical inheritance. We will then consider multiple inheritance, as it is done in Loops and other languages.

Hierarchical Inheritance.

In a hierarchy, a class is defined in terms of a single superclass. A specialized class modifies its superclass with

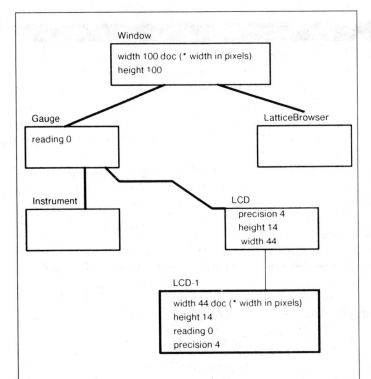

In hierarchical inheritance in Loops, the description of a class is inherited by every subclass, unless it is overridden in the subclass. The instances of the class *LCD* have a class precedence list for getting description—*LCD, Gauge, Window, Object*. The default value for the instance variable *width* is 44 (rather than 100), because *LCD* is closer in the search path than *Window*. In this example, the *doc* property of the instance variable *width* is still inherited by instances of *LCD*—passing along documentation about the use of the variable.

Hierarchical Inheritance of Instance Variables.
Figure 4.

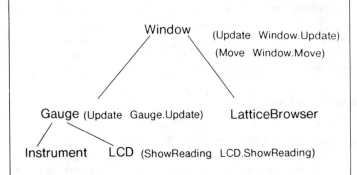

In hierarchical inheritance in Loops, the description of a method is inherited by every subclass, unless it is overridden in the subclass. This inheritance can be characterized as a *first-found* search through superclasses. In this figure, the Move method for the class *LCD* is inherited from *Window*.

Hierarchical Inheritance of Methods.
Figure 5.

additions and substitution. *Addition* allows the introduction of new variables, properties, or methods in a class, which do not appear in one of its superclasses in the hierarchy. *Substitution* (or overriding) is the specification of a new value of a variable or property, or a new method for a selector that already appears in some superclass. Both kinds of changes are covered by the following rule. All descriptions in a class (variables, properties, and methods) are inherited by a subclass unless overridden in the subclass. (See Figure 4.)

The values to be inherited can be characterized in terms of a *class precedence list* of superclasses of the class determined by going up the hierarchy one step at a time. Default values of instances are determined by the closest class in the superclass hierarchy, that is from the first one in the class precedence list. Figure 5 illustrates essentially the same lookup process for methods.

There is always an issue about the *granularity of inheritance*. By this we mean the division of a description into independent parts, that can be changed without affecting other parts. In Loops, any named structural element can be changed independently—methods, variables, and their properties. For example, substituting a new default value for one instance variable does not affect the inheritance of the properties of that variable, or the inheritance of other instance variables. Figure 4 shows this for the independent inheritance of documentation when a default value is changed.

Several approaches for implementing inheritance are possible offering different tradeoffs in required storage, lookup time, work during updating, and work for compilers. For example, the lookup of default values need not involve a *run-time* search of the hierarchy. In Loops, the default values are cached in the class, and updated any time there is a change in the class hierarchy.

The position of a variable is determined by lookup in the class, but the position of this variable is cached at first lookup. Changes in the hierarchy affecting position of instance variables simply require clearing the cache.

In Flavors, the position of an instance variable is stored in a table associated with a method, and is accessed directly by the code. This gives faster access, but requires updating many method tables for some changes in the hierarchy.

Multiple Inheritance in a Lattice.

Inheritance is a mechanism for elision. The power of inheritance is in the economy of expression that results when a class shares description with its superclass. *Multiple* inheritance increases sharing by making it possible to combine descriptions from several classes.

Using multiple inheritance we can factor information in a way that is not possible in hierarchical inheritance. Figure 6 illustrates this in a lattice of commodities.

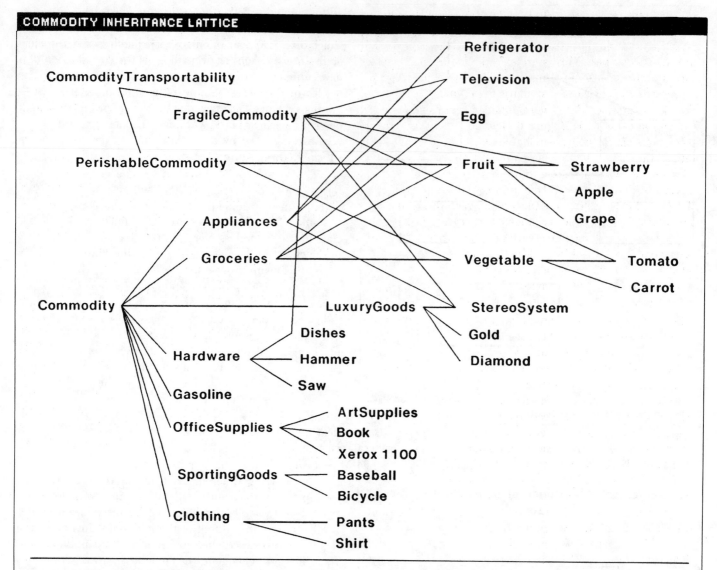

This lattice illustrates the use of multiple superclasses to factor inherited information in a network of classes. Multiple inheritance allows increased brevity in specifications by increasing the ability to share descriptions. For example, the class *StereoSystem* in this lattice inherits information from *LuxuryGoods, Appliances,* and *FragileCommodity.* In a strictly hierarchical system, it would be necessary to duplicate information in the hierarchy—for example by creating classes for *FragileAppliances* or *FragileLuxuryAppliances.* In a hierarchical scheme, the methods and variables associated with "fragility" would need to be replicated for each different use.

Multiple Inheritance in a Lattice.
Figure 6.

The class *StereoSystem* inherits descriptions from *LuxuryGoods, Appliances,* and *FragileCommodity.* The methods and variables describing *FragileCommodity* are also used for *Egg, StereoSystem,* and other classes. It would be necessary to duplicate the information about fragility in several classes such as *FragileAppliances, FragileGroceries, FragileFruit,* and *FragileLuxuryGoodsAppliances* in a strictly hierarachical system. In contrast, multiple inheritance lets us package together the methods and variables for *FragileCommodity* for use at any class in the network.

A class inherits the union of variables and methods from all its super classes. If there is a conflict, then we use a class precedence list to determine precedence for the variable description or method. The class precedence list is computed by starting with the first (leftmost) superclass in the supers specification and proceeding depth-first *up to joins.* For example, the precedence order for *DigiMeter* in Figure 7 first visits the classes in the left branch (*DigiMeter, Meter, Instrument),* and then the right branch (*LCD),* and then the join (*Gauge),* and up from there.

The left-to-right provision of the precedence ordering makes it possible to indicate which classes take precedence in the name space. The "up to joins" provision can be understood by looking at examples of mixins. Mixins often stand for classes that it would not make sense to instantiate by themselves. Mixins are special classes that bundle up descriptions and are "mixed in" to the supers lists of other classes in order to systematically modify their behavior. For example, *PerishableCommodity* and *FragileCommodity* are mixins in Figure 6 that add to other classes the protocols for being perishable or fragile. Another example of a mixin is the class *NamedInstance*, which adds the instance variable name to its subclasses, and overrides methods from *Object* so that appropriate actions in the Loops symbol tables take place whenever the value of a *name* instance variable is changed. *DatedObject* is another mixin which adds instance variables that reflect the date and creator of an object. Mixins usually precede other classes in the list of supers, and are often used to add independent kinds of behavior.

When mixins are independent, the order of their inclusion in a supers list should not matter. Like all classes in Loops, mixins are subclasses of *Object*. If the "up to joins" provision was eliminated from the precedence ordering, then the depth-first search starting from the first mixin would cause all the other default behaviors for *Object* to be inherited—interfering with other mixins later in the supers list that may need to override some other part of *Object*. Changing the order of mixins would not eliminate such interference, since most mixins need to override the behavior of *Object* in some way. The "up-to-joins" provision fixes this problem by insuring that *Object* will be the last place from which things are inherited. Although this effect could also be achieved by treating *Object* specially, we have found that analogous requirements arise whenever several subclasses of a common class are used as mixins. The up-to-joins provision is a general approach for meeting this requirement.

Multiple Inheritance, Revisited.

A major source of variation in object languages that provide multiple inheritance is their stand towards precedence relations. In Smalltalk, multiple inheritance is provided, but not used much or institutionalized. Smalltalk-80 takes the position that no simple precedence relationship for multiple inheritance will work for all the cases, so none should be assumed at all. Whenever a method is provided by more than one superclass, the user must explicitly indicate which one dominates. This approach diminishes the value of mixins to override default behavior.

Flavors and Loops both use a fixed precedence relationship, but differ in the details. The two approaches can be seen as variations on an algorithm that first linearizes the list of superclasses (using depth-first traversal) and then eliminates duplicates to create a class precedence list. In Flavors, all but the first appearance of a duplicate

are eliminated. In Loops, all but the last appearance of a duplicate are eliminated.

CommonLoops takes the position that experimentation with precedence relationships is an open issue in object-oriented programming. In CommonLoops, the precedence relation for any given class is determined by its metaclass, which provides message protocols for computing the class precedence list.

Method Specialization and Combination

One way to specialize a class is to define a local method. This is useful for adding a method or for substituting for an inherited one. In either case a message sent to an instance of the class will invoke the local method. The grain size of change in this approach is the entire method.

A powerful extension to this is the *incremental specialization* of methods, that is, the ability to make incremental additions to inherited methods. This is important in object-oriented programming because it enables fine grained modification of message protocols. In the following we consider two mechanisms for mixing of inherited behavior. The first mechanism ← *Super* (pronounced "send super") allows procedural combination of new and inherited behavior. It derives initially from Smalltalk and is used heavily in the Loops language. Then we will consider an interesting and complementary approach pioneered by the Flavors system in which there is a declarative language for combining methods.

Procedural Specialization of Methods.

Incremental modification requires language features beyond method definition and message sending. In Loops, ← *Super* in a method for selector M1 invokes the method for M1 that would have been inherited. Regular message sending (←) in a local method can not work for this, because the message would just invoke the local method again, recursively.

An example of its use is shown in Figure 8. In this example, *Gauge* is a subclass of *Window*. The method for updating a *Gauge* needs to do whatever the method for *Window* does, plus some initial setting of parameters and some other calculations after the update. The idiom for doing this is to create an *Update* method in *Gauge* that includes a ← *Super* construct to invoke *Window's* method. This is better than duplicating the code from *Window* (which might need to be changed), or invoking *Window's* method by procedure name (since other classes might later be inserted between *Window* and *Gauge)*.

← *Super* provides a way of specializing a method without knowing exactly what is done in the higher method, or how it is implemented. ← *Super* uses the class precedence list to choose when a method appears in more than one superclass. The precedence ordering is the same as that used for object variables.

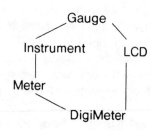

Local supers of DigiMeter: (Meter LCD)

Order of Inheritance:

(DigiMeter Meter Instrument LCD Gauge...)

In multiple inheritance it is possible to inherit things from several superclasses. The precedence of different inherited values is determined by a search as shown.

Order of Inheritance in a Lattice.
Figure 7.

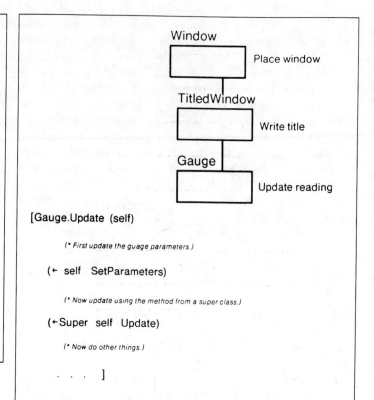

```
[Gauge.Update (self)

    (* First update the guage parameters.)

    (← self   SetParameters)

    (* Now update using the method from a super class.)

    (←Super   self   Update)

    (* Now do other things.)

    . . .   ]
```

In this example, *Gauge* is a subclass of other classes (say *Window*), which have their own methods of updating. The *Update* method for *Gauge* needs to do whatever the method for *Window* does, except that some parameters need to be set first and then some other computations need to be done afterwards. This effect is achieved by using the ← *Super* construct, which allows embedding an invocation for *Window's* method inside new method code for *Gauge*.

Example of Using ←Super.
Figure 8.

← *Super* uses the class precedence list in order to preserve the correctness of protocols under changes to the inheritance lattice. The most obvious definition of ← *Super* would be to search for the super-method from the beginning of the class precedence list. This fails for nested versions of ← *Super*, and even for a ← *Super* in a method which is not defined locally, but is inherited. A second incorrect implementation would use the class precedence list of the class in which the method was found. This gives incorrect results for classes with multiple super classes. To insure that protocols work the right way in subclasses, ← *Super* starts the search in the object's class precedence list at the class from which the current method is inherited. Because ← *Super* is defined this way, inherited methods using ← *Super* consistently locate their "super methods" and common changes to the lattice yield invariant operation of the message protocols.

Combination of several inherited methods is also important. A simple version combines all of the most-local methods for a given selector, that is, all of the methods that have not themselves been specialized. These methods are called the *fringe* methods, and the construct for invoking them all is called ← *SuperFringe*. For example, in Figure 9 the class *DigiMeter* combines the updating processes for *LCD* and *Meter* by using ← *SuperFringe* to invoke the *ShowReading* methods of its superclasses.

For selective combination of methods from different classes Loops provides a construction called DoMethod. DoMethod allows the invocation of any method from any class on any object. It can be viewed as an escape mechanism, allowing one to get around the constraints imposed by message sending. It also steps outside the paradigm of object-oriented programming and opens the door to a wide variety of programming errors. When programs are written using standard message invocations, then protocols keep working even when common changes are made to the inheritance lattice. This happy situation is not the case when programs use DoMethod. Since DoMethod allows specification of the class in which the message will be found, it encourages the writing of methods that make strong assumptions about the names of other classes and the current configuration of the inheritance lattice. Programs that use DoMethod are likely to stop working under changes to the inheritance lattice.

Declarative Method Combination

Flavors supports a declarative language for combining methods at compile time. An important new distinction made in Flavors is that there can be three named parts to a method—a *before* part, an *after* part, and a *main* method, each of which is optional. By default, the *main* method

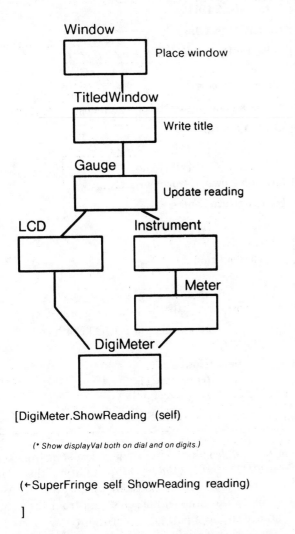

Window

Place window

TitledWindow

Write title

Gauge

Update reading

LCD   Instrument

Meter

DigiMeter

[DigiMeter.ShowReading (self)

(* Show displayVal both on dial and on digits.)

(←SuperFringe self ShowReading reading)

]

In this example, *DigiMeter* combines the classes of *LCD* and *Meter*. To show a reading, a *DigiMeter* must carry out the *ShowReading* methods in both its *LCD* portion and its *Meter* portion. This combination of protocols can be done by using the ← *SuperFringe* construct to invoke the *ShowReading* methods for all of the superclasses. The method above invokes the original *ShowReading* methods of both *Meter* and *LCD*.

Example of Using ←SuperFringe.
Figure 9.

overrides any inherited main method, but the before and after parts are all done in a nested order determined by the class precedence list. Thus a supplier of a method in a mixin can ensure that whatever the main method, its before method will be executed.

A declarative language used in a newly defined method can specify other than the default behavior for combination of inherited method parts. For example, *and* combination of before methods allows the execution of the entire method to stop if one of the before methods returns *nil*. The *defwhopper* combinator allows a compile time con-

struction of the equivalent of ← *Super*.

The concept of organizing methods and variables into classes that can be mixed together for use in combination admits at least two distinct philosophies for assigning responsibility for the viability of the combination. In Flavors responsibility is assigned, at least in part, to the suppliers, that is, to the classes that are being combined. Combinator specifications include things like do this method before the main method, or do it after the main method, or do parts of it at both times. The intention is to get the specification right once in the supplier so that consumers need not know about it. When this kind of specification is successful, it reduces the total amount of code in the system since consumers need only specify the order of superclasses.

In Loops, responsibility for method combination is assigned to the consumer; that is, the local method uses the procedural language and the special form ← *Super* to combine the new behavior with behavior inherited.

It is important to consider the effects on program change when evaluating alternatives like this. How often are suppliers changed? consumers? To what extent are suppliers independent? Do mixins need notations for indicating what kinds of classes they are compatible with? What kinds of changes in the suppliers require changes in the consumer classes?

CommonLoops takes the position that both philosophies are worth exploring, and that continued experimentation in the refinement of method combinators is called for. It provides a primitive RunSuper (analogous to the Loops ← *Super*) in the kernel. Methods are represented as objects in CommonLoops; this means that a system can have different kinds of methods with different techniques for installing them or displaying their sources. Flavor-style methods would be a special kind of object with extra specifications for combinators. These specifications would be interpreted at appropriate installation and reading times by Flavors-style discriminator objects for those methods.

Composite Objects.

A composite object is a group of interconnected objects that are instantiated together, a recursive extension of the notion of object. A composite is defined by a template that describes the subobjects and their connections. Facilities for creating composite objects are not common in the object languages we know, although they are common in application languages such as those for describing circuits and layout of computer hardware. The current Loops facility is based on ideas in Trillium (Henderson, 1986), which is a language for describing how user interfaces for copiers are put together.

Principles for Composite Objects.

Composite objects in Loops have been designed with the following features:

- Composite objects are specified by a class containing a description indicating the classes of the parts and the interconnections among the parts.

The use of a class makes instantiation uniform so that composite objects are "first class" objects.

- Instantiation creates instances corresponding to all of the parts in the description.

The instantiation process keeps track of the correspondence between the parts of the description and the parts in the instantiated object. It fills in all of the connections between objects. It permits multiple distinct uses of identical parts.

- The instantiation process is recursive, so that composite objects can be used as parts.

For programming convenience, the instantiation process detects as an error the situation where a description specifies using another new instance of itself as a part, even indirectly. Instantiation of such a description would result in trying to build an object of unbounded size. An alternative is to instantiate subparts only on demand. This allows the use of a potentially unbounded object as far as needed.

- It is possible to specialize a description by adding new parts or substituting for existing parts.

This reflects the central role of specialization as a mechanism for elision in object-oriented programming. The language of description allows specialization of composite objects with a granularity of changes at the level of parts.

An Example of a Composite Object.

Composite objects are objects that contain other objects as parts. For example, a car may be described structurally as consisting of a body, a power system, and an electrical system. The body has two doors, a hood, a chassis, and other things. Parts can themselves contain other parts: a door has various panels, a window, and a locking system. Objects can also be parts of more than one container: the fan belt can be viewed as a component of the cooling system or of the electrical charging system.

The boxed figure in the next column shows the Loops class definition of *Mercedes240D* defined as a composite object.

Mercedes240D is a subclass of the mixin *CompositeObject* that supports protocols for instantiation that will interpret descriptions of parts. The value of the instance variable *engineSystem* will be filled by an instance of the class *DieselEngine*. In that instance of *DieselEngine*, the value of the instance variable *numCylinders* is initialized to 4 and transmission to *4Speed*.

The *body* instance variable of the *Mercedes240D* will be initialized to and instance of *Body300*. Its instance

---

Mercedes240D
MetaClass Class

  EditedBy (*dgb "15-Feb-82 14:32")
  doc (*This class is a CompositeObject representing a car and its parts.)

Supers (CompositeObject Automobile)
Class Variables

  Manufacturer DaimlerBenz
  StandardCarStuff ((color (@color))(owner(@owner))...)

Instance Variables

  yearManufactured NIL
  owner NIL
  style traditional
  color ivory
  engineSystem NIL
        part (DieselEngine (numCylinders 4)
                (transmission (QUOTE 4Speed))...)
  body NIL
        part (Body300
            (style (@style))
            (color (@color)
            StandardCarStuff))

---

variable *style* is set to the value of the *style* from the *Mercedes240D*, that is, *traditional*. In addition, the *color* property of the *style* instance variable will be set to ivory. These exemplify the propagation of values from the containing instance to those parts contained in it.

The class variable *StandardCarStuff* indicates a number of variables for the body part that will inherit values from the car. For example, the *color* of the body is the *color* of the car. Finally, the instance variable parts will be set to a list of all the immediate parts of the *Mercedes240D*. If any of the parts are themselves *CompositeObjects*, their parts will be instantiated too.

Perspectives.

Perspectives are a form of composite object interpreted as different views on the same conceptual entity. For example, one might represent the concept for "Joe" in terms of views for *JoeAsAMan*, *JoeAsAGolfer*, *JoeAsAWelder*, *JoeAsAFather*. We will first describe perspectives as they are used in Loops, and then contrast this with other languages.

Perspectives in Loops.

Perspectives in Loops are implemented by independent linked objects representing each of the views. One can access any of these by view name from each of the others.

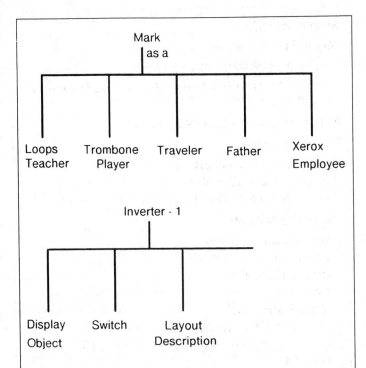

For some applications, it is important to have different perspectives or views of an entity, with independent name spaces. In the upper portion of this figure, the entity *Mark* is shown with perspectives for *LoopsTeacher, TrombonePlayer, Traveler,* and so on. Each perspective offers a different view of *Mark* in a distinct object with its own variables and methods. For example, the *TrombonePlayer* perspective would contain information relevant to Mark's ability to make music. In the example of an inverter, shown in the lower part of the figure, variables with the same name, such as *xCoordinate* and *yCoordinate,* may have one meaning in the perspective *DisplayObject* and another meaning in the perspective *LayoutDescription.*

Perspectives.

Figure 10.

Because the linked objects are independent, the same instance variable name in more than one of the objects can mean different things, and can be changed independently. For example, Figure 10 illustrates an object *Inverter-1* which has the perspective *DisplayObject* as well as the perspective *LayoutDescription.* Both perspectives may have instance variables named *xCoordinate* and *yCoordinate,* but with different interpretations. For a *DisplayObject,* the variables could refer to the coordinates in pixels on a workstation display. For a *LayoutDescription* perspective, the variables could refer to coordinates in the silicon chip on which the inverter is fabricated.

Perspectives were designed in Loops to have the following properties:

- Perspectives are accessed by perspective names.

Given an object, one can ask for its Traveler perspective using the name "Traveler." A given perspective name has at most one perspective of an object. Perspectives

form a kind of equivalence class.

- Perspectives are instantiated on demand.

This contrasts with usual composite objects in which all the parts are created at instantiation time. Additional views can be added as needed to any object.

Perspectives can be compared with class inheritance. In inheritance only one variable is created when there is a "coincidence" in the names of variables inherited from different superclasses. Thus inheritance assumes that the same name is always intended to refer to the same variable. For perspectives, variables of the same name from different classes are used for different views and are distinct. When classes are combined by inheritance, all of the instances of the combined class have the same structure (that is, variables and methods) and all of the structure is created at once. For perspectives, the situation is different. Instances have varying substructure.

Variations on Perspectives.

The term perspective was first used for different views of the same conceptual object in KRL, and later in PIE (Goldstein & Bobrow, 1980). Each view had an independent name space for its slots. However, in neither PIE nor KRL was a perspective a full-fledged object; access to the view could only be obtained through the containing object.

Although the terminology of perspectives is not widespread, some other object languages (*e.g.,* Snyder, 1985) have a similar capability to combine the structure of multiple classes in this way. Snyder suggests that name coincidence in multiple inheritance ought not imply identity. He believes that this violates an important encapsulation principle of object oriented programming—that users of objects ought not to have privileged access to the internals of those objects. He extends that notion to classes which inherit from previously defined classes. For his language, inheritance from a super class means the embedding of an instance of the super class in the subclass. Messages of the super class are to be inherited explicitly, and implemented by passing the message on to the embedded instance.

Examples of Object-Oriented Programming

Examples of programming can be presented at several levels. This section considers three examples of object-oriented programming that illustrate important idioms of programming practice. The first illustrates the use of message sending and specialization. The second example illustrates choices among techniques of object combination. The third example illustrates common techniques for redistributing information among classes as programs evolve.

Programming the Box and the BorderedBox.

Object-oriented programming has been used for many programs in interactive graphics. The following example was

THE AI MAGAZINE

motivated by these applications. We will consider variations on a program for displaying rectangular boxes on a display screen. This example explores the use of message sending and specialization in a program that is being extended and debugged.

Figure 11 gives our initial class definition for the class *Box*. Instances of this class represent vertically aligned rectangular regions on a display screen. The four instance variables store the coordinate and size information of a box. The origin of a box in the coordinate system is determined by the variables *xOrigin* and *yOrigin* and the default origin is at (100, 200). The size of a box is determined by variables *xLength* and *yLength* and the default size is 10 x 30. Operations on a box include moving it to a new origin, changing its size, and changing the shading inside the box. In the following we will specialize the *Box* class and also uncover a bug in it.

Message protocols define an interface for interacting with boxes. Instances of *Box* are created by sending it a *New* message. Size and position of an instance are established by sending it a *Reshape* message. Shade is established by sending it a *Shade* message. These messages provide a structured discipline for interaction with boxes,

that is, a data abstraction. Outside agents need only know the relevant messages. They need not know the implementation of a box in terms of its instance variables.

Suppose that we wanted to create another kind of box with a visible border that frames it in the display. This *BorderedBox* would be essentially a *Box* with a border. This suggests that we employ inheritance and specialize the class definition of *Box*.

In programming *BorderedBox* several choices about the interpretation and representation of the border need to be made. The foremost question is about the treatment of coordinates of the border, that is, whether the border frames the outside of the box or is included as part of the box. For example, is the border included in the length measurements? If the border is on the outside, is the origin on the inside or the outside of the border? The answers to these questions do not come from principles of object-oriented programming, but rather from our intentions about the meaning of the *BorderedBox* program. The answer affects the meaning of the instance variables *xOrigin*, *yOrigin*, *xLength*, and *yLength* inherited from *Box*. For this example, we will assume that the borders are intended only to make the boxes easier to visualize in the

---

Box

MetaClass Class

        EditedBy *(* dgb "31-September-84 11:23")*

        doc *(* Rectilinear box that can be displayed.)*

Supers (DisplayObject)

InstanceVariables

    xLength 10 *doc (* length of the horizontal side.)*

    yLength 30 *doc (* length of the vertical side.)*

    xOrigin 100 *doc (* x coordinate of origin—lower left corner.)*

    yOrigin 200 *doc (* y coordinate of origin—lower left corner.)*

Methods

Move Box.Move	*doc (* Moves box (change origin)in the display)*
	args (newXOrigin newYOrigin)
Reshape Box.Reshape	*doc (* Changes the location and axes of the box.)*
	args (newXOrigin newYOrigin newXLength newYLength)
Shade Box.Shade	*doc (* Fills the inside of the box with a new shade.) args (newShade)*
Draw Box.Draw	*doc (*Displays the box.)*

Instances of this class represent vertically aligned rectangular regions on a display screen. The four instance variables store the coordinate and size information for a box. For example, the origin in the coordinate system is determined by the variables *xOrigin* and *yOrigin* and the default origin is at (100, 200). Operations on the box are defined by messages to the box. They include moving it to a new origin, changing the size of the box, and changing the shading inside the box.

Class Definition for the Box.
Figure 11.

---

display and that for this purpose they will be treated as part of the box.

The next step is to decide whether any of the methods of *Box* need to be specialized in *BorderedBox*. Since a border needs to be redrawn when a box is increased in size, it is clear that at least the *Reshape* method needs some revision. Figure 13 shows a specialized *Reshape* method that uses ← *Super* to invoke the *Reshape* method from *Box*. The specialized *Reshape* also invokes local methods to *Draw* and *Erase* the boundary. These methods plus one for setting the size of the boundary must be added to *BorderedBox*. The *Draw* and *Erase* methods are for internal use, but the *SetBorder* method will become part of the external protocol. Figure 12 shows these methods together with a new instance variable for recording the size of the border.

The use of a variable for *borderSize* brings up a question of how the methods of the original *Box* class work for shading. In fact, they cannot work if the shade is not saved as part of the state of an instance (or is otherwise computable). *Box*'s *Reshape* method should use the current shade in order to fill new areas when a box is expanded. To fix this deficiency, we can now go back to the definition of *Box* to add a *shade* instance variable that will be saved by the *Shade* method. We can also modify *Box*'s *Reshape* method to use this new variable.

After the shade bug is fixed, we should ask whether the specialized class *BorderedBox* must also be changed. *BorderedBox* will inherit the shade instance variable and the revised *Shade* method. Furthermore, the specialized *Reshape* method in *BorderedBox*, which uses ← *Super*, will effectively "inherit" the shade changes from *Box*'s *Reshape* method. In this example, the inheritance mechanisms of the language work for us in just the right way. This illustrates how language features can provide leverage for accommodating change.

Programming the DigiMeter.

Gauges are favorite pedagogical examples in Loops because they use features of both object-oriented and access-oriented programming. They are defined as Loops classes and are driven by active values.

Figure 14 illustrates a collection of gauges in Loops. Gauges are displayed in a *window*, an active rectangular region in the bitmap display. They have a black title bar for labels and a rectangular center region in which they display values. Instances of *LCD* (for "little character display") show their values digitally, but most gauges simulate analog motion to attract visual attention when they change. For example, subclasses of *VerticalScale* and *HorizontalScale* simulate the movement of "mercury" as in a thermometer. Instances of subclasses of *RoundScale* move a "needle" in a round face.

For some purposes it is convenient to combine digital and analog output in a single gauge. The digital output makes it easy to read an exact value from the gauge. The analog output makes it easy to notice when the gauge is changing and to estimate the position of the current value in a fixed range. With gauges like this it is easy to tell at a glance that something is "half full."

The programming of combination gauges gives rise to a choice of programming techniques for combining classes. Figure 14 shows the *DigiMeter* as an inheritance combination of a *Meter* and an *LCD*. Such a gauge needs to combine the programmed features of the two classes. In the following we will consider the arguments for choosing an appropriate technique of object combination.

Here are some goals bearing on the design of a *DigiMeter*:

- The *DigiMeter* should respond in the standard way to gauge protocols.

For example, a single request to *Set* the *DigiMeter* should suffice, without having to send separate messages for the meter and the LCD. Both gauges should display the same correct value.

- The *DigiMeter* should use a single window to display both gauges.

The combination gauge should not have two separate windows and bars. The component gauges should appear in a single window on the display screen that is large enough for both of them.

- The combined description should make direct use of the classes for *LCD* and *Meter*.

DigiMeter should use some method for combining *Meter* and *LCD*. This does not preclude making changes to the classes for *Meter* and *LCD* in order to make them compatible for combination, but we do not want to duplicate code or descriptions in *DigiMeter*. The class descriptions should continue to work whether the classes are used alone or in combination.

The three techniques of object combination supported in Loops are perspectives, composite objects, and multiple inheritance.

Using *perspectives* for combination, we would create a *DigiMeter* with one perspective for the meter and one for the LCD. Unfortunately, the direct approach to this would result in the creation of separate windows for each gauge. We could fix this for all of the gauges in the lattice, for example, by making a window be a perspective of a gauge. The main utility of perspectives is that they support switching among multiple views and instantiating these views on demand. In this application, we always need to create all of the views and the views are very close-

```
BorderedBox
MetaClass Class

        EditedBy (* mjs "1-Oct-84 01:67")

      doc (* Like a Box except displays a black border. The origin is the outside of the border.)

Supers (Box)

InstanceVariables

    borderSize 2 doc (* width of the border.)

Methods

    Reshape BorderedBox.Reshape

    SetBorder BorderedBox.SetBorder doc (* Set a new border size.) args (newBorderSize)

    EraseBorder BorderedBox.EraseBorder

    DrawBorder BorderedBox.DrawBorder
```

A *BorderedBox* is like a box except that it is drawn with a variable-sized border in the display. *BorderedBox* is implemented by specializing *Box*. A new instance variable *borderSize* is added to record the size of border. The width of the border is included as part of the dimensions of the box.

Class Definition for the BorderedBox.

Figure 12.

```
(BorderedBox.Reshape (self newXOrigin newYOrigin newXLength newYLength)

        (← self EraseBorder) (* Erase old border.)

        (* Now Reshape box as before)

        (← Super self Reshape newXOrigin newYOrigin newXLength newYLength)

        (← self DrawBorder) (* Draw new border.)

        ]
```

The specialized Reshape method needs to redisplay a revised border when the shape of the box changes. ← *Super* is used to invoke the *Reshape* method from *Box*. The specialized *Reshape* also invokes methods to *Draw* and *Erase* the boundary. These methods plus one for setting the size of the boundary must be added to *BorderedBox*. The *Draw* and *Erase* methods are for internal use and the *SetBorder* method is part of the external protocol.

Reshape Method for BorderedBox.
Figure 13.

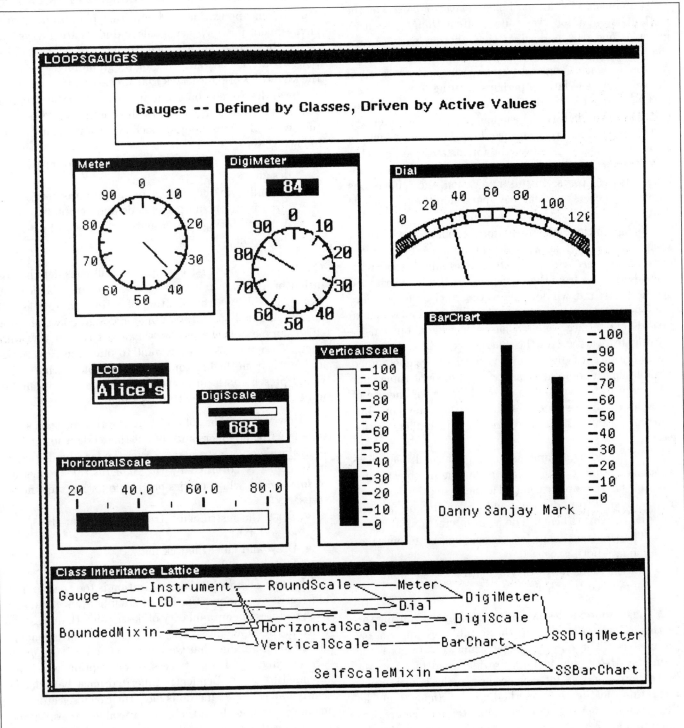

Gauges are tools used to monitor the values of object variables. They can be thought of as having probes that can be inserted on to the variables of an arbitrary Loops program. Gauges are defined in Loops as classes and driven by active values—the computational mechanism behind access-oriented programming in Loops. A browser at the bottom of the figure illustrates the relationships between the classes of gauges. From this figure, we can see that the *DigiMeter* is a combination of a *Meter* and an *LCD*. Other kinds of gauges, mimicing oscilloscope traces or chart recorders, would also be useful.

Gauges in Loops.
Figure 14.

ly associated. Hence, the main features of perspectives don't do much work for us. Using *composite objects* as the method combination, we would create a *DigiMeter* with a meter as one part and an *LCD* as another part. Again, the straightforward combination would yield a separate window for each gauge. As before, we could revise all of the gauges in the lattice, perhaps treating a window as a part of a gauge. In addition, the *DigiMeter* description would need to identify the window parts of the meter and LCD as referring to the same window. The main benefit of composite objects is to describe for instantiation a richly connected set of objects and to differentiate between objects and their parts. In this application, the connections between the parts are relatively sparse and the part/whole distinction doesn't do much work for us.

Using multiple inheritance for combination, we would create a *DigiMeter* as a class combining an LCD and a meter. Since the *LCD* and *Meter* classes inherit their window descriptions from the same place, multiple inheritance yields exactly one window. As in the other cases, we may need to tune parts of the window description to make sure that it is large enough for both gauges, but this is a straightforward use of the inheritance notion. In multiple inheritance it is important to ask whether same-named variables in the combined class refer to the same thing. For this application, we need to be on the alert for the use of variables in *Meter* and *LCD* that have the same name but different meanings, but there are no such conflicts in this case.

The preceding arguments suggest that multiple inheritance is the most appropriate technique of object combination for this application. The next step in designing a *DigiMeter* is to understand and design the interactions between the constituents. The main interactions are:

- The window should be large enough to accommodate both gauges.
- The methods for displaying both gauges should be invoked together.

The first interaction can be handled by specializing the method *(UpdateParameters)* that establishes the window parameters. The major window sizing constraints come from the *Meter*, which must provide room for the calibrated circle and its interior needle. In the Loops implementation the *DigiMeter* method uses ← *Super* to invoke the parameter-setting code for the *Meter* and then revises them to allow extra room at the top of the window for the *LCD*.

The second interaction can be handled by specializing the *ShowReading* method for showing a reading. As shown earlier in Figure 9, this method consists of a simple application of ← *SuperFringe* which invokes the original *ShowReading* methods of both *Meter* and *LCD*. In Flavors this would have involved the application of a *progn* method combinator.

The Evolution of Classes—Gauge Examples.

Most of our applications of Loops take place in a research environment in which new goals and ideas are always surfacing. In such an environment frequent revisions and extensions are a constant part of programming. To cover the kinds of reorganizations that we carry out in our work we have developed some idioms for systematic program change. This section considers three cycles of revision in the design of Loops gauges. Each cycle of revision has the following steps:

- A new goal or requirement is introduced for the design.
- A conflict in the current organization is recognized between sharing of code and flexibility.
- A new factoring of information is chosen to ease the conflict.

Cycle 1.   In our first example we will consider the addition of a *DigiScale* to the class inheritance lattice. A *DigiScale* will be a combination of a HorizontalScale and an *LCD* as in Figure 15. A major design constraint for this example is that the *DigiScale* must be visually compact. To make it small we want to omit the tick marks and labels from the horizontal scale portion. Such a gauge would present both an exact digital value and an analog indication of the value within its range.

However, the plan of omitting the tick marks also interacts with the inheritance of existing code from it HorizontalScale and *Instrument*. In particular, the display of instruments is governed by the *ShowInstrument* method of *Instrument*, which carries out the following sequence of steps:

- Draw the instrument structure (circular dials, an so forth)
- Draw and label the tick marks.
- Print the scale factor.

For the *DigiScale* this organization is too coarse. This illustrates a common situation where inheritance in a subclass requires finer granularity of description than was provided in the super class. The situation arises often enough in our programming that we have a name for it—a *grain-size conflict*. In Loops, pieces of description which are intended to be independently inherited must be independently named—*e.g.*, methods have their own selectors and instance variables have their own variable names. A specific fix in this case is to decompose the *ShowInstrument* method into several smaller methods that we can independently specialize, reorder, or omit.

Cycle 2.   Sometimes a grainsize conflict is the first stage in recognizing new possibilities in a design. In the previous example, we considered the creation of a special kind of horizontal scale that has no tick marks. We could generalize that idea to have vertical scales or even round scales without tick marks. Another observation in

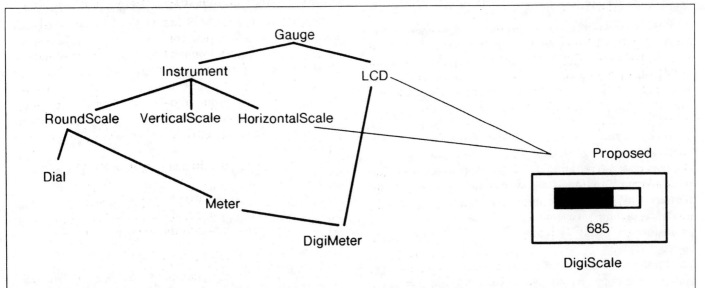

The proposed *DigiScale* will be a combination of a *HorizontalScale* and an *LCD*. An unusual programming constraint in this case is that we want to omit the tick marks from the horizontal scale portion. At issue is the fact that the code inherited from *Instrument* bundles in one chunk the drawing of the gauge and the drawing and labeling of the tick marks.

Programming the DigiScale.
Figure 15.

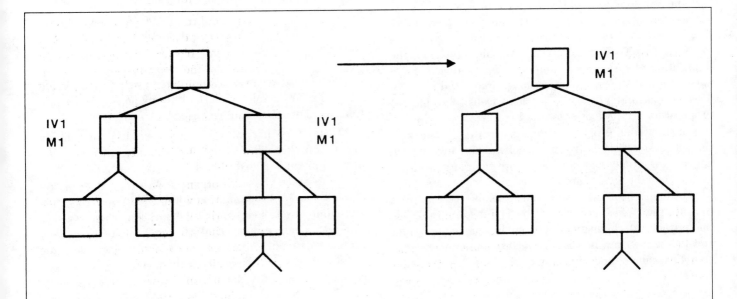

Often there is a motivation to move structure up in the class lattice in order to increase sharing. We call this *promotion* of structure. In this case a method M_1 and an instance variable IV_1 are initially duplicated in two sibling classes. Promotion would move them to their common superclass.

Promoting Methods and Variables.
Figure 16.

the same vein is that the round scale gauges differ from the others in the way that they indicate their values. Round scale gauges use a needle. Vertical and horizontal scale gauges use space filling—like the sliding of a column of mercury. Several other kinds of gauges are possible—such as a PieScale gauge—a round scale gauge that uses an expanding "slice of pie" to indicate its value.

This suggests that there are some independent properties of gauges that we could recognize:

- *Calibration*—gauges can have tick marks and scale factors or not.
- *Indicator style*—gauges can use needles or space filling to present their values.

The recognition that a particular distinction arising in a subclass can be generalized is a common occurrence in object-oriented programming. Often there is a motivation to move structure up in the lattice to increase the amount of sharing. We call this *promotion* of structure. Figure 16 illustrates a simple case of this where a method M^1 and an instance variable IV^1 are initially duplicated in two sibling classes.

Promotion would move them to their common superclass. The Loops environment encourages and facilitates such activities by making them easy to do with interactive browsers that show the inheritance structure, and allowing menu driven operations to make changes.

Figure 17 shows a first attempt to organize a class lattice for these distinctions. In this attempt, instruments are partitioned into *CalibratedInstrument* and *UncalibratedInstrument*. This partitioning tries to exploit the observation that the best-looking uncalibrated instruments are also the space-filling ones. The classes *VerticalGraph*, *HorizontalGraph*, and *PieGraph* are created as uncalibrated space-filling gauges. The main problem with this approach is the duplication of code. For example, code is duplicated between *HorizontalScale* and *HorizontalGraph*, and between *VerticalScale* and *VerticalGraph*. This leads to a different proposal for a lattice as shown in Figure 18.

In the second proposal, a mixin is created for the code that generates tick marks and labels. The gauge lattice appears essentially the same as before the reorganization except that the classes are now uncalibrated. Classes like *VerticalGraph* have calibrated subclasses like *VerticalScale* that use the *CalibratedScale* mixin. The mixin establishes the procedural connection between instrument drawing and tick mark drawing. Each subclass also supplies specialized local methods for arranging the tick marks and labels.

Cycle 3. Gauges have upper and lower bounds for the values that they display. When data go out of range, the standard behavior is to light up an "out of range" indicator and to "pin" the gauge to the maximum or minimum value. This highlights a nuisance with analog gauges. Their readings become useless when data go out of range. One idea is to have gauges automatically recompute their extreme points and scaling factors as needed. For example, if a gauge goes out of bounds, it could automatically increase the maximum reading by about 25 percent of the new high value subject to some constraints of display aesthetics.

The rescaling requirement is *independent* of the style of display, that is, it is independent of whether we are spinning a needle or driving mercury up and down. This suggests using a uniform technique for revising the scale for all the gauges. The natural choice for additive behavior is a *mixin*.

Unfortunately there is a difficulty in doing this for the *BarChart*. The *BarChart* is unique among the gauges in Figure 14 in that it displays several values at once. A *SelfScalingMixin* could be easily defined that would work for all of the gauges except the *BarChart*. This mixin would just use the value of the gauge in computing a new maximum. For a *BarChart*, it is necessary to look at all of the bars to determine the maximum. This seems to lead to the following design choices for using mixins:

- We could design two mixins. One for the *BarChart* and one for all the other gauges. (Equivalently we could just mandate that the gauge mixin should not be used with *BarChart*.)
- We could design one mixin that worked differently for the *BarChart* and the other gauges. The method for computing the maximum would need to check whether it was being used in a class with *BarChart* as a super class.
- We could modify the definition of the single-value gauges by adding a method to simply return the value when asked for the "maximum" value.

The first two choices do not extend well if we later add additional multi-value gauges. In our Loops implementation, we chose the third option.

Usually we think of mixins as classes that we can mix in with any class whatsoever. For example, when the *DatedObject* mixin is added to class it causes instances to have a *date* instance variable initialized with their date of creation. Some kinds of mixins are designed to be used with a more limited set of classes. This example illustrates a case where the "mixees" can fruitfully be modified slightly to accommodate the mixin. The modification broadens the set of classes with which the mixin is compatible.

Conclusion and Summary

Objects are a uniform programming element for computing and saving state. This makes them ideal for simulation problems where it is necessary to represent collections of things that interact. They have also been advocated for applications in systems programming since many things with state must be represented, such as processes, directories and files. Augmented by mechanisms for annotation, they have also become important in the current tools for knowledge engineering.

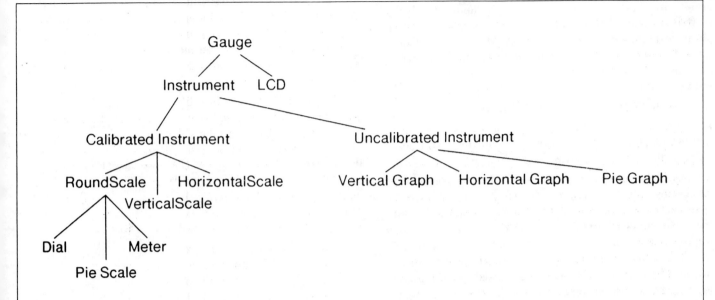

This lattice shows gauges partitioned into *CalibratedInstrument* and *UncalibratedInstrument* which exploits the observation that the best-looking uncalibrated instruments are also the space-filling ones. However, code is duplicated, for example, between *HorizontalScale* and *HorizontalGraph*.

Rearranging the Lattice of Gauges.
Figure 17.

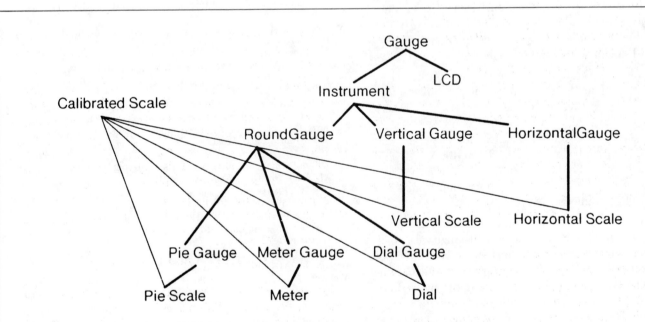

In this arrangement, a CalibratedScale mixin is created for tick marks and labels. In this reorganization there is a *CalibratedScale* mixin which is added to uncalibrated classes to create tick marks. For example, *VerticalScale* is a subclass of *VerticalGraph* and uses the *CalibratedScale* mixin.

Rearranging the Lattice of Gauges, Again.
Figure 18.

As object languages have become widespread, considerable interest has been expressed in developing standards so that objects could be used as a portable base for programs and knowledge bases. Towards this end, the Common Lisp Object-Oriented Programming SubCommittee is now considering several proposals to extend Common Lisp with objects.

The diversity of language concepts discussed here suggests that research is very active in this area. Standards will need to provide the kind of open-endedness and flexibility that enables languages to endure.

As object-oriented programming has taken hold in the mainstream of AI languages, they have reinforced a more general principle. There are multiple paradigms for programming. Procedure-oriented programming and object-oriented programming are but two of a larger set of possibilities that includes: rule-based programming, access-oriented programming, logic-based programming, and constraint-based programming. Different paradigms are for different purposes and fill different representational niches.

In this article we have not tried to describe all of the ways in which features of object oriented programming have been achieved in the context of other systems. For example, logic programming has inspired a number of interesting mergers. In Concurrent Prolog (Shapiro, 1983), objects are represented by processes, and messages are passed to the process along a stream. Delegation is used to achieve the effect of inheritance. In Uranus (Nakashima, 1982) objects are bundles of axioms in a database. Inheritance is done by following links in the databases, using a logic-based language to express the methods.

In Uniform (Kahn, 1981) objects are represented by expressions, and methods as operations on objects that would unify with the "head" of the method. Inheritance is implemented by viewing one expression as another (through an axiom that states, for example, that (SQUARE X) is equivalent to (RECTANGLE X X)). This has the nice property that "inheritance" can go in both directions—from specialization to super, and from super with the right parameters to specialization.

Languages that combine multiple paradigms gracefully are known as hybrid or integrated languages. Languages that succeed less well might be called "smorgasbord" languages. In any case, language paradigms are no longer going their separate ways and attempting to do all

things. Separate paradigms now co-exist and are beginning to co-evolve.

References

Bobrow, D.G., Kahn, K., Kiczales, G., Masinter, L., Stefik, M., & Zdybel, F. (1985) CommonLoops: Merging Common Lisp and Object-oriented programming. Xerox Palo Alto Research Center: Intelligent Systems Laboratory Series ISL-85-8, August 1985.

Bobrow, D.G., and Stefik, M. (1981) The Loops manual. Tech. Rep. KB-VLSI-81-13. Knowledge Systems Area. Xerox Palo Alto Research Center.

Bobrow, D.G., & Winograd, T. (1977) An overview of KRL, a knowledge representation language. *Cognitive Science.* 1:1, pp. 3-46.

Borning, A. (1979) A constraint-oriented simulation laboratory. Stanford University. Stanford Computer Science Department Report: STAN-CS-79-746.

Dahl, O.J. & Nygaard, K. (1966) SIMULA—an algol-based simulation language. *Communications of the ACM.* 9: 671-678.

Drescher, G.L. (1985) The ObjectLisp USER Manual (preliminary). Cambridge: LMI Corporation.

Henderson, D.A. (1986) The Trillium user interface design environment. (submitted to Computer Human Interaction. Boston: April.)

Fikes, R., & Kehler, T. (1985) The role of frame-based representation in reasoning. *Communications of the ACM.* 28:9, pp. 904-920.

Goldberg, A., & Robson, D. (1983) *Smalltalk 80: The language and its implementation.* Reading, Massachusetts: Addison-Wesley.

Goldstein, I., & Bobrow, D.G., (1980) *Descriptions for a programming environment.* AAAI-1.

Goldstein, I.P., & Roberts, R.B. (1977) NUDGE, a knowledge-based scheduling program. IJCAI-5, pp. 257-263.

Kahn, K., (1981) *Uniform—A Language based upon Unification which unifies (much of) Lisp, Prolog, and Act 1.* IJCAI-7, pp. 933-939.

Lieberman, H., (1981) A Preview of Act 1. Massachusetts Institute of Technology. Artificial Intelligence Laboratory Memo No. 625. June.

Minsky, M.A. (1975) A framework for representing knowledge. In P. Winston (Ed.), *The psychology of computer vision.* New York: McGraw-Hill.

Nakashima, H. (1982) Prolog/KR—language features. Proceedings of the First International Logic Programming Conference. Marseille, France: ADDP-GIA.

Rees, J.A., Adams, N.I., & Meehan, J.R. (1984) The T Manual, 4th edition. Tech. Rep. Yale University. January 1984.

Shapiro, E., & Takeuchi, A. (1983) Object oriented programming in concurrent prolog. *New Generation Computing* 1, 25-48.

Smith, R.G. (1983) Structured object programming in STROBE. Schlumberger-Doll Research: Artificial Intelligence Publications: AI Memo No. 18. September.

Snyder, A. (1985) Object-oriented proposal for Common Lisp. ATC-85-1. Palo Alto: Hewlett Packard Laboratories.

Stefik, M., Bobrow, D.G., & Kahn, K. (1986) Integrating access-oriented programming into a multi-paradigm environment. To appear in *IEEE Software.*

Stefik, M. (1979) *An examination of a frame-structured representation system.* IJCAI-79, pp. 845-852.

Weinreb, D., & Moon, D., (1981) Lisp Machine Manual. Symbolics Inc.

Author Biography

Gerald E. Peterson is currently a Principal Investigator in Automated Reasoning for McDonnell Douglas Aerospace Information Services Company, St. Louis, Missouri. He holds B.S. (1961), M.A. (1963), and Ph.D. (1965) degrees in mathematics from the University of Utah. He taught at the University of Utah, Brigham Young University, the University of Missouri at St. Louis, and Southern Illinois University at Edwardsville prior to joining McDonnell Douglas on a full-time basis. From 1981 to 1986 he worked part-time in software engineering methodology for McDonnell Douglas Astronautics Company. During this time he developed an interest in object-oriented computing. He is the author or coauthor of several research papers in mathematics and computer science.